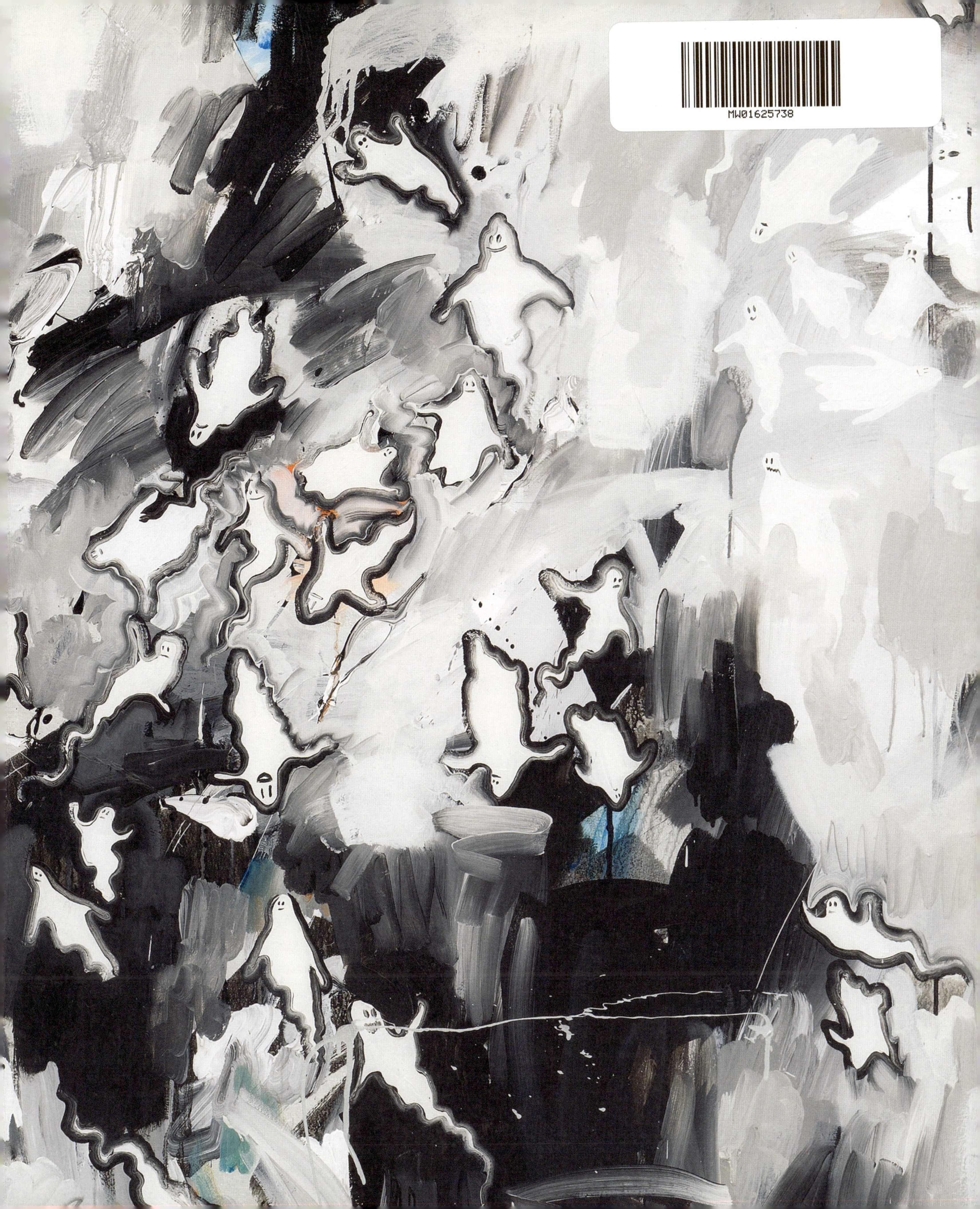

MW01625738

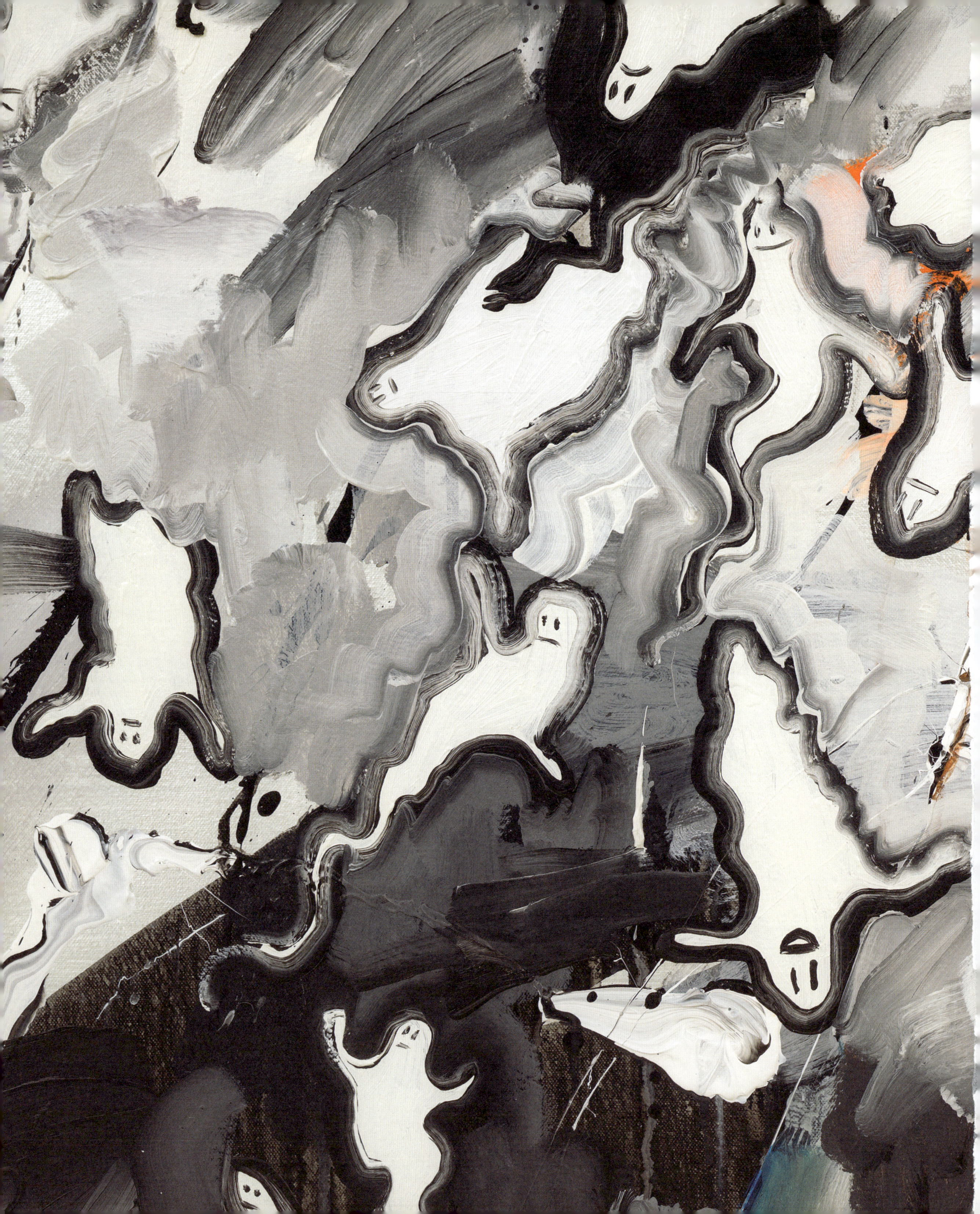

This cannot go on.

Henri Fantin-Latour

SAM

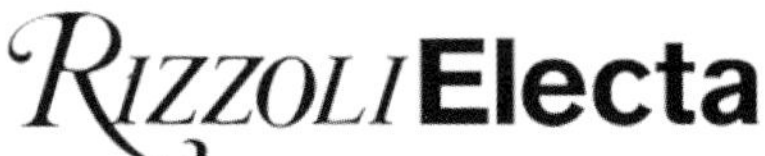
Rizzoli Electa

McKINNISS

With Jarrett Earnest and Natasha Stagg

CONTENTS

STAGG McKIN-NISS

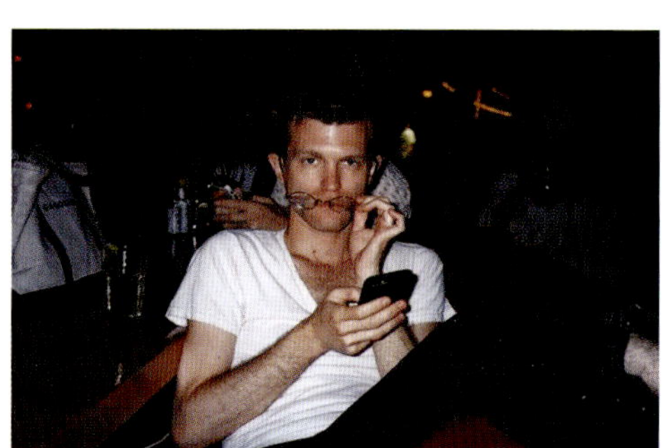

NATASHA STAGG:
When you appropriate an image, you are putting yourself in a trajectory, instead of coming up with the image that may later be appropriated. This somehow feels humble, as if you are saying, who am I to come up with a brand-new idea? I'm part of an existing process.

SAM MCKINNISS:
Yeah, I'm part of the problem.

NATASHA:
Not the problem!

SAM:
But that's how I feel about it, really. Feeling that way gives me levity. The opposite of that levity is feeling trapped in consumerism. There's no escaping it, and there's no other way to experience culture in this time and place; that is the culture.

NATASHA:
Consuming.

SAM:
It was a conscious decision that I made several years ago, to not introduce any new imagery. I wanted to copy all of it because that acknowledges my complicity inside of a system there's no escape from anyway. And it gives me a little bit of control, a little bit of power, and a little bit of authorship inside of this giant marketplace that's really top-down already. All the drama and narrative structures that come to give meaning to our lives, it's very top-down.

NATASHA:
Right.

SAM:
And then I decided I could redeem some of my time here in that system, not by fighting that, but by stealing it. This is not a new idea, but what is new probably is the specific way that I handle paint and have studied and developed a skill set that is more classical, requiring my time, effort, and attention. There's a redemptive aspect to learning how to use paint effectively and gorgeously in order to promote beauty. The content is never as interesting to me as the activity of making the painting. It's time well spent. And time gets shorter and shorter. I don't know how that got started.

NATASHA:
Do you mean for you, yourself?

SAM:
For all of us. Every day feels like we're running out of time.

NEW YORK, NY 04.04.24

NATASHA:
Well, and every time you're consuming, it feels like there's more to parse. That speeds up time.

SAM:
If I'm not mistaken, when I was 16, 17, 18 years old, you could believe that there was a way to resist this arch-consumerism. And it makes me uncomfortable now that it has become even more pervasive. It's like, do you enjoy breathing oxygen? Do you enjoy drinking clean water? Do you enjoy this advertisement? Do you enjoy the entertainment industry?

NATASHA:
Do you have any say in what will be in your vicinity?

SAM:
I'm saying that I do not, because I don't know how to infiltrate that area of content creation or the way it's disseminated. I'm admitting defeat in a lot of ways, by copying.

NATASHA:
But you're taking the most pervasive images and freezing them. In a way, you're slowing down the process of those images pervading your thoughts by seeing each detail while you're painting them.

SAM:
And that slowing down process, that's a big part of the redemptive quality. And not in a Christian sense, but in the way you redeem a coupon or a gift card.

NATASHA:
In your show, *Egyptian Violet* [at Team Gallery, New York, 2016], I noticed the lighting, as in the colorful light that you saw and then painted, in pictures of Prince, Diana Ross, swans, and movie stills. It feels as if you were working out the manipulative quality of someone or something bathed in purple light, the images that stick to us and why.

SAM:
I named that exhibition *Egyptian Violet* to put the material front and center. The content, the figures, the characters, and the scenes depicted in that show, in those paintings, I wanted that to be secondary to the formal processes that I needed to get a handle on to make the work. And I named the show after that one tube of Williamsburg brand paint, Egyptian Violet, because depending on how densely one uses the color, it can appear nearly black, or you could dilute it down to a lovely, faint shade of royal violet. That's not true with every tube. It was especially true with that one. It has a kind of translucency and excellent

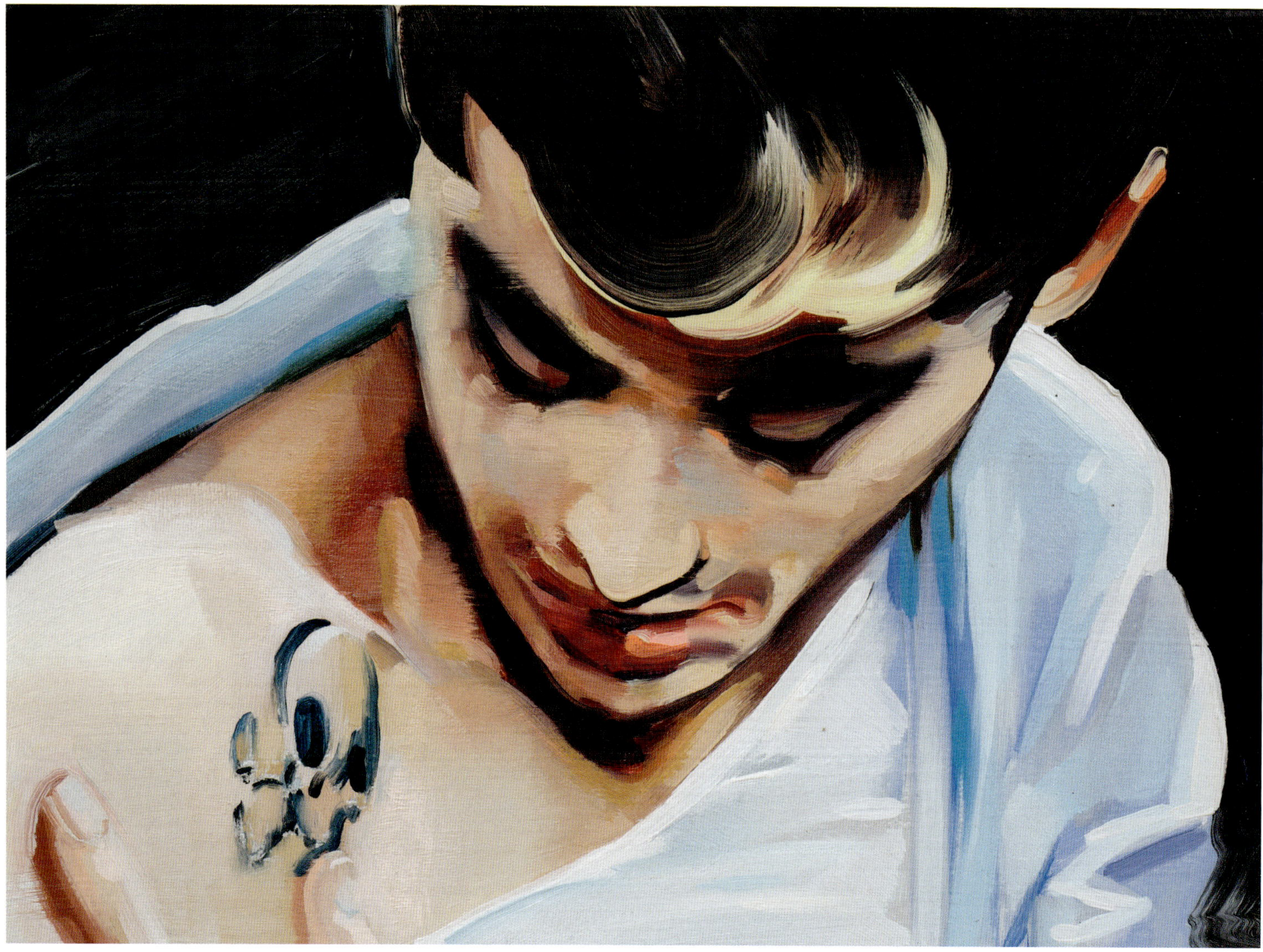

lightfastness. When you get to discussing light and shadow, it's not so different from what cinema does. That was all formal stuff that I wanted to get right to serve the mood of the show. The content also served the mood of the show, but in my mind, less dramatically than the material. If I did not know how to use the color effectively, the drama of these characters would not be enough to make the show as delightful as it was to look at. The content was exciting, and it felt meaningful, but at the same time, the paint came first in my mind.

NATASHA:
Even the name, Egyptian Violet, is very evocative.

SAM:
I was accused, on Facebook, I remember, of misappropriating a racial identity because Egypt is obviously in Africa, and that's taboo, for a white artist to take something from the African continent and claim it as theirs.

NATASHA:
I assumed it was a more distinctive way of referring to the flower, African Violet. But when you get into etymology, there are always these problems.

SAM:
At the time, I understood that there was potential for me to be viewed as racially insensitive, but there was also glamour in it, in the same way Egyptian cotton bedsheets are labeled that way, as a marketing strategy. Making a large painting of Prince's likeness was also possibly taboo for a white artist. But again, he was selling that product. The product was his music and the movie *Purple Rain*, which is available for anybody to consume. I didn't feel like I was maligning Prince's legacy. Don't get me wrong; Prince was a genius. Showing that painting felt like a bold gesture, like I was stepping in to celebrate him right after he died, while also borrowing his star power.

NATASHA:
Our society has become more narrow-minded about who can represent what. Has that affected the way you choose your images?

SAM:
When I was younger, I used a camera to take photographs of people in my life, and then, if I felt strongly about one of those amateur snapshots, I would make that into a painting, in a diaristic way, not dissimilar to examples set by Nan Goldin or Jack Pierson or

Mark Morrisroe, the Boston School. They were photographing their intimates within their personal and romantic lives, and I was really attracted to that. I would go the extra step of turning those photographs into paintings.

NATASHA:
When did you stop?

SAM:
The last big project I did like that was for Sarah Nicole Prickett's *Adult* magazine in 2014. I did a cover story for issue number two, which was the last issue she was able to make. There were maybe ten paintings based on a photo shoot that I did with three of my hot friends. I asked them all to take their clothes off and hang out with me while I shot pictures—because it was an erotic magazine and so I had to make a centerfold type story. Soon after that, I gave up on involving the people in my life in my paintings because I started to think: I want you to be my friend, I don't want you to be my model. I don't want to need you in that way. I want to need you because I love you, and I love being your friend, and I love having you in my life. I don't want you to inspire my art.

NATASHA:
It felt exploitative.

SAM:
A little bit.

NATASHA:
I'm sure your friends loved it.

SAM:
They loved it, but certain boyfriends didn't. And I was friends with people who, the way they looked, I didn't necessarily love, and they would get offended that there wasn't a painting of them.

NATASHA:
Right, and then you start making friends with hotter people because you think it'll benefit your work. As in, other artists have surely done this.

SAM:
You might sell more paintings, yeah. I didn't want to have those thoughts and negotiations. There was already precedent for the kind of appropriation-based paintings that I wanted to make, but I wanted to make them my way. The point is, there are so many pictures, and I knew there was a way for me to describe a mood, or a narrative, or a cobbled-together kind of drama with all this stuff that I could borrow from pre-existing material.

NATASHA:
And you have.

SAM:
There's a shaky suspicion that bothers me about our lives now. I suspect it's easier to remember an experience when you are consuming content. It's harder to remember scenes from your own life that nobody has

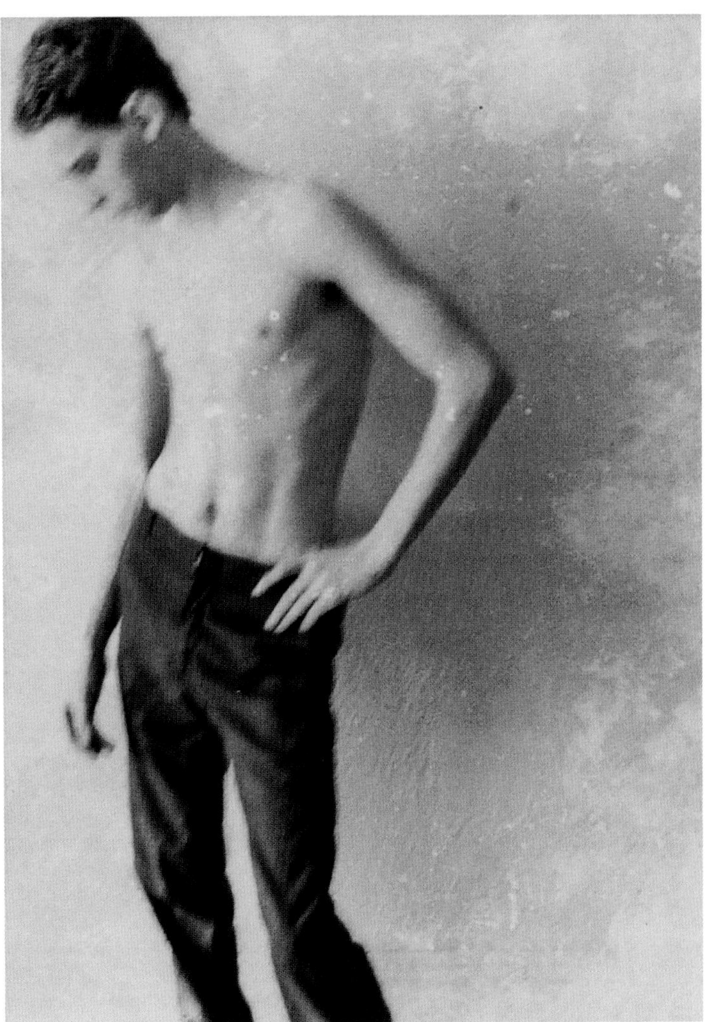

bothered to photograph. So, what you do is you take twenty iPhone pictures a day. It doesn't mean that you'll never, ever look at them again, but it might. This accumulates into an enormous backlog of photographic material. When do you find the time to go through it in any meaningful way? You could take a thousand pictures every day, many people do this, and I'm afraid of the thoughtlessness, the ease of that. Pics don't feel as commemorative as they used to. It's a washout.

NATASHA:
It's like making your friends look at your vacation photos on a slide projector, what used to be a metaphor for the most boring possible evening spent, is now our everyday.

SAM:
And it's been made to be addictive. It's horrifying.

NATASHA:
You've said that swans, all of them, are celebrities.[1] Swans' necks, when doubled, make a heart, and even the heart is ridiculous because it is an abstraction of a human organ that doesn't have much to do with love. Each of these images depicts other images, and then those images depict objects or people that are largely objectified. That idea, in a sense, describes what it is to be a celebrity: we have romanticized their bodies

and movements to such an extent that we can't look at someone without seeing them as a sentimental object.

SAM:
Correct.

NATASHA:
So, the fable of the ugly duckling is melancholic, because once the duckling develops into a swan, it has already gotten so much shit for looking the way it did, for trying to fit in, it will never feel understood. And then it stands out among the ducks; it is wanted disproportionately for its beauty. It still doesn't fit in, and so it is alone. I loved when you said that a swan is a celebrity.

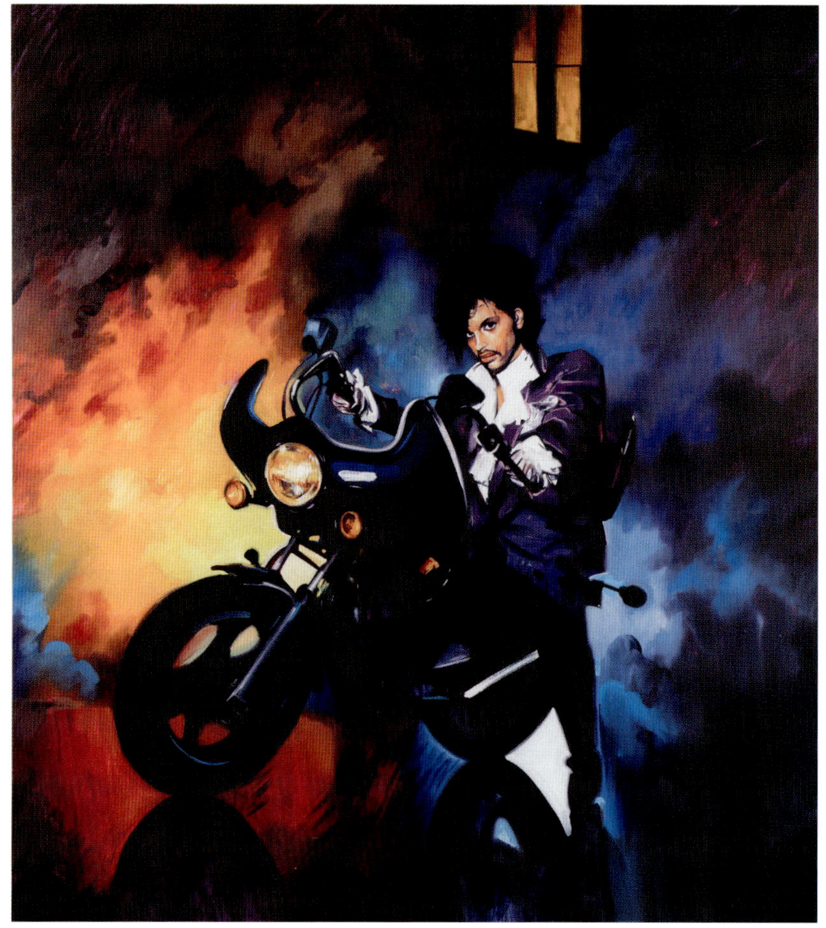

SAM:
I'm glad you feel that way because sometimes when I talk to publications that are more interested in the entertainment industry and pop culture, there's the assumption that I'm devoting my effort to this practice because I find celebrities and their activities and their products and show business in general incredibly moving, which is just not true. I think that movies and TV are, for the most part, extraordinarily boring and not worth our time. I do acknowledge their power, however, and that I can't resist looking. The melancholy comes after consuming so much, and I wonder what would've happened instead, had I spent any of that time just living my life, or pursuing my drama, the stronger elements of being alive that do not involve film and video.

NATASHA:
It takes a lot of mental effort that you're not in control of to transform something into the sentimental object that it is. I think that's really apparent when you talk about a swan, or Whitney Houston. You can't un-see the image as visually meaningful, and you'll never know that being's interiority.

SAM:
You can't know that, in the same way I don't know what's going on inside of your mind and you don't really know what's going on inside of my mind, even though we're having this conversation. It's even more removed when it's happening on TV.

NATASHA:
Right, right.

SAM:
But there's a flip side to this. I'm not cynical about every picture that I've ever made in terms of its content, such as the Whitney Houston paintings. I've made a few of them. I find her body of work quite meaningful, even though, by and large, I am stuck wondering if all this entertainment that takes such a demanding presence in our lives is an enormous waste of time and an insult to my intelligence. There are these excep-

tions that prove the rule, such as Whitney Houston, especially in the instance of her singing the national anthem at the Super Bowl in 1991, which I made a painting about. That performance was profound.

NATASHA:
But any interaction you have with media is as profound as you let it be. Sometimes when I am a fan of a celebrity, I can care so much about that person's talent that I would rather not know the real them. I care more about those profound things that come out of consuming the product. I would also rather not know how anyone else's experience with this product is going. I am only interested in my own.

SAM:
You're individuating. However, even if I can recommend the experience of becoming an individual, the thing that makes me sad and anxious and nervous is the undeniable fact that it's still a mass media that's being offered to us. It's the same stuff being offered to everybody on a massive scale. This is a classic, high school problem. If we're all unique, but we only have access to the same media, how unique are we from one another?

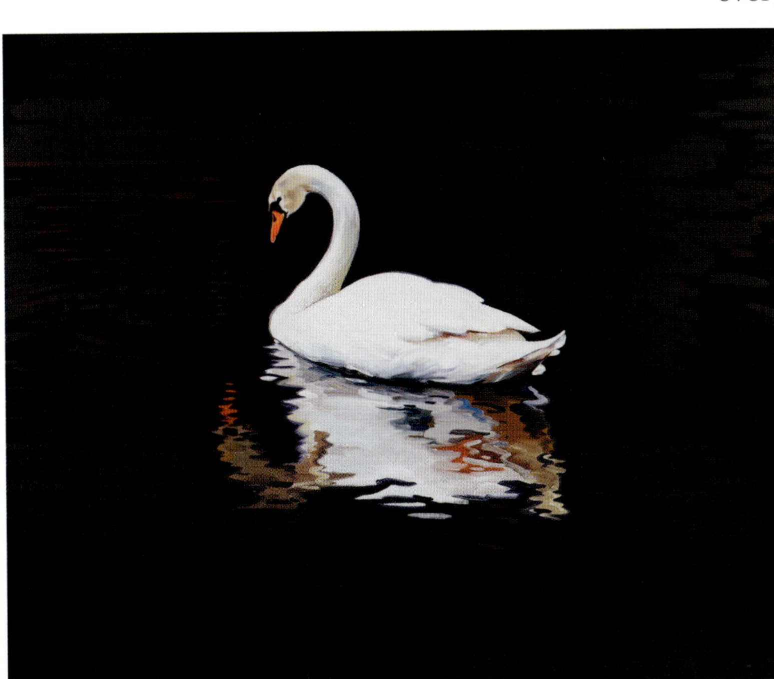

NATASHA:
Well, that is what your art is getting at, in a way. We're all looking at stock images and we're all reacting to them in our own ways inside of ourselves. On one end of it, you can say you don't care and that none of this is you, but you're still involved in consuming the product, and what that means for you is different from what it means for me. And then you can try very hard to have nothing to do with mass culture, to seek out the obscure. But everything eventually is mass.

SAM:
Well, that's why you and I get along, we both feel aware of the trap. We're trapped at the decline of an advanced capitalist society, in a future-less present.

NATASHA:
So, you might as well get into it.

SAM:
At the bare minimum, I wake up every day and if I want to work, which is most days, it's an opportunity to talk back to the power that controls our understanding of reality and have my way with it, at least for the time that I spend devoted to the painting practice. And that's the redemption. But I don't know how my art, or any art could mount an offense against the system that controls all of that. That would be truly revolutionary. It would have to become violent. It wouldn't be art.

NATASHA:
If something becomes so obviously anti, it isolates itself from anybody who was interested in that subject

to begin with. So, you're not graffitiing over all these images and saying, don't look at this. Instead, you're saying, look at this. This is what this looks like.

SAM:
To that I would add, there's an insistence on finding pleasure. Painting is not only a practice and a discipline requiring vision and training, it is a pleasurable activity. To bring paintings from start to finish is mostly a pleasurable experience. And arranging them, displaying them, all of that is pleasure.

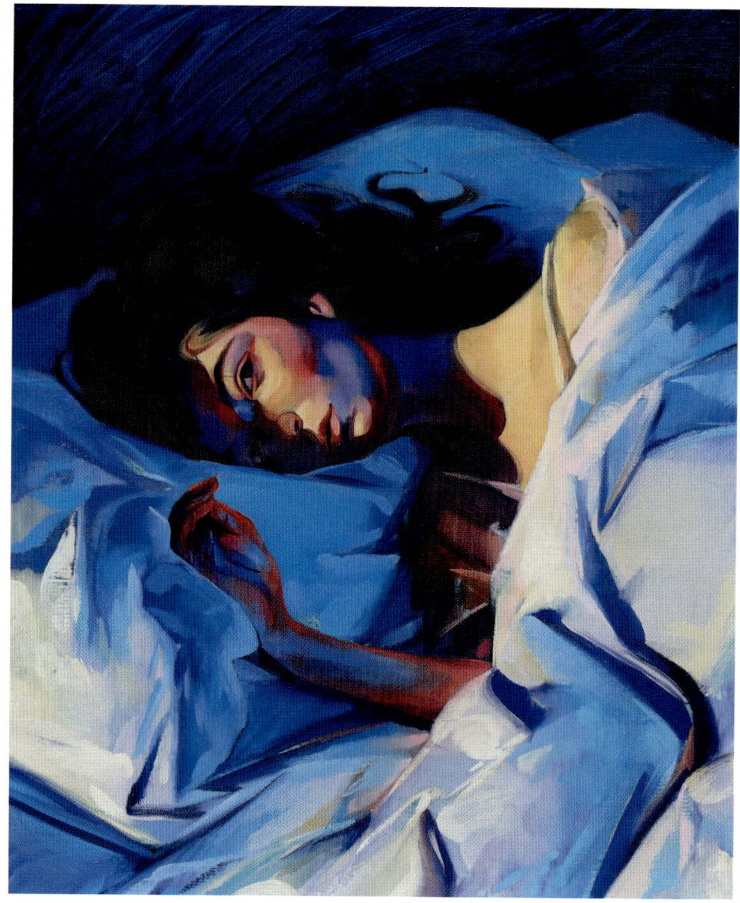

NATASHA:
What about coming up with the images that you choose to paint?

SAM:
Sometimes I find it humorous, which is pleasure. And then sometimes I find it difficult to continue saying I'm going to keep on putting my thing out into the world. That takes a little bit of work to get myself up to the level of boldness. It's a tad arrogant.

NATASHA:
When we were watching the Oscars the other day, I was wondering, do you watch something like that and say, I might get something from this to paint?

SAM:
With something like the Oscars, I'm trying to understand what the official cultural party line is. I'm trying to determine what a celebration of the absolute top of the entertainment and image industry is. With all that pageantry, what's the story that they're trying to sell? Not because I need to agree or disagree, but if I'm going to participate in that image culture, I'll use that information to try and position myself. How do I interact with this? How do I participate on my level, which is much smaller and less resourced?

NATASHA:
You've chosen this area of entertainment and you've defined the lines of it. And you also haven't made your paintings into anything other than paintings. Lorde's album cover [for *Melodrama*] was not your idea, for example.

SAM:
It was her idea, and we talked about it a lot, but, yes, after that happened, I didn't go out and try to get more record cover painting gigs.

NATASHA:
You weren't like, the next show is all album covers. Because that lends another dimension to how images get used on different surfaces. You're not doing a Warhol thing and asking, what's the next media, and the next, and the next? What you've said is you are painting to slow things down. Let's look at what each of those images are doing. Let's further contain them.

SAM:

I can't completely do away with what the content means when I make it into art. I must be aware that all these well-known figures, by virtue of their being well-known, signify something to their publics. When I've looked at someone, understood their messaging, enjoyed a performance, disliked a performance, whatever, something significant happens. One magazine interviewer asked me, what does Dolly Parton mean to you? That was a pretty basic question, but it turned interesting because she's been so famous for so long, I really had to think about it. People continuously see her image and her significance, and they enjoy her talent. This makes them feel strongly. The answer to that question was something like, I believe she signifies glamour. However, the glamour is so abundantly obvious, it turns into a self-deprecating joke. Ultimately, what she then signifies is good humor and generosity of spirit. It was interesting to try and map how that trick works because her surface appearance is so hyperactive. But because there's a certain level of self-awareness in her performance and the way she describes herself, it becomes about joy, about laughing at her, laughing with her. That's part of my process, too, trying to interpret celebrity presentation. I've said this before, perhaps even to that same interviewer, that part of what I'm trying to understand is that which gives our era its cause for celebration, ergo, I look at celebrated personalities closely.

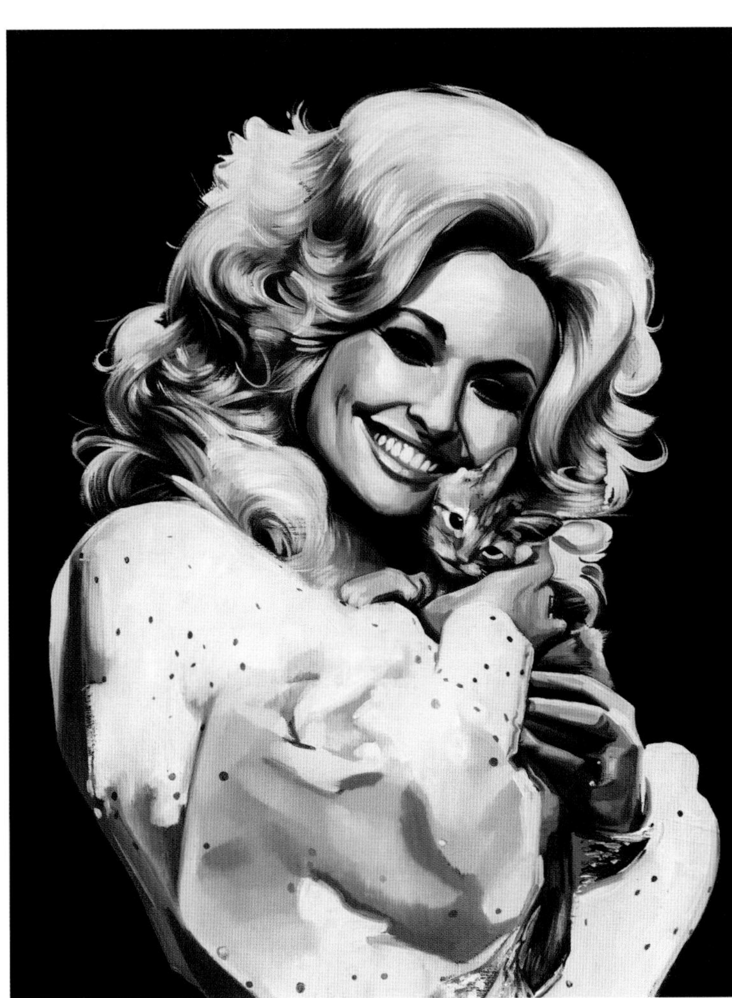

NATASHA:

I seem to recall that when people ask Dolly Parton, what's with all the spangles? She always says something like, I'm just a simple country girl from the Smoky Mountains. She's become this camp persona that performs something else, humility as flamboyance. And that image being elevated to a painting adds another dimension.

SAM:

And the added dimension is quality and time invested. It's not just a fleeting impression somewhere in the world on some screen or tabloid that's really hoping to sell you something at the end of it. Assigning time and labor to it provides a longer opportunity for me to sort out the message and where the meaning comes from, how that inflects upon or incorporates into your self-definition after having seen it, the way that you understand your time on earth, your relationships to the world, to other people, to yourself.

NATASHA:

I've noticed that you get asked this question, the one concerning your feelings on a subject of your work, a celebrity, and your response is usually the same, sort of unprepared, or unenthused. Someone will assume

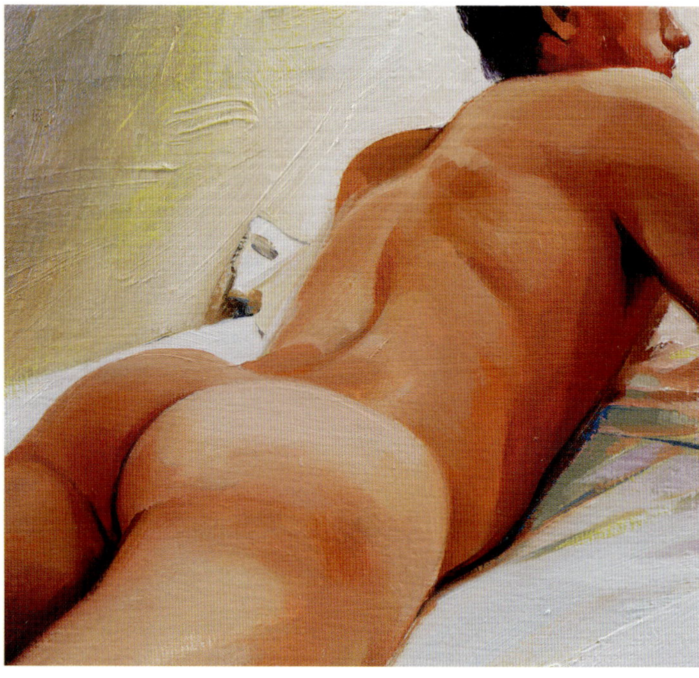

you are a huge Prince fan, or a huge Dolly fan, and you're like, sure, who isn't? They're great.

SAM:
It's never about fandom as the ultimate end.

NATASHA:
That is something that has maybe been misconstrued about your work.

SAM:
That I just love celebs, end of story.

NATASHA:
That you're a super fan and the bigger the celebrity, the better. I wonder how many people think that you're a very different person than what you are.

SAM:
Well, everybody wants to know that about themselves.

NATASHA:
But I wonder if more people would be surprised by your demeanor in person after having only seen your work. There are a few people you've painted that would be considered gay icons, and the term gay icon is weird and convoluted in that it ends up meaning an exploited person.

SAM:
Judy Garland is the template.

NATASHA:
The most tragic celebrity.

SAM:
This does get bandied about from time to time. I am a gay guy, and there is a lot of diva worship, historically speaking, within the gay guy community. It's almost antiquated. The concept is of a certain vintage, even if it persists. It's not the reason I get up and make art, that I feel compelled to deliver another instance of unexamined hype for its own sake. Certainly not.

NATASHA:
Every diva that puts her all into it is worth a painting.

SAM:
That is a funny assumption, and it's funny to let people think that, but the cliché about being gay that I relate to more is growing up into a kind of abject dissatisfaction with the society we live in, what with the bullying, the unfair expectations around sex and gender roles. I relate to the disaffection in a lot of gay life and attitudes, but I grew out of diva worship a few years ago. It kind of died out around age 32. It was like, I can't do this anymore.

NATASHA:
Why not?

SAM:
Because there's no real payoff for me. For other people, there is a payoff, and I envy their enthusiasm.

NATASHA:
There's a relationship between diva worship and image worship and maybe worship of a very distilled existence that is darker than a lot of people give it credit for. Judy Garland lived a miserable life.

SAM:
And more recently, Britney Spears, right?

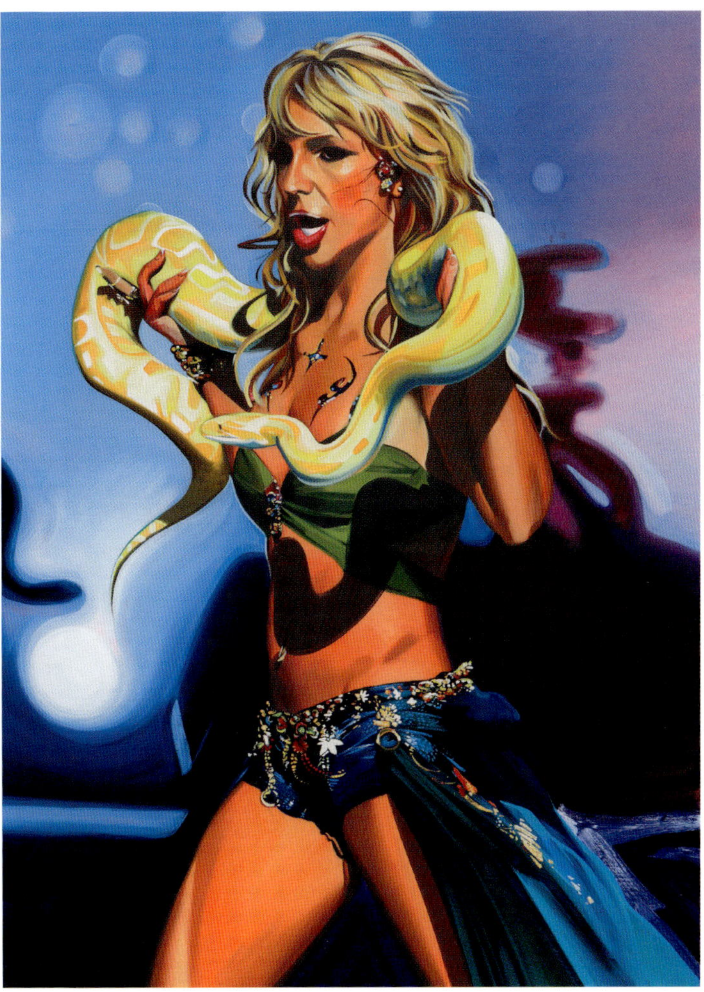

NATASHA:
You create a conversation about image worship, showing that there's a type of misery in that.

SAM:
Yes, but I didn't invent it. That's in line with the practice of painting as an iconographic tradition, beginning with the Catholic Church. When oil paint was invented, it was to depict the Christ, the Word becoming flesh. It was developed so light could enter an image through translucent layers of color suspended in oil on a plain surface to better imagine the Holy Ghost entering Christ, the mother of Christ, the saints, et cetera. It's about the divine joining man through the miracle of sanctification, the same way light hits the surface of any painted figural depiction in oil as a process of literal illumination. It's a one-to-one analogy, which is what made painting so successful as an art form and the Christian Church so successful as an edifying world power, at least in part. It's materialism. By deploying this fabulous visual technology, they were able to strong-arm a lot of average, garden-variety pagans into believing they might gain access to God's heaven and a way out of their own misery, speaking of.

NATASHA:
Or, according to other religions, it's wrong to worship any image.

SAM:
Of course. That's what we call iconoclasm. But the icons are vastly preferred. Dave Hickey once observed, correctly, that nobody really likes what the Taliban did to those Buddhas in Afghanistan.

NATASHA:
When you have recreated older paintings, I wanted to ask how you chose which ones to paint, but then I thought, the process is likely not different from choosing the other images you paint. Still, the history of art is very daunting.

SAM:
I suppose it is daunting to contend with the long history of art as a subject. One thing that I like to do to relieve some of that pressure is, I've kind of made up my mind that there's no such thing anymore as an important artist. Things have gone way off the rails geopolitically and environmentally, so the idea of there being an important artist is just an absurdity.

NATASHA:
That sounds right.

SAM:
Functionally, in terms of an exhibition, adding something that does not come strictly from the popular media complicates that viewing experience. Adding content from a different period confuses the situation in a way that is fun for me as the designer of the exhibition, but also hopefully for the viewer to try and work out. It also supplies evidence to the viewer that there's a sophistication, an awareness of art's long history. Every painting I include is there because it felt essential to the group dynamic. A gallery is an arena. This is a space where only these discrete parts are allowed to contend with each other. There's no singular reasoning, but if I've included it, it seemed necessary according to my subjective feelings or intuition.

NATASHA:
It reminds me that these are paintings of pictures instead of traditional portraits. More recently, you've

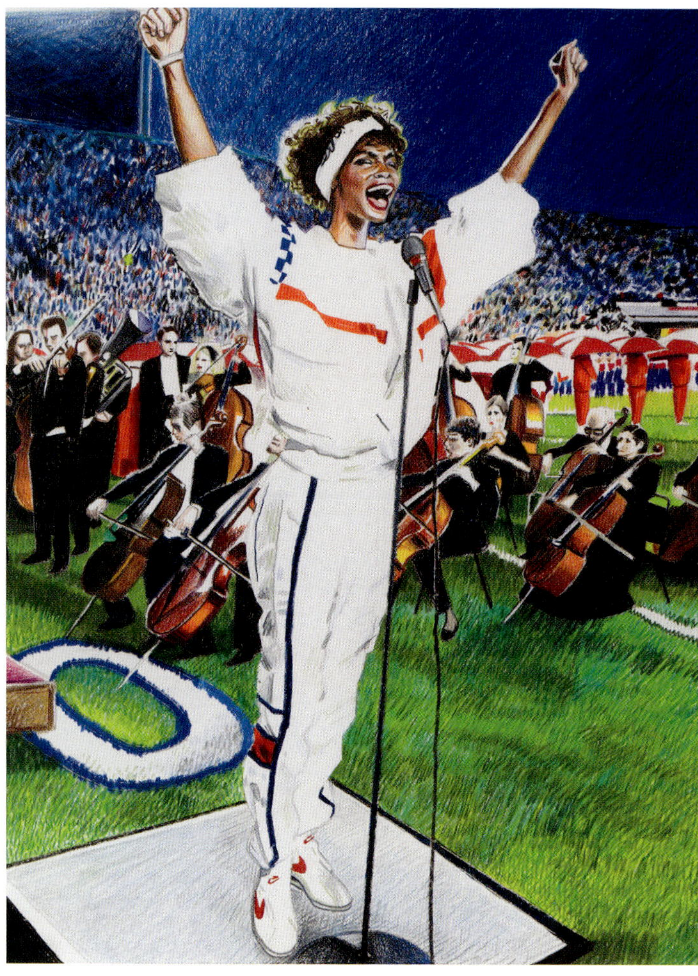

painted the Holstein cows and the Golden Gate Bridge from stock images. You can walk into a room and see a painting of the Golden Gate Bridge and not necessarily think of it as something that was copied from a Google image search. One could say, maybe this artist was struck by the beauty of the Golden Gate Bridge in person. But then when you're in a room of several similarly iconic ideas, it is clearer that these are concepts that have resonated with you for a longer while.

SAM:
The enormity of art history doesn't stress me out as much as the enormity of the image catalog contained on the internet. That is way more daunting than the canon. The canon is tiny compared to what the internet contains.

NATASHA:
The commons.

SAM:
It's like a monster. And it's working hard to replace the way our memory functions. I've painted a lot of copies of Henri Fantin-Latour's floral still lifes. That work is mysterious to me. I can't say exactly why I continue to be interested in it. In an exhibition, I like the way they give pause. They exist there as decoration. They also hearken back to 19th-century France—among other things, an explosion of technical ingenuity and commerce in the European picture trade. Injecting a little of that energy into what I'm doing with other appropriated material seemed like a good idea.

NATASHA:
Those paintings feel a little more joyful than most of your others. Maybe you're reminding yourself that you love painting and its history and probably the experience of seeing paintings in museums.

SAM:
I think that's fair. All of this reminds me of something Robert Glück said to the *Paris Review*, and this applies to everything. He was quoting Jesus in the Apocrypha. "When an image replaces an image, then you will be in heaven." Glück appropriates a lot in his writing, and then so am I, of course, in my paintings, but copying anything is a way of passing through it in order to touch something special. Maybe that's the joy that you're picking up on in the floral still life copies.

NATASHA:
It's interesting that you bring up writing, because I consider you a writer and I know you read a lot of fiction. If you consider using images as tools to pass through an emotion, writers do that, too, because all we have are words. All writing is appropriation because we're using the language at hand.

SAM:
We already have the alphabet; it's established.

NATASHA:
And it's proven to work. You have faith in that alphabet.

SAM:
Let's call all the images that are available to me to use for making paintings the vocabulary. I'm refusing to use anything but the vocabulary that is given to me by the major studios or the image industry or whoever. I take that for granted. But when you have a limited vocabulary, you have a limited understanding of the world. That's the melancholic part. On the other hand, I still need to understand the vocabulary. I need to learn it. I feel compelled to that labor, to that job, to that effort.

NATASHA:
Words aren't just words, and images aren't just images. You must make decisions to present those to an audience. Even if you're stuck in the realm of the word, the vocabulary is still not simply itself. It must be represented with a typeface and a size and a color and a context, for starters.

SAM:
There are covert meanings, as in a Freudian subconscious, especially in advertising. How does it operate inside of you once it permeates your surface and goes into your dream space? That's an endless analysis. This is something I think about: Do we know anyone who has invented a cliché?

NATASHA:
Personally?

SAM:
Yeah. You would have to be a genius if you hit on something that then gets to be endlessly repeated in the mouths of countless other language users.

NATASHA:
Right, exactly. And there is joy in cliché. I don't see your work as cynical.

SAM:
I think I can acknowledge the cynicism of the times we're living in without becoming a full-time cynic myself. I don't think my work is cynical. I acknowledge the existence of cliché and the repetitive nature of making copies like this. It can start to feel lousy, being bombarded with so much unoriginal material, so many unoriginal ideas and unoriginal people. However, by cutting out the requirement to invent something new, I can pass through these clichés to enjoy the thick, essential meaning held inside of each and in that way, experience elemental emotions every now and then. I think that becomes possible. Hopefully, that rubs off on those who come to see my art. If I had to guess, they can't just be enjoying my work because they love celebrities so much.

NATASHA:
Well, if they are, then so be it. But you can't expect the worst from your audience.

SAM:
That would be cynical.

NATASHA:
Every time I see a new painting of yours, no matter how surprising it is, it's not a surprise. That reminds me of when we were children and a new Disney movie would come out, and I'd think, yeah, of course. Disney used to only produce fairy tales, stories we'd heard. There was a comfort in that these stories should continue to be retold in an updated way, that there should be constants within progress.

SAM:
Angela Lansbury sings it in *Beauty and the Beast* when she's describing the plot thus far: It's a "tale as old as time." The audience is sitting there in the movie theater, arms crossed, eyes on at the screen, hearing the lyrics, with this old British actress in the role of a lifetime—a singing cartoon teapot—and they're agreeing with her, passing through this tale that's been told countless times. And yet, they are moved by it.

NATASHA:
You can have a complacent feeling about it, or you can think in a more pornographic sense and say that *Beauty and the Beast* is a horrific psychodrama. And because it's so old and has been retold so many times, it may have changed the course of history and the way we think about relationships. There are so many reads of that passing through, even.

SAM:
And only with effort and concentration can you attempt to get to the bottom of where that cliché ends up guiding human behavior. And what is painting, but concentration and effort?

1. Bill Powers, "A Talk with Sam McKinniss," *ARTnews*, October 13, 2016, accessed at https://www.artnews.com/art-news/artists/it-has-to-be-tragic-or-somewhat-manic-depressive-a-talk-with-sam-mckinniss-7125/.

P. 8, *Zayn Malik's Death Tattoo*, 2015; p. 9, Mark Morrisroe, *Untitled (Man Posing Without a Shirt)*, c. 1986, © The Estate of Mark Morrisroe (Ringier Collection) at Fotomuseum Wintethur; p. 10, *Prince*, 2016; p. 11, *Swan*, 2016; p. 12, *Lorde: Melodrama*, 2016; p 13, *Dolly Parton with kitten*, 2021; p. 14, *Sam's Ass (ADULT)* (detail), 2014; p. 15, *Britney Spears*, 2021; p. 16, *The Star Spangled Banner*, 2022

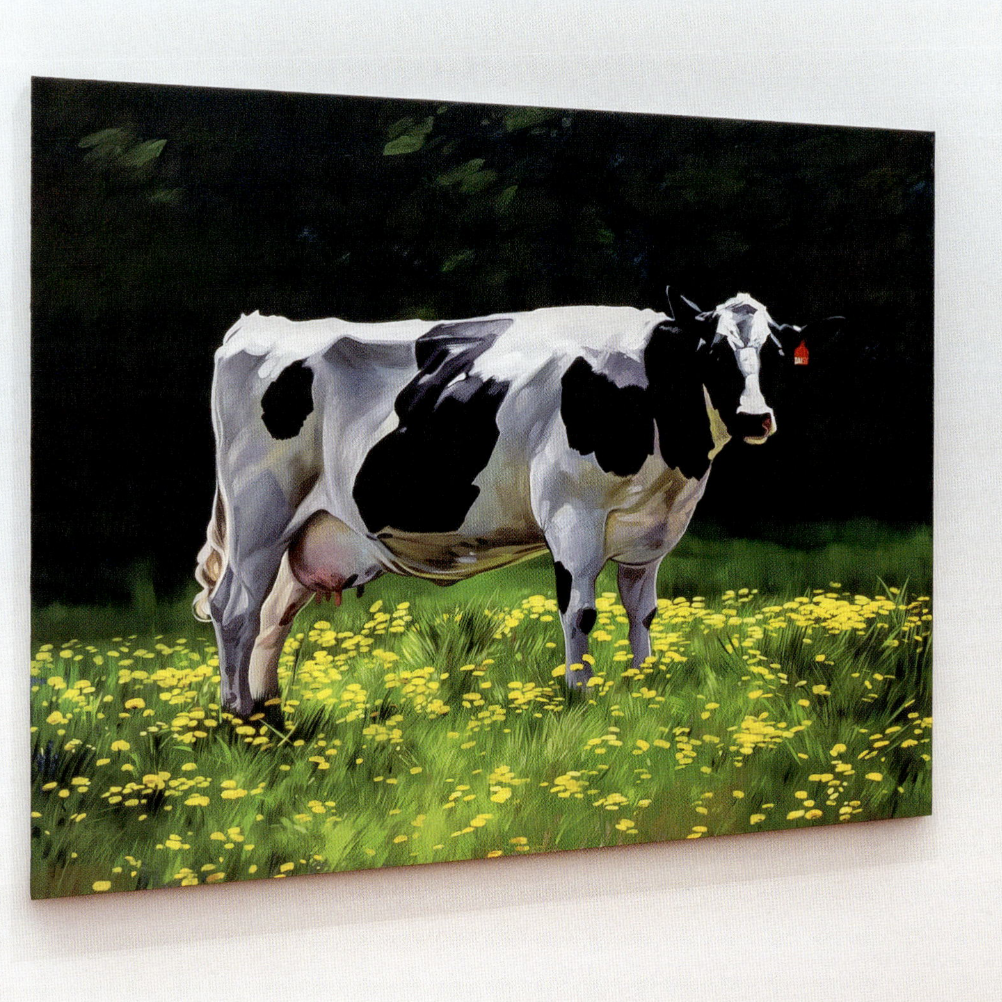

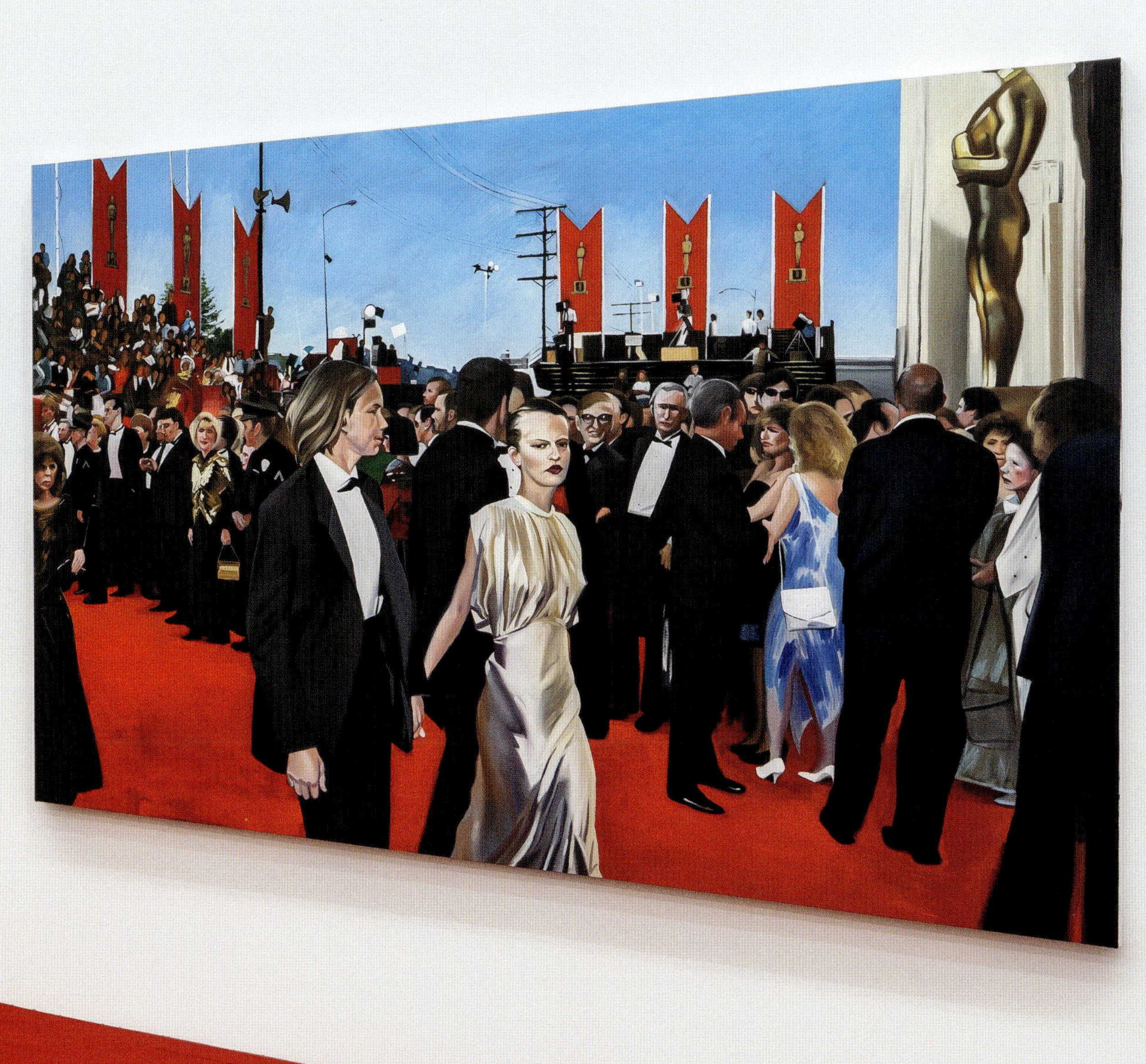

PAINTINGS

Sometimes I think I'd rather be a movie star than an artist.

Mark Morrisroe

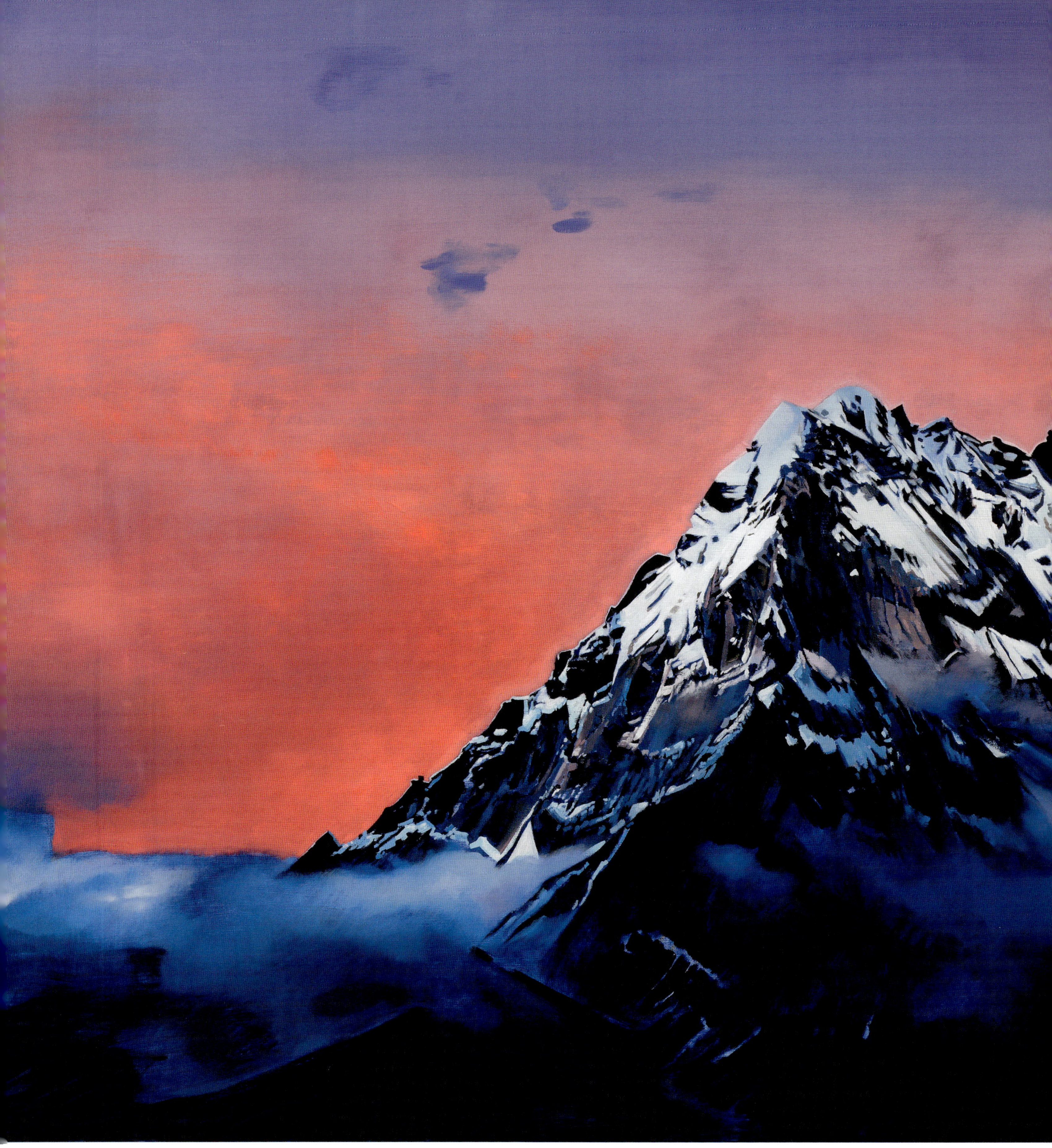

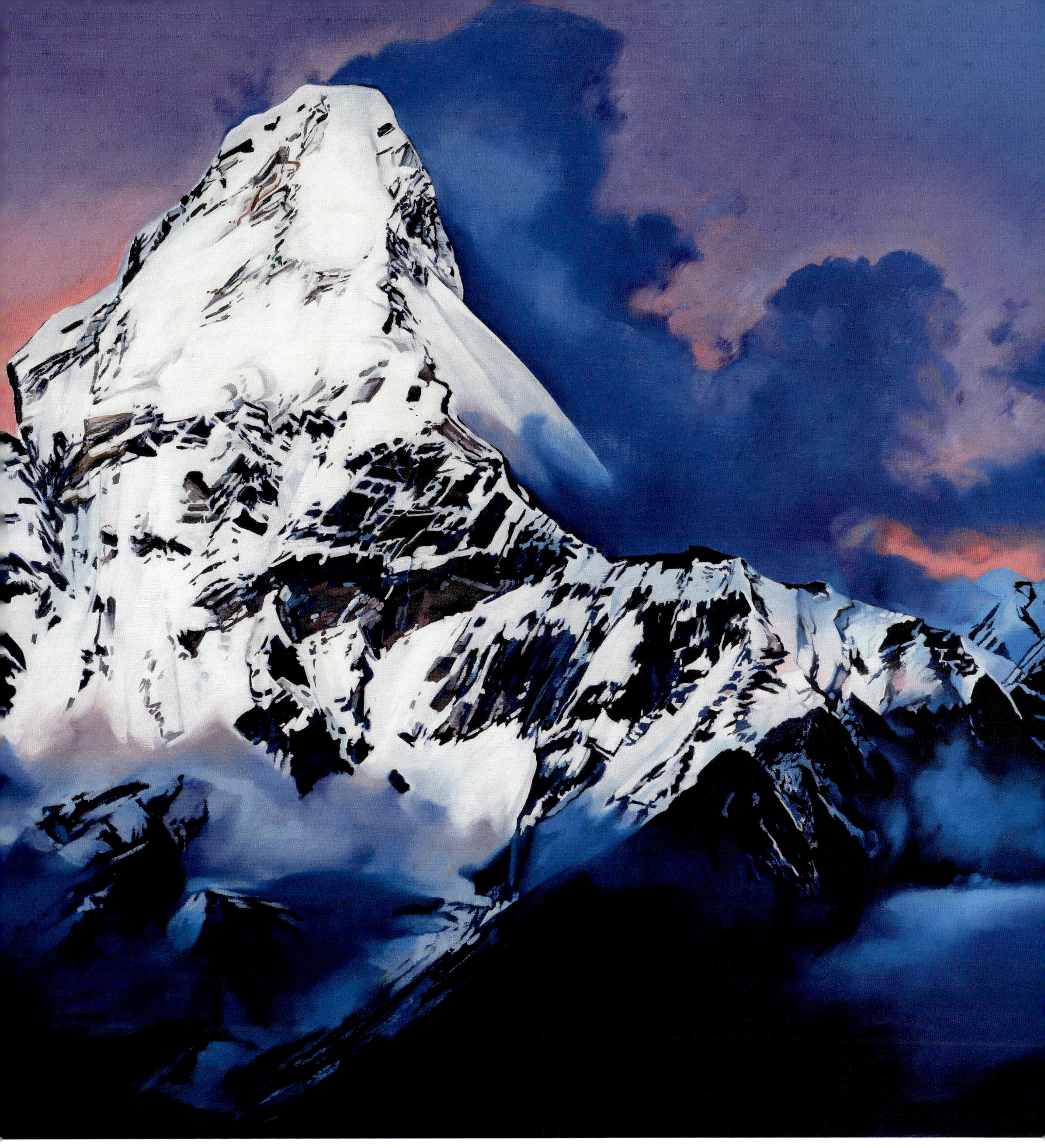

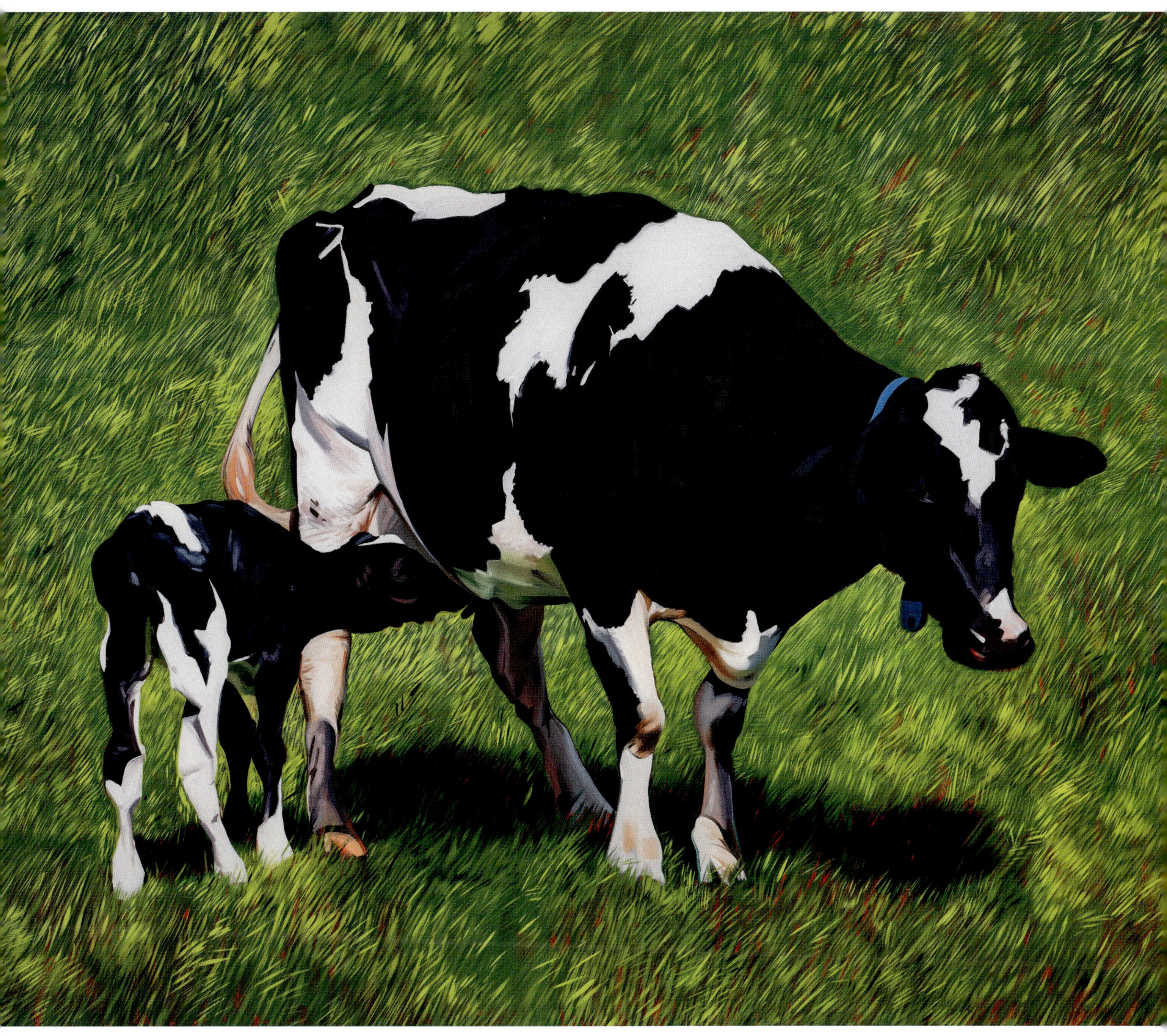

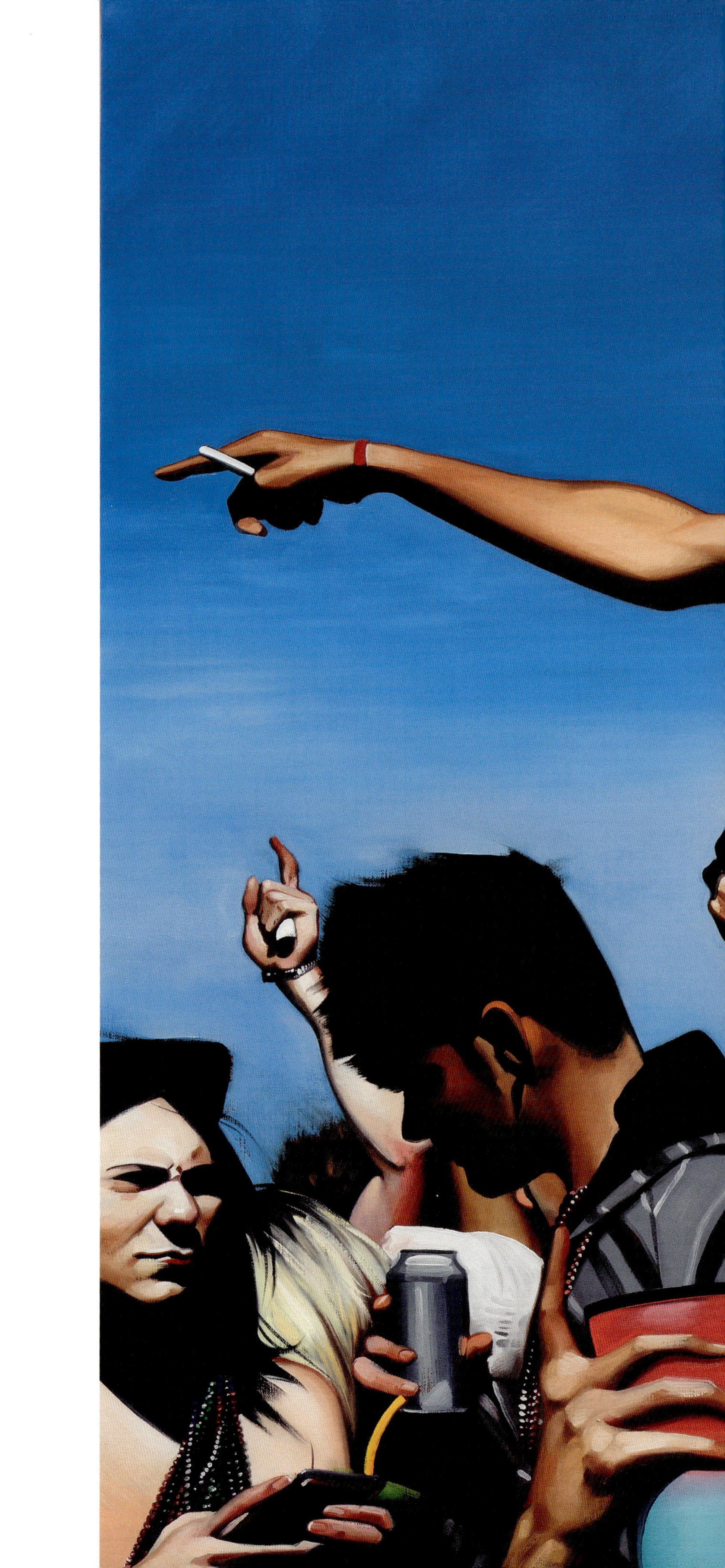

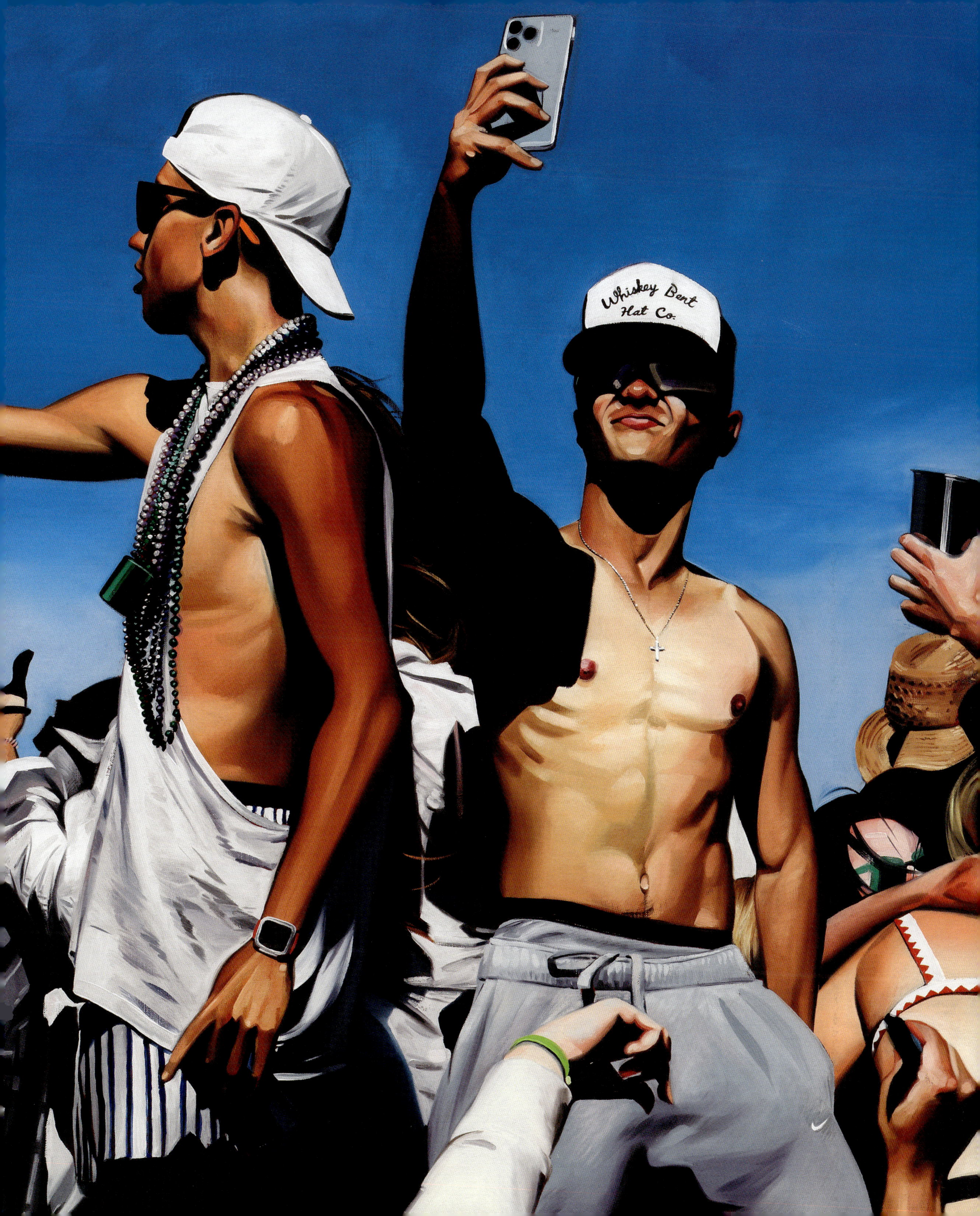
Whiskey Bent
Hat Co.

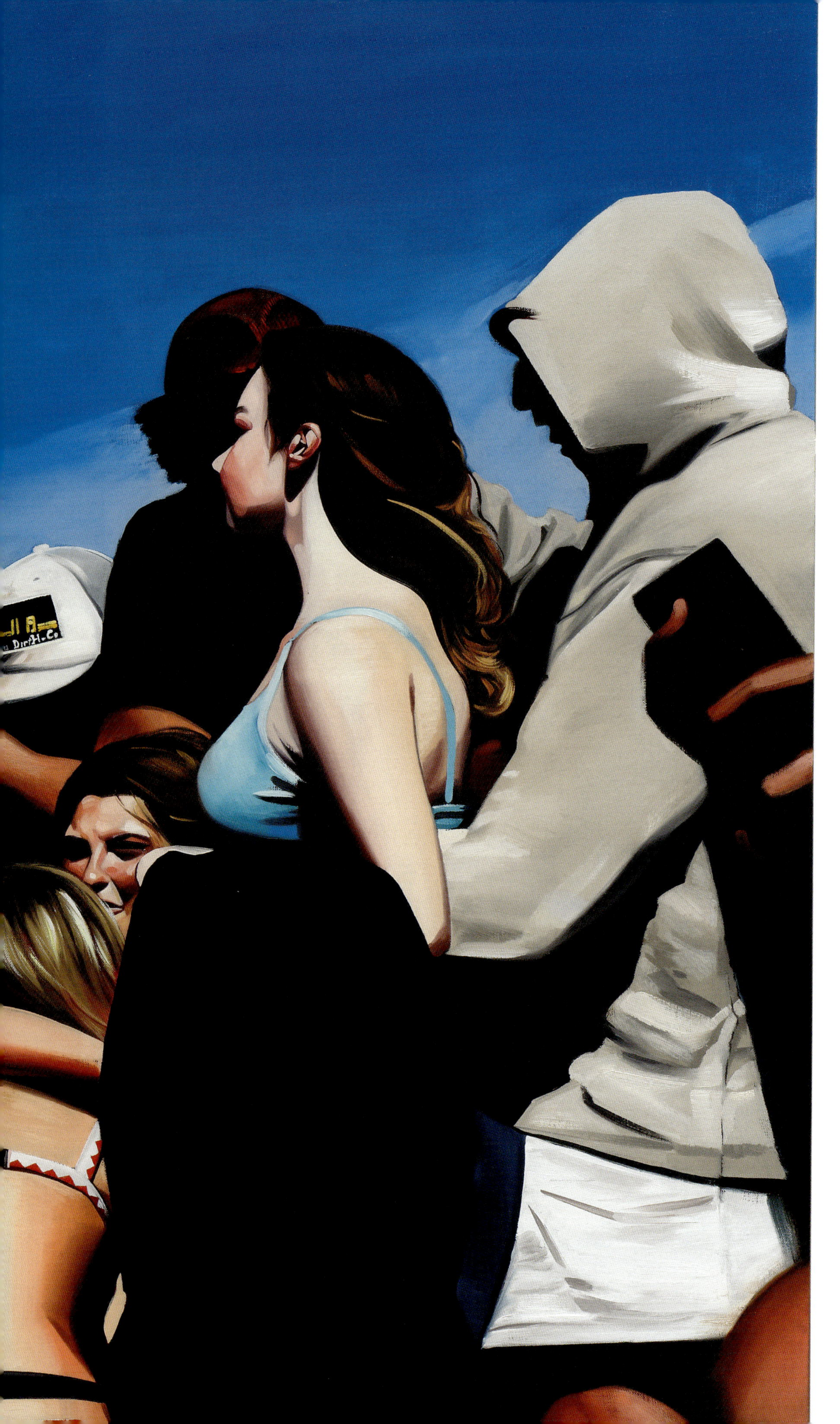

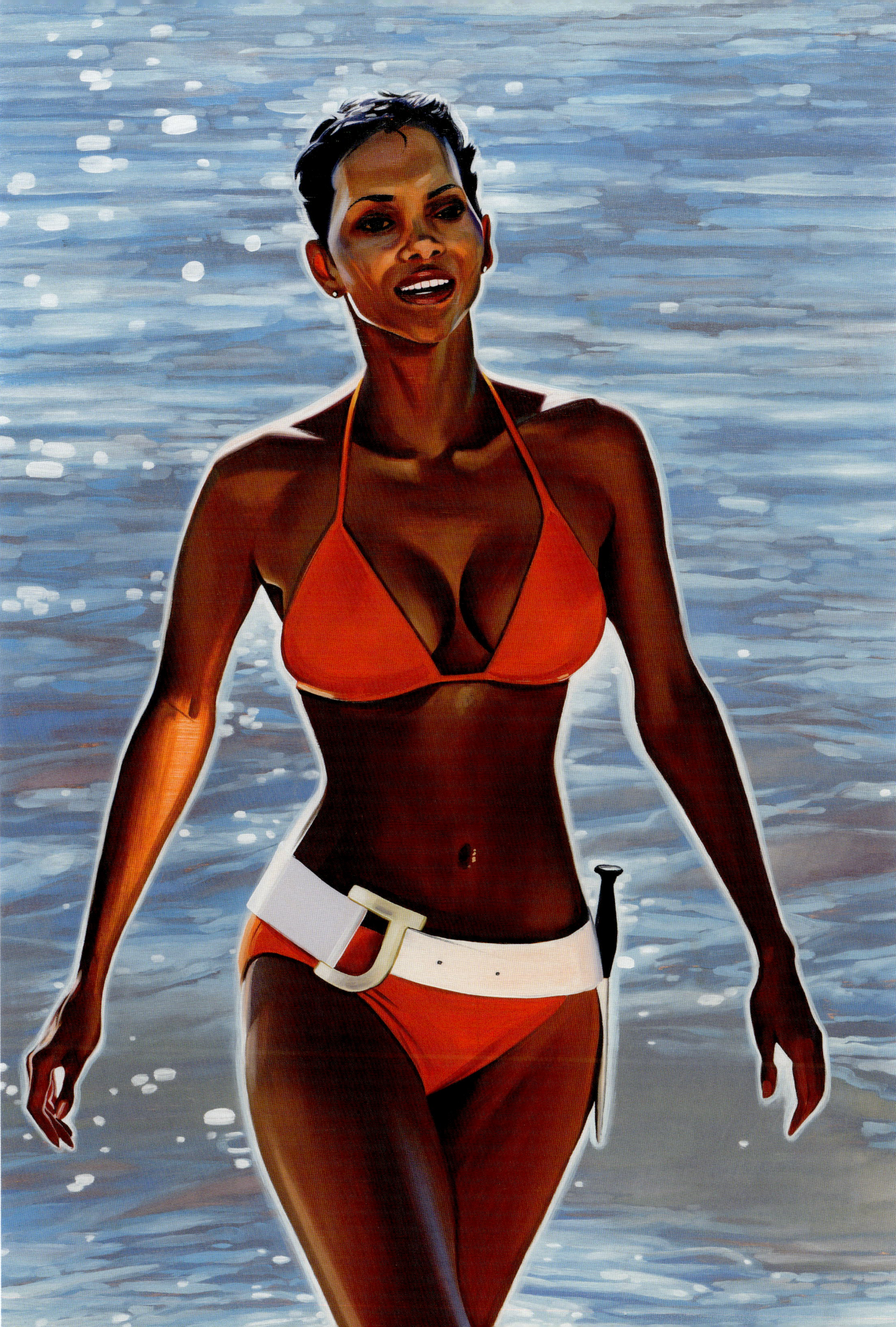

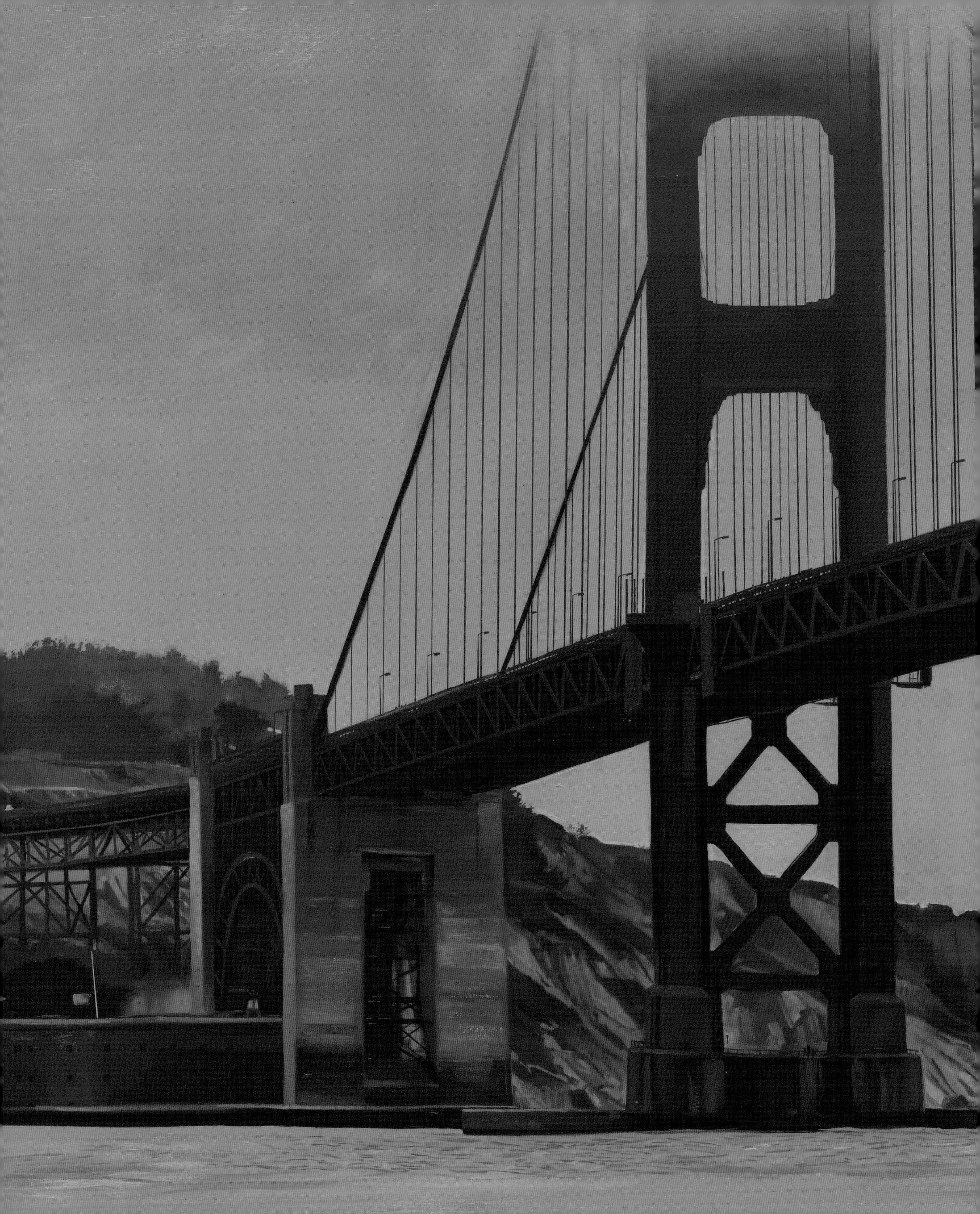

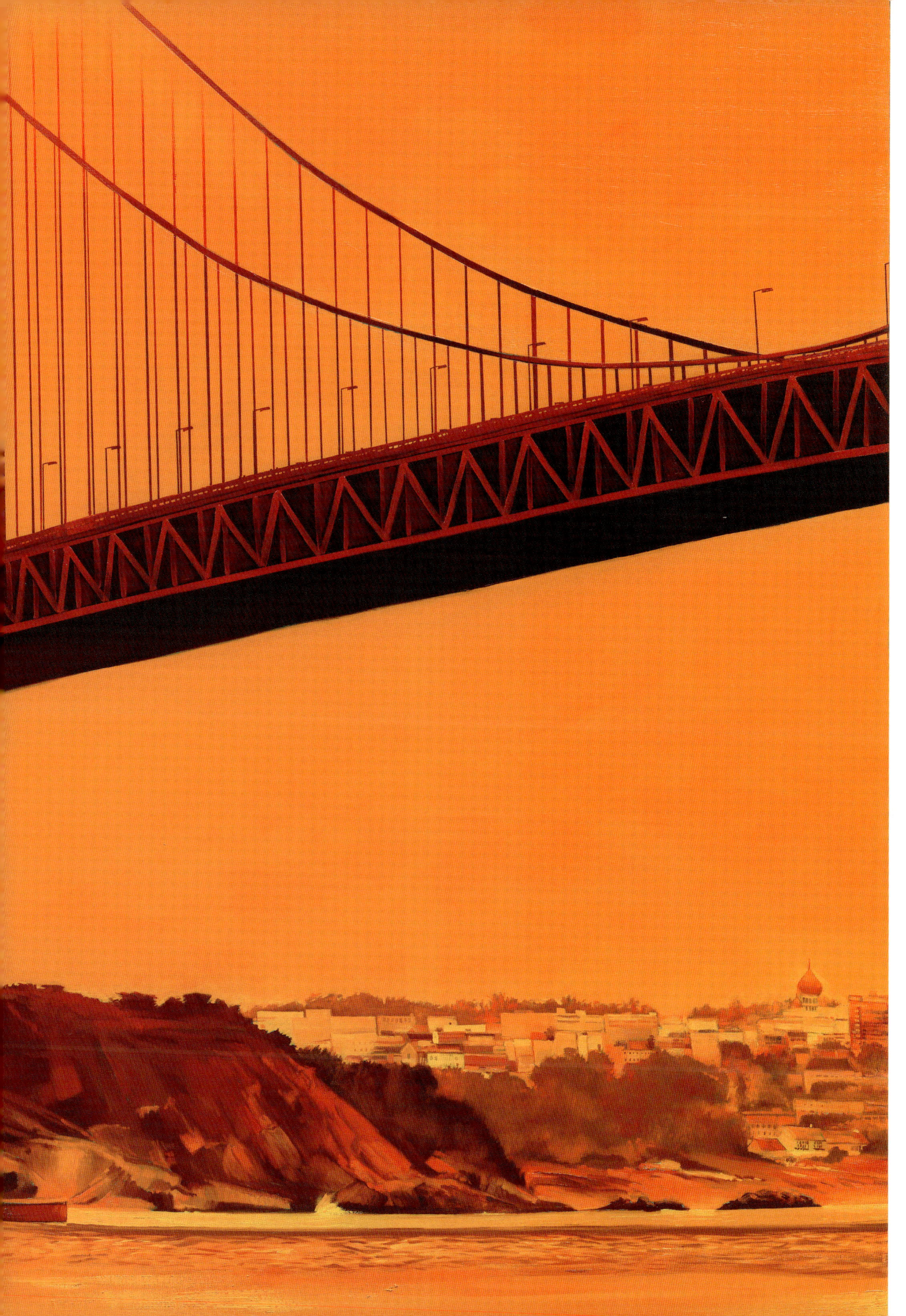

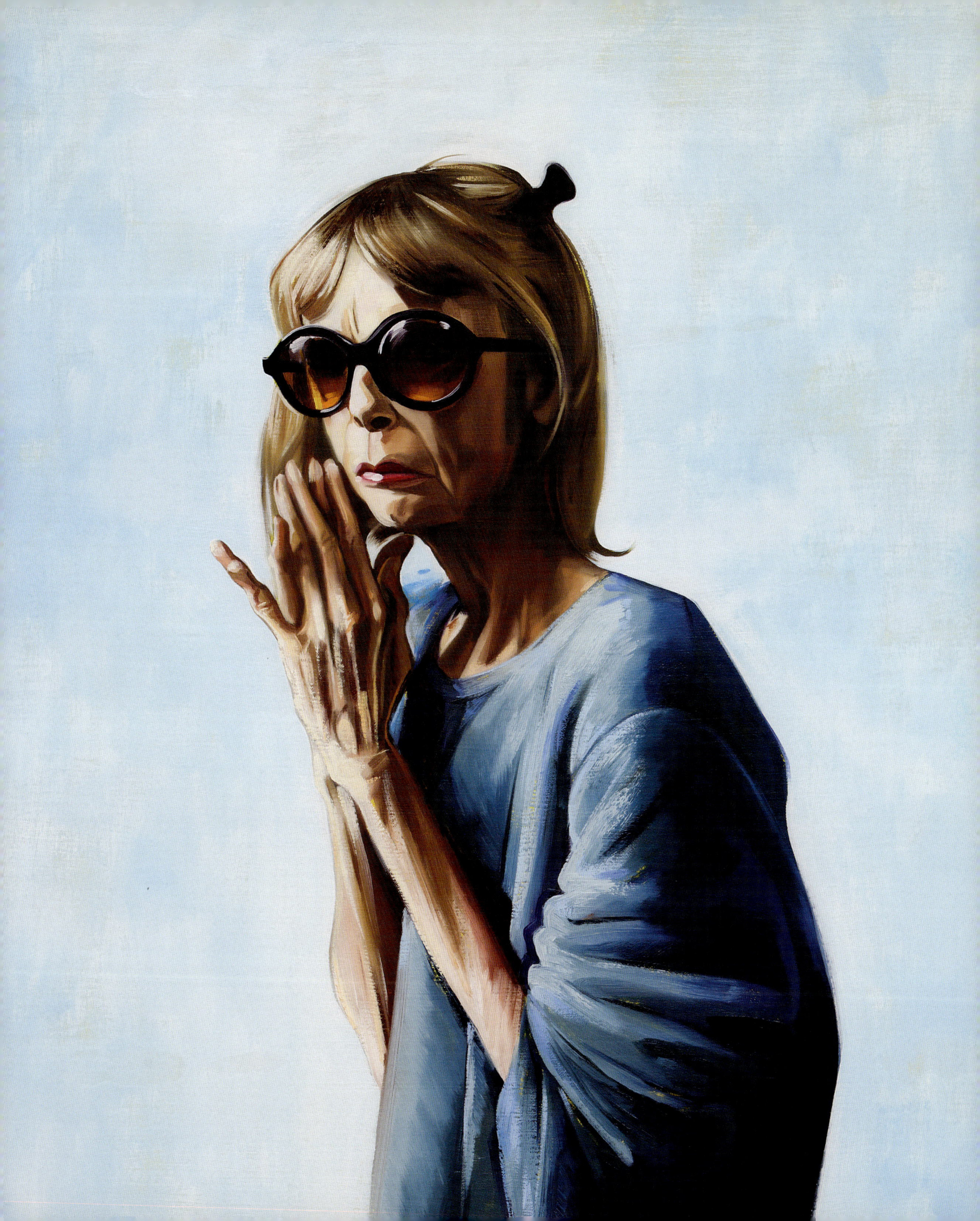

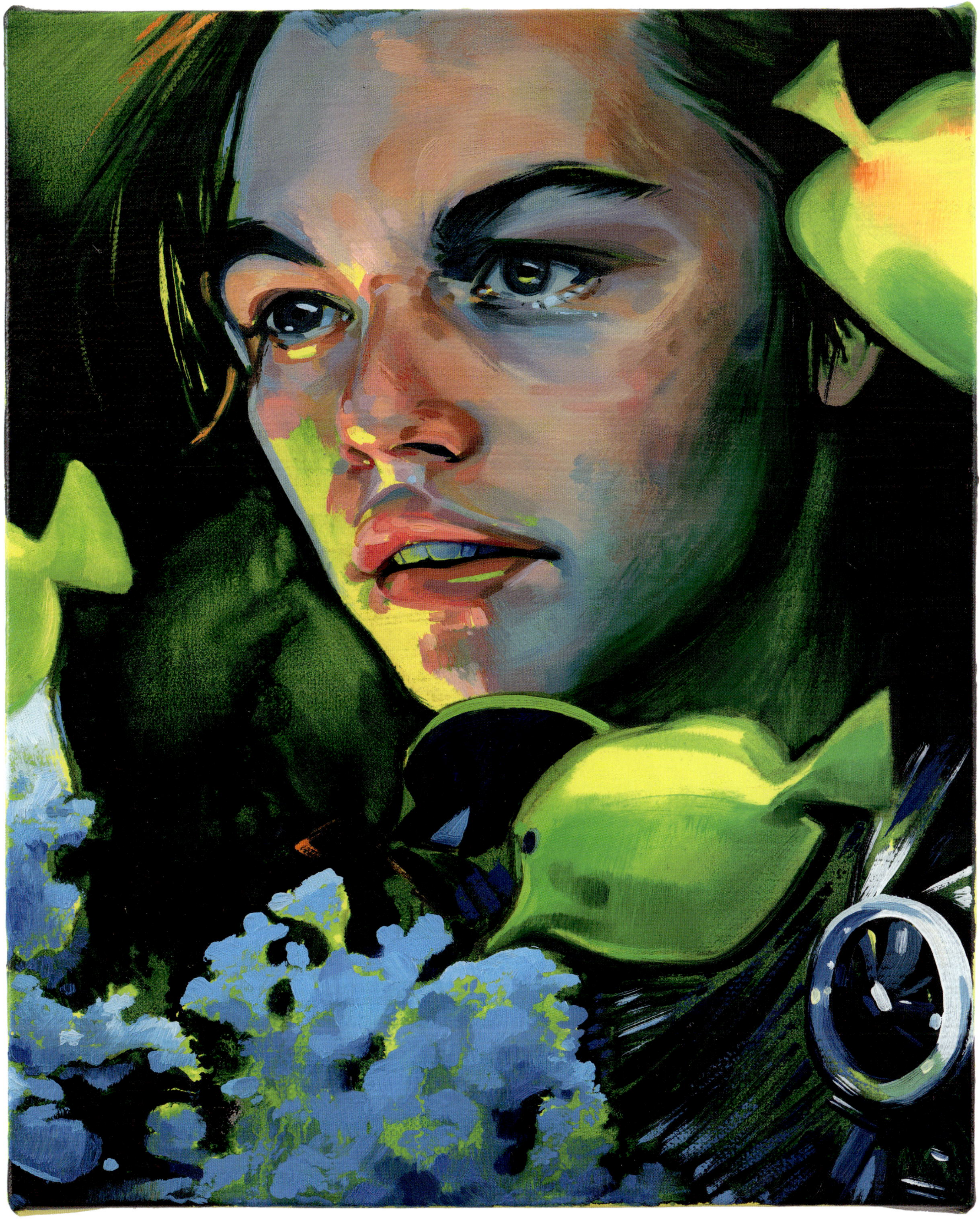

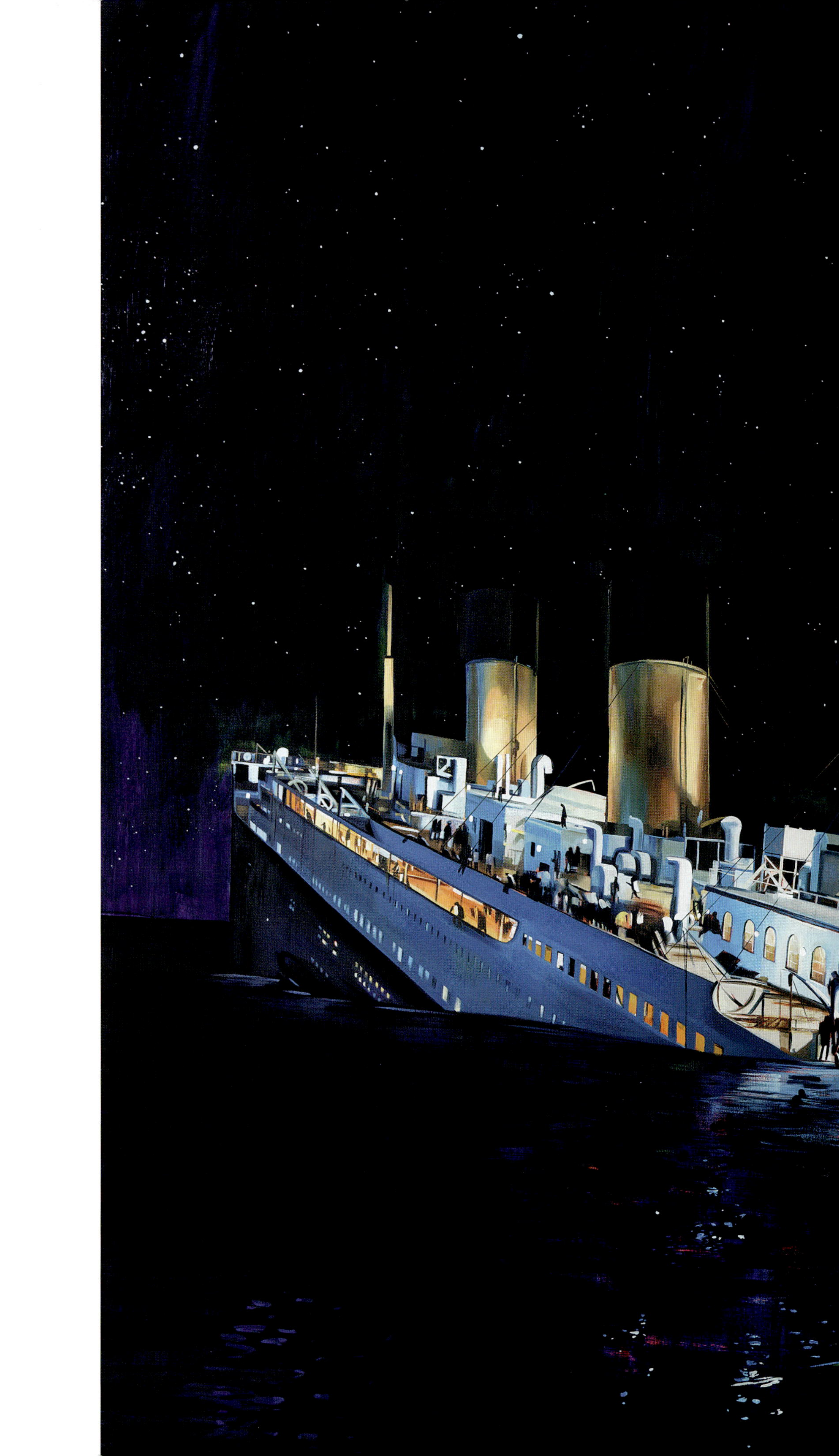

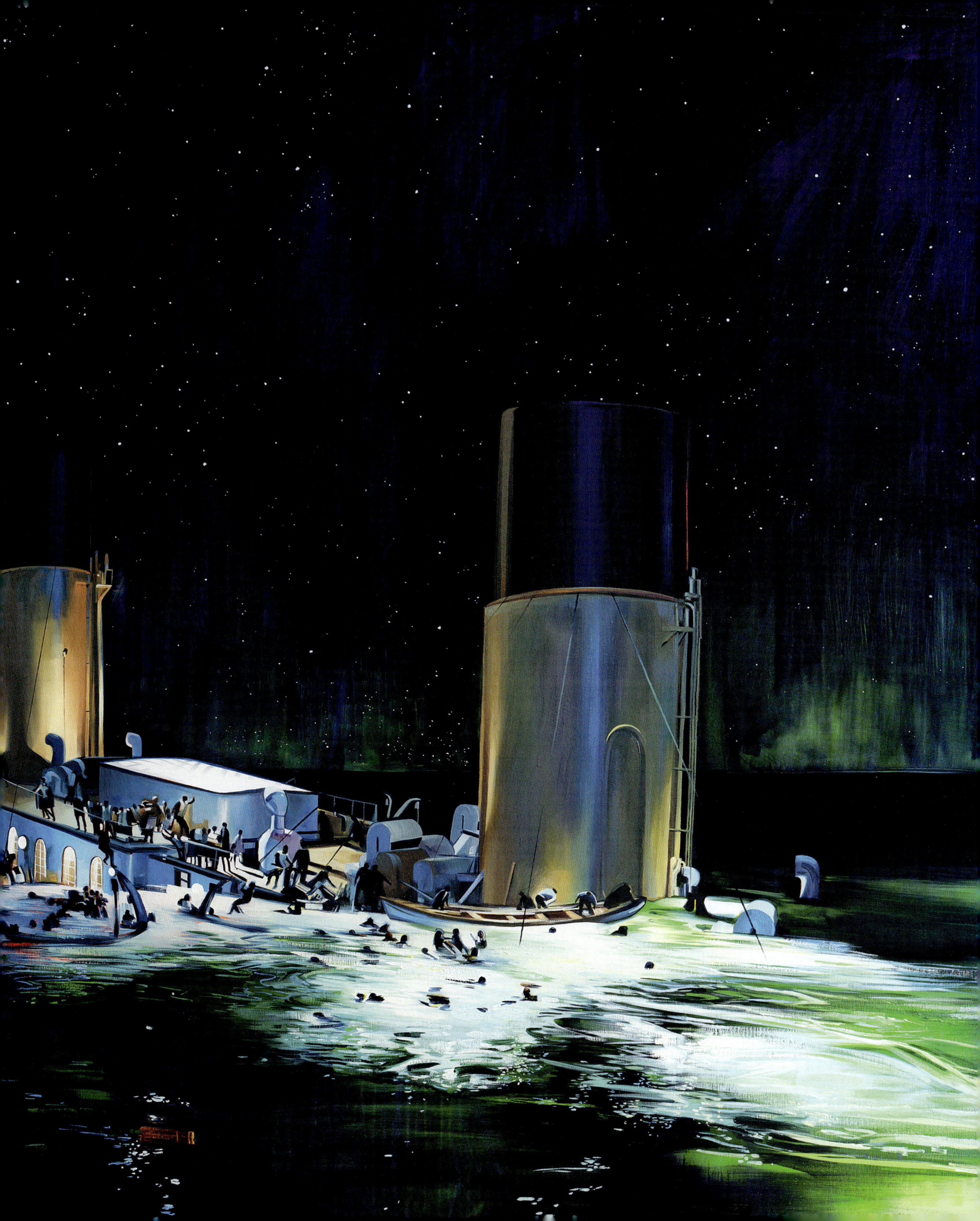

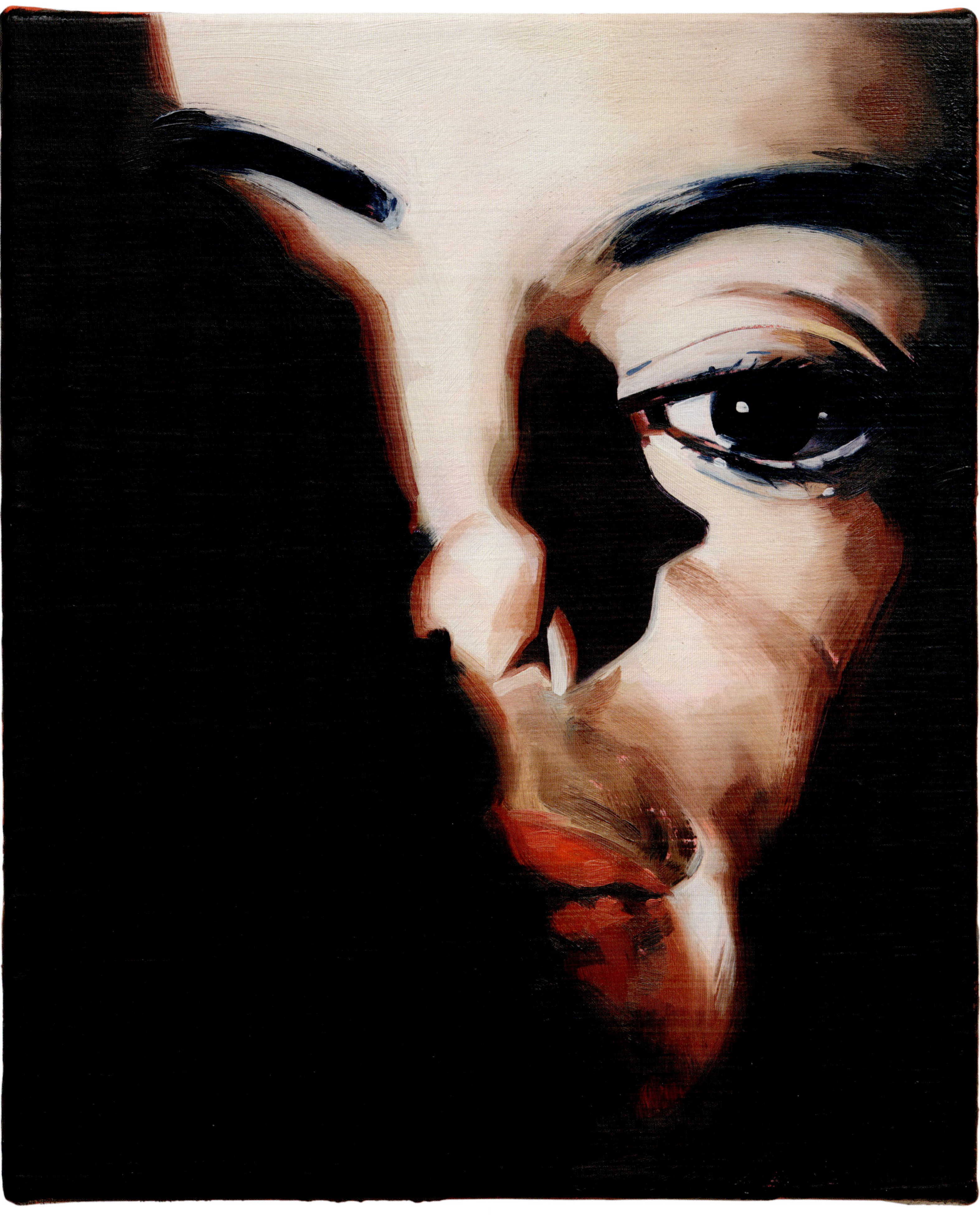

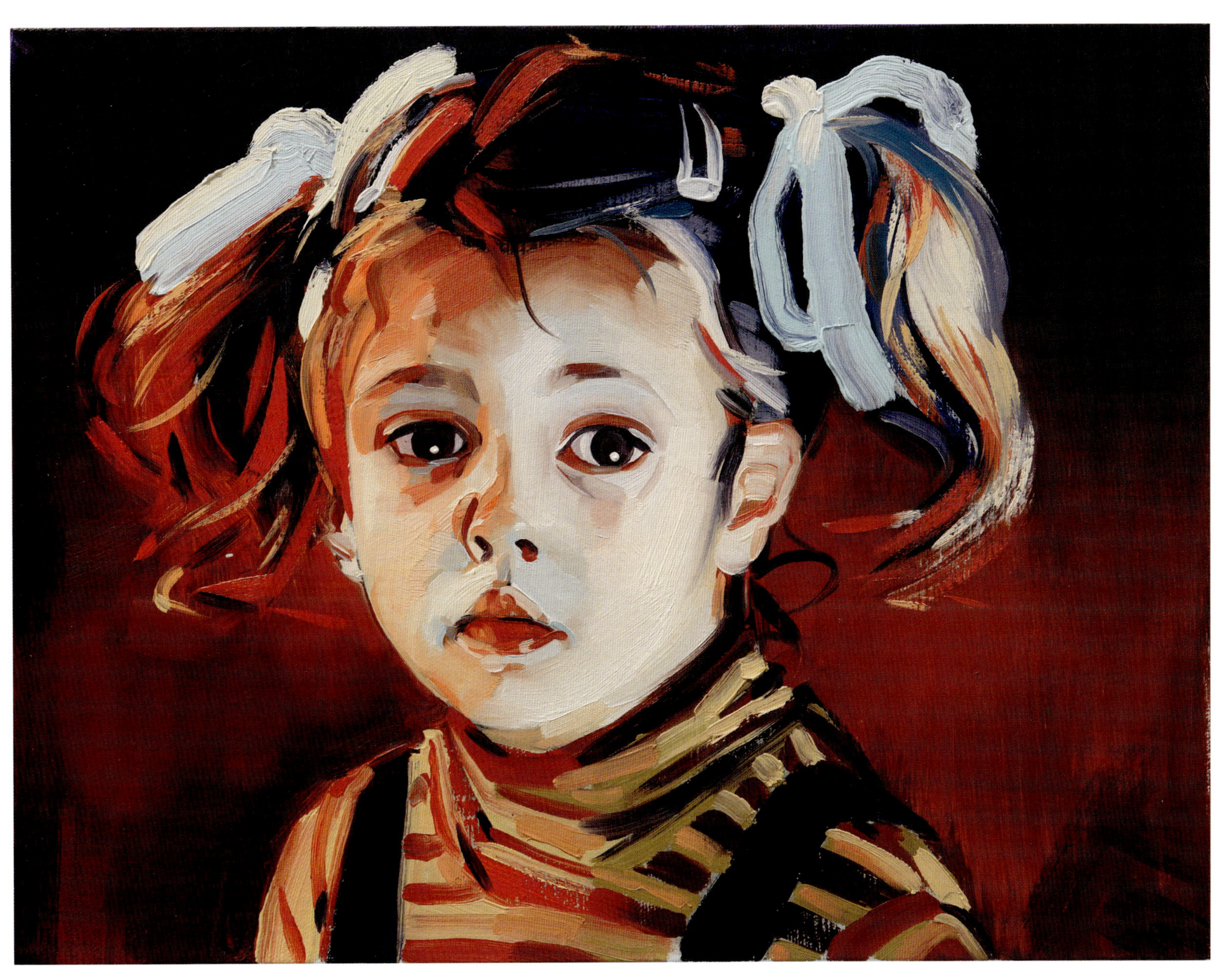

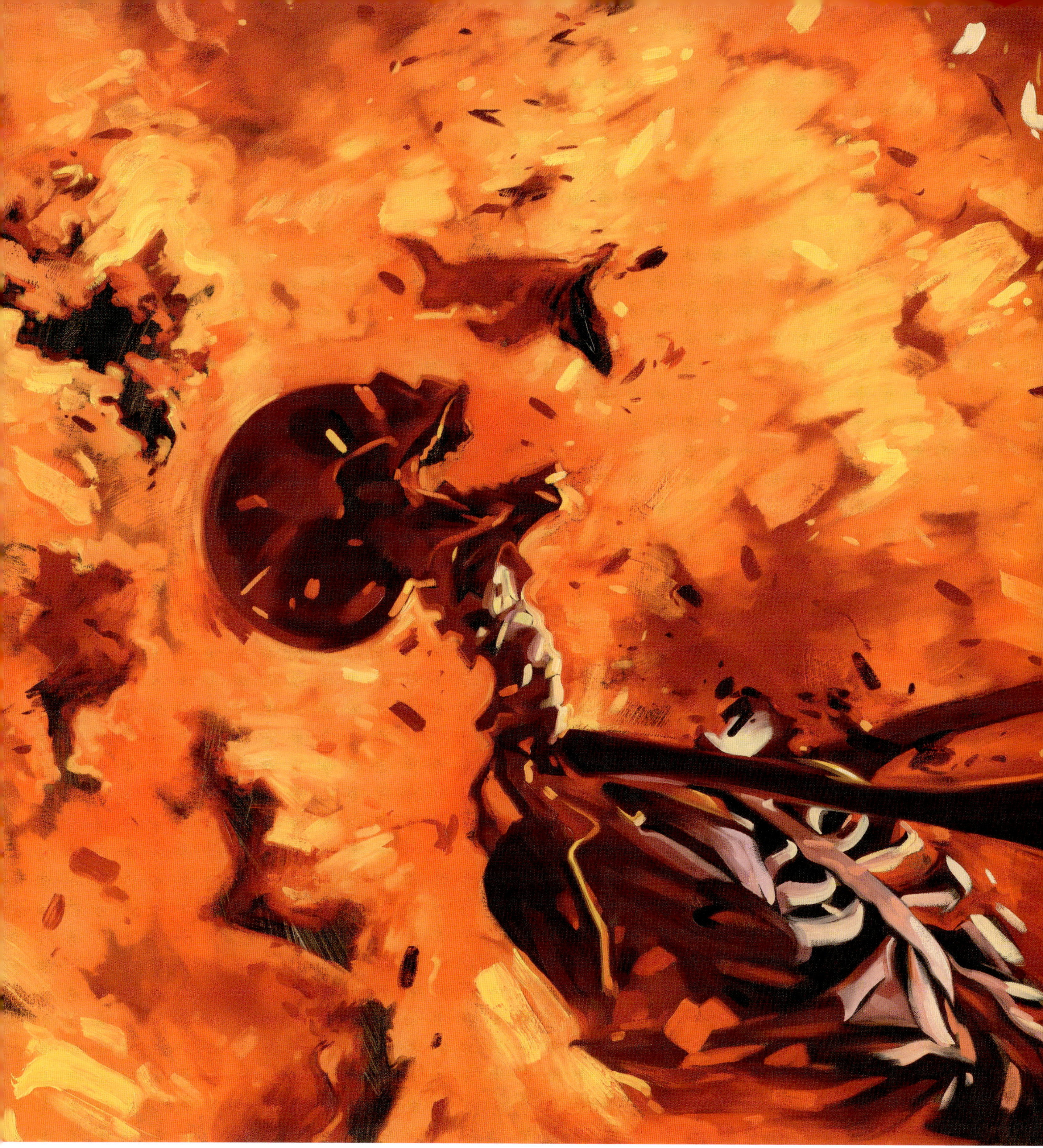

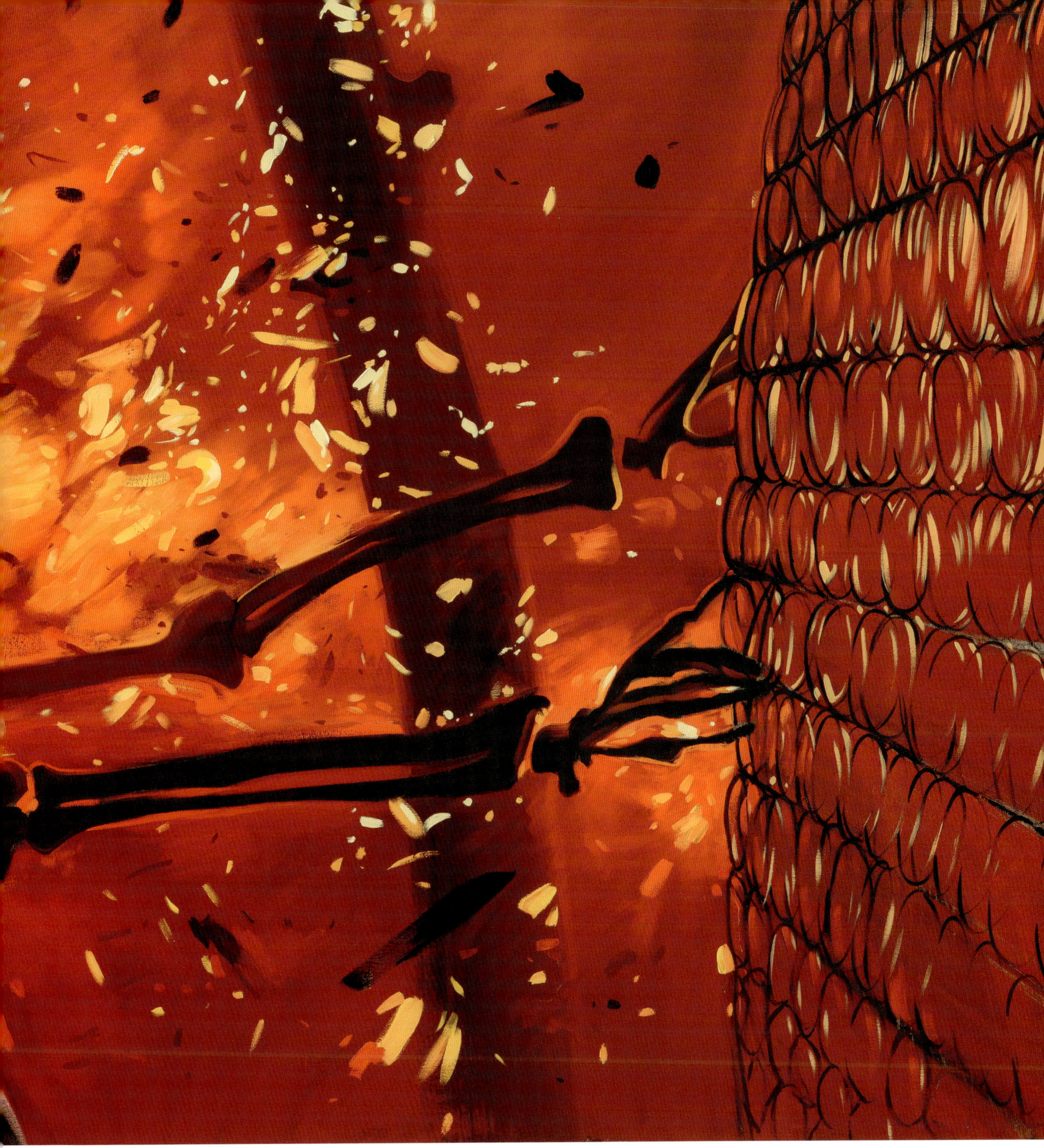

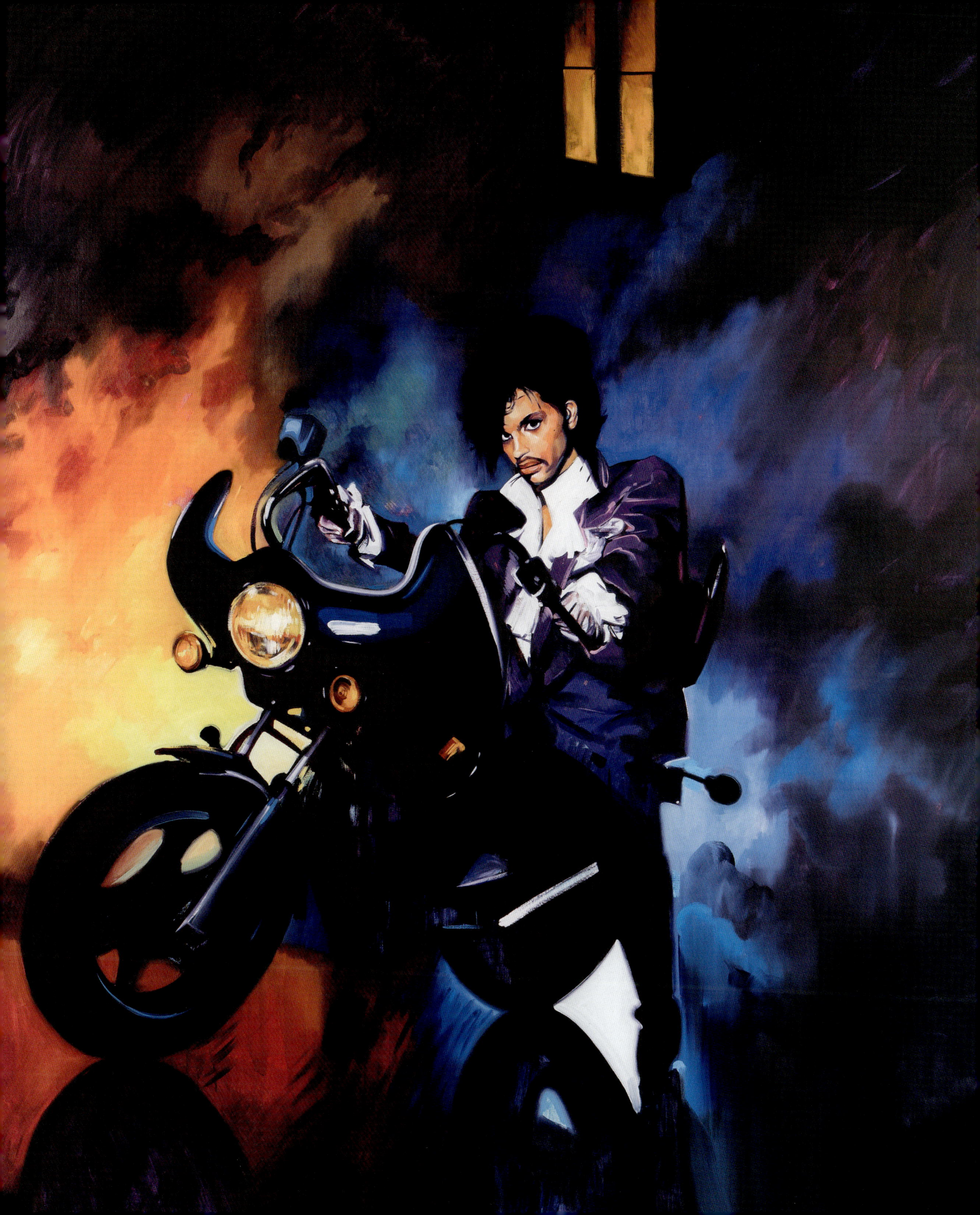

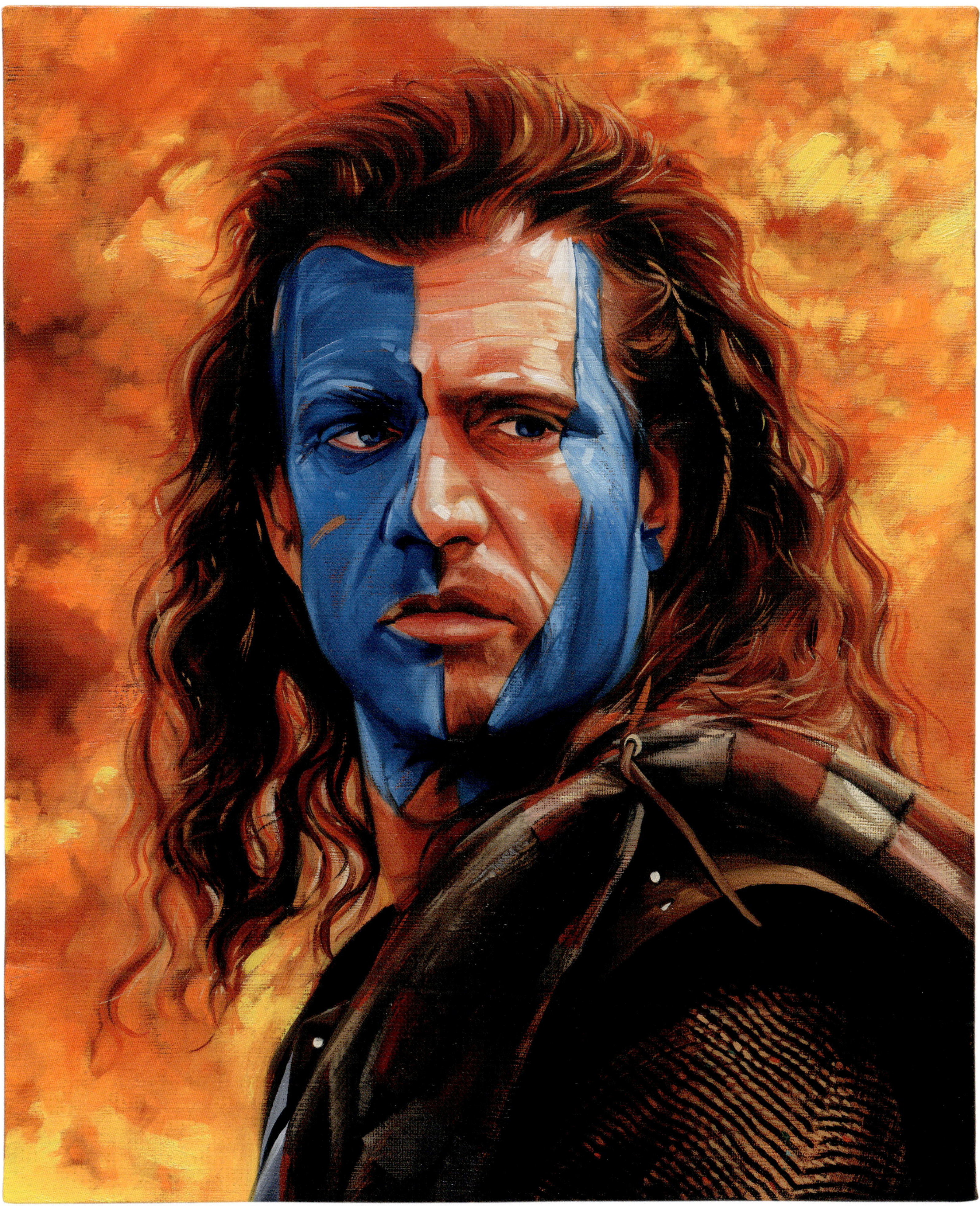

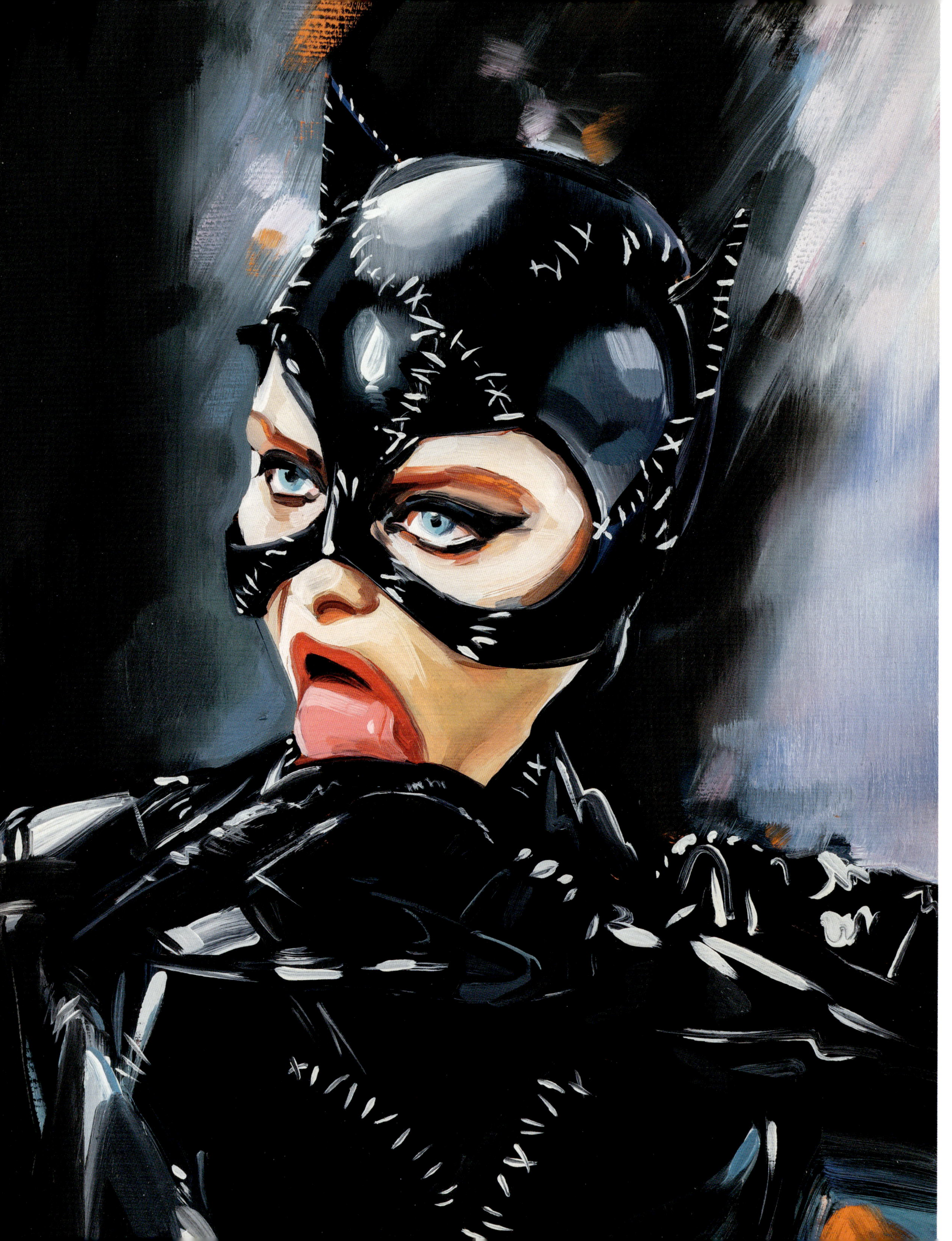

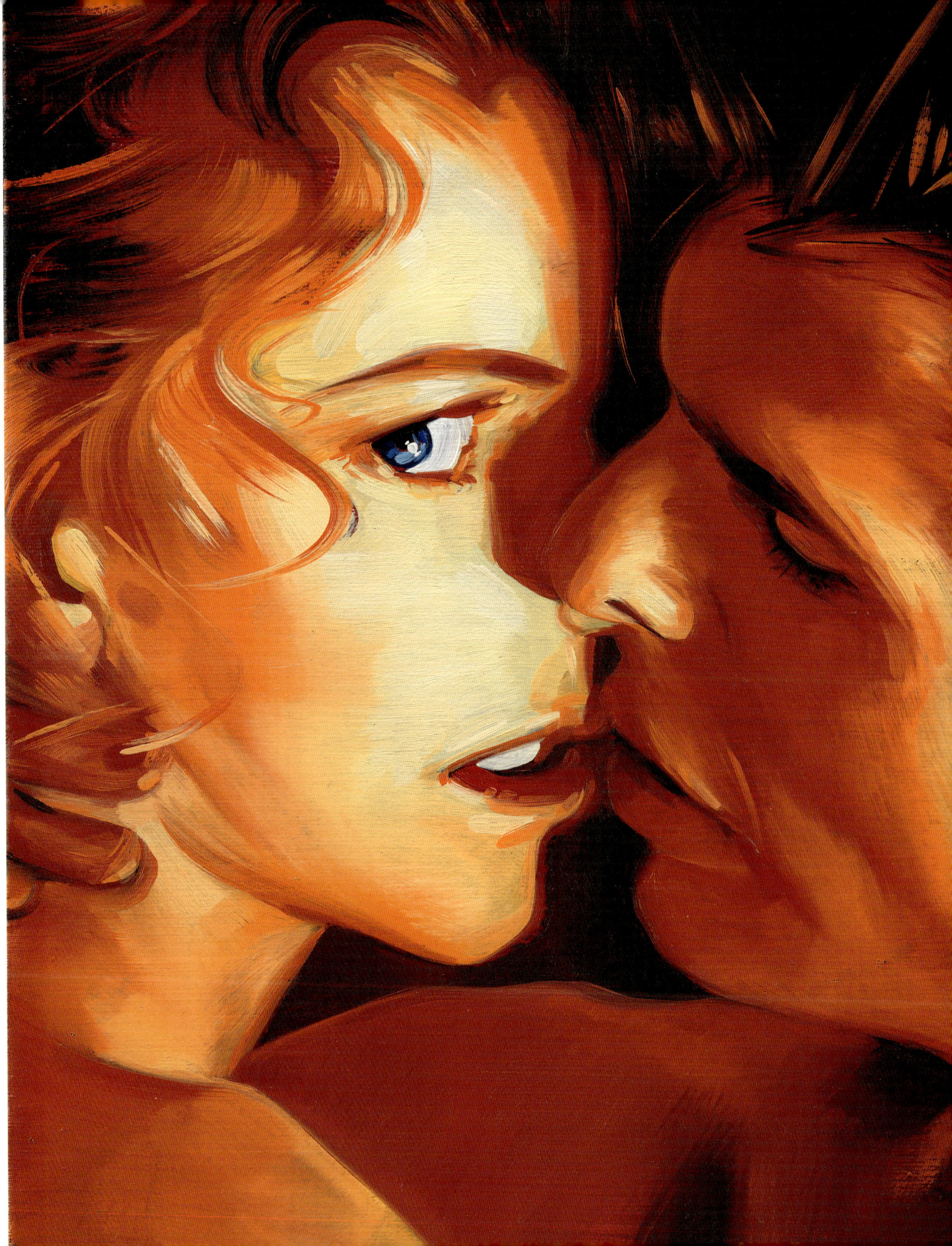

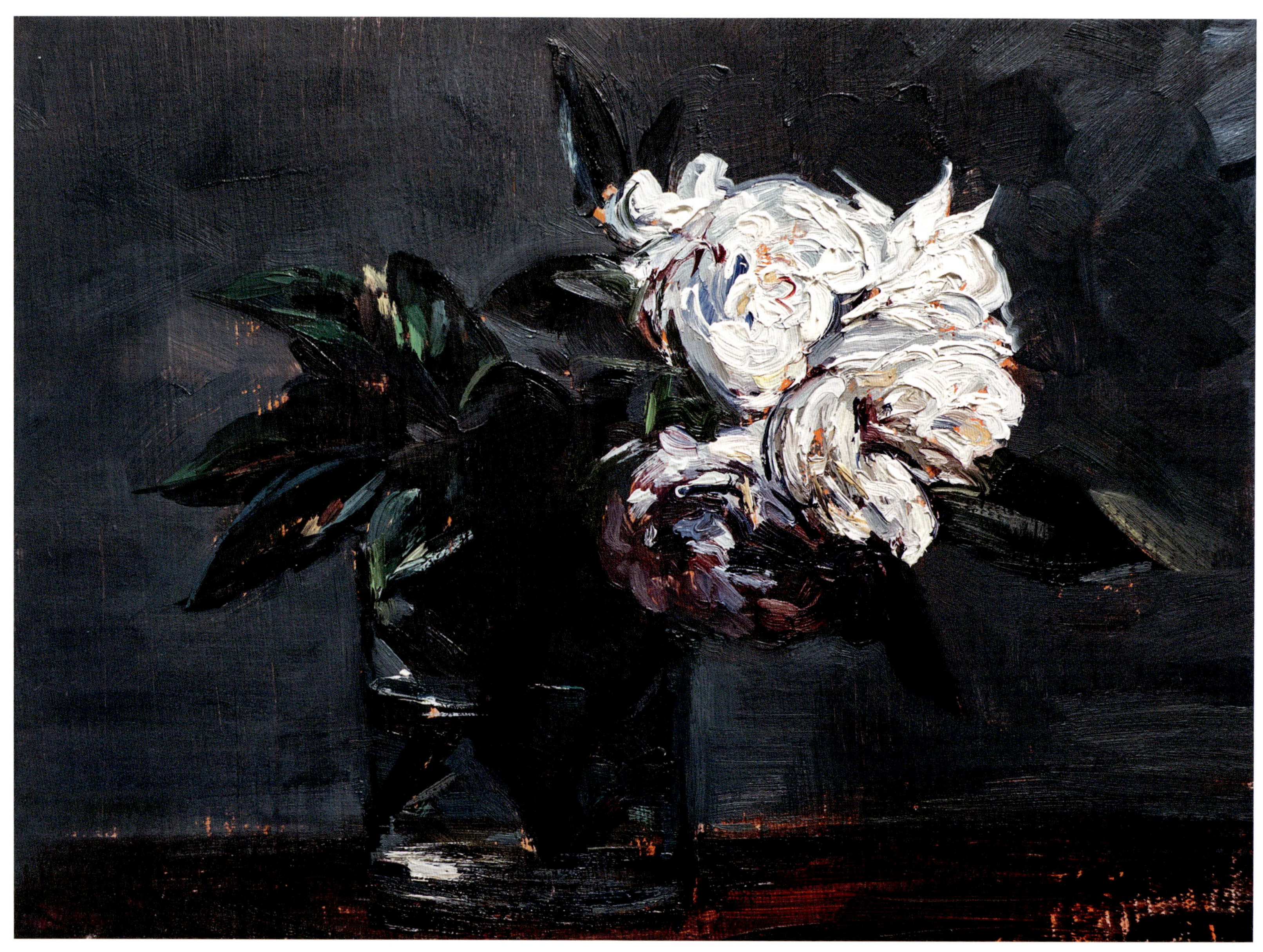

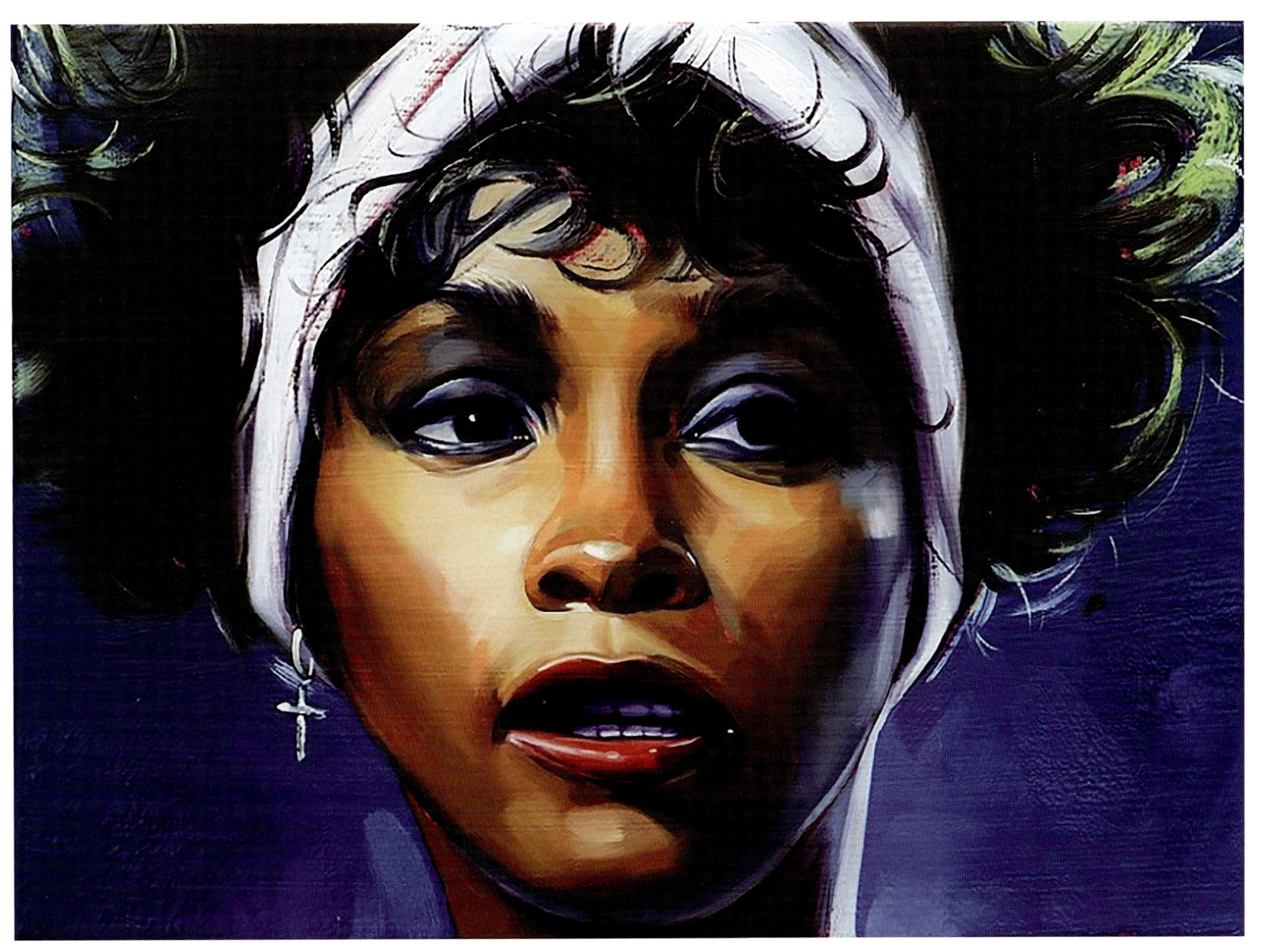

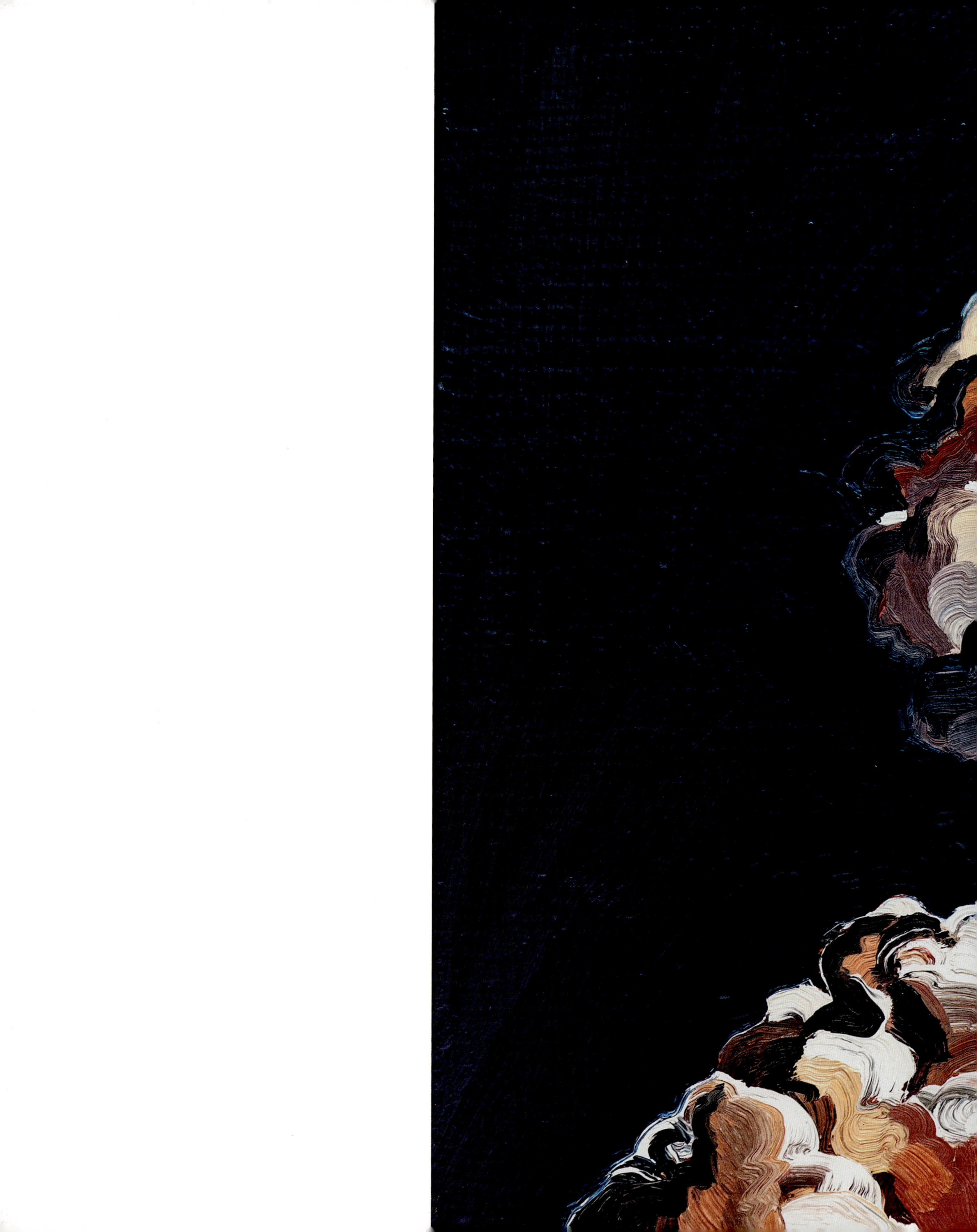

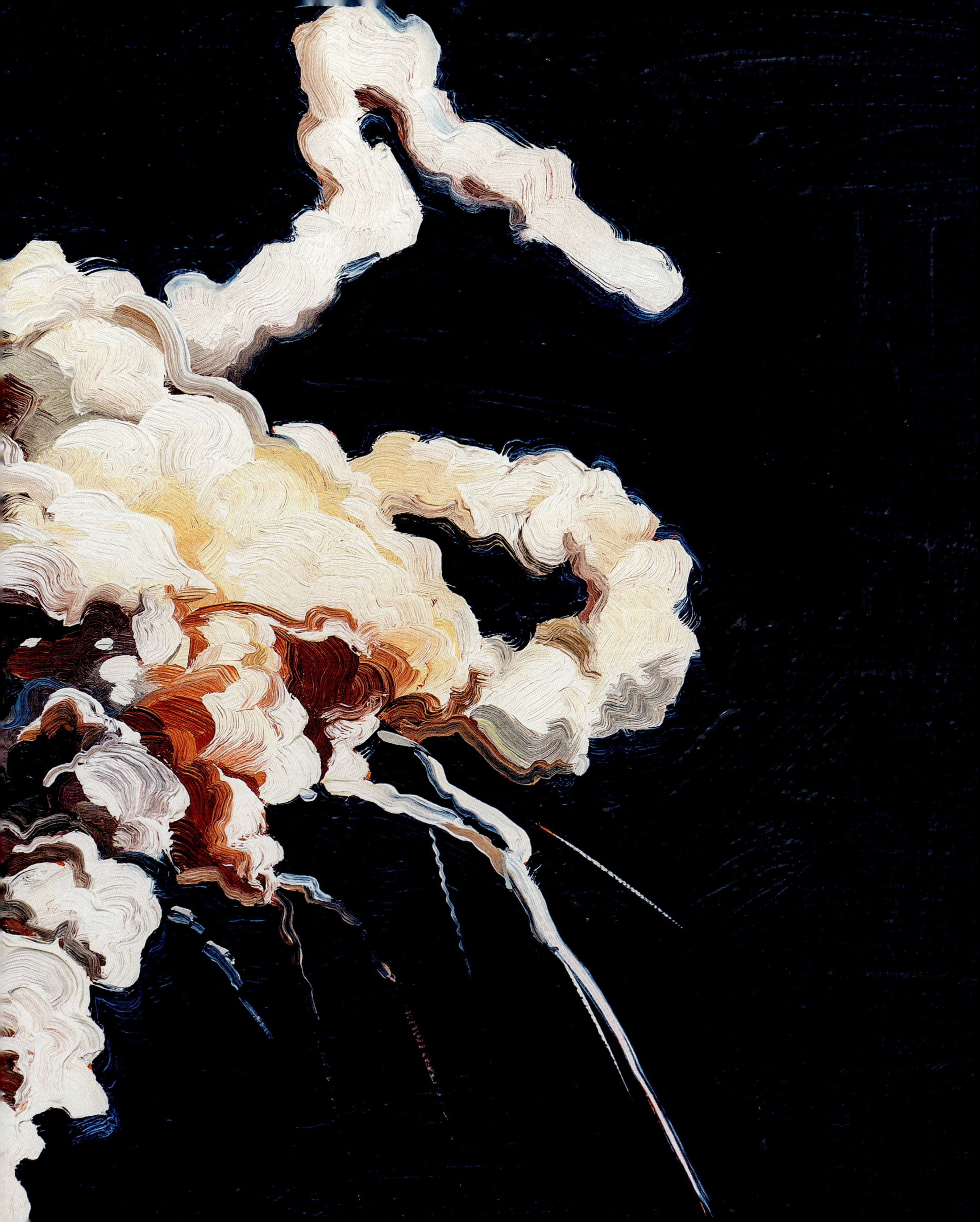

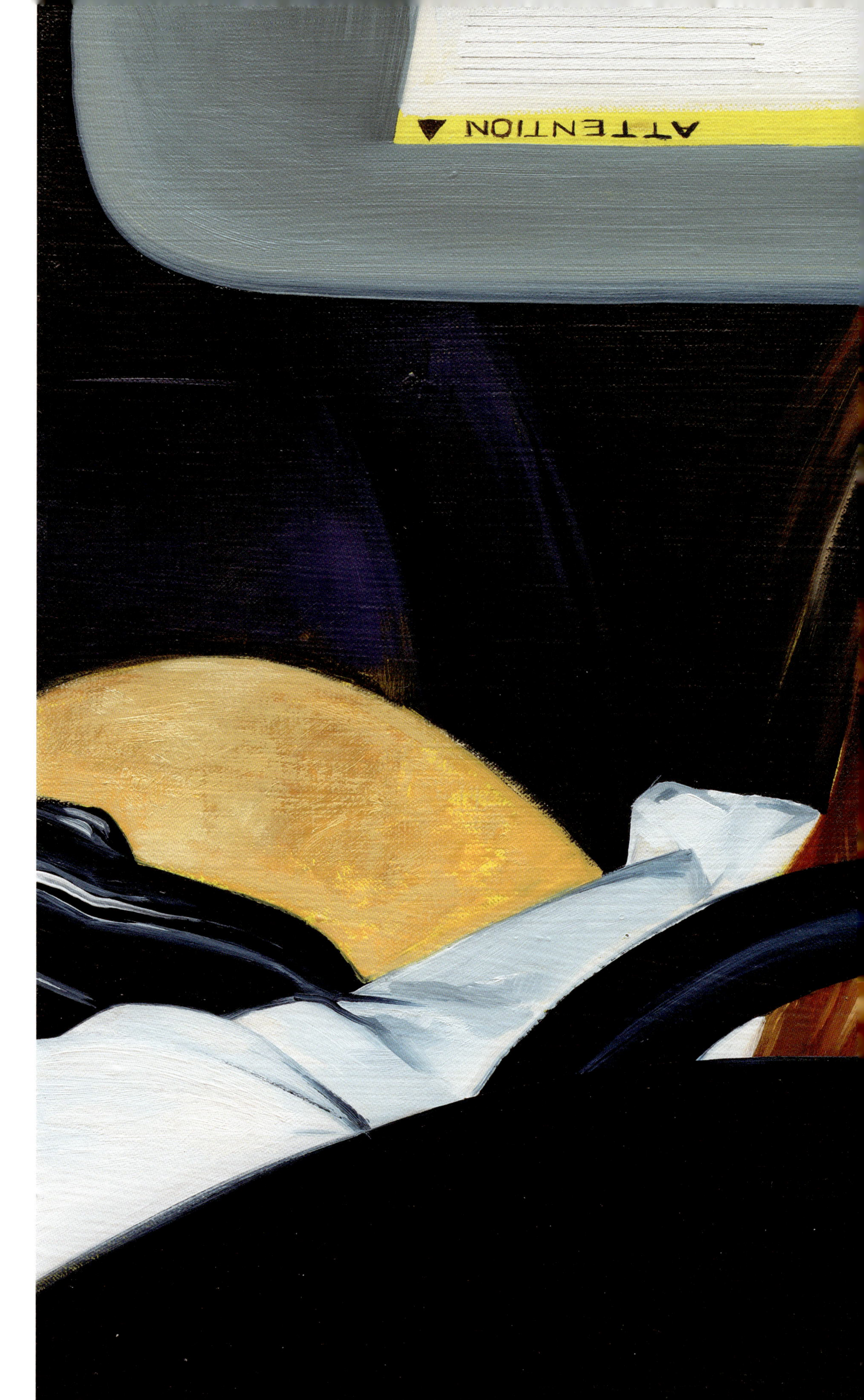
ATTENTION

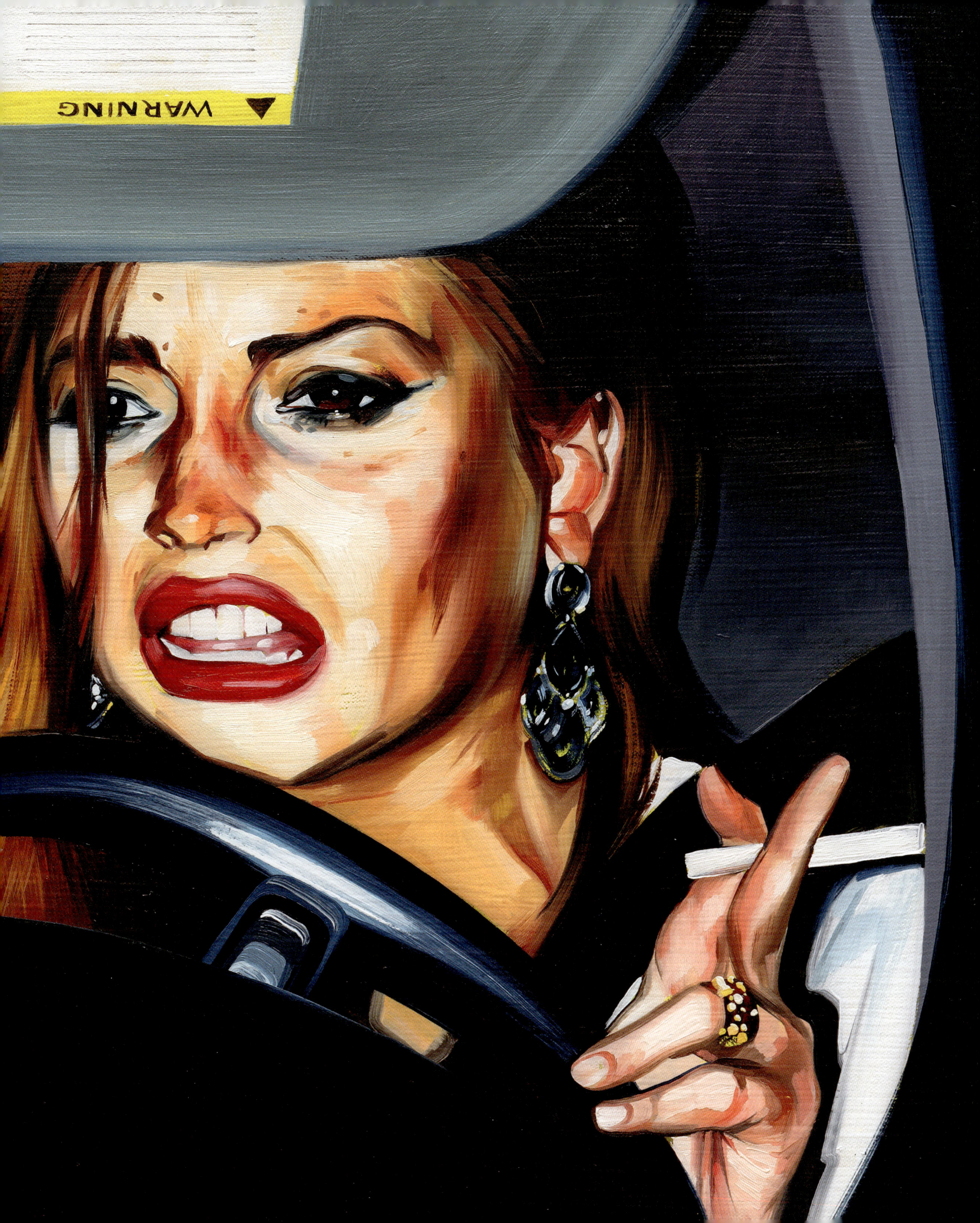
WARNING

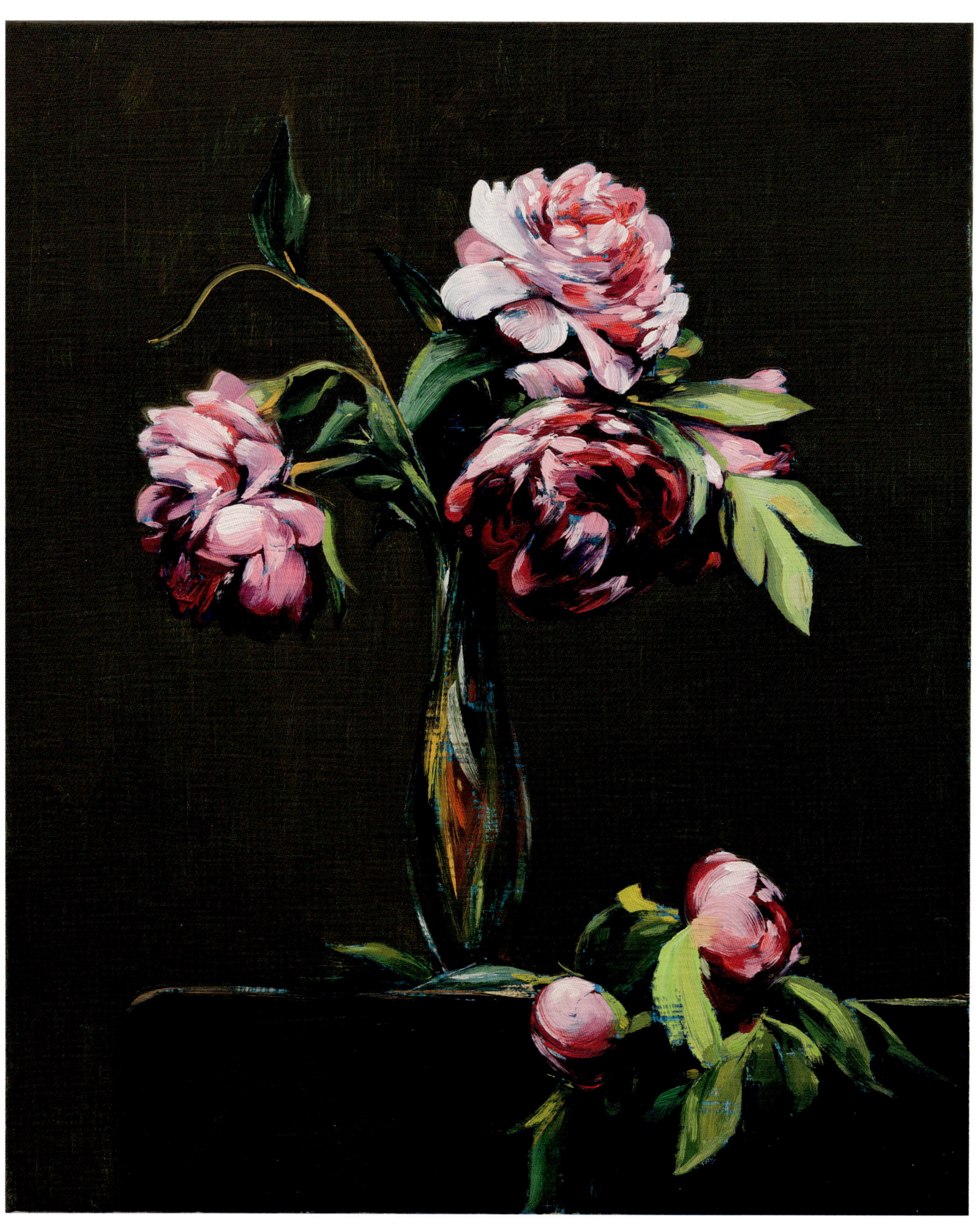

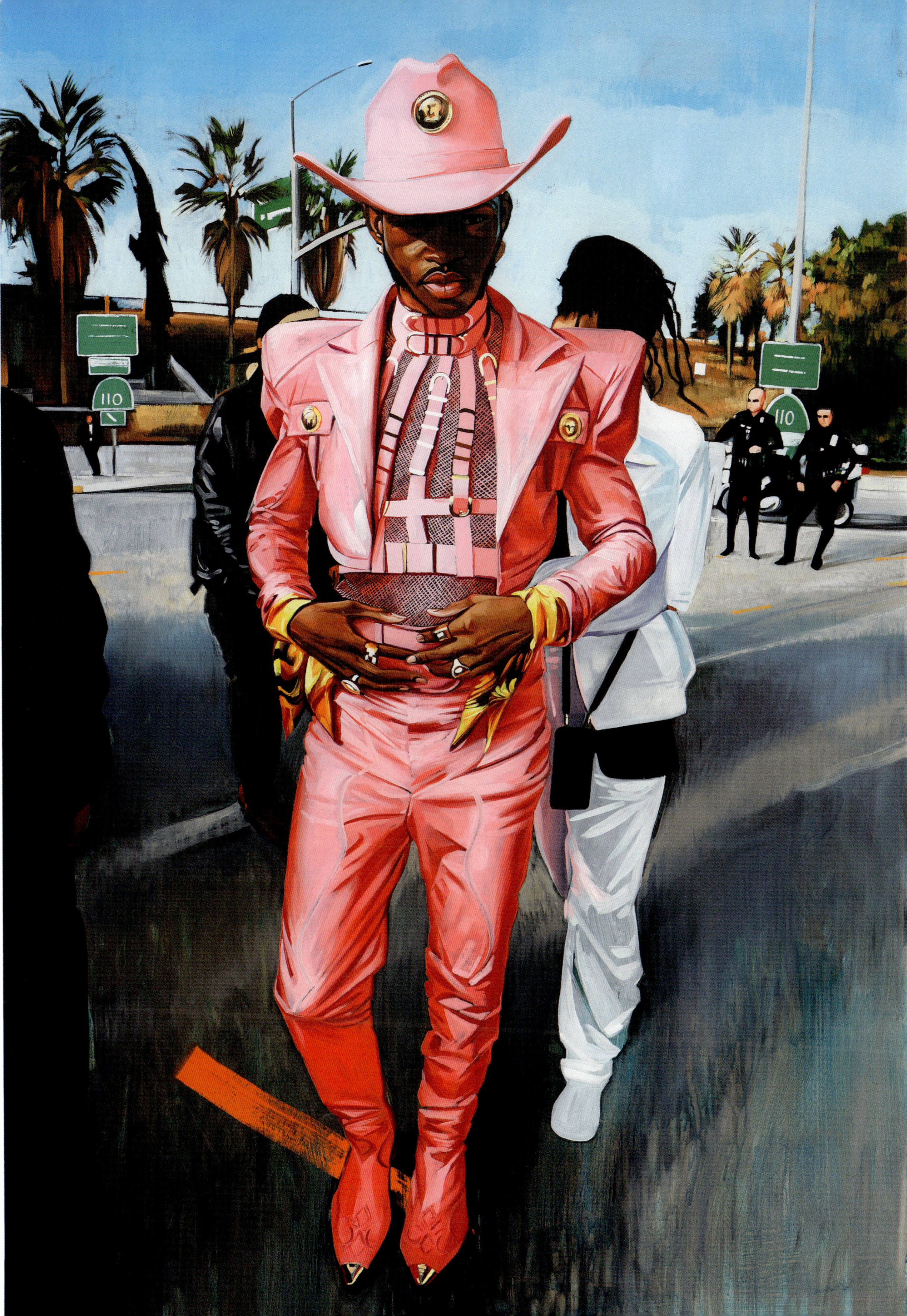
110
110

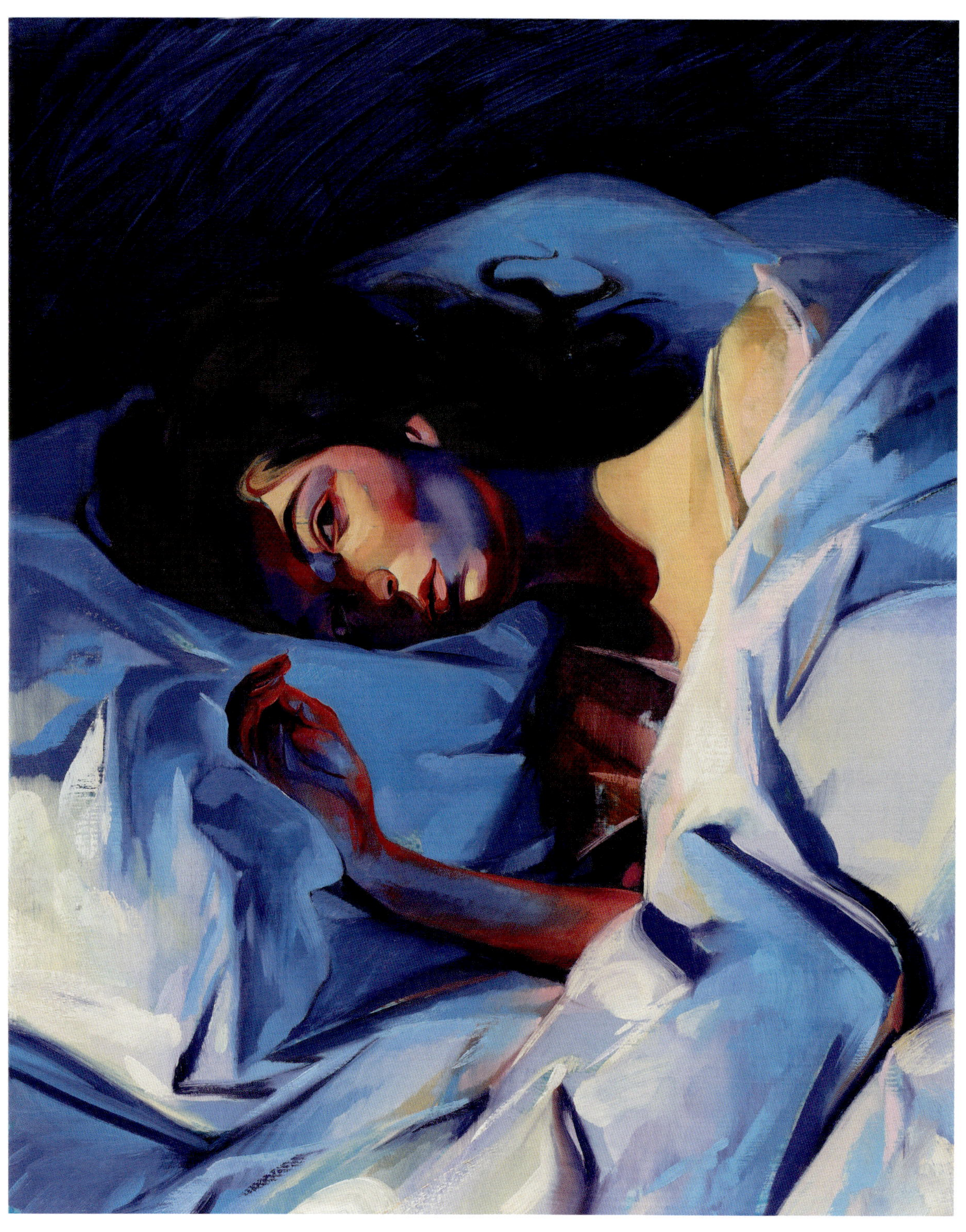

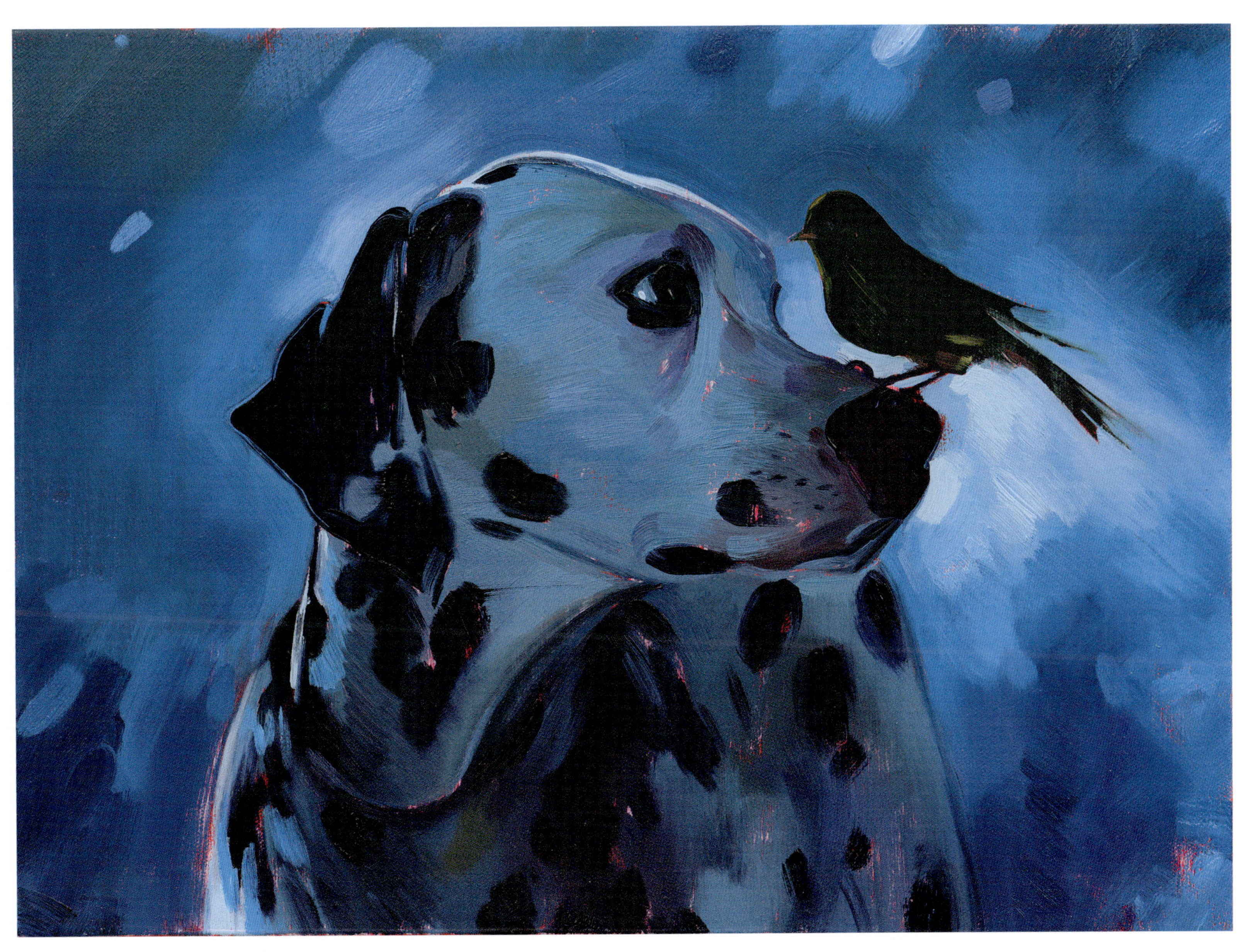

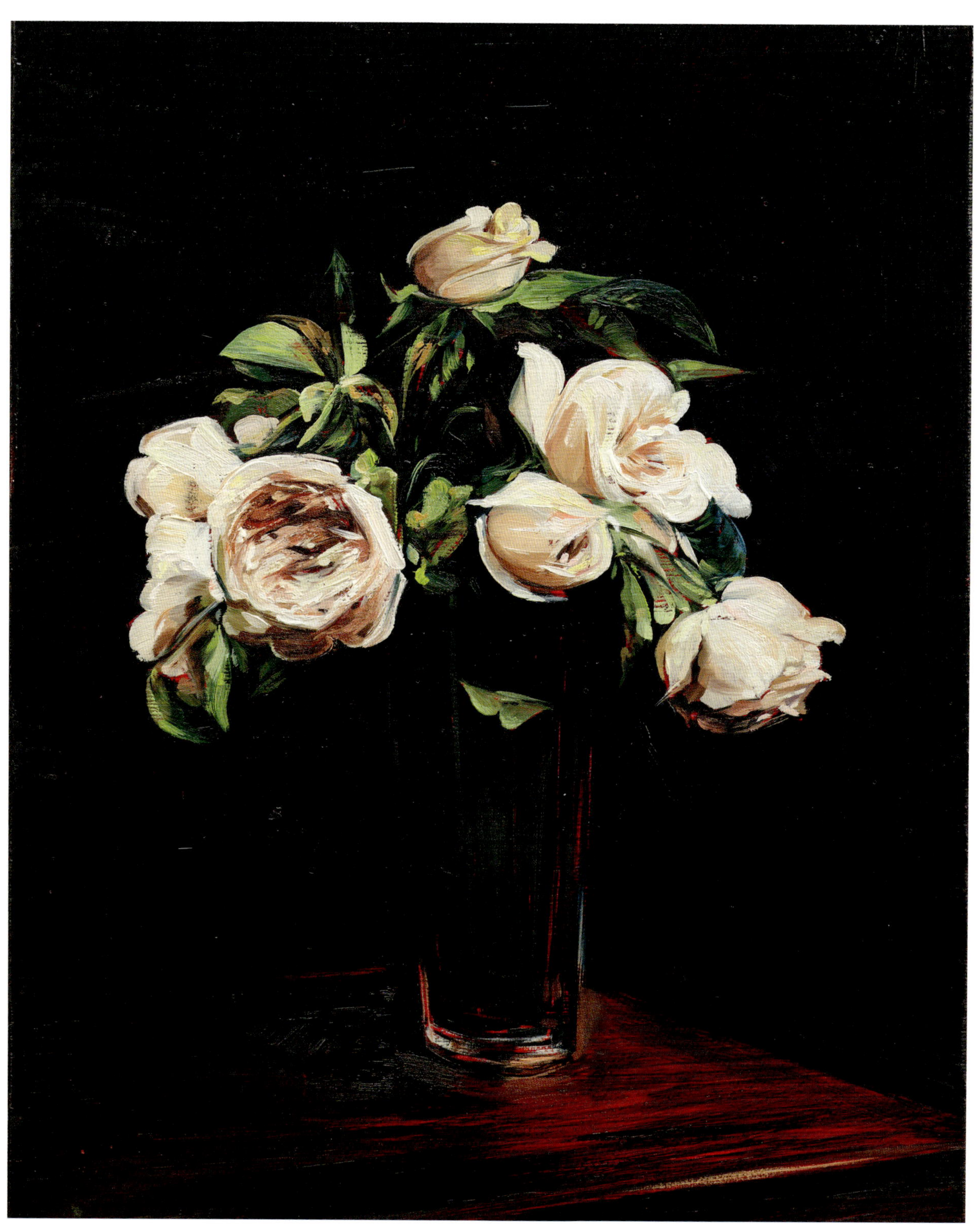

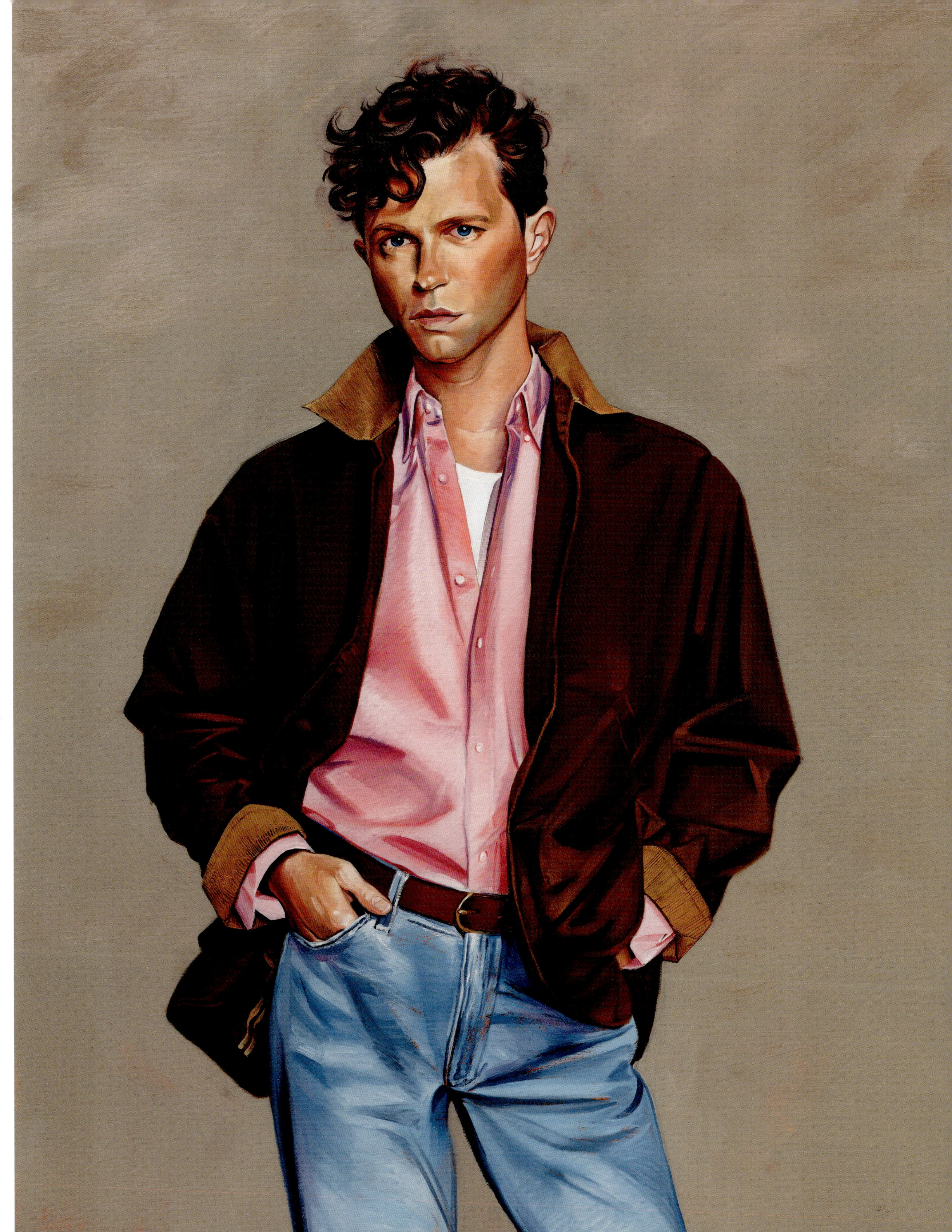

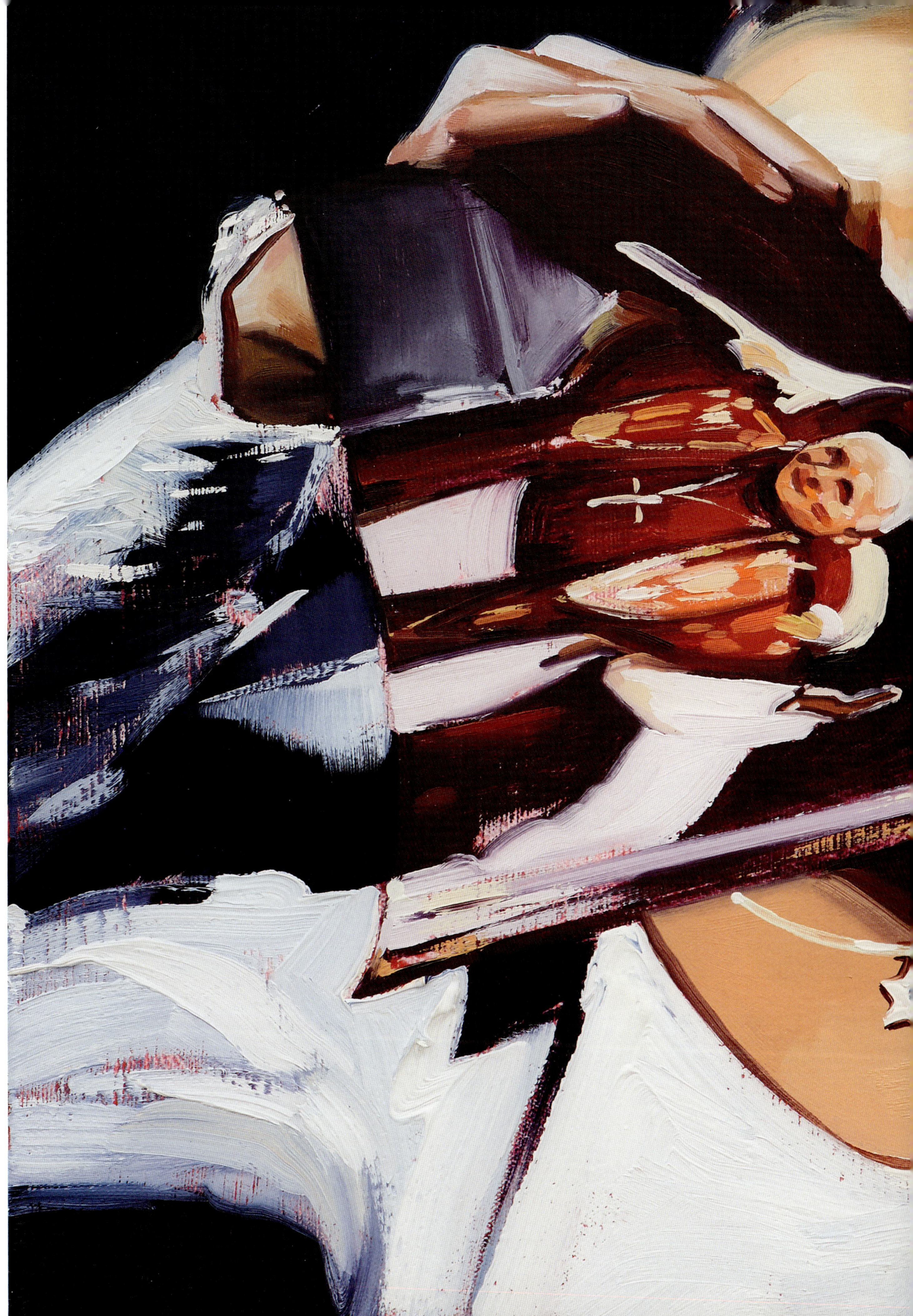

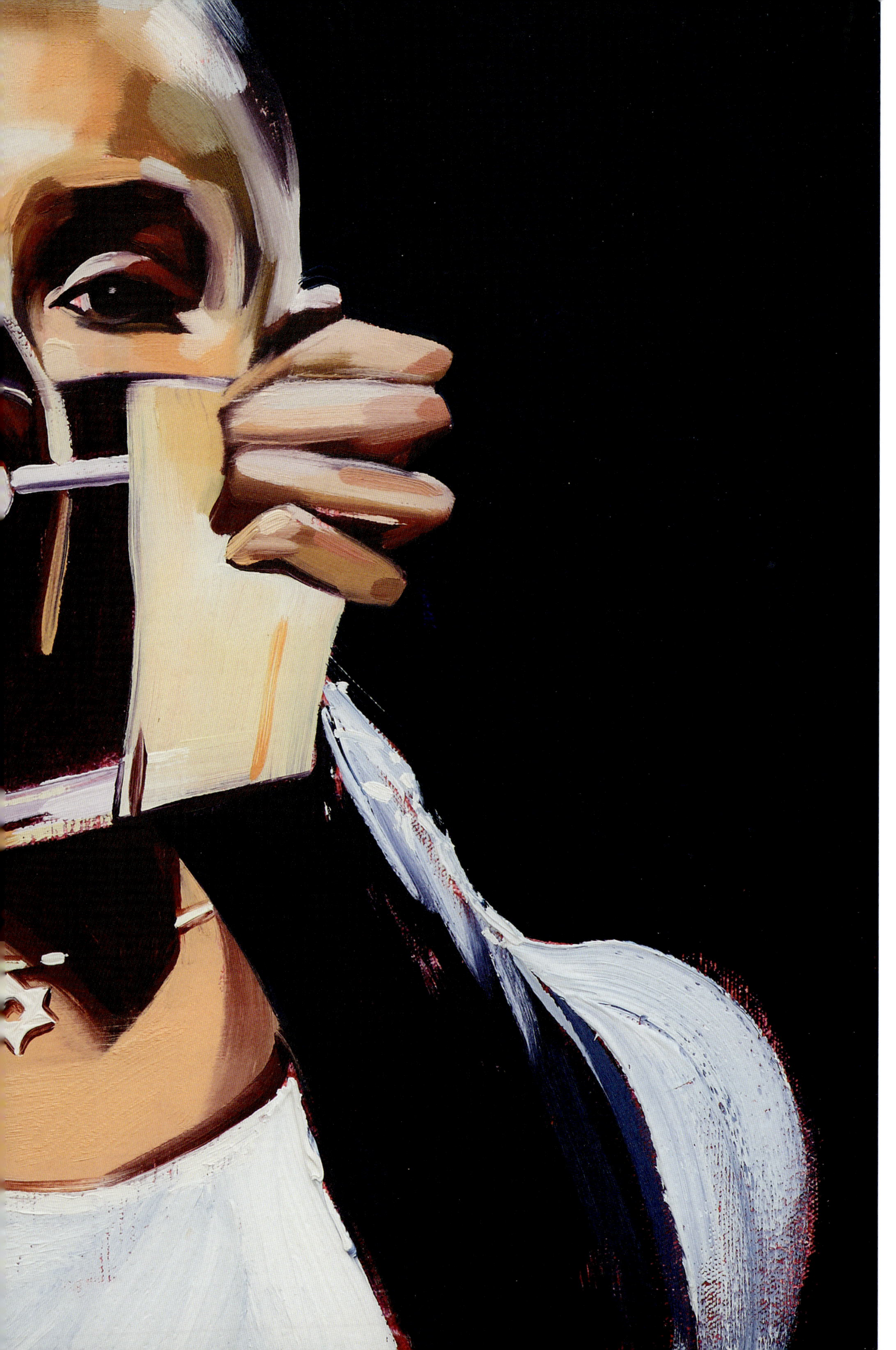

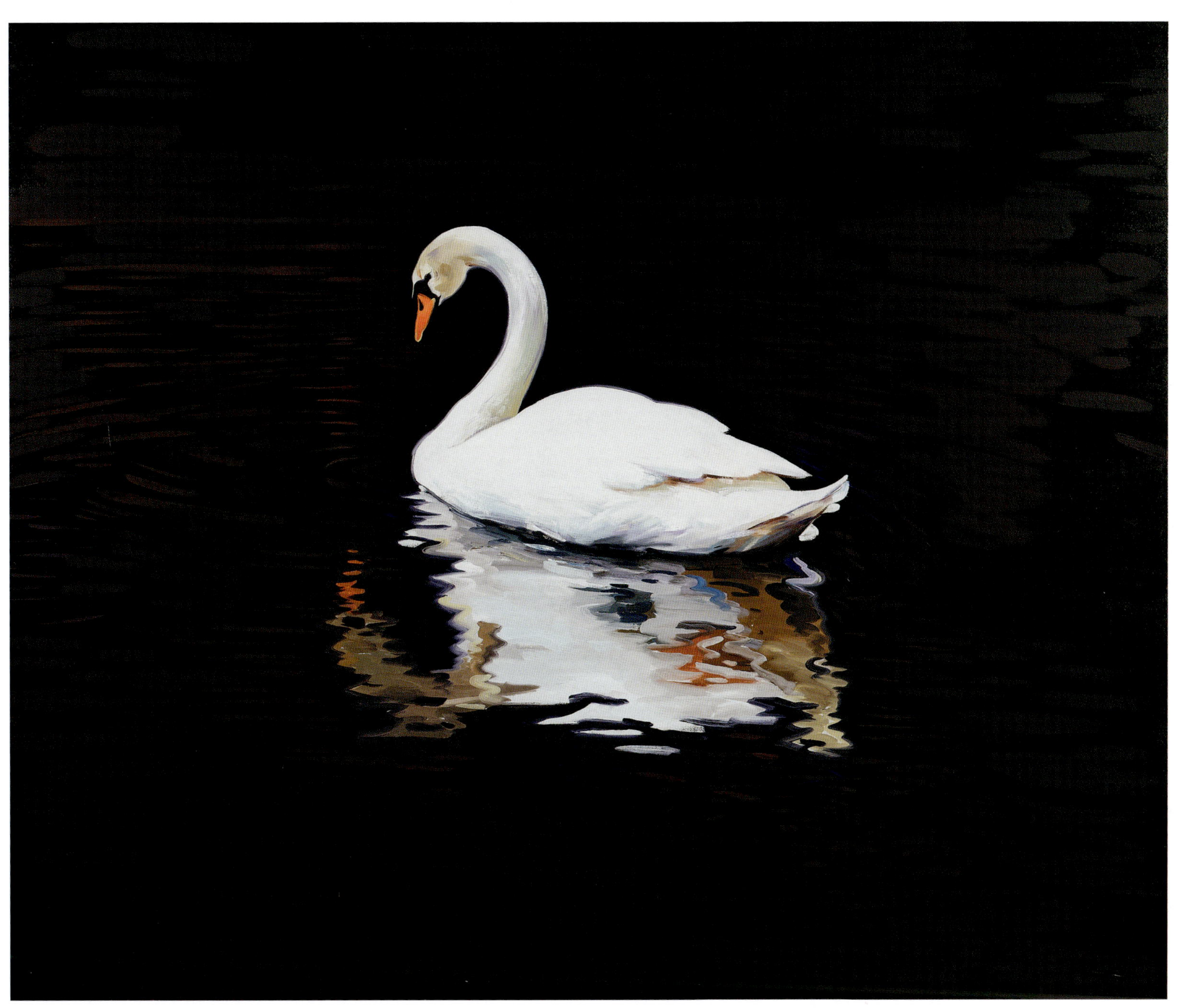

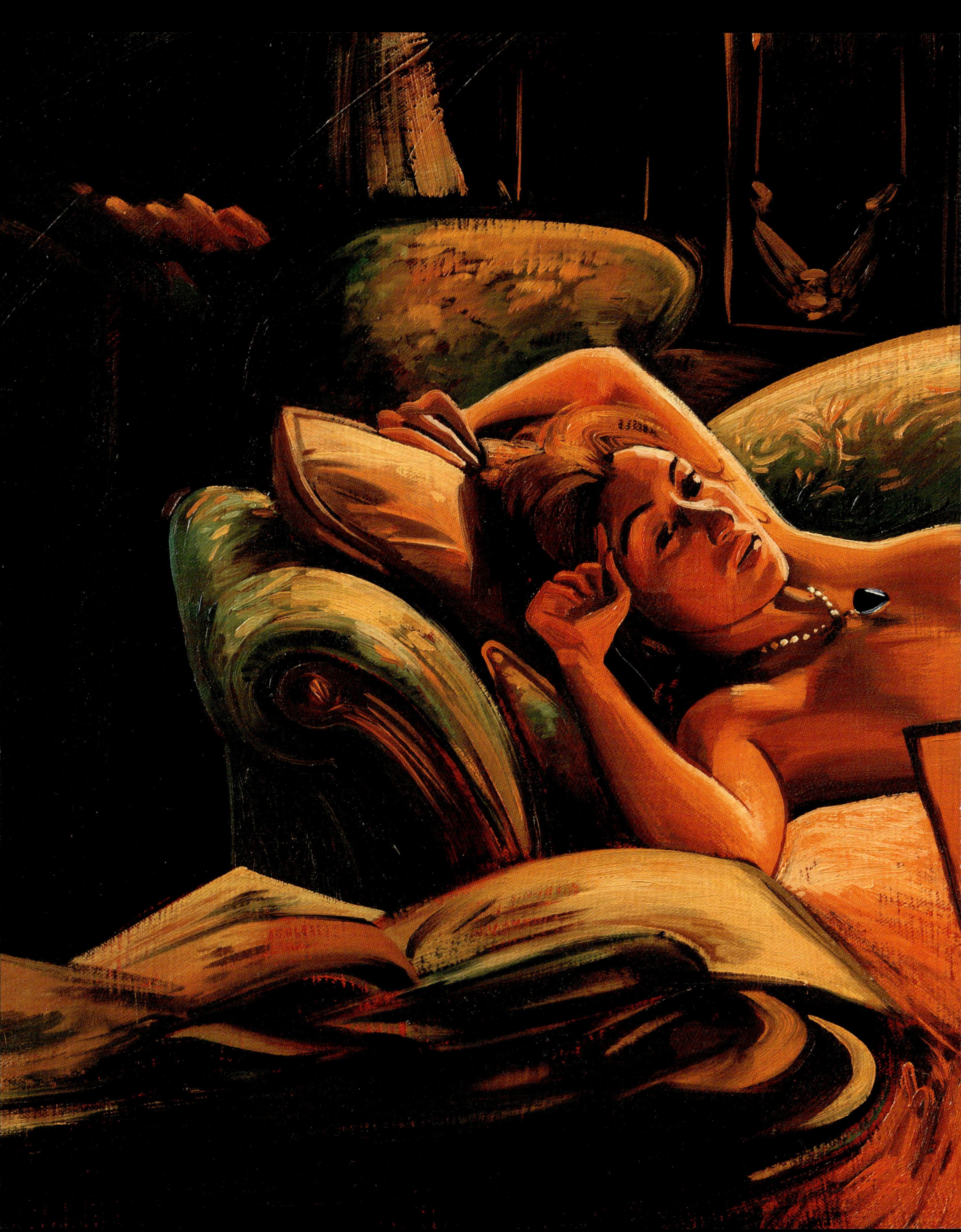

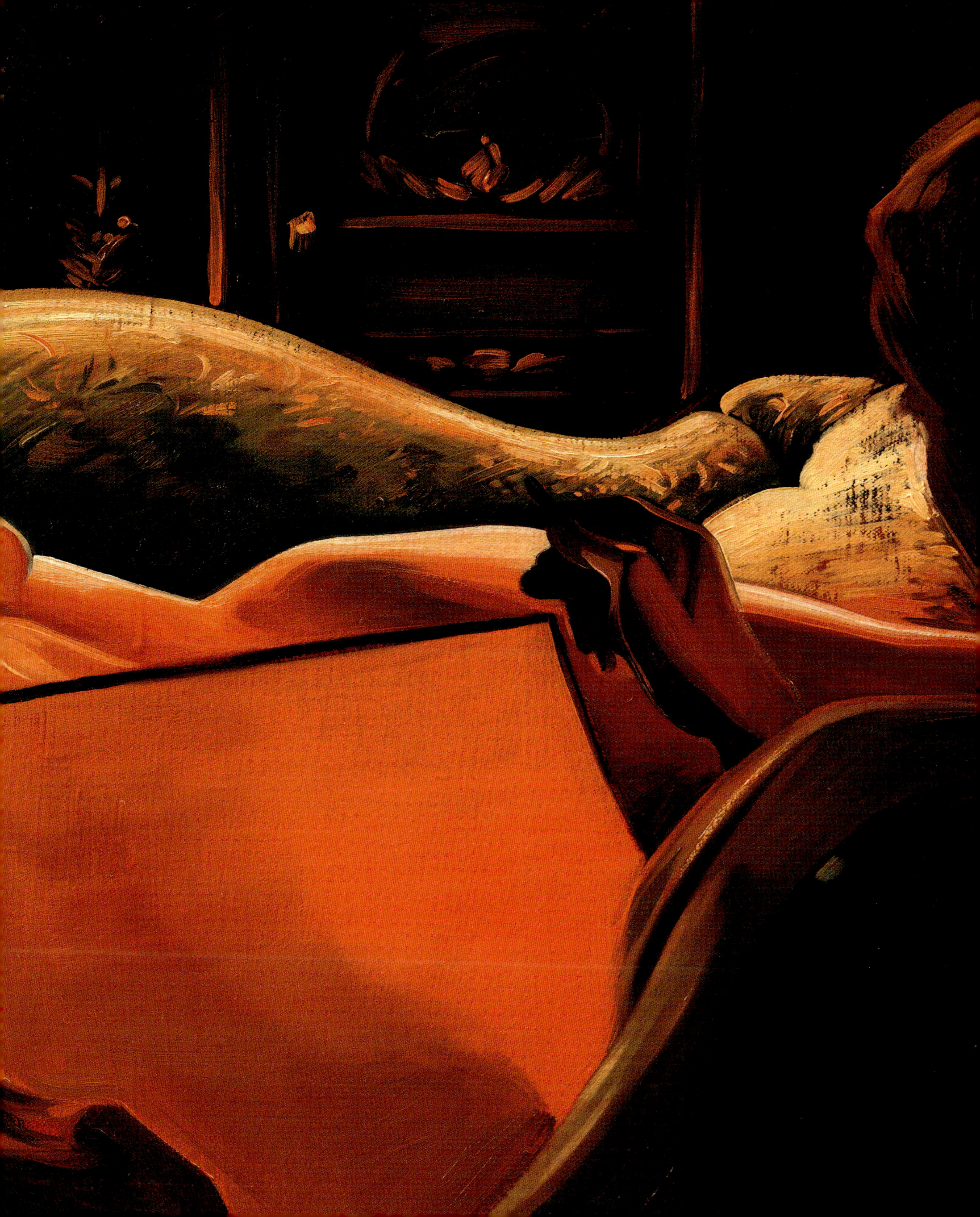

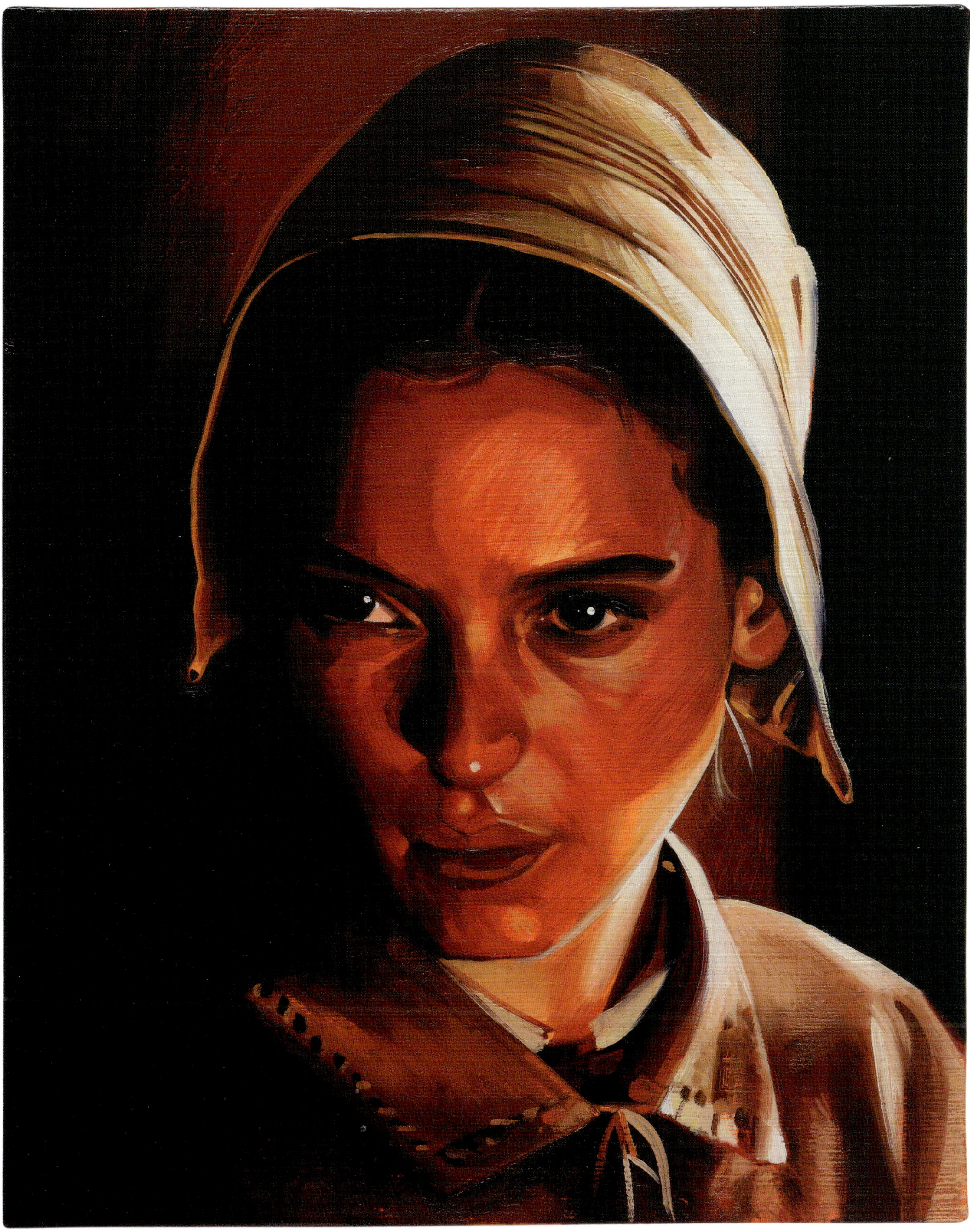

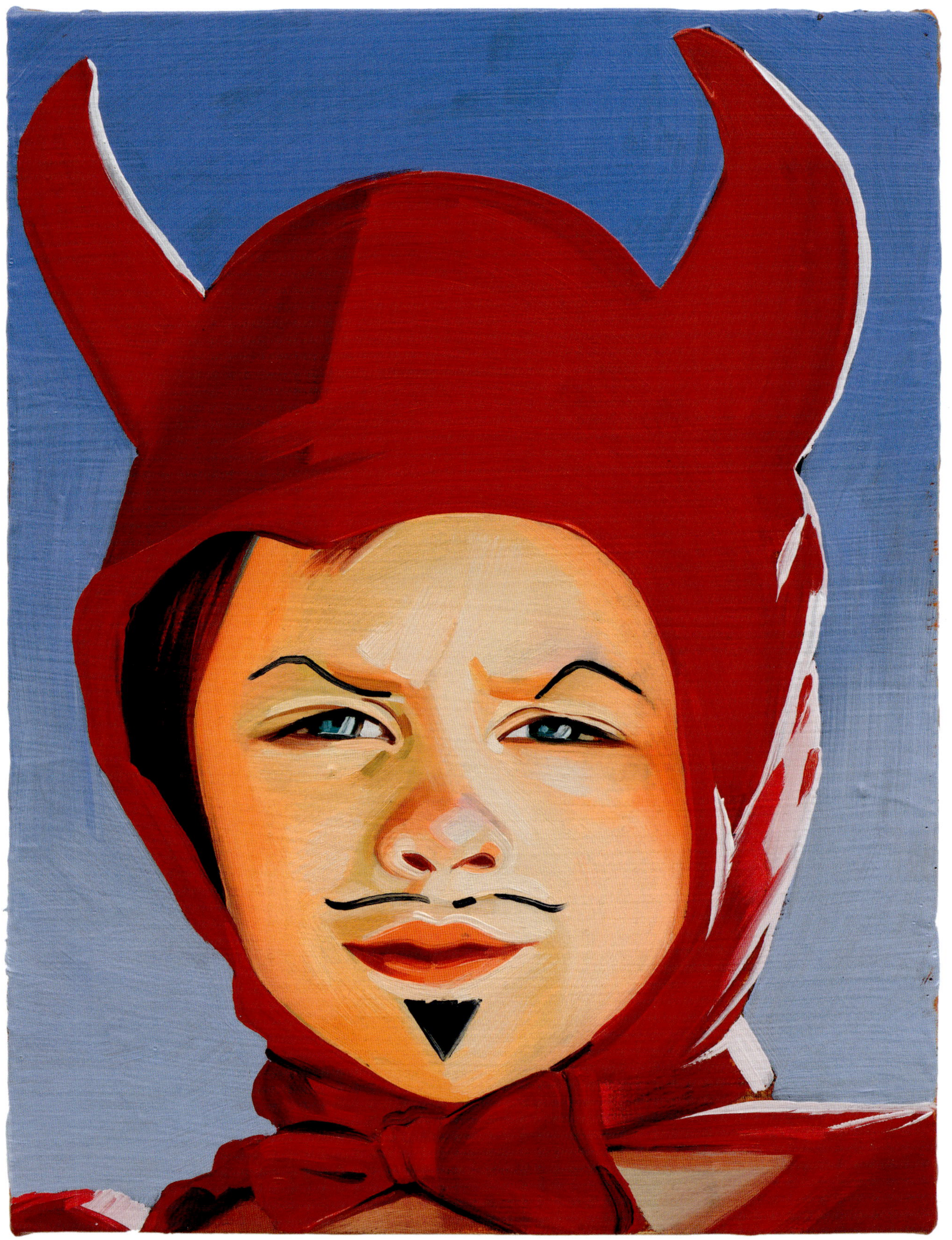

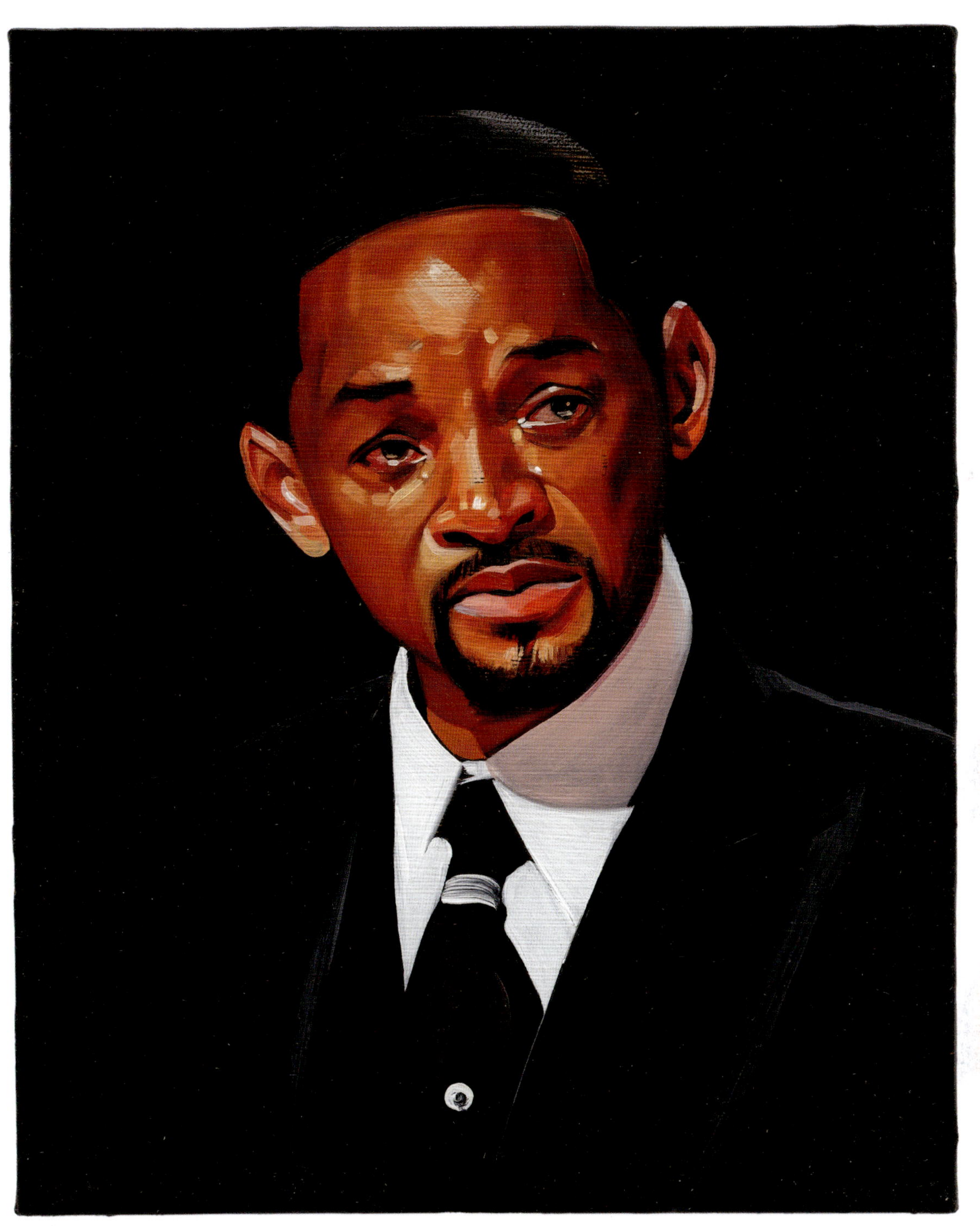

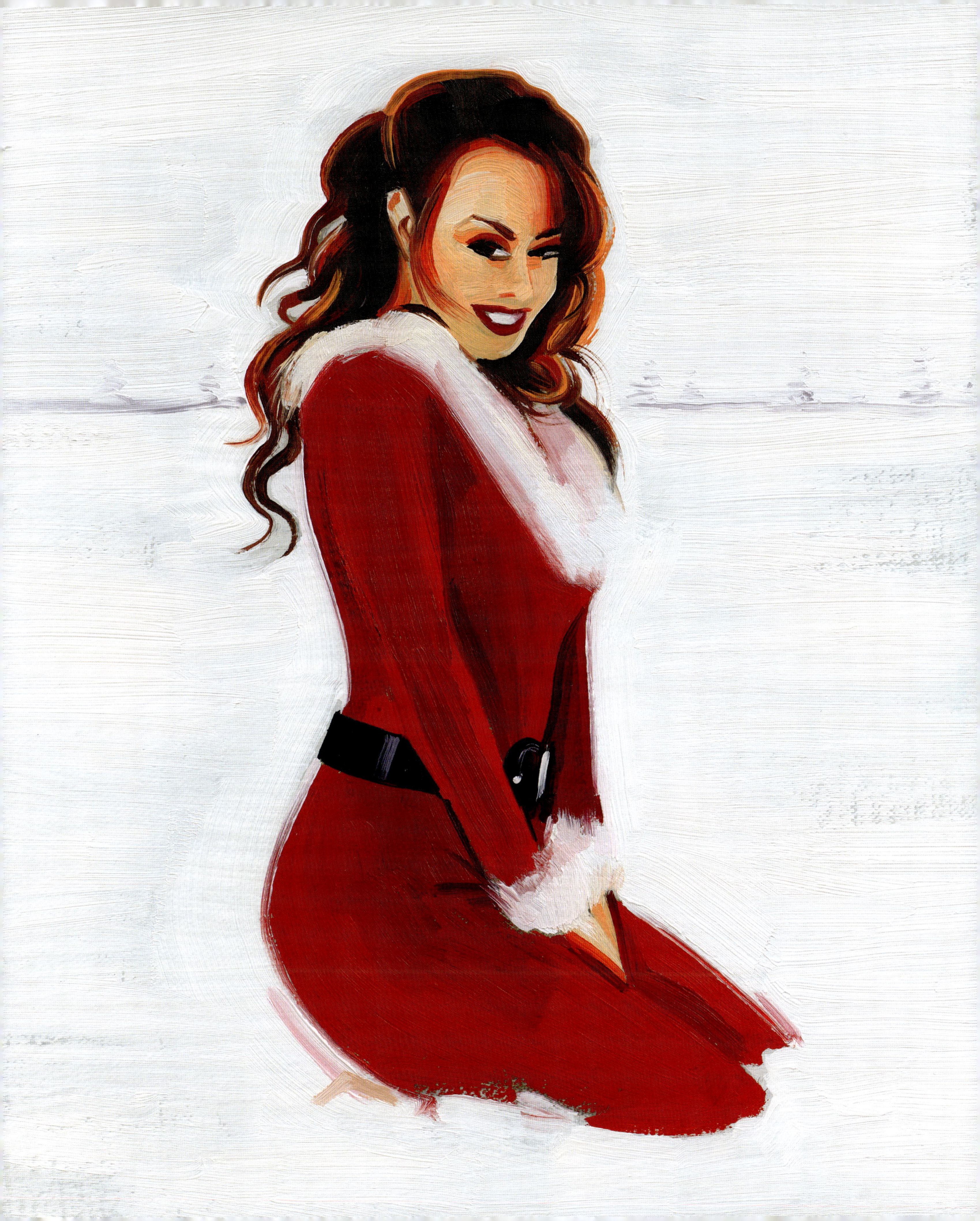

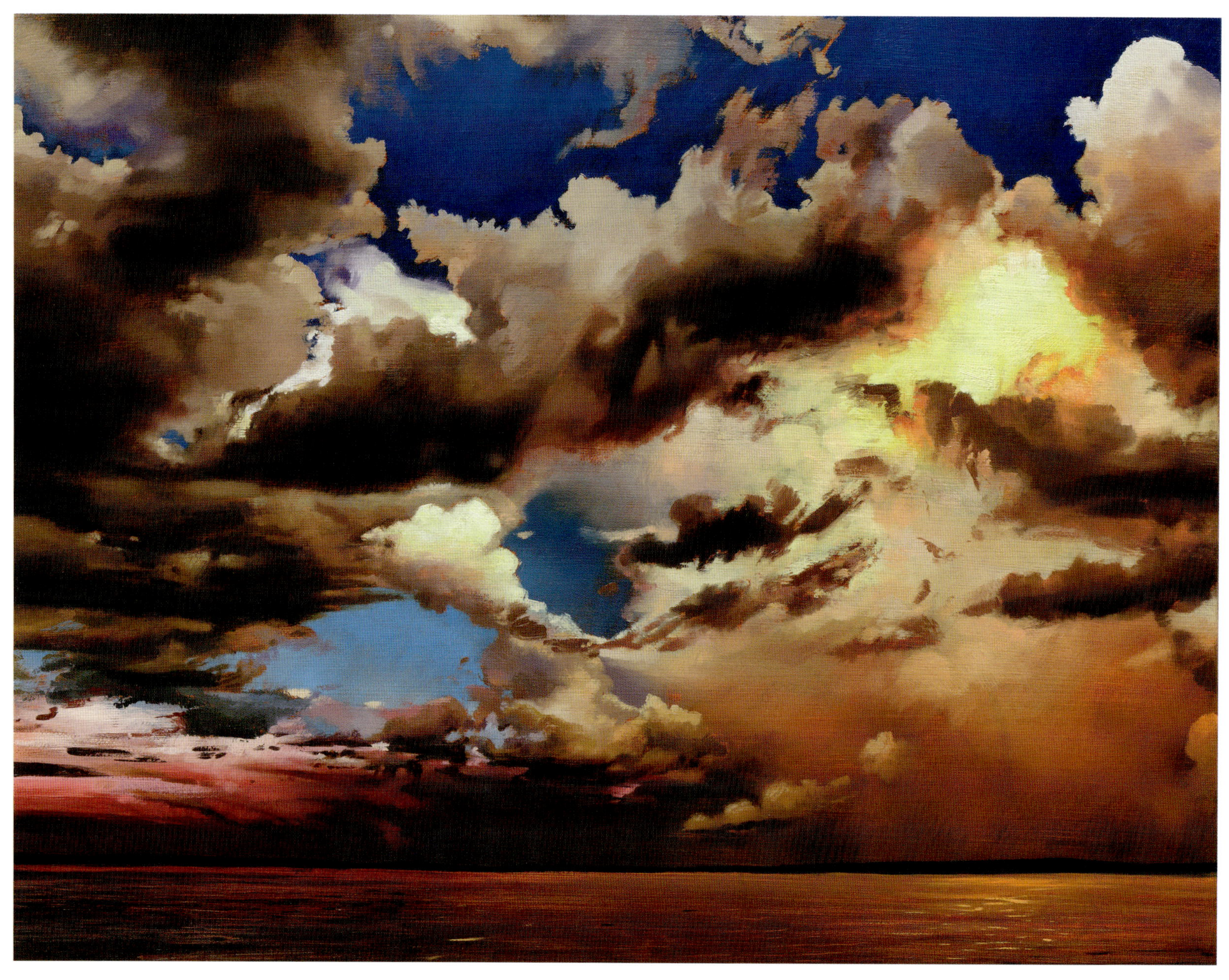

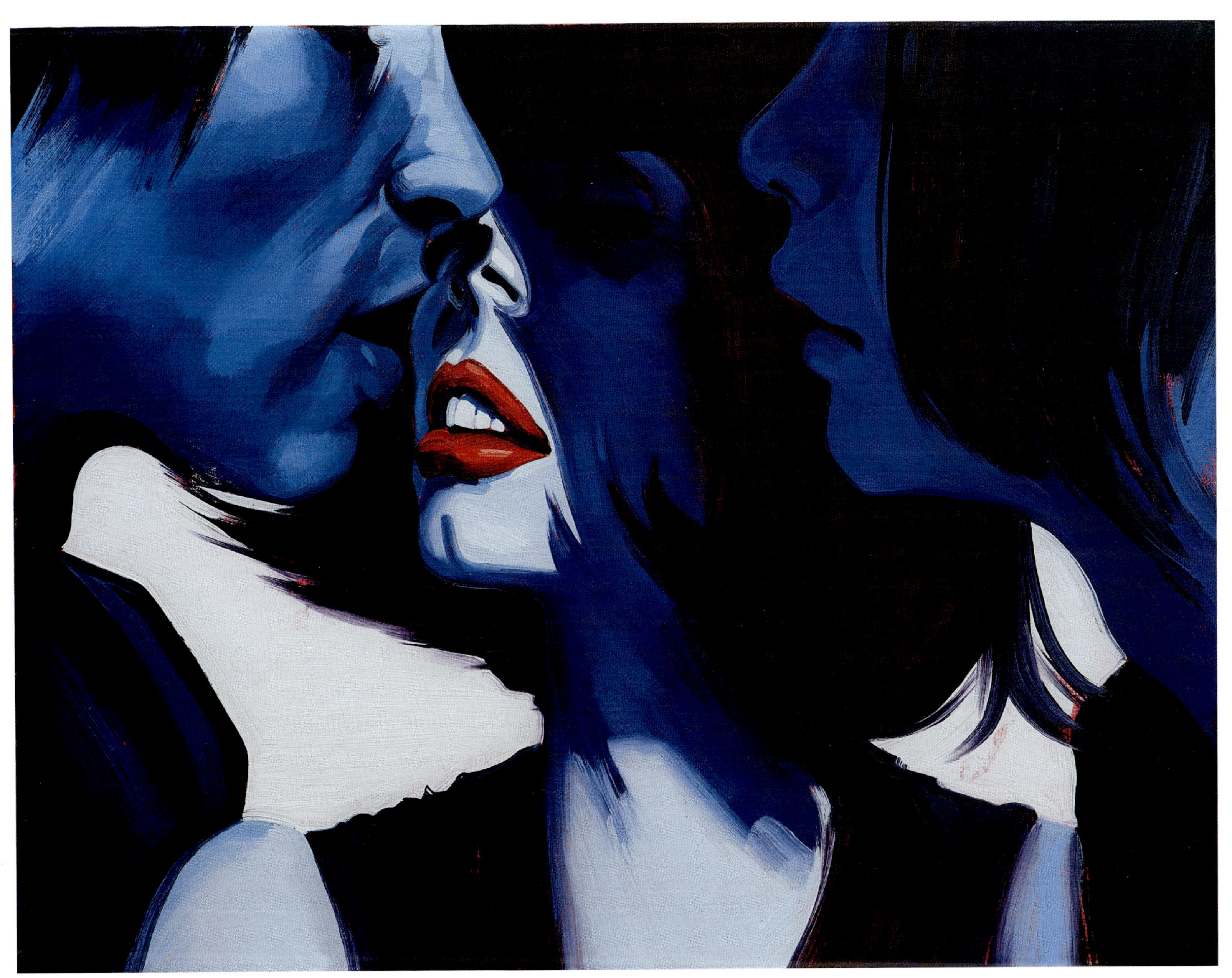

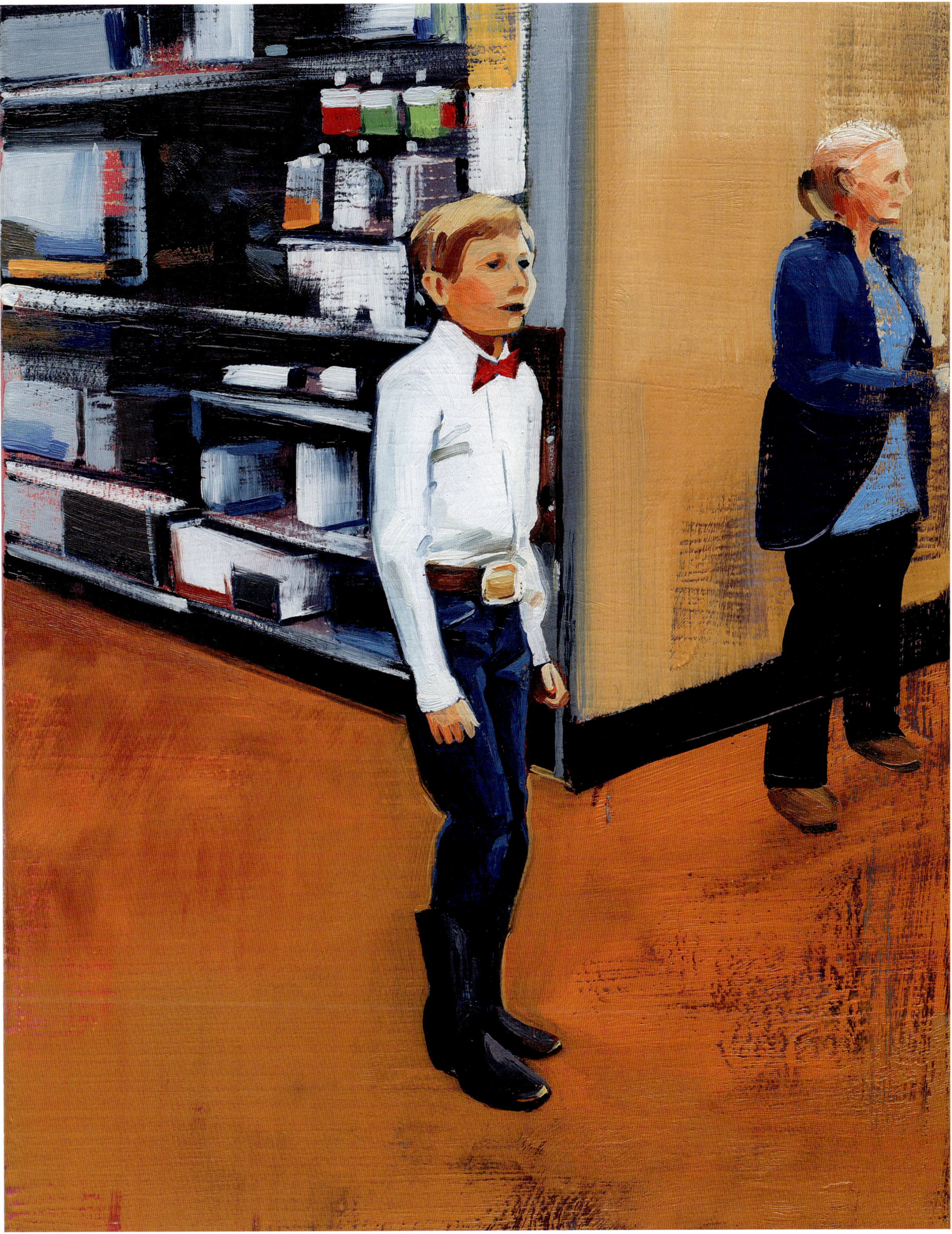

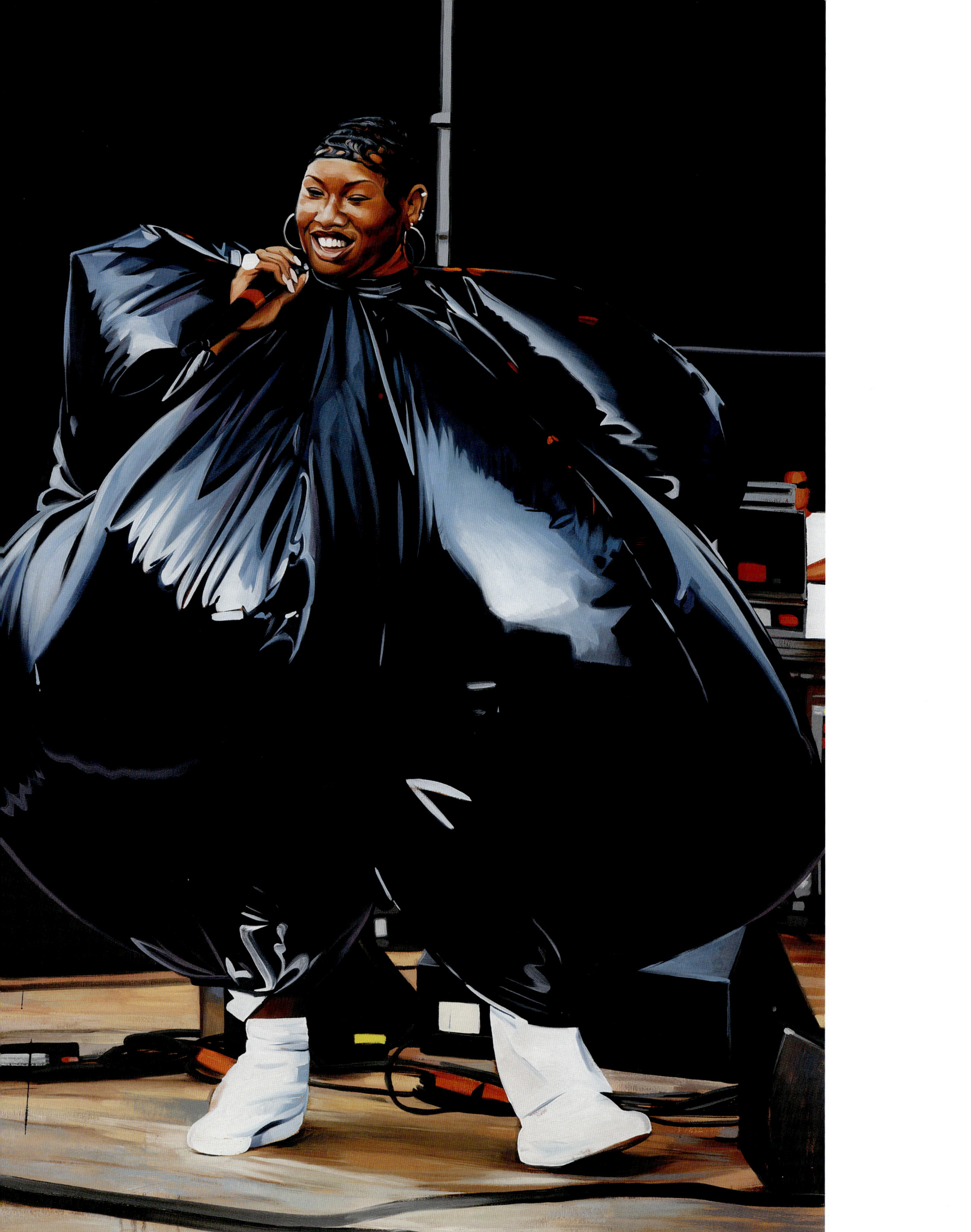

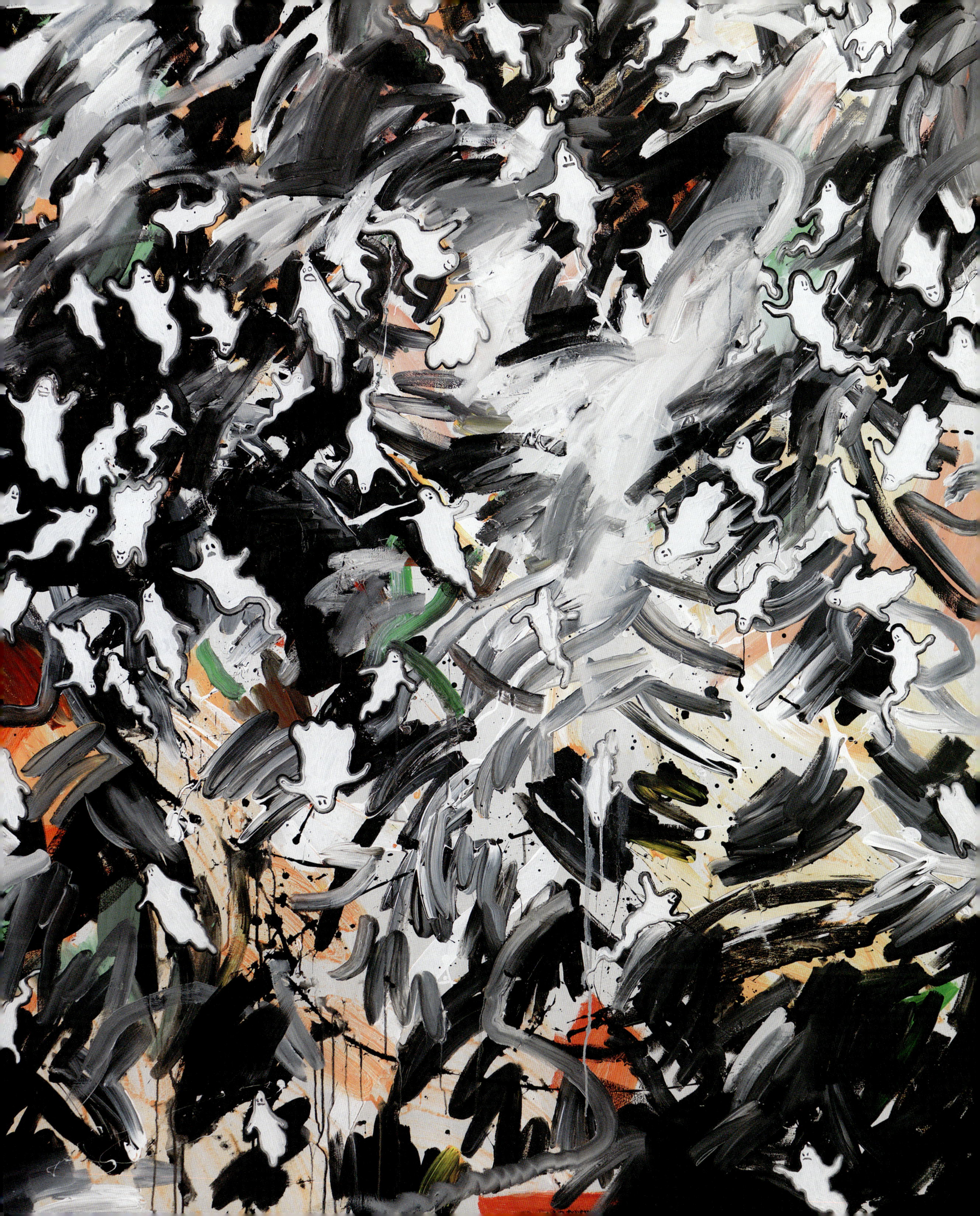

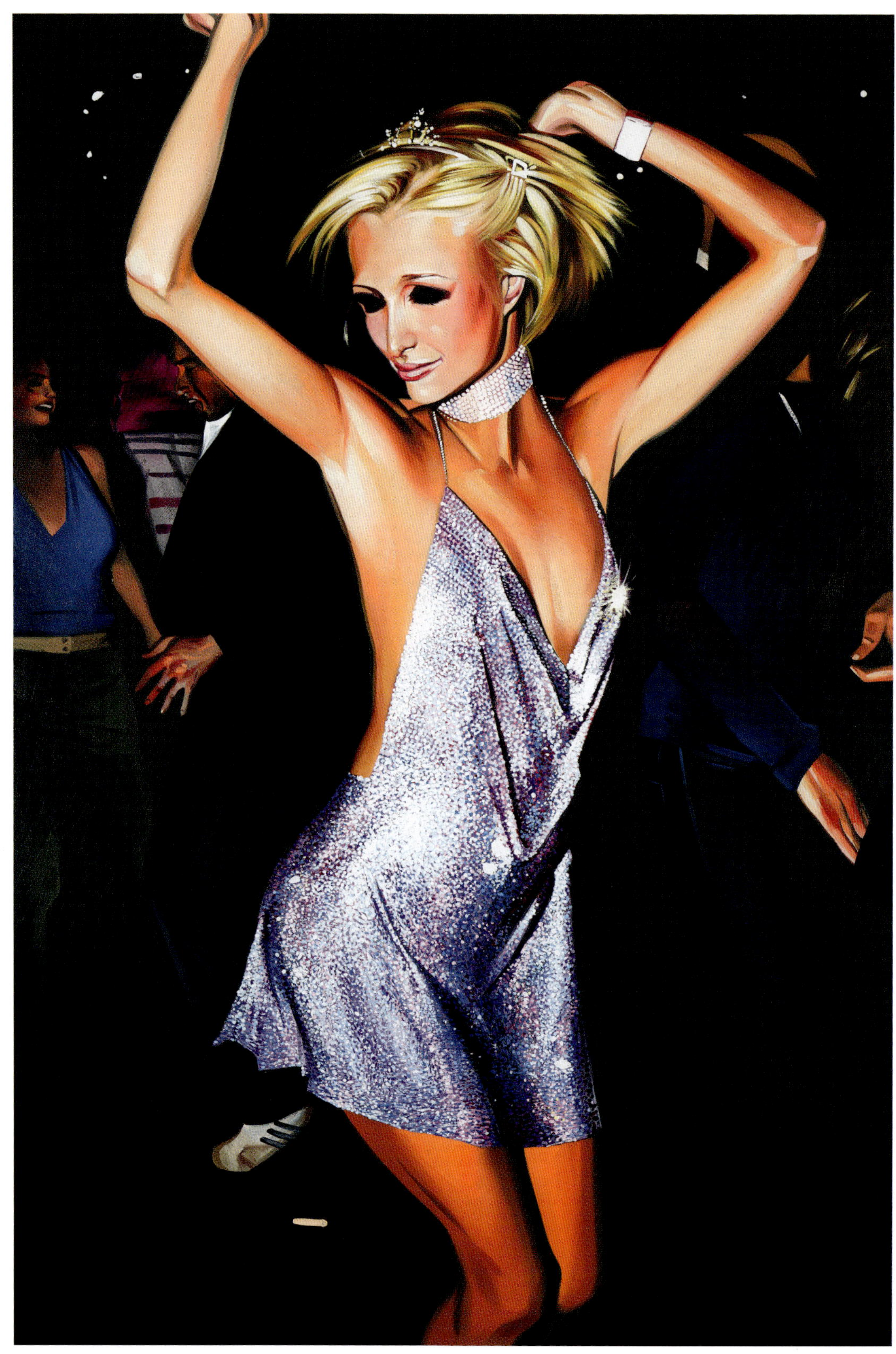

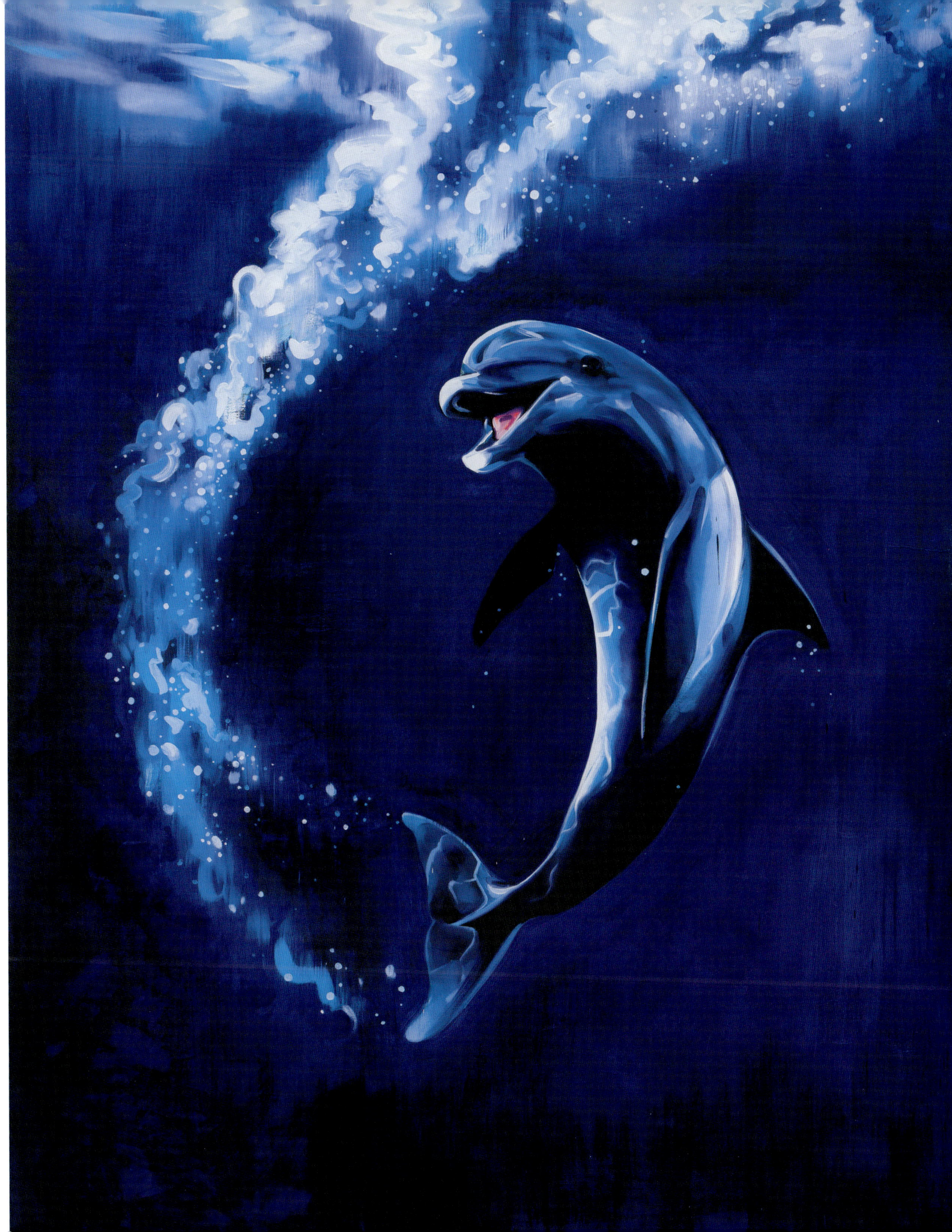

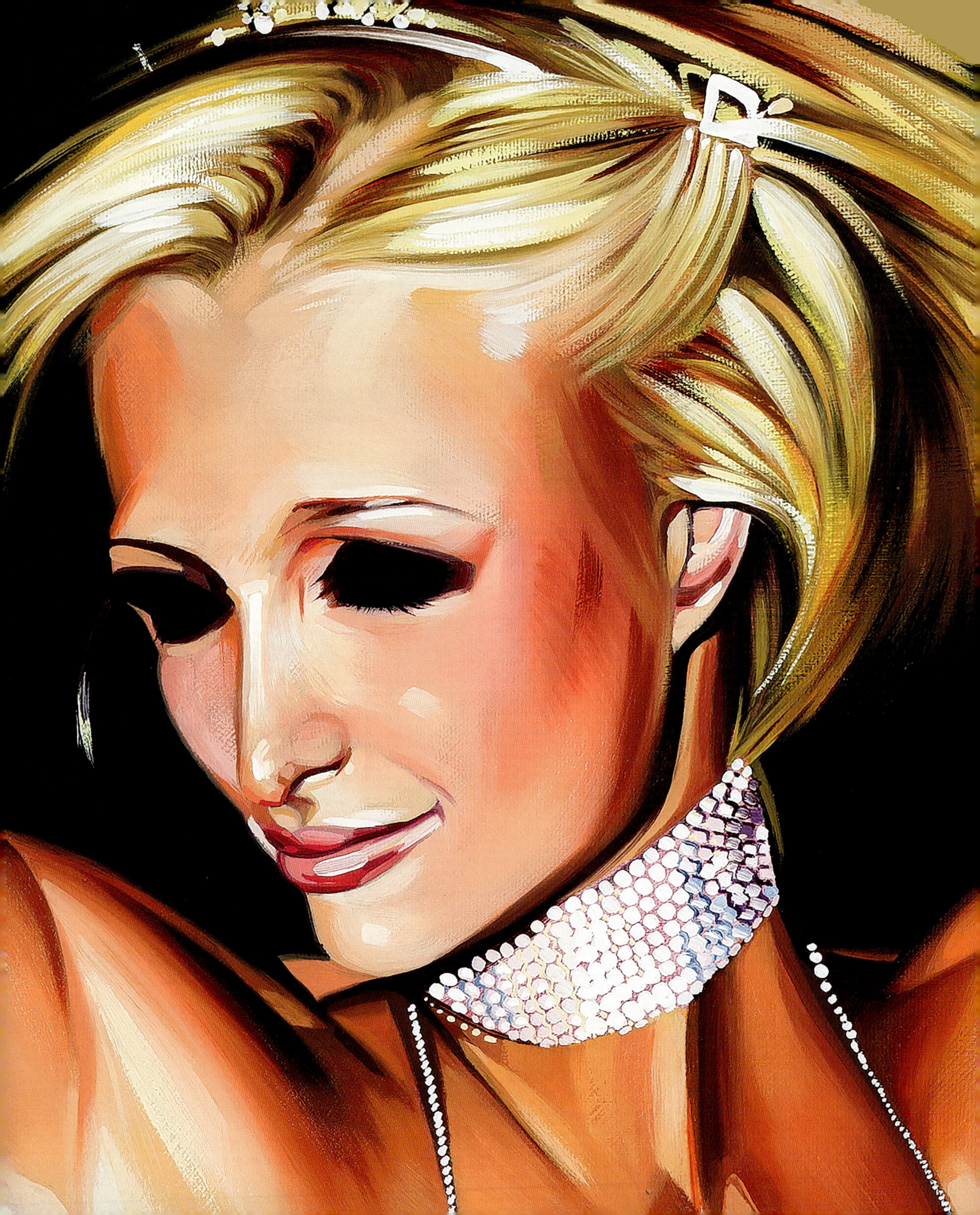

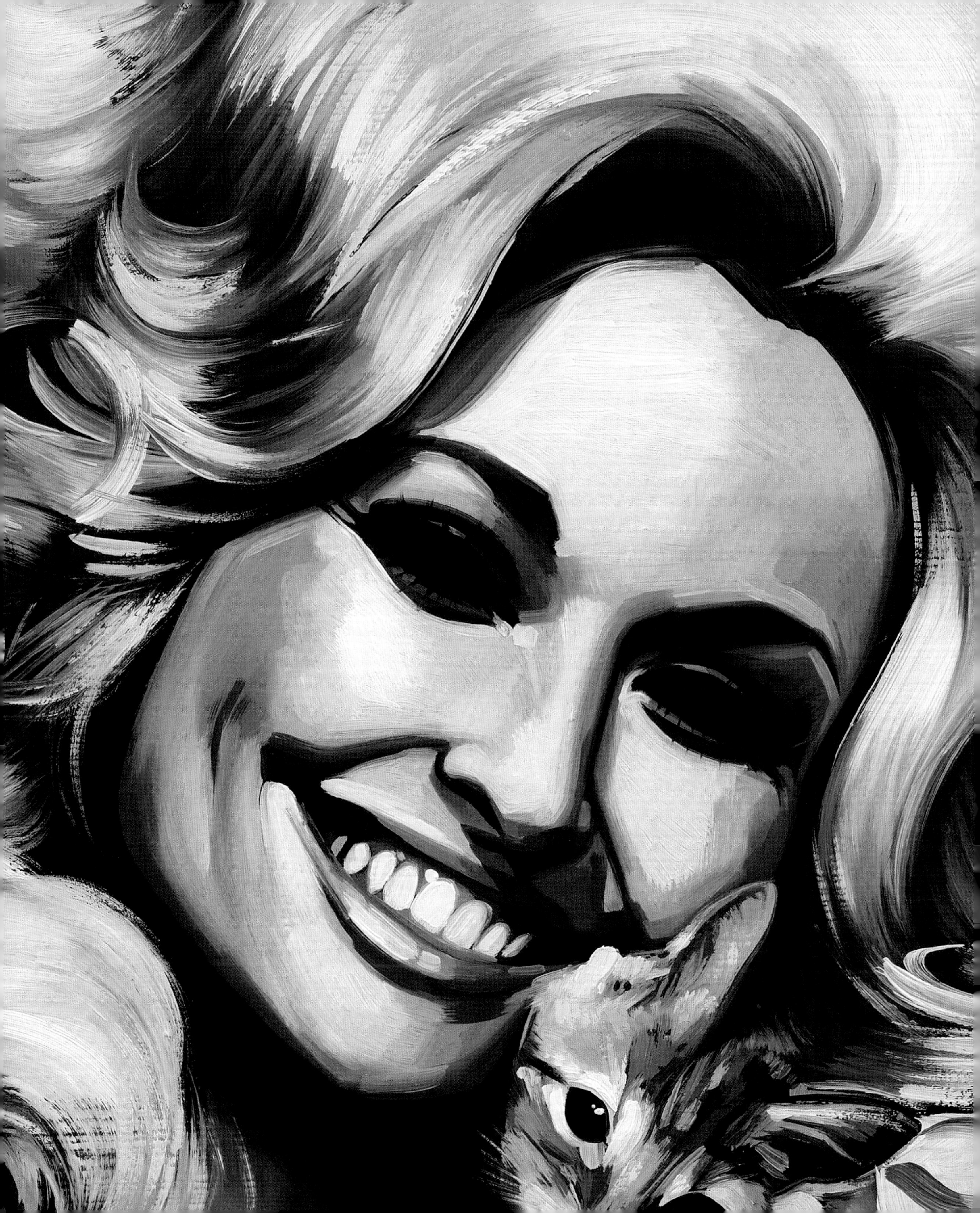

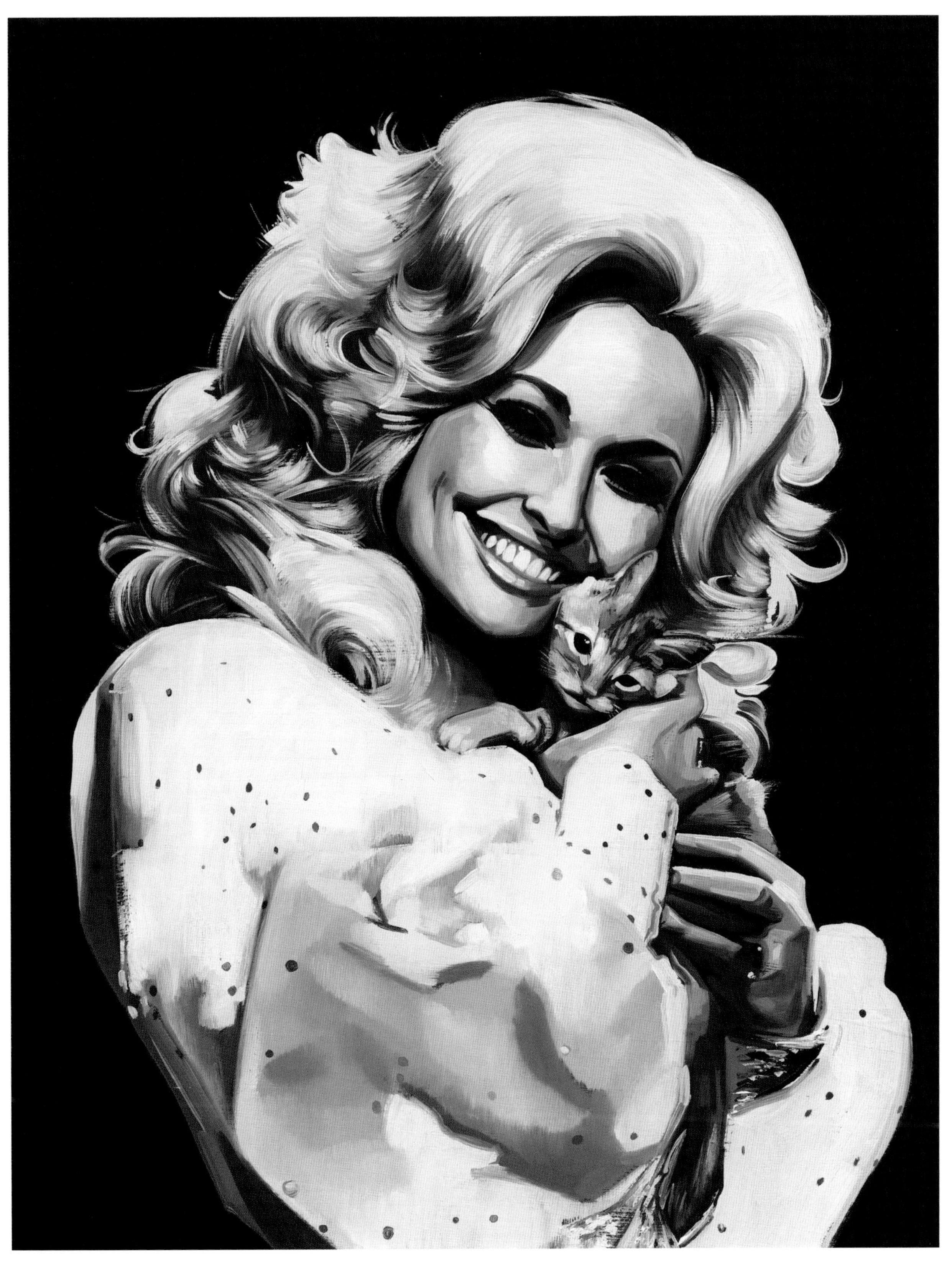

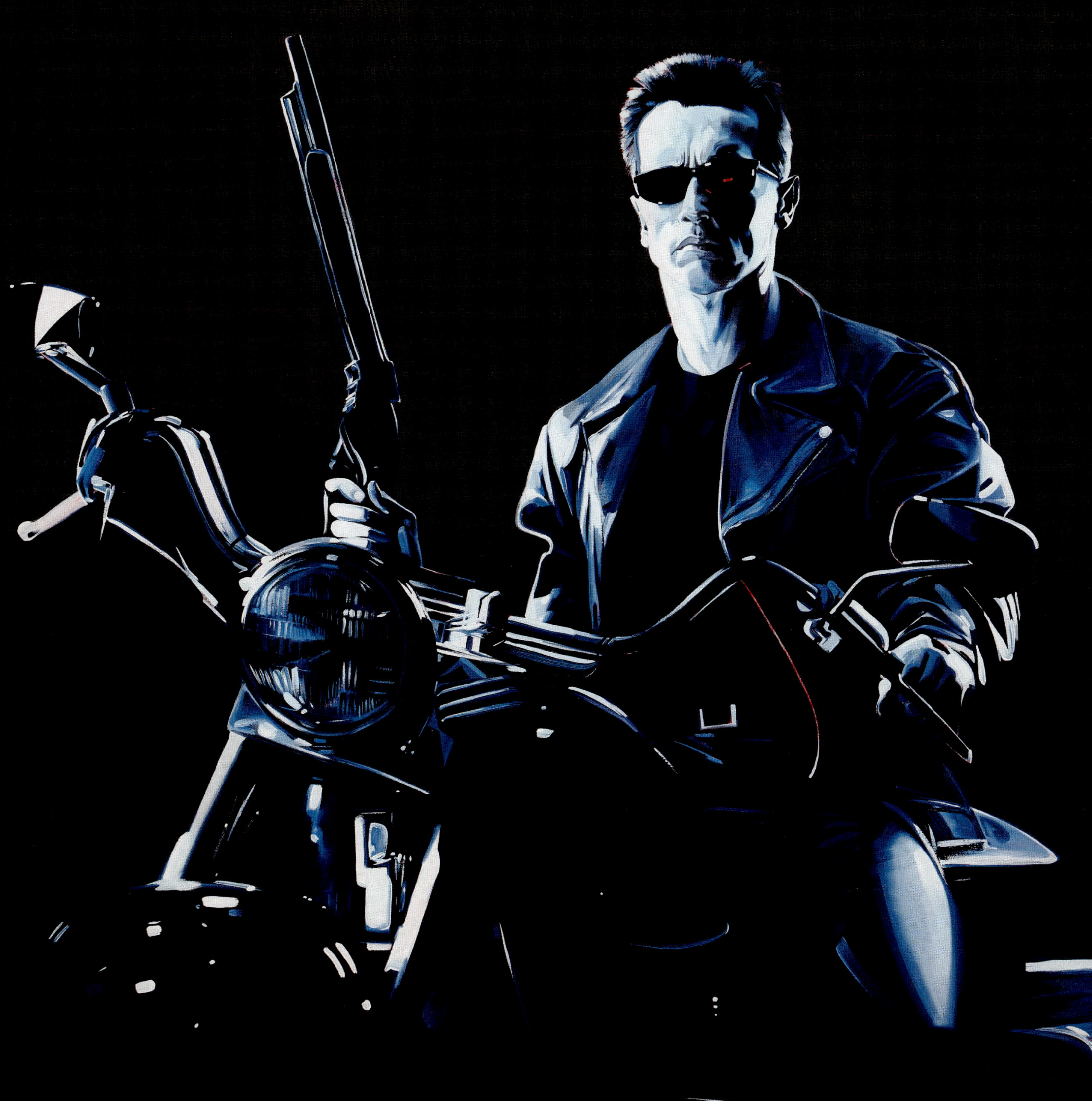

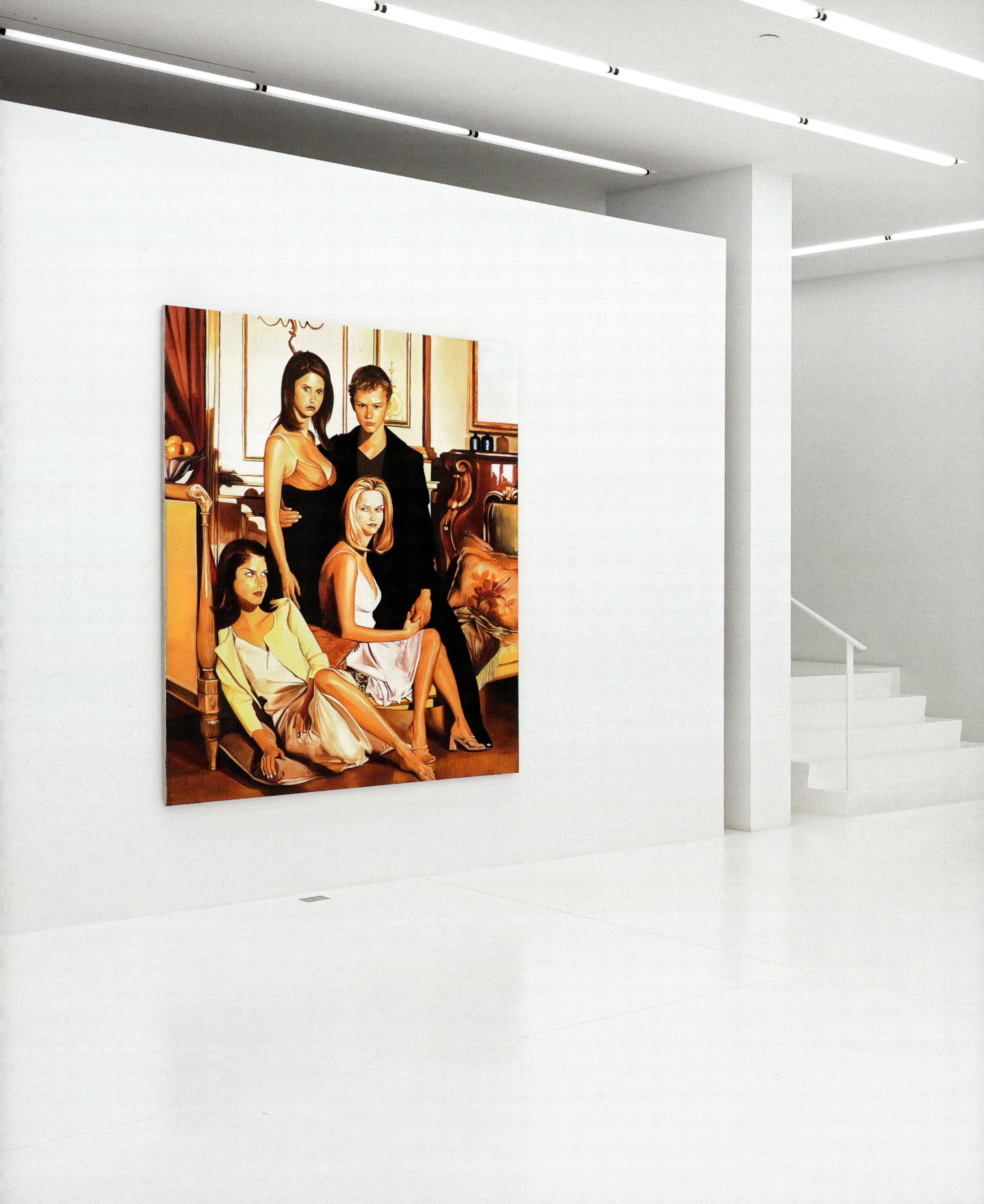

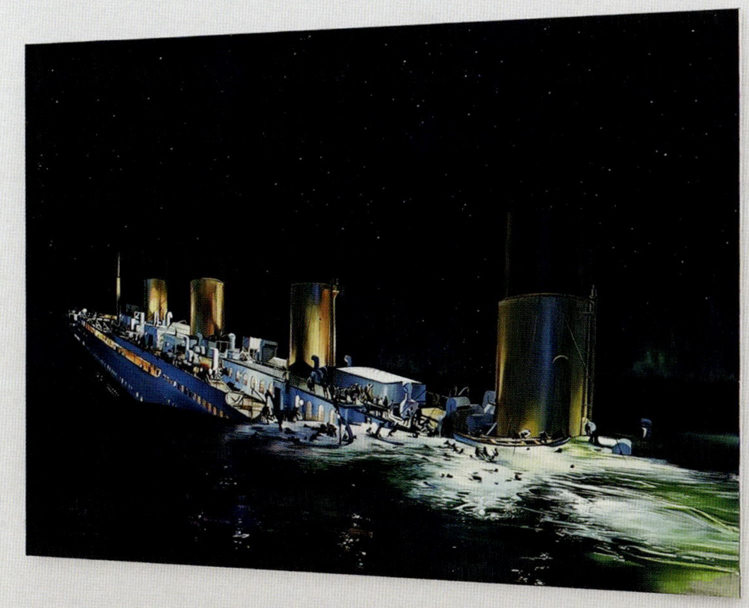

Entertainment Tonight Jarrett Earnest

Duh—it's like a famous quote. —*Clueless* (1995)

I

When I think of it now, it's less a narrative than a sequence of particularly intense images strung together by peculiarly erotic feelings. I was seven or eight years old. I caught it on television without my parents knowing. Not that it was *naughty,* or that I was especially secretive about it, but it felt like something I shouldn't necessarily be watching—so glamorously *adult.* My heroine has extremely pale skin with dark blush, wildly over-drawn eyes, and blood-red lips. Her black bouffant has messy bangs and tendrils dangling over her shoulders and down her back. The lower-than-low-cut dress frames her enormous breasts, pushed up and out into perfect globes. An ornamental dagger pins her wide leather belt; the slit in her gown goes all the way up to the waist, revealing incredibly long legs atop spiked heels. She looks like a heavy metal fantasy, but her affect is more valley girl. She's not afraid to be corny and horny and because of that, she is irrevocably cool.

After a confrontation with her sleazeball boss in the opening scene, Elvira quits her job hosting b-horror movies on late-night television and needs a wad of cash to bring her act to Las Vegas. At just that moment she gets a message that a hitherto unknown great-aunt has died ("I didn't know I had a good aunt, much less a *great* one!") and left her something in the will. She sets off on a cross-country road trip in her "macabre mobile"—a black and chrome convertible with faux-leopard seats and barbed wire around the rearview mirror—which breaks down just as she arrives at her destination, a conservative small town in Massachusetts.

Dressed in all-black high-femme drag, she is an existential threat to the pastel townsfolk and a freedom fighter for the sexually repressed teenagers. Elvira's bummed to find out that she inherited not a lump sum, just her aunt's house, an old book, and a dog. As a consolation, she discovers that her mother and aunt were in fact legendary witches. ("Here I am knocking myself out as a horror hostess . . . when I'm actually descended from like a major metaphysical celebrity!") With this power comes responsibility; it is her occult duty to vanquish her demonic uncle, liberate the town from themselves, and garner enough cash to stage her Vegas show. *Phew!*

Elvira's phantasmagoric nightclub act is revealed in the final scene. She wears a sparkling spider bikini with silver tassels that she rotates first clockwise with one breast, then counterclockwise with the other, alternating like propellers. Cut to a close-up of her smiling, winking face—living her dreams. One of the best endings to a movie, *ever.* To this day I cannot watch it without laughing out loud.

In 2021, the same year that Cassandra Peterson, who created and played Elvira, came out as a lesbian in her memoir, Sam McKinniss painted and exhibited *Elvira,* a large horizontal canvas, seven feet wide and just over three and a half feet tall, which shows the self-proclaimed "Queen of Halloween" slinking across the floor, her legs stretching along the bottom of the canvas, arms holding her top half upright. Pink and purple lights illuminate the dry-ice fog rolling around her, the shape of her wig haloed with white against a jet-black backdrop. It's the kind of cheeky high-power pop culture image McKinniss has become known for translating into densely chromate paintings.

Seeing Sam's *Elvira* activates my emotional and psychic armature from childhood onwards—with all its attendant connotations of slutty and silly queer outsiderness—in exactly the same way Renaissance depictions of *Virgin and Child* unconsciously mobilized the entire war machine of Christian theology and European political history. In trying to regard such paintings strictly as "form," where exactly do they stop being a representation of God and his miraculous mother? When we strip them from narrative recognition so they're just figures, any woman and baby? Or when they're reduced to being colored shapes arranged on a two-dimensional flat surface? When the paintings can function as some purely optical phenomenon.

What is it about this particular image or the kinds of images McKinniss unfailingly paints, that is so powerful? Why do I feel like I, in particular, should have it? An oil painting of a woman lying horizontally on a body-sized horizontal canvas, Sam's *Elvira* is another in a long art historical tradition, i.e. the woman on display as courtesan. But as soon as these spectral nudes arise, whether they are Manet's *Olympia*, Goya's *Maja*, or Titian's and Velazquez's *Venus*, the comparison feels absurd. Elvira is not actually naked and yet is sexier; she's on her stomach, not on her back. Nevertheless, hundreds of years of pictorial form are present, providing the chassis of the painting. Furthermore, as one of the icons of the 1980s, Elvira was herself a pastiche of an earlier television horror host in the 1950s, Vampira, whose look had been inspired in turn by Charles Addams's glamorously gothic Morticia from the 1930s *The Addams Family* comics and subsequent 1960s TV show, conjuring each character with her own evocations. And it's all just hovering there between me and the picture, each with attendant potential meaning blowing hot and cold, high and low.

On the most basic level, I relate to the *Elvira* painting as honoring my childhood idol, and I respond immediately, supplying the love or lust it seems poised to receive. But there are many people for whom the character of Elvira is irrelevant, just another bit of mainstream schlock; to such a viewer, the painting might be recuperated as a biting critique of media culture, satirizing the art market for gimmicky baubles, and the fallen taste of contemporary collectors—giving everyone what they want. But whether it's intended as criticism or celebration, the artist does not tip the scales one way or the other. In this I've come to regard McKinniss's work as diagnostic, circulating through the worlds of commerce and display, testing our relationship with images and the status of painting in the 21st century.

II

In the 2010s the overall aesthetic in the New York art world was sterile—rehashed conceptualism funneled into conservative sellable objects, inspired by the emergence of social media as a major venue for seeing and selling new art. The most hyped works by young artists were decoratively abstract: mirrored, splattered, or bleached. A lot of stuff was shiny and air-brushed—because that somehow signified the "internet." These works were eventually dubbed "Zombie

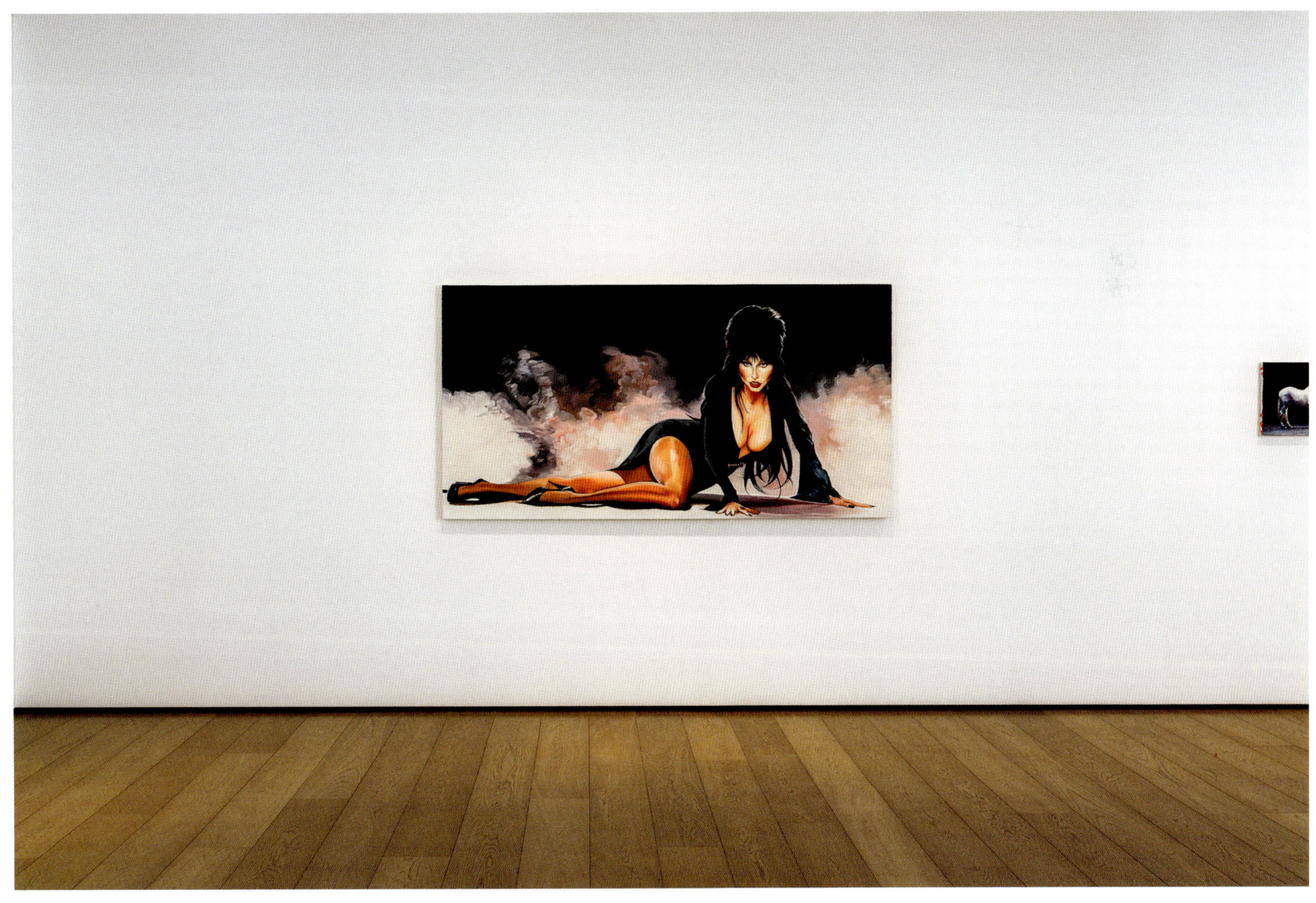

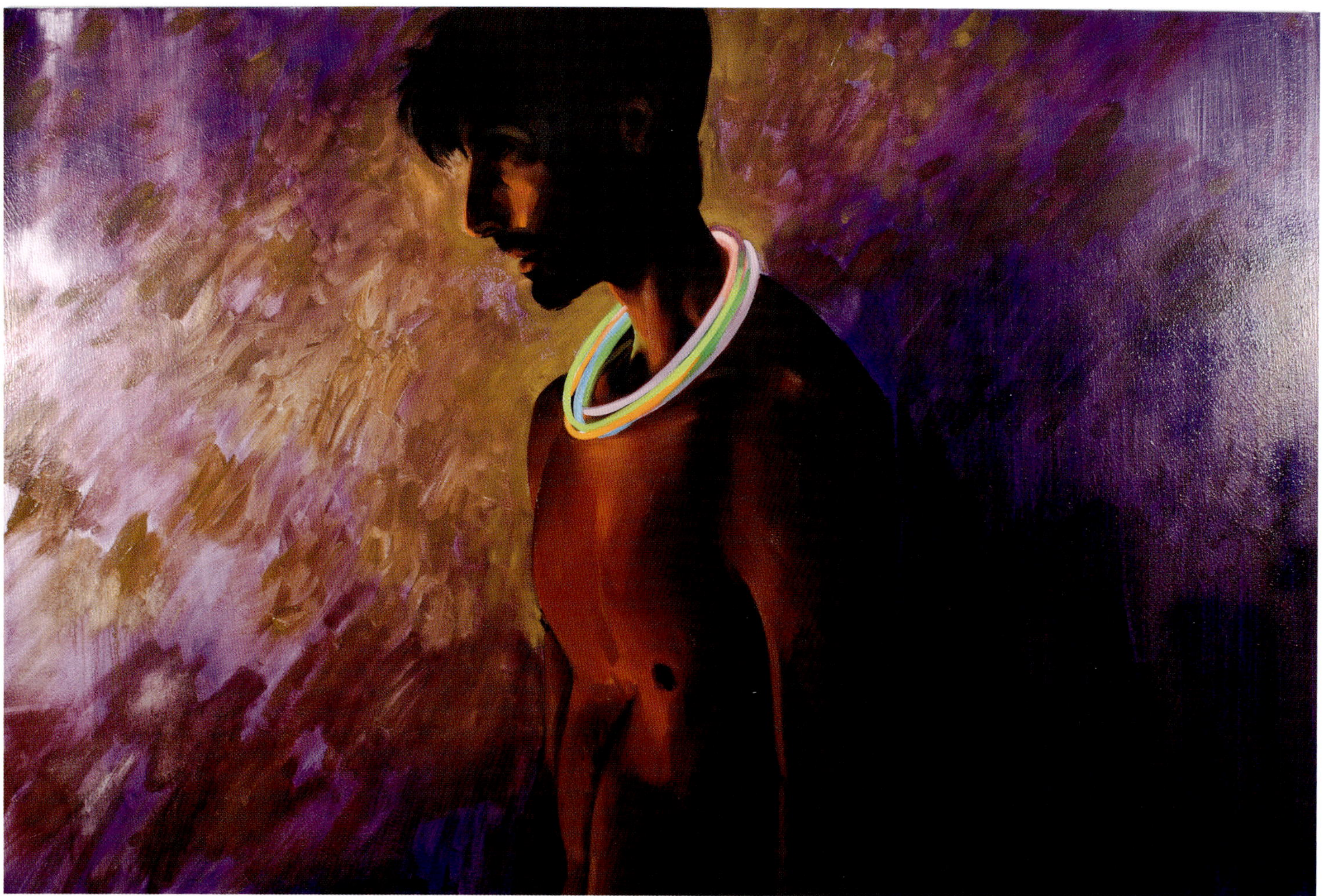

Formalism" by the artist and critic Walter Robinson, a disparaging coinage that immediately stuck. The cohort of insurgent figurative painters, artists as different as John Currin, Lisa Yuskavage, Elizabeth Peyton, and Kerry James Marshall were treated somewhat as individual exceptions to the general rule of contemporary art, which was dominated by large-scale installation, video, and performance art, spectacles perfect for that age of international biennials.

When I arrived in New York in 2010, with time-honored brattiness, I disliked all the art I saw and how it was being discussed. Somehow I just couldn't get excited for showrooms full of torqued semi-reflective metals or Plexiglas objects, neon lights, and dayglow detritus scattered amid coyly institutional furniture. Post-financial crash, there were, however, little gangs starting to do their own work outside of museums and galleries. Three friends and I started an experimental space on Essex Street called 1:1, a messy rejection of everything that was being put forward from our generation at places like the New Museum's Triennials. As always with youth cultures, nightlife played an outsized role. There was the multidisciplinary performance collective House of LaDosha, Venus X and Shayne Oliver's roving party GHE20G0TH1K, the DIY queer club in Bushwick called Spectrum, the performance art drag family Chez Deep, and the group that started DIS magazine. Because we had a physical location in Manhattan, 1:1 became a kind of clubhouse where friends from all these projects mixed, did events, made movies, and hung out.

A lot of people came through, and looking back at photos it's a who's-who of the future-famous, but because we were so resistant to visibility, it remained suitably under the radar. Despite the art world's numbing financialization, I knew that there were artists my age doing interesting things, and I wanted to find them. In early 2013 I made a list of ten people in their twenties I considered good artists and interviewed them. I then asked them to give me the names of three artists they were interested in, and I interviewed all of them too. The working title of this never-published project was "After the Doom Generation." We all loved that Gregg Araki movie, but also it gives you a sense of how it felt for us then and how it always feels for ambitious young artists trying to find a place for themselves in a world that's not interested: *things suck, what's next.*

Colin Self, then doing high-concept drag in Chez Deep, now a successful musician and performer living in Berlin, sent me to Sam McKinniss—*you'll love him.* Sam was graduating with an MFA from New York University, and I met him at his painting studio down in the financial district and recorded our conversation. I was struck by his flat, highly affected way of speaking which flashed a blistering intelligence. Also, he's very funny.

McKinniss had studied painting as an undergrad at Hartford Art School at the University of Hartford, Connecticut, near where he grew up, which has a strong emphasis on the rudiments of technique and observational figure painting. There he made large and small oils of solitary figures, his friends and lovers, lounging their lean bodies in atmospherically empty spaces. Faces were often turned away or obscured, allowing their beautiful physiques to be studied at length, refined into extreme artifice.

In an artist statement from 2008, he said: "I want to fall in love with pictures over and over again and expect to receive nothing but heartbreak in return. For the same reasons why sad songs are the best pop songs, unrequited love is the best love because it incites the most intensely felt emotion." What might sound capricious is in fact a pretty straightforward description of painting's appeal: the attempt to halt a quality of light, a feeling, before its inexorable change. Creating the illusion of a presence circumscribing an absence. This is a capacity of art so fundamental most people pretend it doesn't exist.

At NYU McKinniss continued in this vein, making decidedly queer, sexy, and sad portraits of beautiful boys from his own photographs. Most striking was a series of large oils of darkened figures in even darker spaces, bodies illuminated by glow-stick necklaces, casting a gently neon articulation on their anatomy that felt both anachronistic and utterly contemporary at the same time. It was like a joke, to apply the efforts and effects of the Caravaggisti to a solitary raver.

I remember an almost too clever painting called *BOYTWEETSWORLD* (2013) of a guy with his ass out, stomach down on a bed, immersed in the now familiar handheld illumination of a then relatively new iPhone. In his written master's thesis, McKinniss described this figure, "his intimate attentions are forwarded to an alternative, simultaneous reality outside of the picture plane, like a Fragonard letter-reader brought to speed on the latest telecommunications technology. I am looking for a sinister ray of light. Like moonlight hitting narcissus's pool, the soft glow emanating from a smartphone screen is incredibly seductive."

All these paintings were slightly too early to be considered part of what is now called "queer figuration," which solidified into a defining trend by the year 2020 and applied to the work of fellow artists like Doron Langberg, Jennifer Packer, or Salman Toor, who were concurrently making their early work in the city. By contrast, I always felt that McKinniss's painting contained a critical edge that is wholly absent from the feel-good intimacies painted by our peers. Around the time of *BOYTWEETSWORLD*, he was also making a series of all-over abstractions populated by cartoon ghosts. I understood them as a response to the demand for highly commercial Zombie Formalism, a haunting from painting's past. Shimmering atmospheric effects of light and dark were interrupted by white ghosts, insouciant and chic. It was as if the entire history of painting and its capacities for representation and expression were coming back to tease the vacuity of the present discourse. Painted luscious and wet, these dematerialized cartoons spurt across their surfaces like so many money shots, a material revenge on the digital or spectral: as Sam put it, "*beaucoup la petites morts* flying around." The *ghosties* were attended by little experiments in color and brushwork that he was calling "cosmetic abstractions," as though painting was make-up covering empty space.

Reading the transcript of our first conversation more than a decade later is to see an artist formulating the work for which he would become known but had not yet made. Because we were both young and neither of us had anything to lose—the interview didn't have a public destination, and indeed was never published—there is a riveting honesty mixed in with the full-throttle intellectual and artistic aspirations. An excerpt:

JE: How do you think about the "decorative" dimensions of your paintings?

SM: That it fits instantly into a commodities market where people are attracted to painting initially based on what it looks like and how it fits into proving their lifestyle, or improving their lifestyle, or decorating their lifestyle—that does not bother me at all. Painting has multiple duties because it carries immense meaning within it—it has the possibility to sustain several different conversations by holding complex forms onto one surface, but while it's doing that it is stimulating a viewer's eye through aesthetic appeal, through line, pattern, color, shape—it's a confluence of all those things.

JE: But what do you *want* from painting?

SM: I want it to be elegant—I think painting is supremely elegant. There are things that, even though they were invented a long time ago, continue to succeed, and painting is one of them. Human beings have a lot of fluids entering and exiting their bodies; we have a tricky relationship with our own fluids. Painting to me is where you rescue

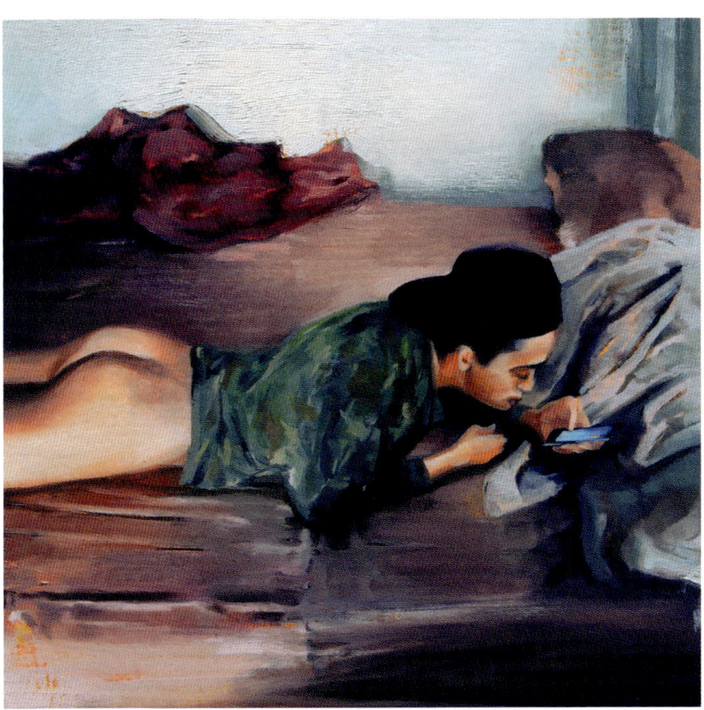

and civilize a man's relationship to fluids. Being able to manipulate, organize, and set in place liquid material in a way that sets up something powerful, impactful, and beautiful, is ultimately very civilized. And through that, you conquer this thing that freaks everybody out, which is the messiness of fluids. But I want painting to terrify me a little bit and turn me on while becoming an image of something extremely refined.

JE: Are you interested in "style" as in fashion?

SM: Style is important—how could it not be? People have to get dressed so it should matter what you put on. That is another reason I'm totally obsessed with painting—it's all surface—it's all shallow. Somehow paradoxically within that shallow surface is a depth of a multitude of other meanings, for lack of a better word. That potential gets me excited. Who is the best painter for that? Fragonard is basically my favorite artist. His paintings are so light, they are so stupid, frivolous, they are totally in the service to power, but the *colors*—his sensibility with touch, and gesture, and the airiness within layers of paint which can go from a top layer to a base layer yet seem to go on infinitely. Then the sexuality, perversion, or playfulness within most of that work as content is very exciting and looks contemporary.

JE: One of the things I like about your work is that you're playing the aesthete—the sensibility is funny and maybe cruel, but they are not ironic.

SM: Irony fucking sucks. You have to feel it. You have to. And, it's that old cliché—you know how all comedians are depressed or basically suicidal, that is the secret edge. If you don't mean it, don't feel it, I don't think you are in touch with the urgency that we exist in. My type of painting is not impersonal, ironic, or a complete acquiescence to the academic-industrial complex. A lot of people make work that has to position itself to seem "savvy." When I see some of the ironic-critical practices I just think "What do you want?" So why am I in this city that is a grind, doing this thing that no one cares about?—because it matters that I love it. It's romance.

I make them for the contact high, for the proximity of being near them. A painting is not just an object, it is an activity. I don't want to portray myself as overly pathetic, but I think they come from a place of dissatisfaction and sadness—in image-making I can arrest a moment and have it stay in front of me in order to efficiently obsess over it. The let-down is that there are so many moments that will not wait for you, and you are reminded every time you notice one that you want something you can't have—you want to have a moment of time swell up and remain still.

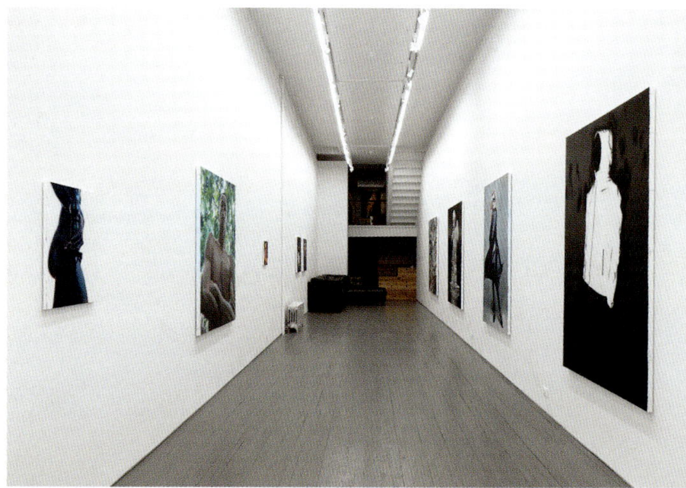

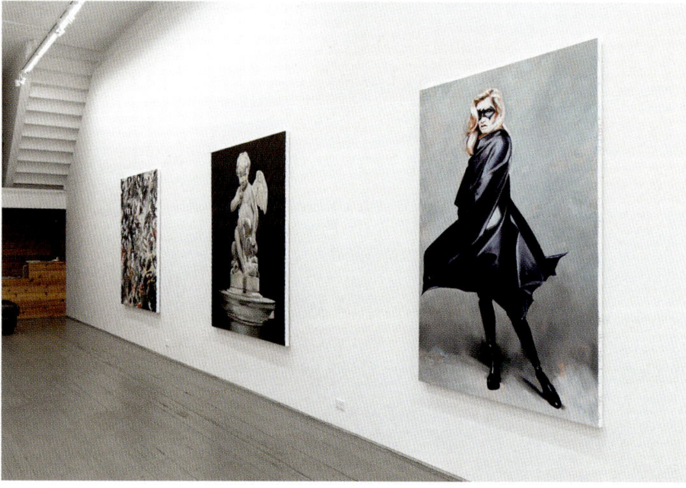

JE: Talking about Fragonard is so interesting because the subject matter of class is over the top there—maybe in painting itself—how do you think about that?

SM: My work is class-passing. They try to trade up, it's fairly obvious, just as it is with me—I'm one of the most affected people I know. I had a lot of good things in my life growing up, but money wasn't one of them. I'm from Connecticut where everyone is absurdly wealthy, even people in the middle class don't look like the middle class of the rest of the country. I think painting knows where it's going to end up eventually. It's unavoidable. I don't want to pretend and say I think these things have revolutionary potential—I don't want to lie and say that I think they have working-class solidarity because they don't. My dad is a pastor, he has a church, which is basically like any other not-for-profit entity, very *budget*. But as a result, I'm also really in touch with some sort of Christocentric metaphysical cosmology. Light and dark and color—those things have inherent metaphysical power directly related to every religious symbolism on the planet. Like I actually believe in Heaven, and I'm constantly comparing things to Hell. I don't think that stuff is incidental.

I remember leaving the studio slightly dazed and delighted to have someone new to argue with. Also I just instantly liked Sam, that he was so different from me while seeming equally passionate about painting as a human endeavor. It was rare to find anyone in those days to talk about Fragonard—and, in fact, it still is. Yet I was unsure. He was close with a group of what were then called Net artists whose work I never liked—I thought it was at best cynical and at worst merely ugly. And despite all the talk about romance and art history, there was a coldness in Sam's work that attracted and disturbed me, which was perfectly captured by something he said in that first meeting: "What is most important to me—having the last fucking laugh."

III

In 2015 Sam McKinniss opened *Black Leather Sectional*, his first solo show in New York at Joe Sheftel Gallery on the Lower East Side. Named for a rented couch he installed at the back of the space, it featured a dozen paintings of varying sizes and seemingly disparate imagery. Along one wall was a quartet of large canvases. At the end was a ghostie abstraction followed by unexpected variations on a theme. There was a depiction of Etienne-Maurice Falconet's *L'Amour Menaçant,* an 1857 marble statuette (made for Madame de Pompadour's garden) of an impish cherub smirking and holding his finger up to his mouth, which makes a cameo in Fragonard's Rococo iconic work *The Swing*. In Sam's painting, it's blown up and dramatically lit, a white figure against a black ground. Used as the press image for the exhibition, its title encapsulated the seemingly contradictory attitude of the work: *The Menacing Love.*

Beside the angel was a full-length portrait of actress Alicia Silverstone dressed as Batgirl, taken from a publicity portrait by Herb Ritts for the blockbuster campfest *Batman and Robin* (1997). She's all high-gloss black in a swirling leather cape against a gray backdrop. Last in the row was an almost entirely black painting of a nearly invisible figure, described by what seems like a bright photo flash bouncing off of a reflective hoodie, in the vein of Sam's graduate school paintings made from his own pictures. The formal elements echoed: lights to darks, hoodie to ghost, wing to cape.

The rest of the show built on these juxtapositions, with a small portrait of downtown it-girl and future Hollywood actress Hari Nef made from a selfie placed beside a mid-sized painting of T. J. Lane, the 17-year-old who shot six classmates in Chardon Ohio, killing three in 2012 without discernible motive or remorse. The source image was a self-portrait from the shooter's Facebook page and shows his lean white pubescent body flexing shirtless in the woods, the image from below so we look up at the merciless young man, face in shadow, arms folded across the bottom of the canvas. If you didn't know the reference, it would be easily mistaken as gay porn. On its other side was a small painting of a close crop of Donatello's teenage twink *David*, in profile from mid-stomach to mid-thigh, framing his hand resting lightly on the sword's big phallic handle that he's just used to decapitate the giant. What did all these things have to do with each other except a kind of dread, frigid and frivolous, fit to be numbly yet stylishly displayed above your couch?

The choice of Batgirl felt emblematic. To underscore her importance, there was actually a second Batgirl in the show, a smaller head-and-shoulders portrait of the actress from the same photoshoot, turning and tilting her head so that her blonde hair gently cascades over the top of her cape, the rubber bodysuit showing a breast with the nipple in profile (as did that iteration of the movie's corresponding Batman and Robin costumes). The painting represents a nexus in pop culture, the point at which a character in the seventy-year multimedia *Batman* franchise overlaps with the career trajectory of a real-life ingenue. After starring in a trio of Aerosmith music videos ("Cryin'" and "Amazing" in 1993; "Crazy" in 1994), Alicia Silverstone was cemented as the archetypal teen dream when she played Cher Horowitz, the Beverly Hills rich girl with a heart of gold in *Clueless,* Amy Heckerling's loose adaptation of Jane Austen's *Emma* in 1995. Pictures of Silverstone in any of these earlier incarnations would have been immediately beloved, a synecdoche of the star and American teenage desire at the end of the 20th century. She's the prettiest, coolest, kindest, and unwittingly hilarious version of adolescence imaginable. *As if!*

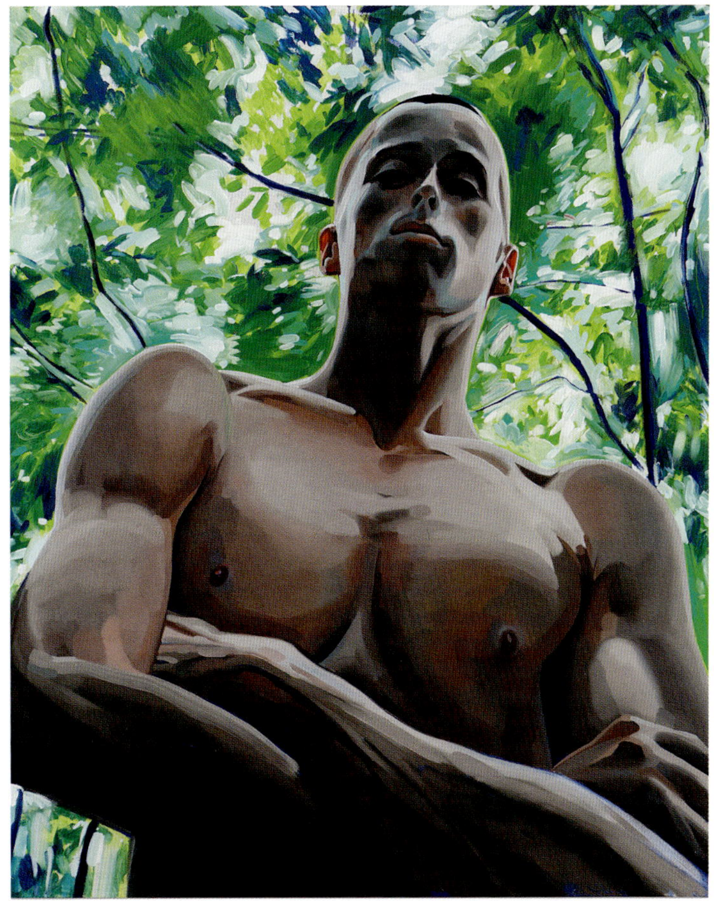

However, when the twenty-year-old actress donned the rubber suit as Batgirl, there was much public conversation about her changing body. Articles in *Entertainment Weekly* discussed her need to lose weight for the role, while less "thoughtful" publications simply called her "fat girl." So it's understandable that watching *Batman and Robin*, Silverstone just doesn't seem like she's having any fun, especially while delivering stinkers like: "Using feminine wiles to get what you want? Trading on your looks? Read a book sister. That passive-aggressive number went out long ago. Chicks like you give women a bad name." (Meanwhile, Uma Thurman is chewing the scenery and having a blast as Poison Ivy.) The movie was a critical bomb, with Silverstone singled out for her poor performance.

A big oil painting commemorating Alicia Silverstone's turn as Batgirl is a totem of her debasement, or at least her entry into more complex territory than the universal adoration bestowed upon her Cher character, representative of our culture's favorite game of tearing apart its most beloved starlets. At the same time, the amped-up homoeroticism of *Batman and Robin* (the product of gay impresario Joel Schumacher) that imagines Batgirl in fetish gear is itself a kind of queer triumph embedded within the most mainstream popular culture, its own kind of "bat signal" for gay kids like Sam and me. (I remember seeing *Batman and Robin* as a nine-year-old in a theater with my family then going across the street to Taco Bell; thanks to $20 million spent in cross-promotion, we drank soda out of "collectible" plastic cups with the actors' faces on them.) And yet any nostalgia-fueled fandom that could explain the Batgirl painting is challenged, undermined, and held in check by the inclusion of T. J. Lane, which is rendered

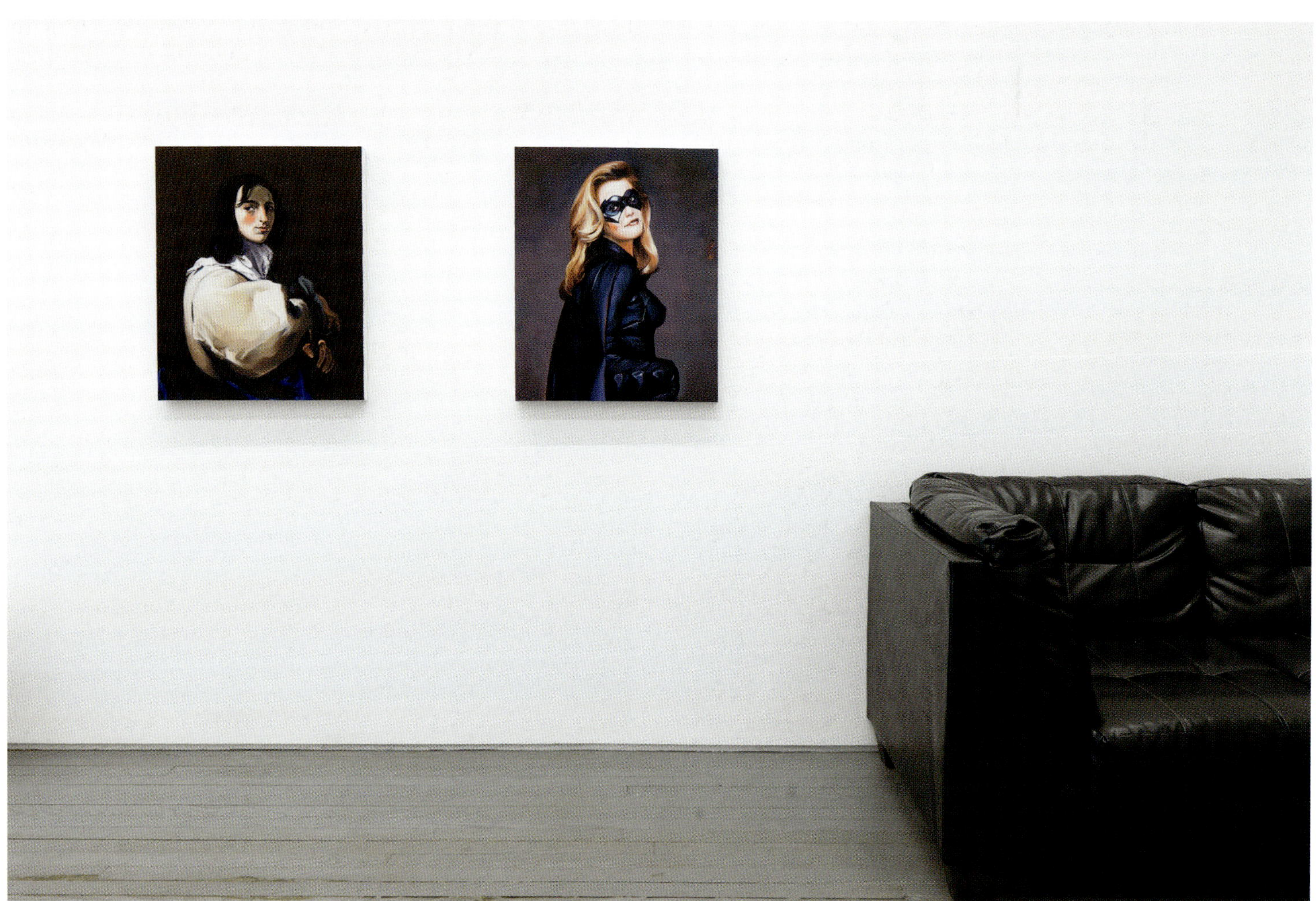

with the same facile "impressionistic" brushwork, with slight distortions of drawing and keyed-up colors. I didn't understand what was going on in the show as a whole—in my memory *nobody* did—but it was obvious that these new paintings of images harvested online had an electricity, markedly different than all the subjects that he had painted before, and that their associations had a greater capacity for sustaining the "several different conversations" that he attributed to painting itself, "by holding complex forms on a surface."

IV

The next year, in mid-October, Sam McKinniss opened his breakthrough exhibition *Egyptian Violet* at Team Gallery in downtown New York. I remember showing up to the opening and it was *mobbed*—you couldn't pack another body in the room, much less see the paintings. In her memoir Ronnie Spector talks about the unmistakable experience of having a hit record: it's a feeling in the air around you, palpable in the nuance of what people said and what they didn't. McKinniss's show radiated that feeling of a *hit*, whatever that is. It was clear that night he had connected to something deep in the culture, offering the first full view of his work as we now know it. Ghosts were gone, portraits of friends too were banished, replaced exclusively by "found" images pulled from the recent past, largely from the pop culture of our childhoods: Princess Leia in George Lucas's *The Empire Strikes Back* (1980); the album cover for Prince's *Purple Rain* (1984); Laura Dern as Sandy in David Lynch's *Blue Velvet* (1986); Winona Ryder as Lydia Deetz in Tim Burton's *Beetlejuice* (1988); Michelle Pfeiffer as Catwoman in Tim Burton's *Batman Returns* (1992); the dolphin star from the remake of *Flipper* (1996); Jonathan Rhys Meyer as Brian Slade, the fictional homage to Ziggy Stardust, in Todd Haynes's *Velvet Goldmine* (1998); Whitney Houston in the video for "It's Not Right But It's Ok" (1998); Lil' Kim getting jiggled by Diana Ross onstage at MTV's VMAs (1999); Snoop Dogg in the movie *Baby Boy* (2001). All images so instantly recognizable, specifically pinpointing a position deeply within and yet slightly outside of the dominant culture.

In addition, there was a shadowy swan floating on glittering water, and three small recreations of nineteenth-century French painter Henri Fantin-Latour's still lifes of flowers on otherwise empty tables. This information regarding the source material wasn't supplied; you knew it or you didn't. The canvases were united only by the recurrence of the purple paint of the exhibition's title and the brisk, fluid paint handling, which integrated all his impulses from the earlier "cosmetic abstractions" and *ghosties*, especially into the brushy backgrounds. The intention resided at the selection and the conceptualization of them as a "show," each painting individual yet tethered to the other works in the room, just as every singular image conjured a host of other invisible images and cultural meanings.

Donald Trump was elected on November 8, 2016, affirming and intensifying the exhibition's "glitter and doom" atmosphere. The show was reviewed in the major art magazines, *ARTnews, Art in America, Modern Painters,* and *Artforum*, as well as receiving mention in mainstream outlets like *The New Yorker.* The response was positive, though not altogether certain about the painting's implications, lingering on the ambiguity of imagery and questioning the artist's intentions. In *Artforum* critic Johanna Fateman captured the overall tone when she observed, "The emotionalism of his canvases is high-pitched but not very vulnerable, which also makes it seem at least partly ironic. But would it be possible for an American artist to paint Prince on April 22 [the day after his death] ironically, in an emotional state not overtaken by, or at least tinged with, grief? I hope not." *Prince,* the largest painting in the exhibition at 96" x 84", did strike the dominant chords of the show, tuned to his sudden death six months earlier, furthered by the portrait of Whitney Houston who died tragically in 2012. But then, a few feet away you had a large painting of *Flipper*, doing an underwater trick, seeming to smile broadly, in a whirl of silver bubbles.

Writer Alissa Bennett—doyenne of a particular downtown literary and art scene since her move to New York City in the 1990s—is the smartest person I know for theorizing our emotional and psychic relationships with popular culture and the detritus of the past. When Sam's show opened, she was working as a director at Team, and I recently asked her to describe her experience of *Egyptian Violet.* She told me that working in a gallery attunes your eye to the "best painting" in the show, the one you knew would connect with everyone, but the curious experience with McKinniss's work is that there was no telling who would connect with which painting, "It was like playing Go Fish." Alissa continued:

> *When I watched people stand in front of them, there was some kind of romance between the spectator and the object, and it was almost like I could see them thinking, No one deserves to be with us like I do. No one will understand it like I do. And it's protective, it's narcissistic, it's jealous—this sort of jealous gesture about needing to be with this particular image. With Catwoman—you looked at that painting and you were like, that's going to sell in one minute. And it sold in one minute and you could have sold it a hundred times. They all sold and sold very quickly. Those paintings got their hooks in people in a way that was interesting to watch because I'd not seen it before.*

How does she account for this extreme desire? Alissa Bennett explained that she believes there is a category of niche images where the only way that you can identify them or locate them within time is that you were directly engaged with them at the moment of their genesis in the culture. The intense identification with these particular images is about the viewer in the past. "For instance, I remember someone being really desperate to buy this painting of Macaulay Culkin in *Home Alone*. It's not an 'incredible' painting *per se,* but the collector really begged for it. He felt so connected to it somehow. It emotionally completed a circuit. There's no other reason to have this kind of symbolic relationship with that film except that it reminds you of an easier, younger, less fraught time. And I think a lot of Sam's paintings do that."

V

So far I've dealt with Sam McKinniss's work iconographically, which is pretty much the only way they ever get discussed. I think critics don't even realize that they're talking about them as *images*, as though they're transparent emanations of their signified, rather than attending to the sensuous specificity of them as painted signifiers. In responding to Bennett's observations, it becomes important to foreground the works not just as images but as paintings, moving from apparent subject matter to how they actually function in the world. McKinniss's work has to do with a selection of charged images that have a particular visual structure: a single figure usually isolated against an amorphous background, intensifying the viewer's identification with the subject, opening the kind of "emotional circuit" as described, the closure of which is always deferred.

Sometimes these images are stills from a film or video, but usually, they are images made readily available as a result of being selected (and cropped or otherwise tweaked) by professional photo editors for print and online publications. It is interesting to note how many of the pictures are in fact publicity portraits, in which the actors in costume are posed in gestures that crystallize and condense, made to stand in for the entire movie. McKinniss drolly refers to hours scrolling on Google image search as his "drawing practice." He is not "constructing" his compositions as so-called "representational" or figurative painting would, but simply identifying them. The artist understands himself as the end user of a chain of highly paid and incredibly intelligent media professionals who have forged pictures of maximum appeal.

Sam McKinniss paints the image in a way that performs itself *as paint,* leaving every brushstroke visible with buttery assurance, more or less conforming to the thing they describe, often with each color its own mark.

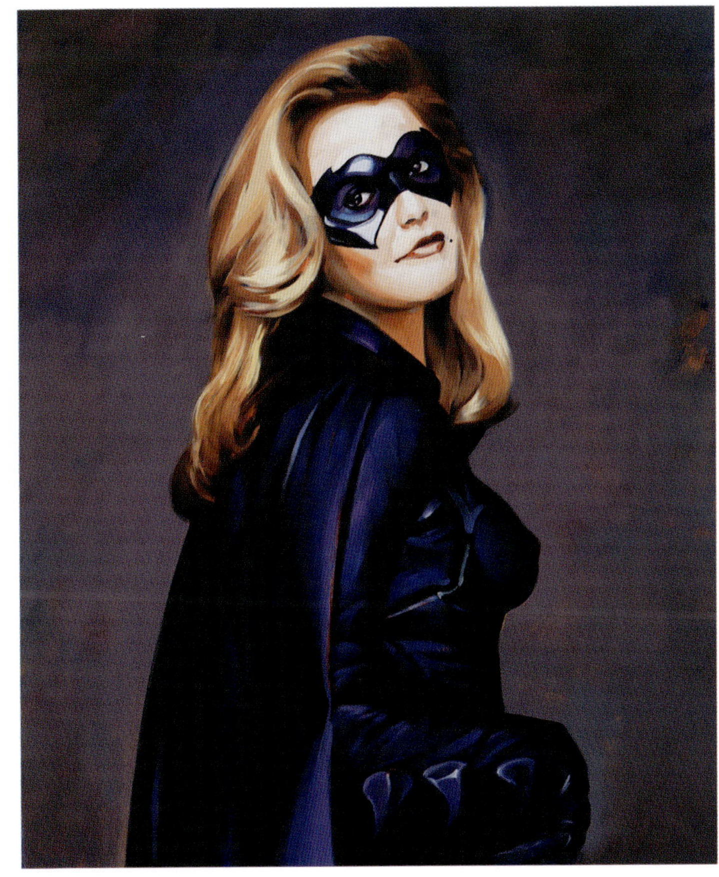

The paint sits right on the surface and does not open into illusionist space, although such spaces are "described" by the image. Faithful to the original image in part, his process of painting it himself by hand, rather than through photomechanical transfer or farming it out to assistants, entails slight distortions in the drawing, heightening the sense of artifice. These paintings are not made with the academic realism of figurative paintings nor with the deadpan precision of photorealism. It is rather a kind of emotional impressionism in which the image is transcribed into a painterly shorthand. In this way, the work opens onto the kinds of projections that Bennett describes, a relationship that is less about the source image than the way we connect with them.

Scale shifts are important, playing with and against their subject matter (that the emotionally vacant *Flipper* and *Swan* paintings were the other large works beside the overdetermined pathos of *Prince* in *Egyptian Violet* is a case in point.) Most important for me are the preponderance of small paintings, around 9" x 12", intimately scaled to be cherished at home. They are the ultimate fetish objects, radiating a desire protracted indefinitely, from which their physical presence seems to offer a temporary reprieve. These enact most clearly one of the structural transformations that drive the work: to make a public image into a private devotional object, something you can possess. At that size the brushwork is more broadly descriptive, intensifying the "abstraction" of the original, asking you to get close to savor every inch of its surface, at which point the image paradoxically recedes in legibility, replaced by the luxuries of color and touch.

There has been a surprising lack of serious criticism around the recent commercial boom and heightened cultural prominence of figurative painting, which has helped return painting to a level of vitality it has not seen since the mid-twentieth century. Reading art criticism of the late twentieth century the consensus opinion, against which all arguments were pitched, was that painting was dead. Its apparently exuberant returns in the 80s and 90s were regarded as reactionary, retrograde, or oblivious to the state of the discourse—and in fact some combination of all three. In art school in the mid-2000s, students like McKinniss and I were still dutifully taught essays like Douglas Crimp's "The End of Painting" and Benjamin Buchloh's "Figures of Authority, Ciphers of Regression" which retained their stranglehold on the discourse well into the early twenty-first century.

Painting's returned prominence coincides with seismic shifts in our cultural, physiological, and psychological relationship with images. We encounter more images today than have ever existed in history, and the overwhelming majority of those are encountered *immaterially,* digitally appearing on a screen before disappearing in an infinite scroll. Just colored light, they are fluid, able to dissolve in an instant, while giving us the illusion of choice and the fantasy of connection. This torrent of images seems to bypass our conscious mind, flowing right into the unconscious. Internet technologies are not an extension of a neutral public square; they are optimized by the richest corporations in the history of the world to sell our attention to advertisers, making images the most powerful force in contemporary life. They affect our deepest connections—how we regard our own bodies and each other, how we encounter our very consciousness itself. These are existential and urgent questions that painting is uniquely positioned to address.

It's worth reflecting on how swiftly this revolution has taken hold, and how wholly it's become entrenched. I graduated from high school in 2006, the year Facebook first opened itself to anyone with a valid email address. The following year the first iPhone appeared, as did the microblogging platform for content aggregation, Tumblr. It was three more years until Instagram launched in 2010. The image ecology of social media reached a recognizable form a few years later, and Sam was painting naked boys staring into the glow of their phones. That decade saw a profound shift in how digital images function socially, becoming an indelible part of our lives. In this context, figurative painting returned full throttle.

Painting is a specific and extremely old image technology that has persisted unabated for thousands of years. One aspect of painting that was unremarkable for most of its long history was its material existence—it was an image that was also an object—a fact without need of comment because there was no alternative. But with the apotheosis of immaterial images in the 21st century, the implications of painting's materiality grow in importance. As opposed to a digital image on a screen, the painted image is a physical embodiment that addresses the viewer in time and space. It discloses itself through the way it is made; one can follow how different strokes or gestures add up to make a surface, and that surface has its relationship to the depicted image. A painting's image can hit all at once, but looking at the object enables us to regard it not as static but as a sequence of moves and material qualities that attenuate the image—expanding it, complicating it, slowing it down—allowing the viewer to form a relationship with it. Being with a painting allows for a kind of thinking and experiencing that is wholly different from looking at the same image on a screen. Thus painting itself, as one of the oldest art mediums, unassisted by critics and theorists, has emerged as a site from which we can reflect on our shared condition, as embodied people in a physical world today.

VI

Finding artist-predecessors of McKinniss's work proves more deceptive than might first appear. It's impossible to escape Andy Warhol, who used a headshot of Marilyn Monroe to make his first silkscreen portraits, her celebrity evoking the visual power of the Byzantine icons of his childhood. Created in the wake of her death in 1962, the source image he used was a publicity photo for the film *Niagara*, a movie from a decade earlier. In the monumental *Marilyn Diptych* (1962) he printed grids of fifty images on a pair of canvases, side by side. On the left side are twenty-five Marilyns, with skin painted pink, hair yellow, lips red, against an orange ground; on the right side are twenty-five more Marilyns, this time with the black photographic image screened directly atop a silver field, allowing the variations in over-inking to blur her features across the iterations. The provocation was not just the subject matter but the form, the use of a commercial printing technique to make a painting, one that suppressed the artist's hand. The intense repetition seemed to speak to the libidinal drives of commodity fetishism and the collective obsession with the actress. It's hard not to interpret Warhol's painting of Marilyn as animated by both queer devotion and camp sensibility, as long as both are understood as wholly sincere. Meanwhile, noting Warhol's collapsing of so-called high and low cultural forms, critics debated the artist's intentions as either celebrating or critiquing the burgeoning economy of images, but the work itself refuses to reconcile those contradictions.

After several generations of theory-driven appropriation and conceptual art, in the 1990s a new crop of artists took up image-based painting with a renewed cultural force. Among them were Elizabeth Peyton's small fey paintings of her beautiful friends as well as heartthrobs and rock stars, all reduced to elegant calligraphy. She created indelible icons of the Gen X sensibility, placing a portrait of Jackie O. brushing back her son's hair next to Liam Gallagher, young Prince Harry, re-paintings of art historical works by Jacques-Louis David, and many wan and worshipful renditions of Kurt Cobain. Through her distinctive style, they all look recognizably like their subjects while also looking like Peyton paintings. Describing her images and what she does with them is more or less indistinguishable from what McKinniss embarked on a generation later, with one massively important distinction. In the case of Elizabeth Peyton's subject matter, one always has the sense she paints things she likes, that she is driven by her own private tastes and personal fandom, and that these disparate sources have been equalized by crossing the horizon of her affection. By contrast, I don't for one second think that Sam McKinniss has profound feelings about *Home Alone, Batman,* or *Flipper;* his work is not about *his* fandoms—but *ours.*

In this McKinniss reminds me of a very different painter who helped define painting at the end of the twentieth century, Luc Tuymans. Few artists have interrogated the power of images more systematically, and none, to my mind, more ruthlessly. Working at a time when figurative painting was all but intellectually discredited, he employed painting to make spare, abstract analyses of photographs, diagrams, and film stills, overburdened with historical and political meaning. One small painting famously depicts a beige room, sketched out in high contrast with a few dark-gray squares to indicate the loose contours of an interior—door, window, some unidentifiable forms on a ceiling and floor—which snaps into horrifying focus with the title *Gas Chamber* (1986).

Through hundreds of paintings and his collected writings and interviews, Tuymans is contemporary art's reigning philosopher of images. In 1996, before the full impact of digitization, he wrote his prescient thesis "On the Image" which sets out an analysis of how the media landscape impacts the individual and the entire social order:

> *Whereas we have never been so literally detached from the image, the impact on the viewer, which cannot be defined as anything but physical, has been maximized. The instant of experience has been banished and alienated from any real-time span, and the instant has become a code that is perfectly able to skim across the surface of the existing reality. The information, reduced to its most rudimentary form, which means impulse and reaction, is virtually total; what follows is addiction. The image as such has become invisible, unknowable, and anonymous, its meaning undiscoverable as a result of being fragmented into thousands of possible interpretations.*

I met Luc Tuymans around the same time Sam was working on *Egyptian Violet.* He told me that as soon as he saw the iPhone he wanted it, wanted to touch it, seduced by its promise of seamless creation and manipulation of photos. In 2008 he embarked on his first paintings in response to this initial desire. He recounted a story about using his iPhone to photograph a man standing by a tree in a garden, a scene frequently found in paintings throughout art history. He then made a painting based on that photo. When he placed it next to an actual 19th-century painting of the same subject, "the contrast was shocking," he told me, "The light was totally different, and mine clearly came out of a digital age. My painting had nothing to do with the 19th century even though the imagery was the same, which means every age has a specific quality to it that you will be able to retrace via the visual itself."

It is in this sense that I interpret Sam's re-painting of various floral still lifes by Fantin-Latour, which he has made and exhibited consistently across his career, like recurring control images. In remaking these artworks from the nineteenth century, emulating stroke after stroke, of a subject just as fresh for us today as flowers from the bo-

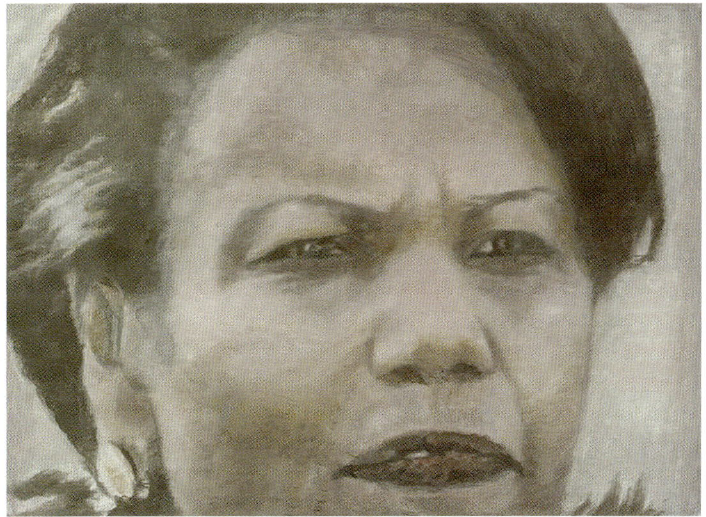

dega, the point is not Sam's painterly virtuosity in achieving similitude, but the yawning gap of difference between then and now they display. While Sam's versions absolutely resemble the Fantin-Latours as pictures, they look nothing like them as paintings. Changes in the science of the pigment and ground cannot account for this difference; each painting is some mysterious measure of an irrevocable distance traveled, one which, as Tuymans observes, is embedded in the light, at the level of the visuality. It is an aspect largely hidden at present, but I imagine this is the quality that will emerge as these structures of visuality change with technological advancement and social change. That is their true content, to be seen in the future.

Tuymans has continued his decades-long process of breaking down images, making his images more obscure and less amenable to online distribution, restraining the color which always tilts toward grays, draining the power from the image itself to draw attention to its operations and the physicality of the painting. Coming of age mere

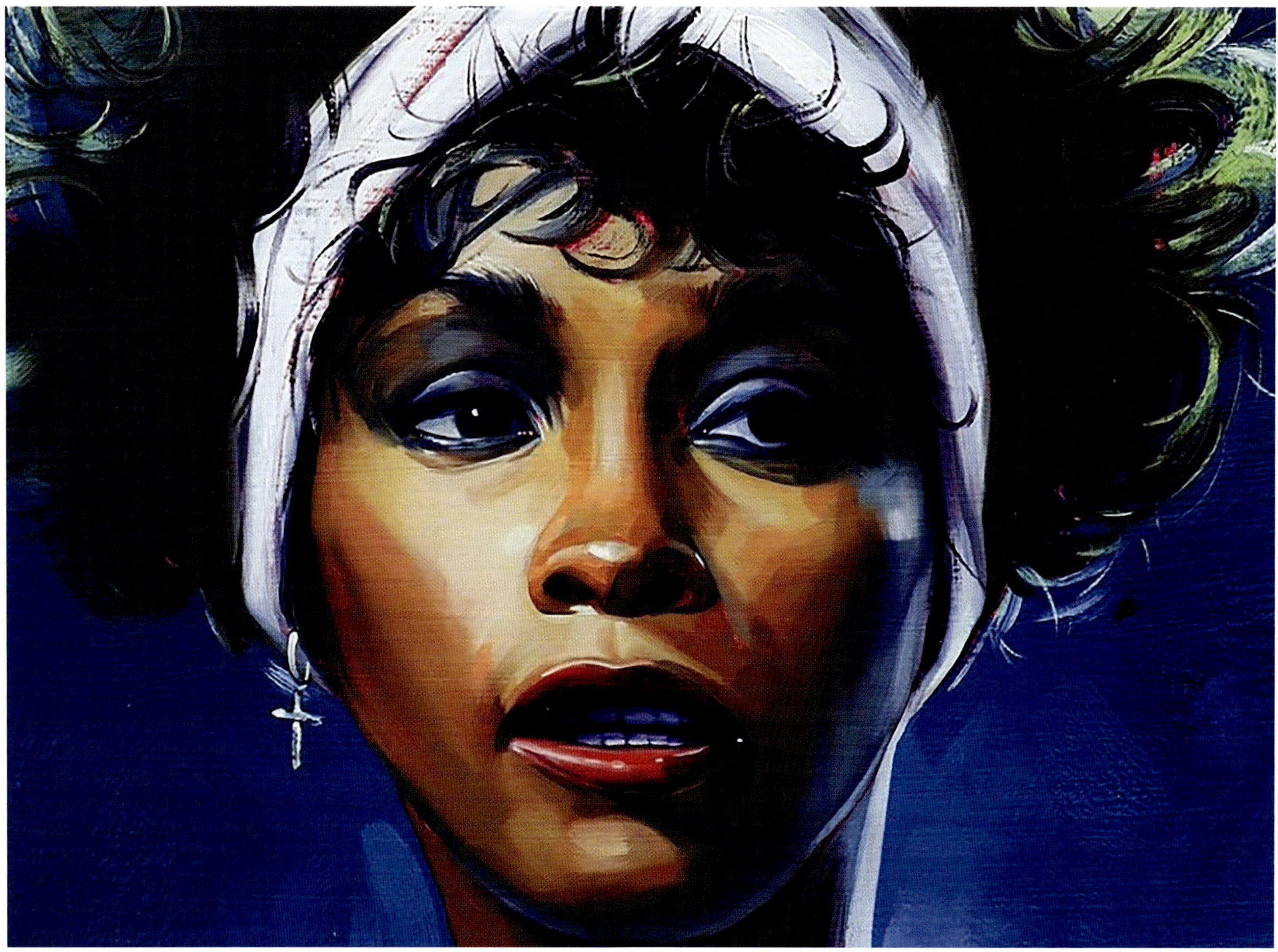

moments before this new media ecosystem achieved total ubiquity, McKinniss has taken the opposite tack: juicing the image with oversaturated high-chroma color, trying to find pictures that could be so flooded with desire that they burn out before your very eyes in a blaze.

Contrast Tuymans's very famous, drab-colored, tightly cropped painting of Condoleezza Rice, *The Secretary of State* (2005; p. 99), made during the throes of the US "War on Terror," with McKinniss's *Star Spangled Banner (Whitney)* (2017), which he told me he consciously approached in relation to the Tuymans painting. Both share the dynamics of white men using an image of a Black woman of undeniable excellence and astonishing achievement to make statements about America in general, if not deadly American exceptionalism in particular. The paintings' similarities are uncanny. Both feature a close crop of the face, both are orientated within wide, horizontal rectangles, and both pairs of eyes move to the right of each painting, the two open mouths. One difference, however, is that while Tuymans's picture of Rice was received as an uneasy but undeniable critique when it appeared in the contemporary art world, McKinniss's depiction of Whitney Houston was largely misunderstood as unqualified, if pathos-laden, adoration. Another difference is each subject's position with regard to either hard or soft power. One takes the highly consequential form of a top state official in wartime, as opposed to the chart-topping star given to soaring propaganda just as one's boss's dad invades Iraq for the first time around.

But the image of Houston triumphant, as she was in this career-defining, 1991 performance of the National Anthem, from source material televised at the start of Super Bowl XXV and the early days of the Persian Gulf War, morphs into an image of her eventual martyrdom (while as of this writing, Rice remains alive and at large). As viewers, we know the rest of the story just as well as we know the fate of the baby Jesus in a Bellini painting. Whitney even has a little crucifix earring, visibly glinting on the left side of the painting; the future *Preacher's Wife* poised and ready to die for our sins.

What seemed to be missing in the discussion of McKinniss's painting, which witnessed our communal grief, not only for Houston herself but also in co-occurrence with the ongoing Movement for Black Lives, was a sense of viewers' own complicity in its tragic, intentional cruelty. Our ravenous interest in her celebrity, in the story of her personal abjection as much as her artistic glory and international significance, makes McKinniss's painting a highly conflicted artwork. It depicts a recording artist isolated by her audience's worship and by the financial necessity of maintaining that celebrity at all costs, an isolation which ultimately culminated in her untimely death. This very painting is yet another symbol of that fused exploitation and adulation, just like Warhol's *Marilyns*. Except instead of the repetition of the silkscreens, in which the image muddies and warps in reproduction across the surface, McKinniss's painting compresses all those conflicted meanings into a single image, to be bought and sold for the profit of others, hard and cold as a diamond, its facets sparkling with the "sinister light" of a screen.

VII

Sam McKinniss has continued to expand his cavalcade of divas: Britney Spears (performing with the yellow python Banana from 2001 VMAs), Nancy Reagan, Joan Didion (emaciated in her oversized glasses), Drew Barrymore (as a child in *E.T.* and in the 1990s with a daisy in her hair), Michael Jackson, Nicole Kidman (in roles for *Batman Forever* and *Eyes Wide Shut*), Little Nas X (in hot pink Versace cowgirl bondage suit), and Dolly Parton (just being perfect with a kitten). These are enriched by high-drama mountain views and charismatic animals of various types—swans, cows, dogs. They go on and on . . . there is seemingly no end to beautiful images of people, places, and pets who fascinate, amuse, or horrify us. Taken together I see Sam's work as profoundly queer, albeit an acidic queerness in the tradition of Kenneth Anger's *Hollywood Babylon*, which his collected works might one day be for our own age—*Entertainment Tonight*, forever.

Actors predominate. Their function is emphasized by naming: the painting is titled not "Alicia Silverstone" but *Batgirl*, not Cassandra Peterson but *Elvira*. When McKinniss's subject matter comes closer to the present, the actors sometimes give way to celebrities as themselves but are treated as characters nonetheless, since online a person is not a human being but an avatar, a digital mask. No matter the subject, the conversion is from person to persona, like Elizabeth Grant into Lana Del Rey. The torrential rise in remakes and reboots of existing intellectual property which dominate the cultural sphere in the past decade knowingly embraces this transformation. And of course that is the very subject behind so many of Sam's images: his paintings of Christina Ricci as Wednesday Addams from the 1990s remakes of the long-established spooky family, of Leonard DiCaprio in Baz Luhrmann's *William Shakespeare's Romeo + Juliet* (1996), of Lindsay Lohan twinning out in the 1998 remake of *The Parent Trap* (1961), and of course all the Batman stuff. Often these are images that pre-date internet culture, but have been absorbed by it, unproblematically churning in its visual reservoir. The reference as *mise en abyme*.

This highly curated yet apparently random selection speaks to the present experience online, where images float, separated from their context, a non-place where everything simply co-exists, sliding whatever their meaning might be onto the qualities of the image itself and the infelicities of the people sharing them. When taken offline, when painted and put into an art gallery or museum, that seeming loss of context is inserted into another highly coded framework, one of art history, self-consciously entering into dialogue with thousands of other artworks.

Paintings have emerged not only as a tool of potential resistance from the online image attention economy but can themselves become the most complicit. Photographs of certain kinds of paintings move easily online, the primary way art audiences and collectors around the world "see" art today, appearing more alluring via reproduction on Instagram or through attached PDFs. This has produced one strand of contemporary painting in response that is illegible as images (I think this accounts for the increasing pictorial emptiness of Luc Tuymans's current paintings, as well as whole swathes of highly nuanced minimal abstractions), while other artists take an accelerationist approach, producing painted images that move even faster in reproduction. Many recent figurative—or what I would call "image-based"—paintings are in this latter category, and McKinniss's paintings are the shrewdest embodiment of this tactic. Above all else a painting is made to be seen, and for the majority of human life that meant to be in its presence. Through continued personal and cultural interactions it accumulates meaning, far beyond the intentions of the person who made it. This is one way that paintings do their much-needed work of opening up, slowing down, and complicating our physical and psychic interaction with an image. When seen online, the effect of Sam's work is almost like a "painted" Instagram filter on images we already know. His choice of pictures acknowledges the disjunction between how paintings function online versus the experience of being seen in person, stretching apart and compressing back together like the bellows of an accordion, again and again.

Back in 2013, Sam described his work: "I think they come from a place of dissatisfaction and sadness—in image-making I can arrest a moment and have it stay in front of me in order to efficiently obsess over it." What is being framed by his paintings is the online vacuum of context, a vacuum we rush to fill, with our personal identification. The experience of looking at Sam McKinniss's work re-enacts our contemporary image world *samsara*, which I believe to be his true subject. These images have power over us, for those who recognize them and are recognized by them, and his paintings seem to offer something tangible to hold, to momentarily light upon in the flood of pictures, to promise respite, a place where we might reflect, take stock of how we changed, what we've lost, who we have or haven't become. Sam McKinniss's paintings turn me on and piss me off. Yet I recognize their reality, the reactions they solicit, and his need to make them. Just behind what seems silly and flippant is something so utterly attuned to the psychic and emotional needs of this moment, flickering light across the surface of an aching void. His paintings pretend to tease, when in fact they haunt and are haunted. They are pictures with a hole in their heart.

1 Luc Tuymans, "On the Image," in *ON&BY LUC TUYMANS*, ed. Peter Ruyffelaere, of *Whitechapel: On & By* (Cambridge, MA: The MIT Press, 2013), 49. 2 "LUC TUYMANS with Jarrett Earnest," *The Brooklyn Rail*, July/August 2016, https://brooklynrail.org/2016/07/art/luc-tuymans-with-jarrett-earnest/.

P. 91, *Elvira*, 2021, installation view, *Country Western*, Almine Rech, London; p. 92, *Max in Ecstasy*, 2014; p. 93, *BOYTWEETSWORLD*, 2013; p. 94, Installation views, *Black Leather Sectional*, 2015; p. 95, *T.J. Lane*, 2015 [destroyed 2021]; p. 96, *Young Man with a Sword (after Eustache Le Suer)*, 2015 (left), and *Batgirl (after Joel Schumacher)*, 2015 (right), installation view, *Black Leather Sectional*, 2015; p. 97, *Batgirl (after Joel Schumacher)*, 2015; p. 99, Luc Tuymans, *The Secretary of State*, 2005, © Luc Tuymans; p. 100, *Star Spangled Banner (Whitney)*, 2017

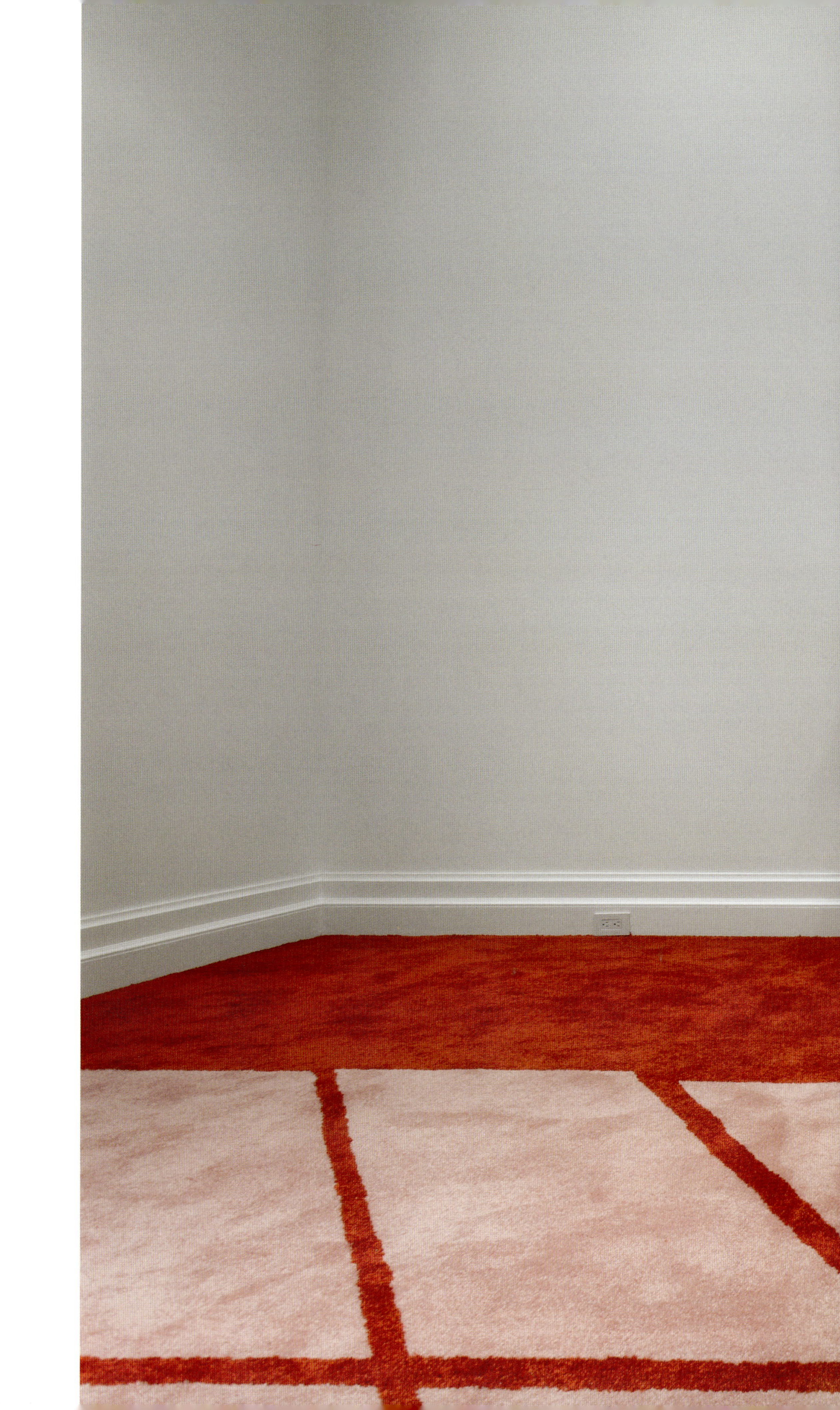

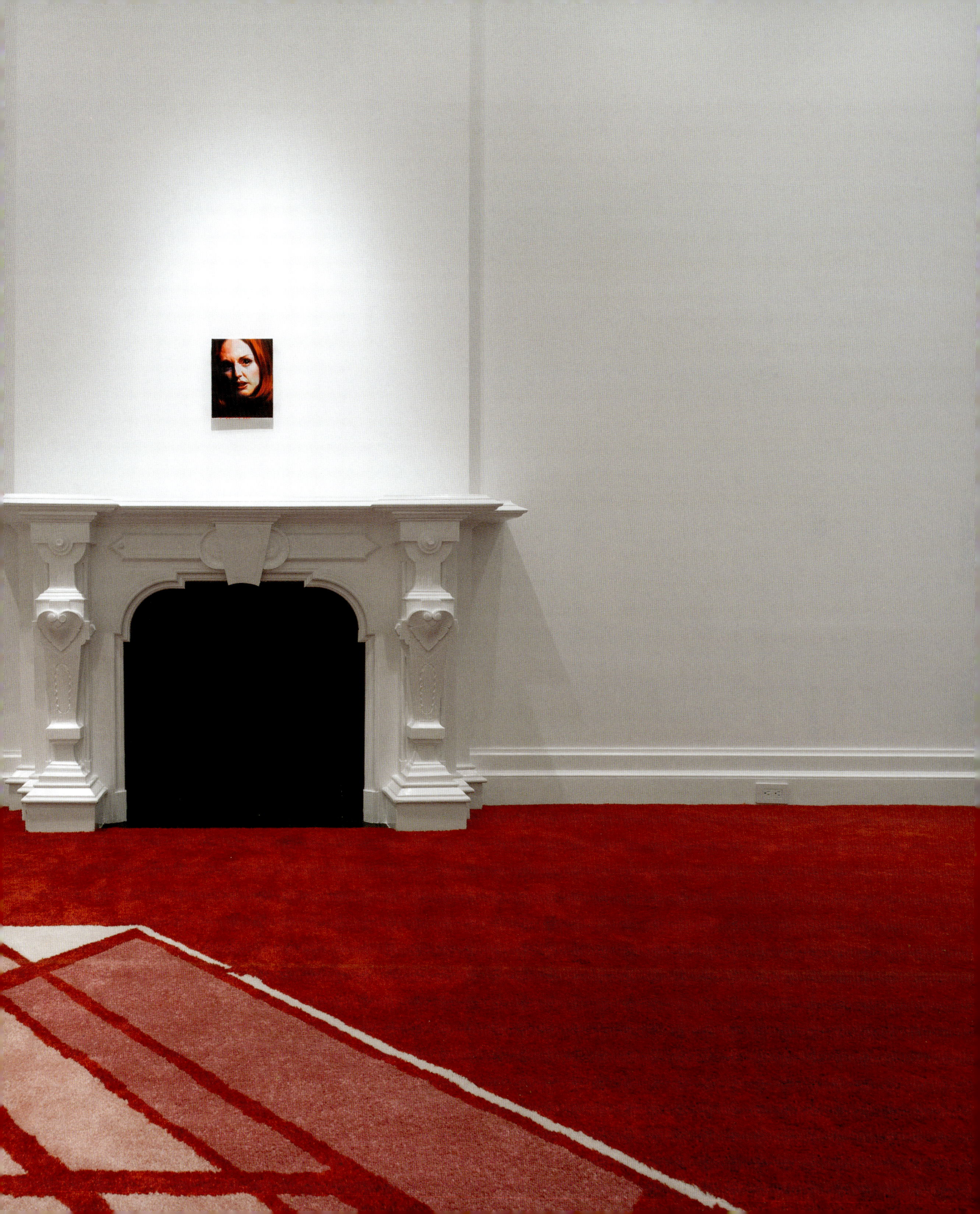

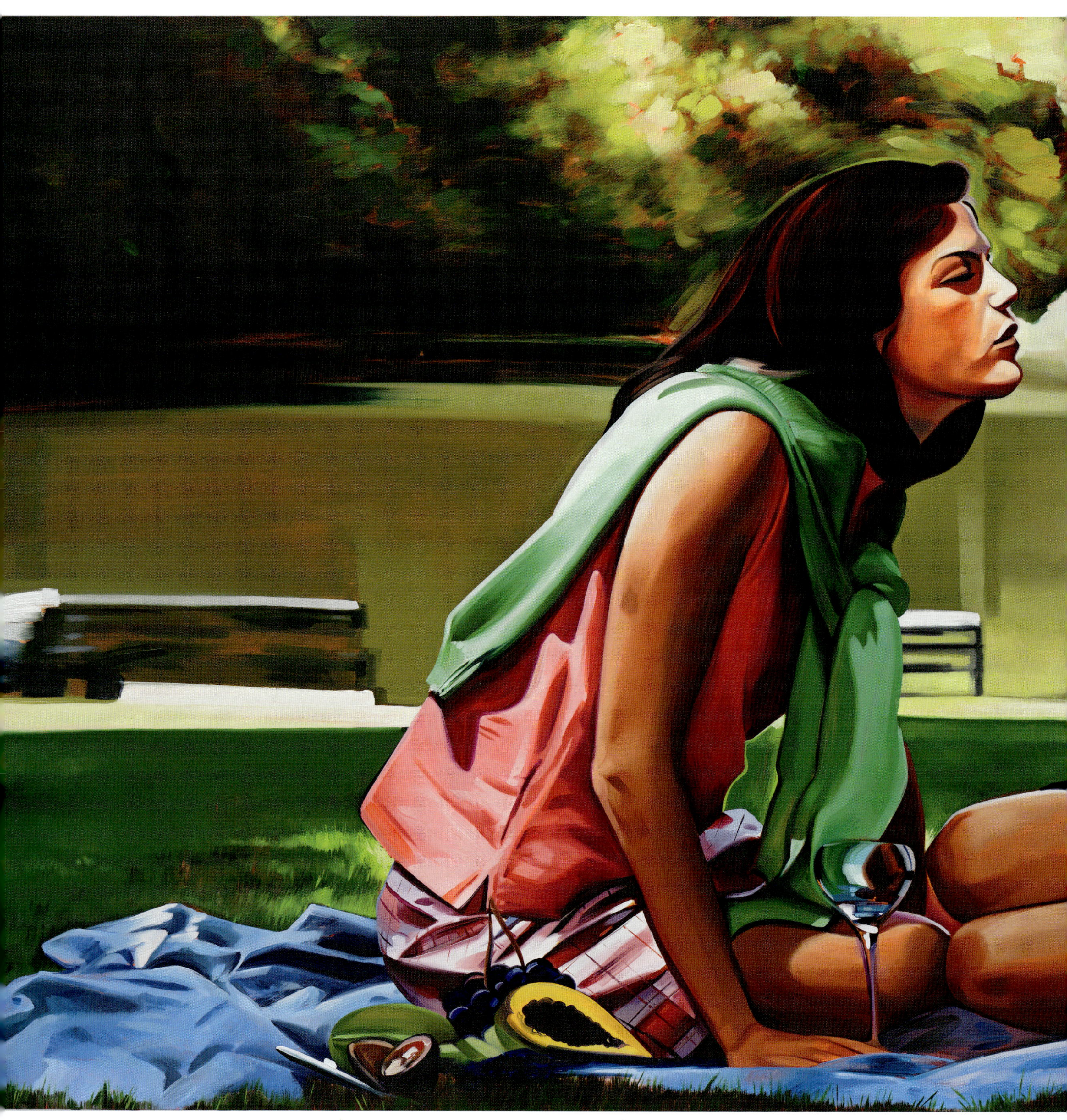

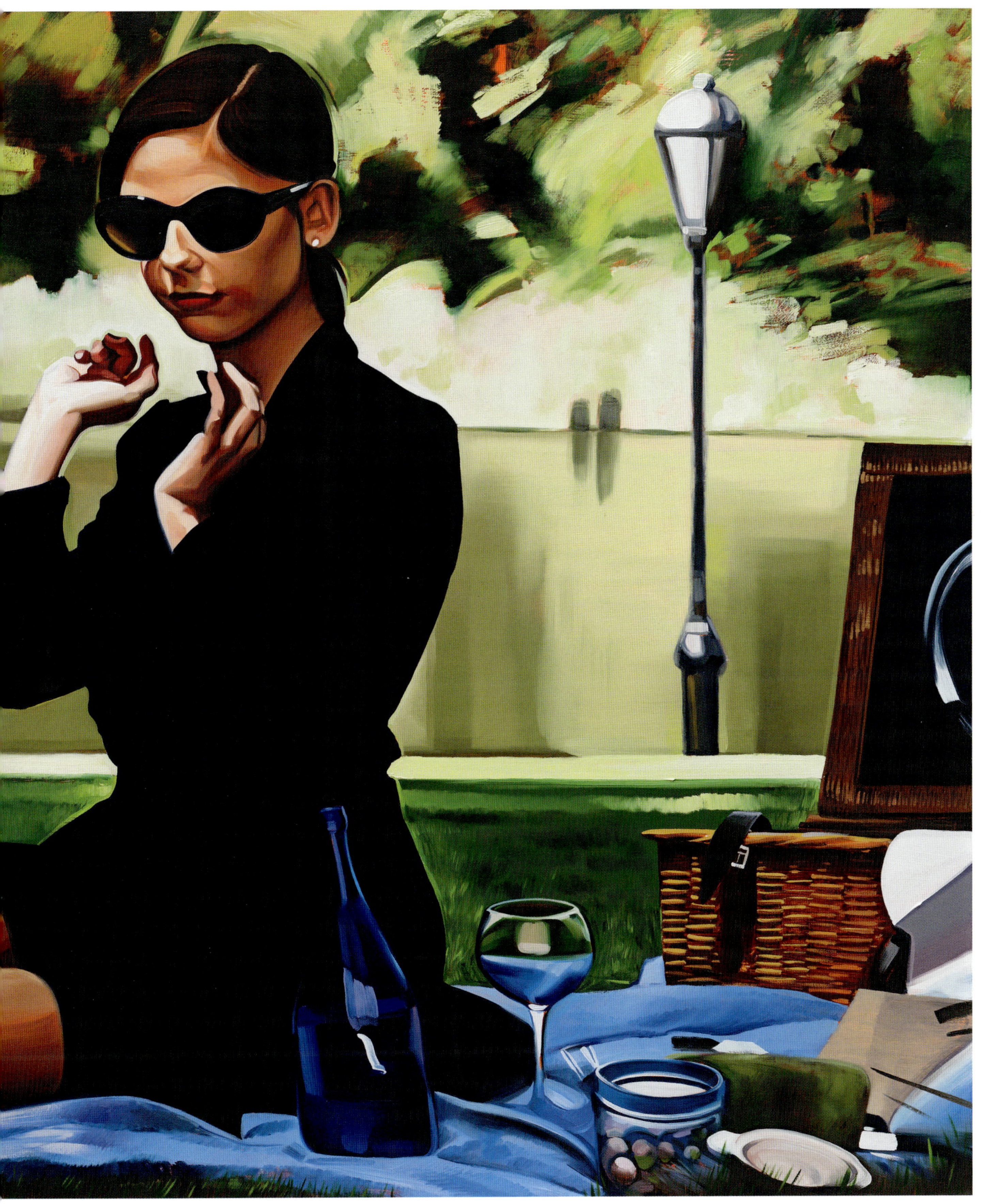

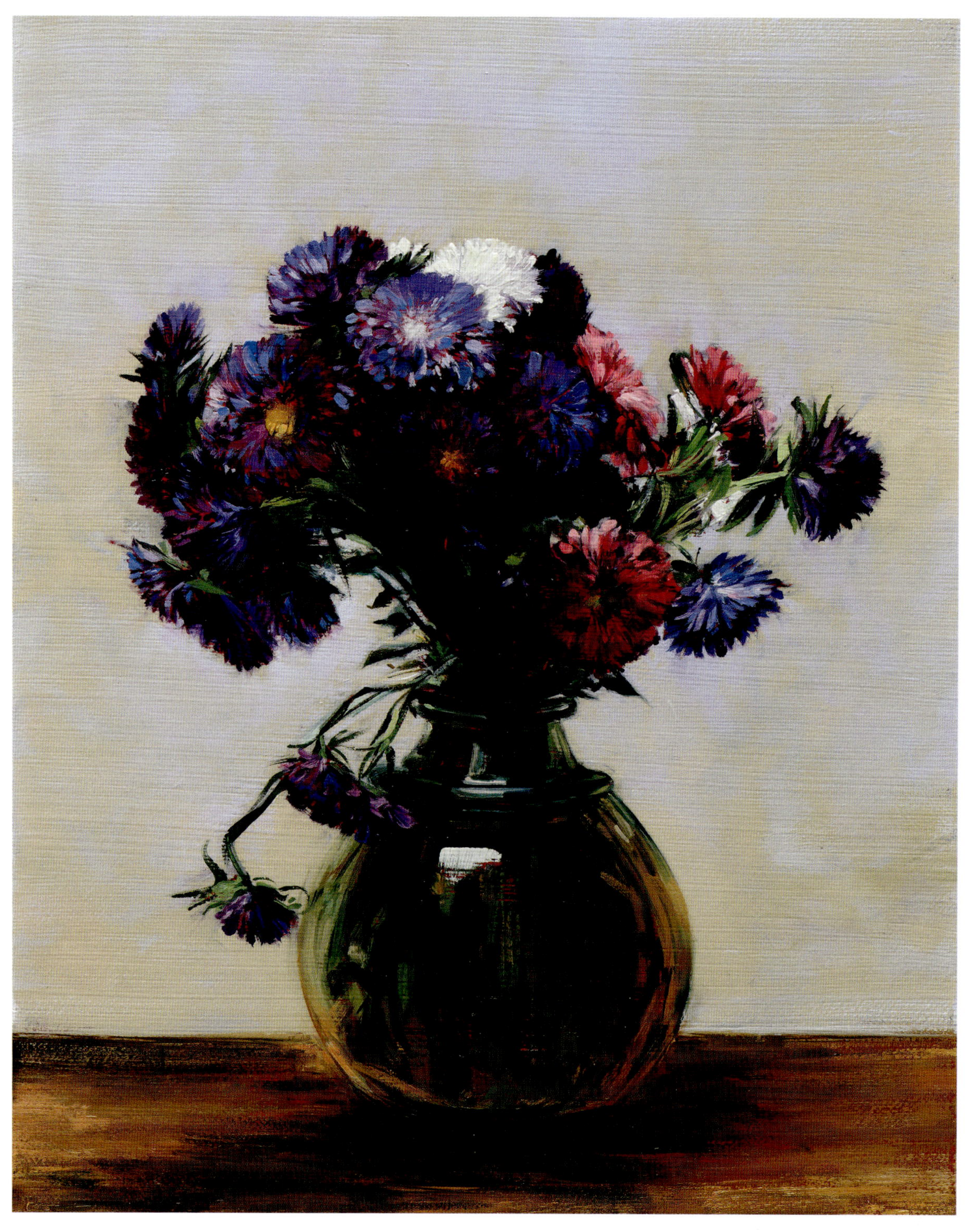

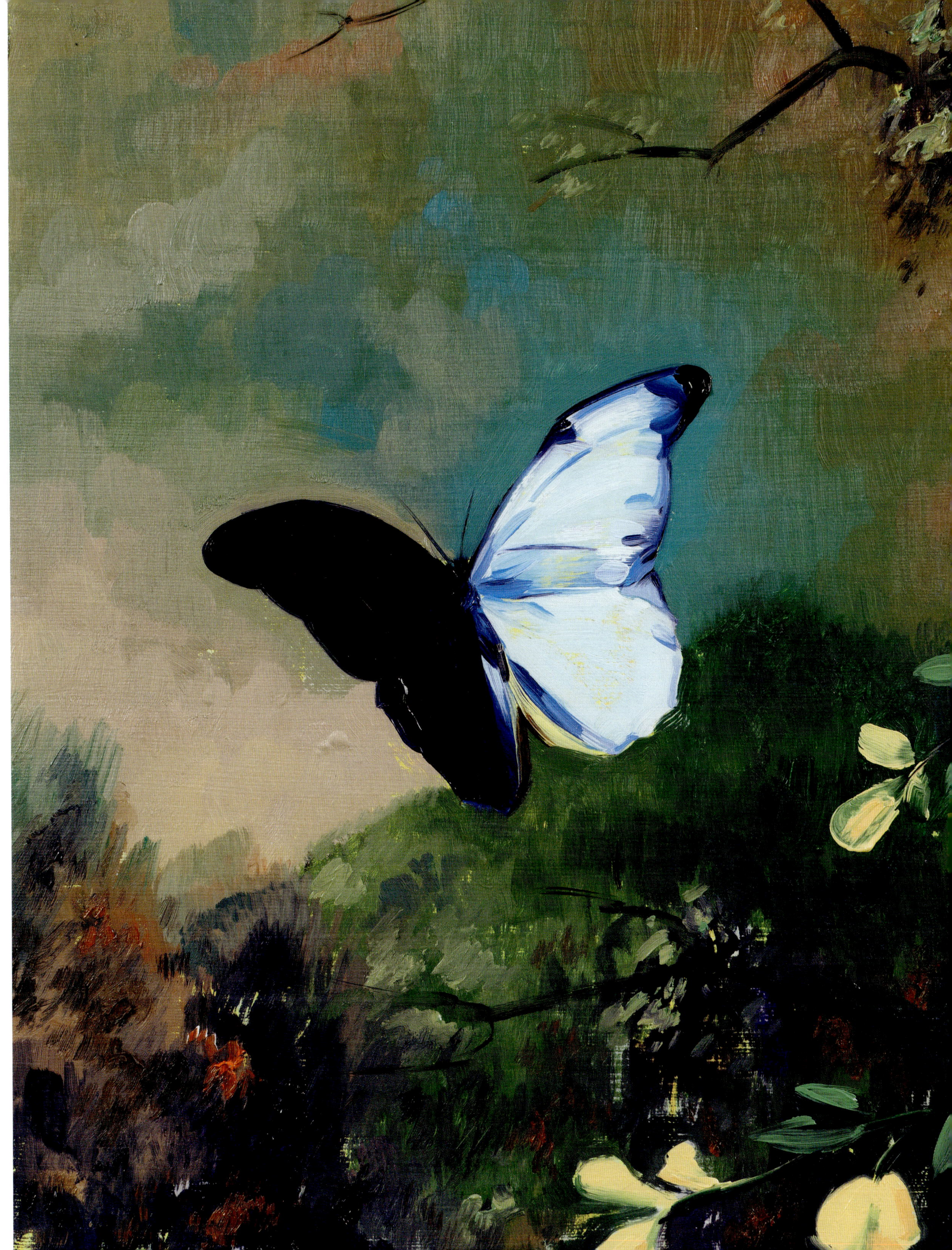

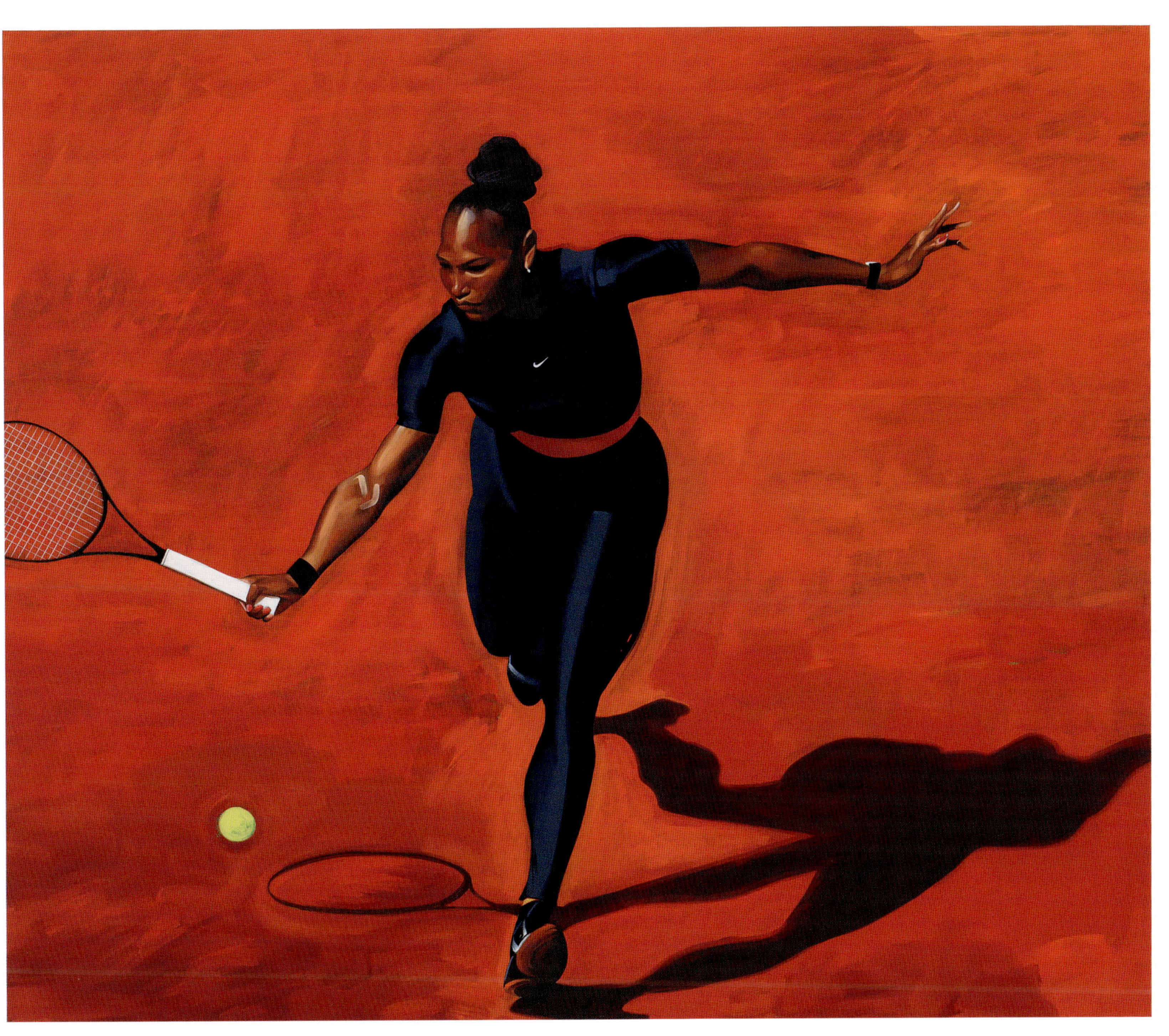

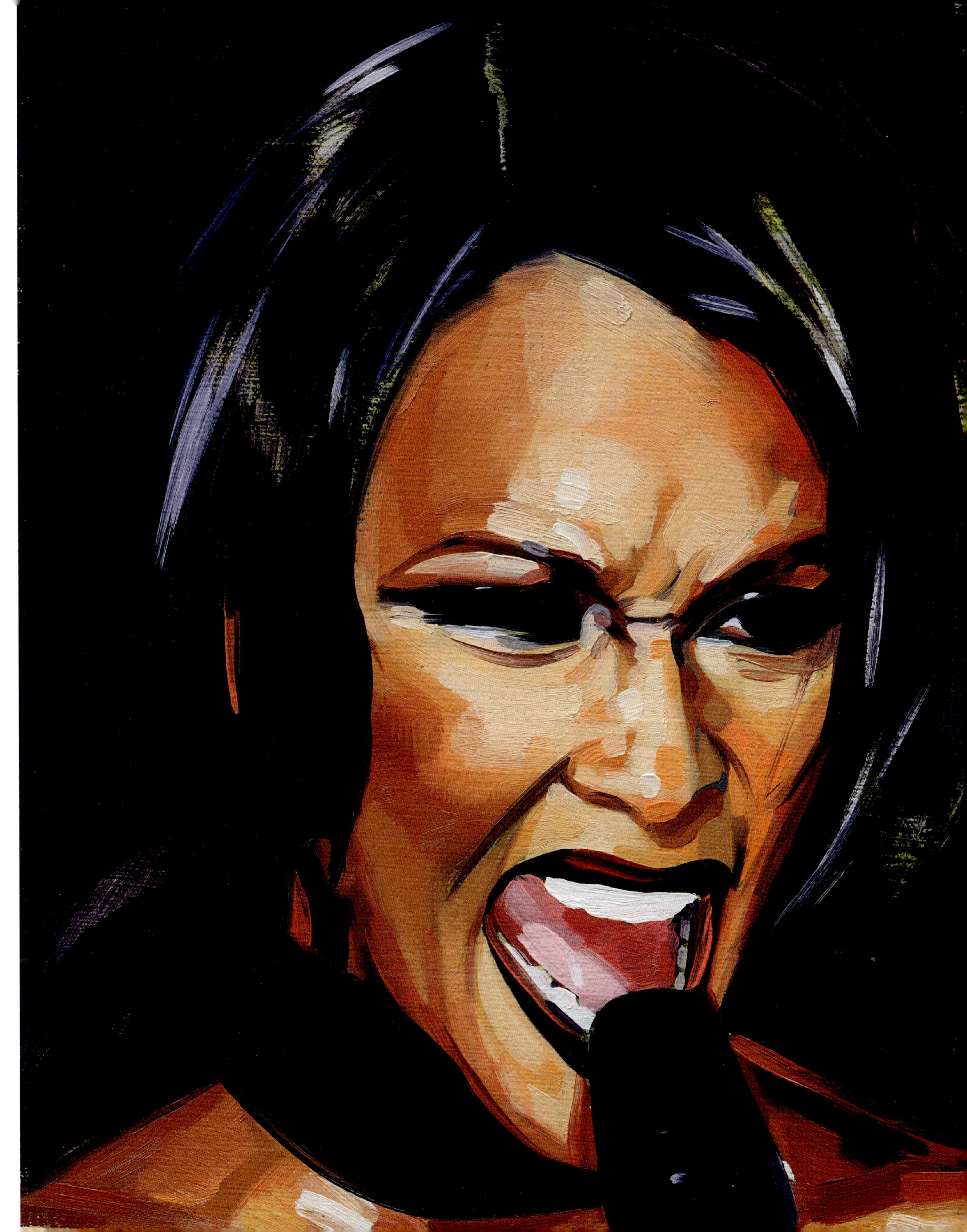

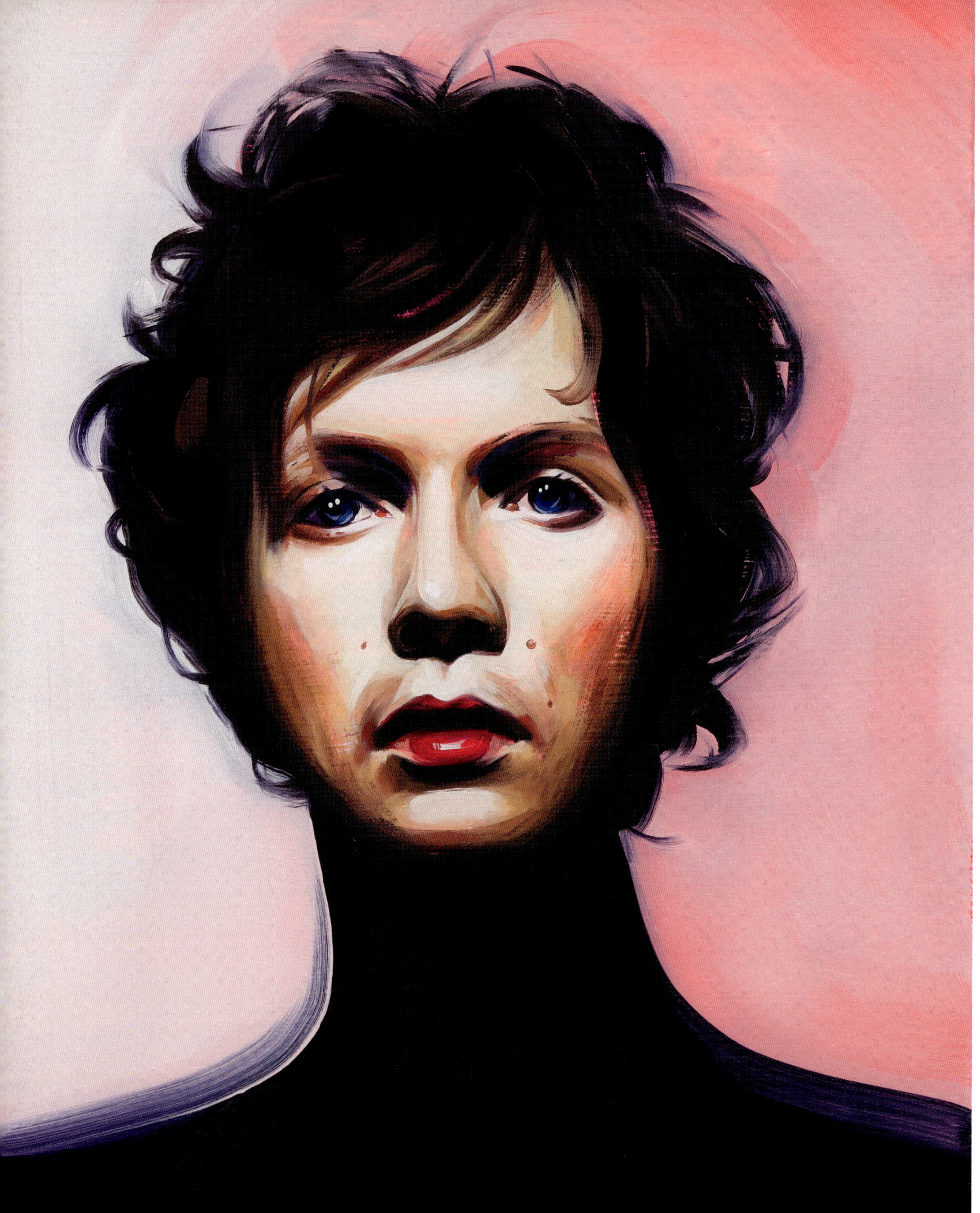

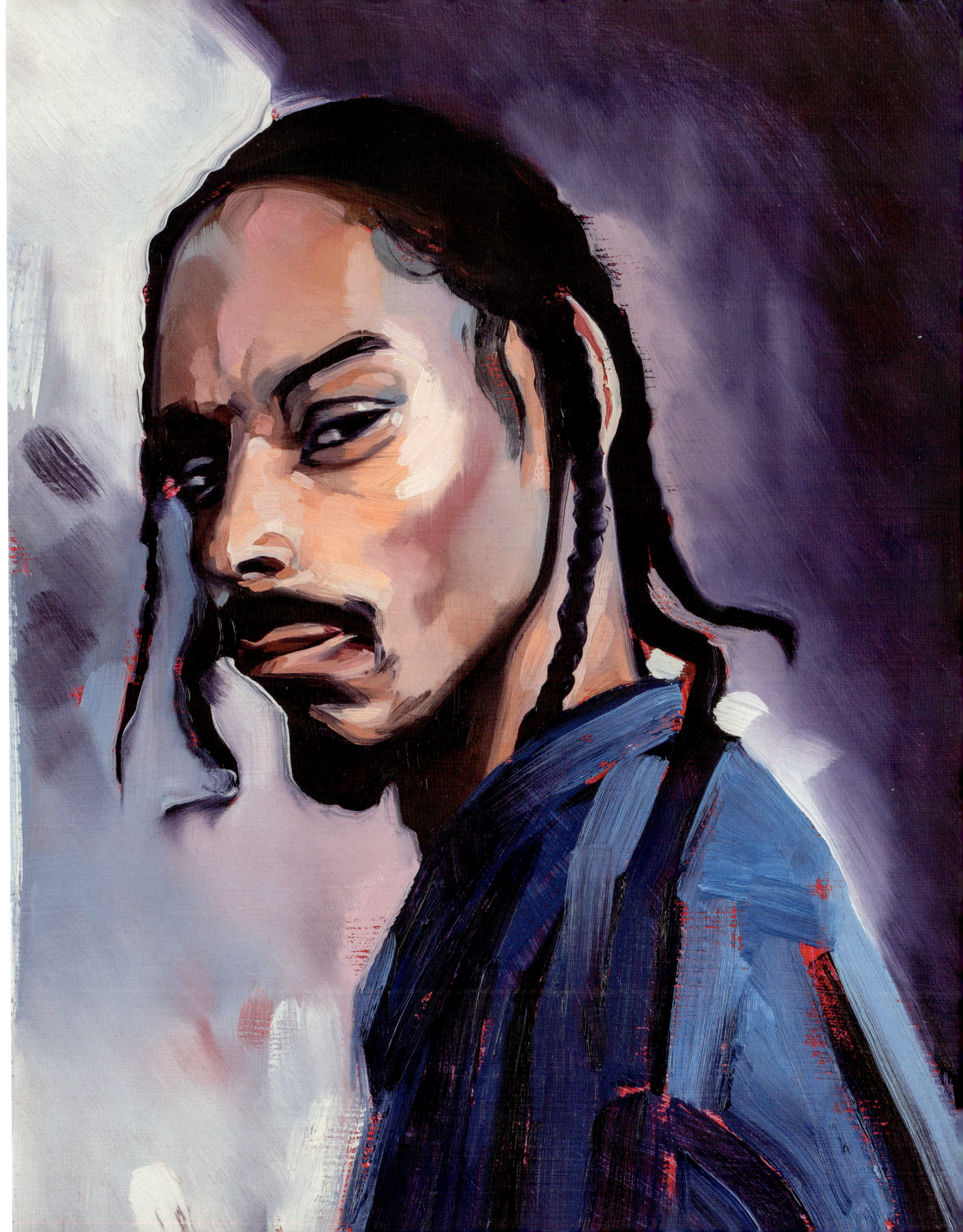

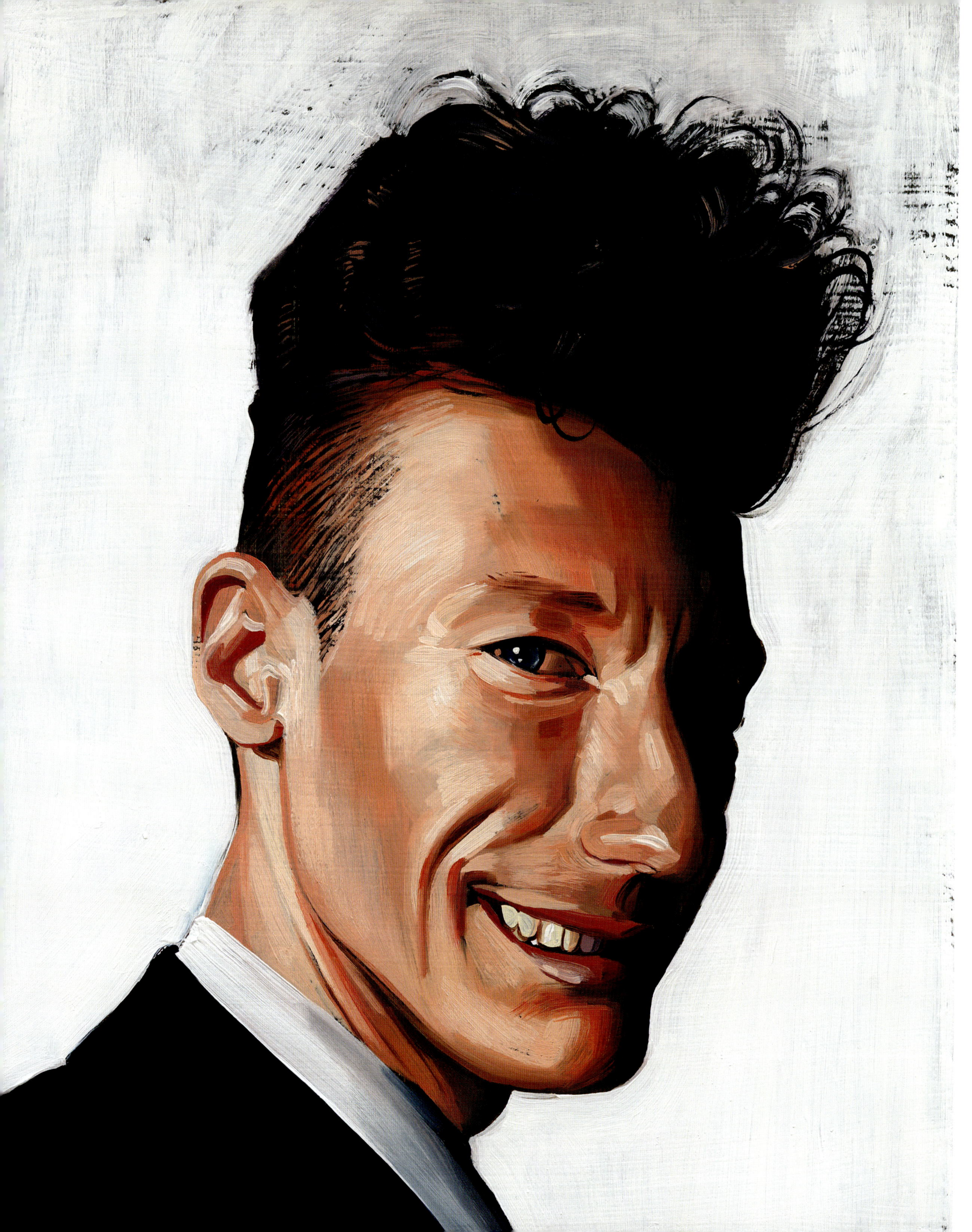

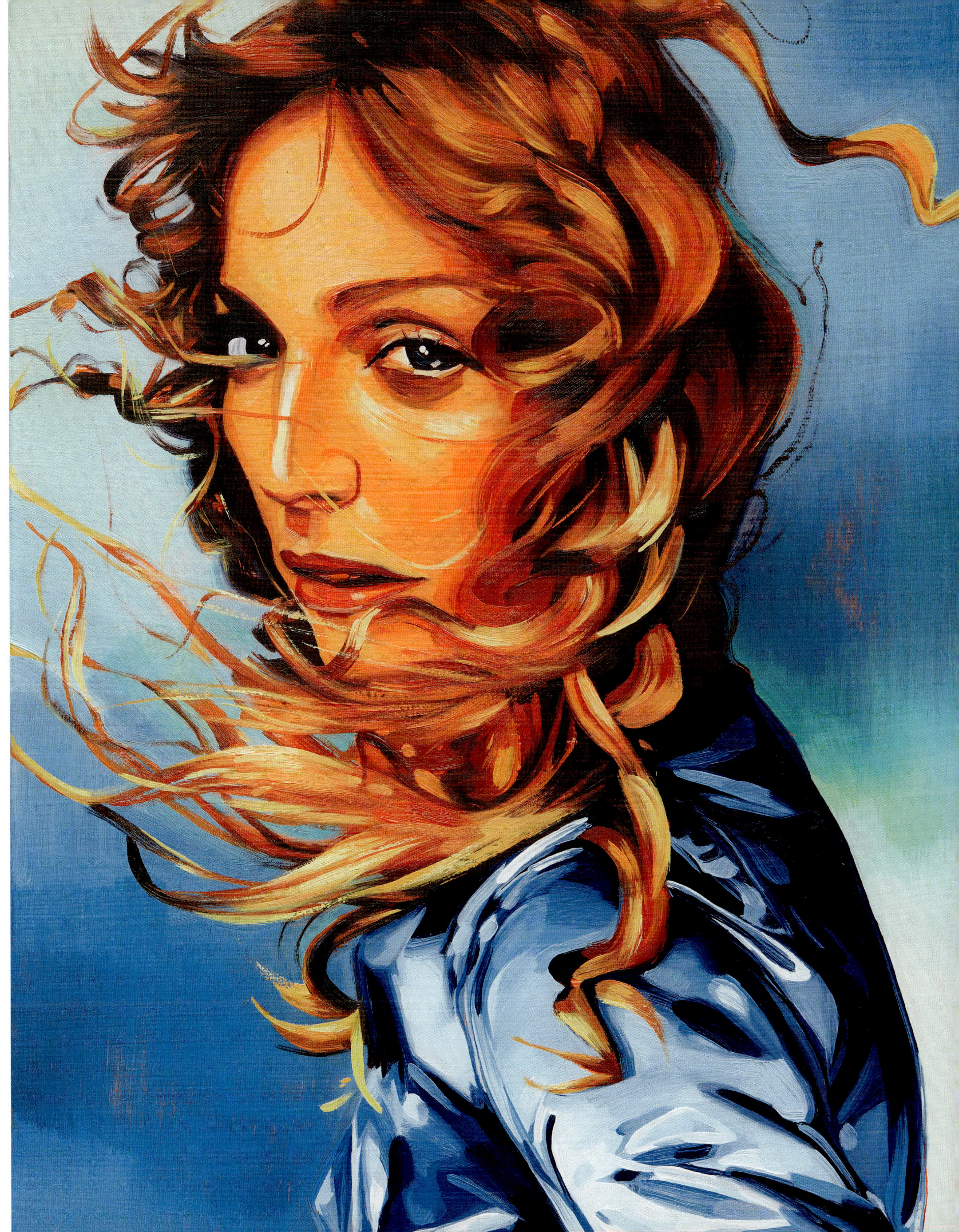

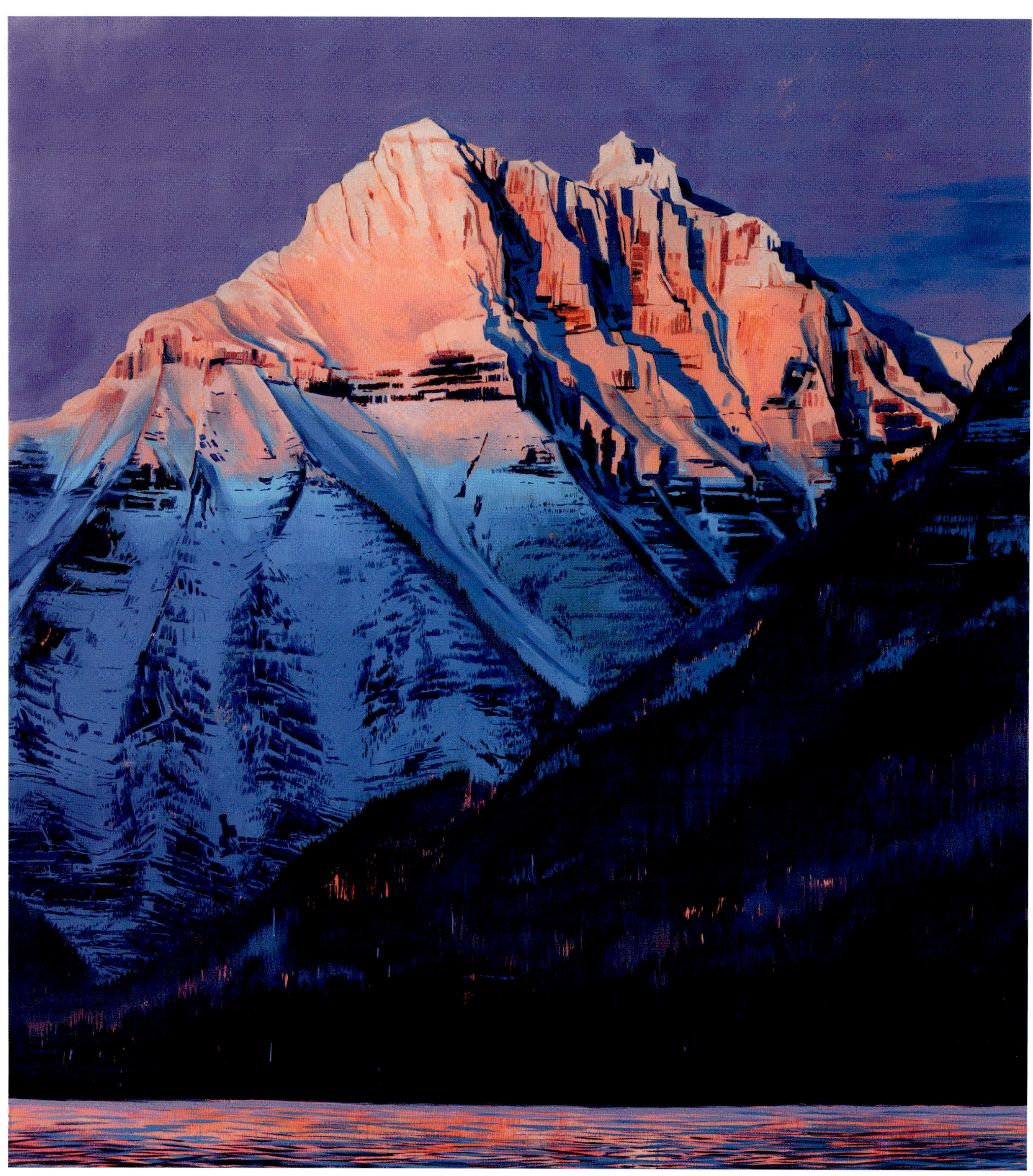

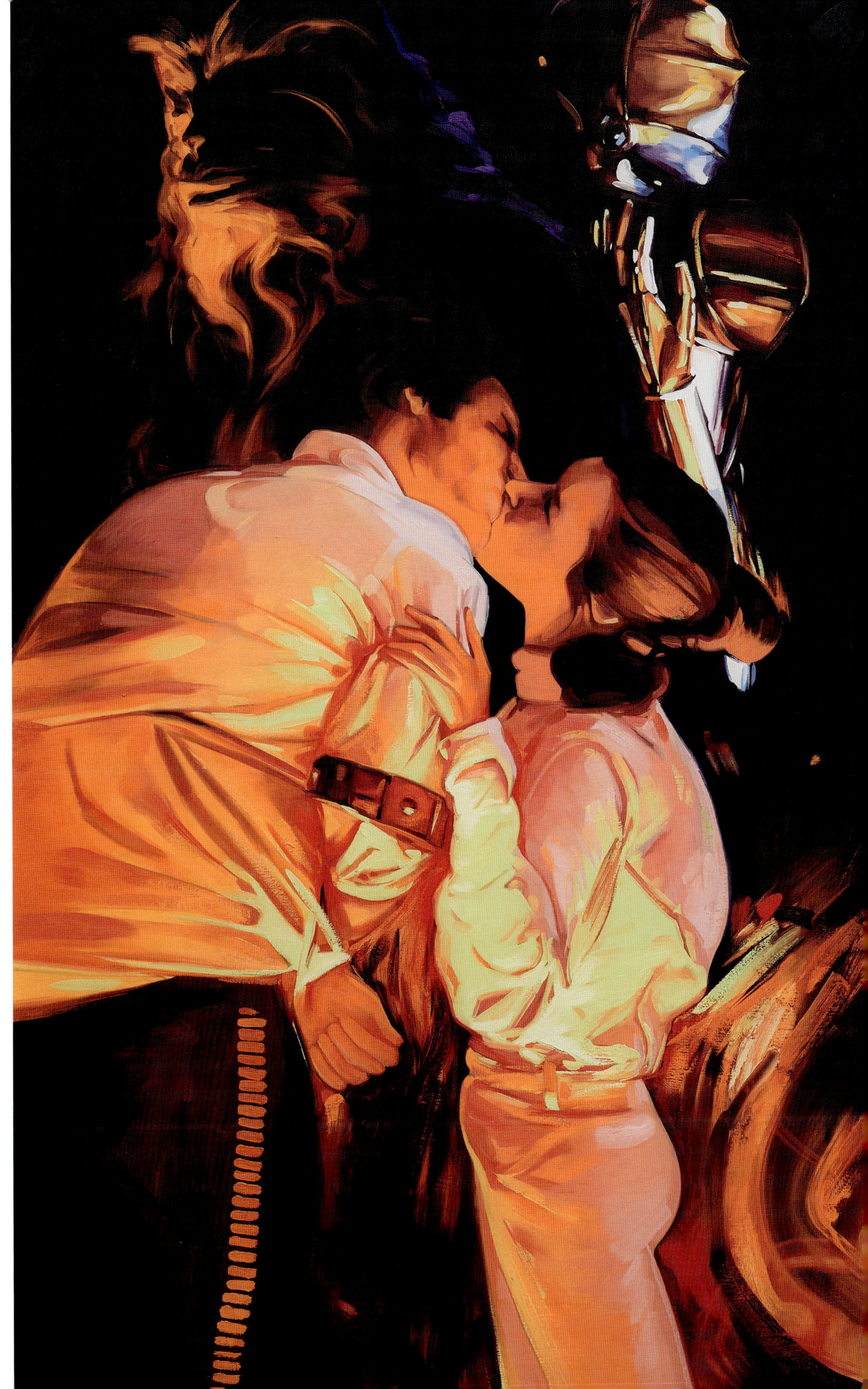

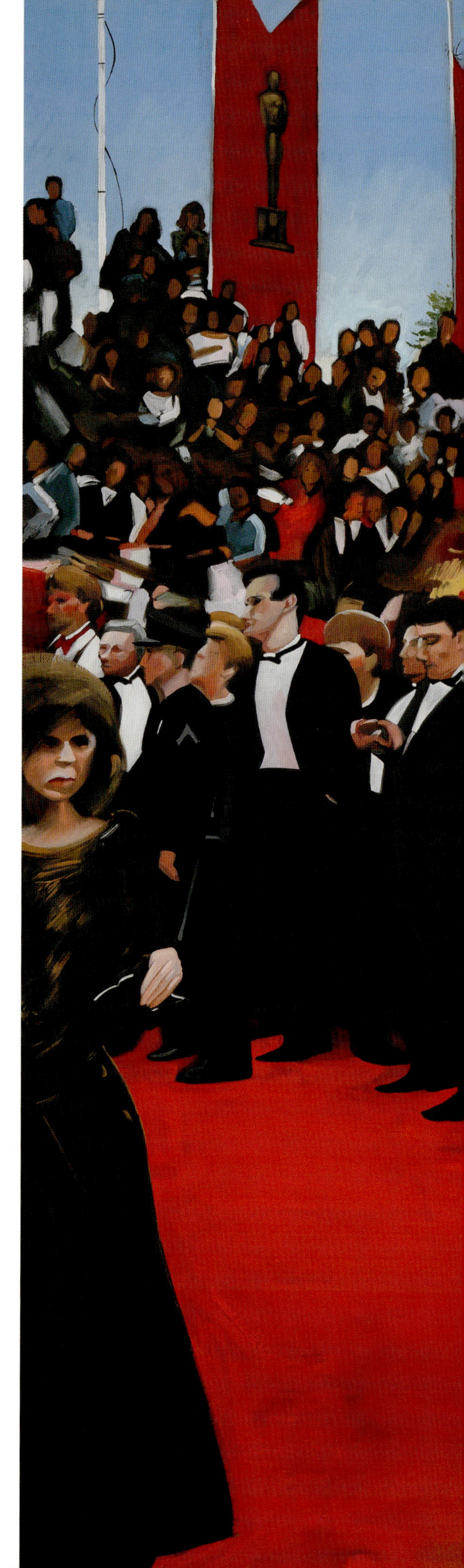

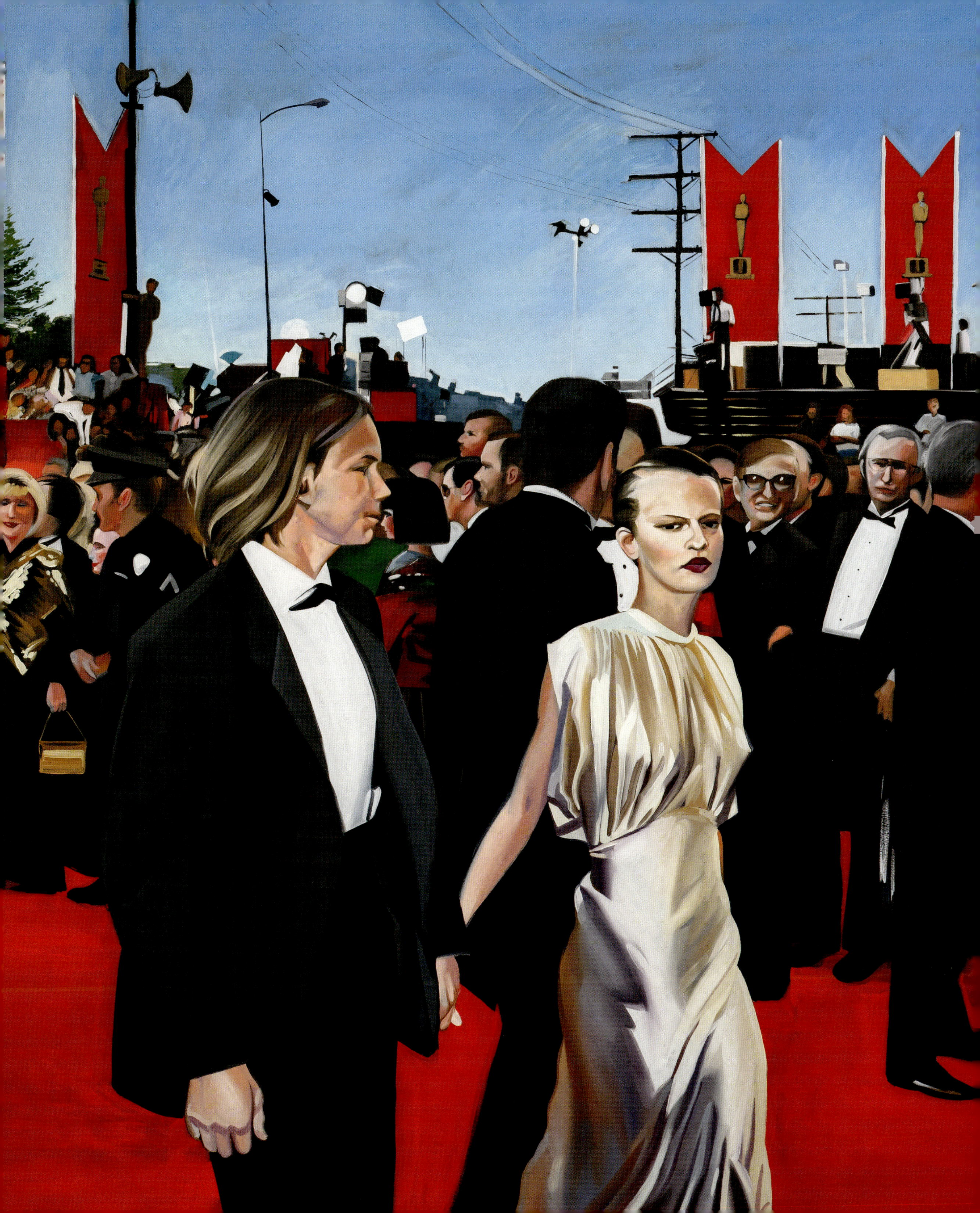

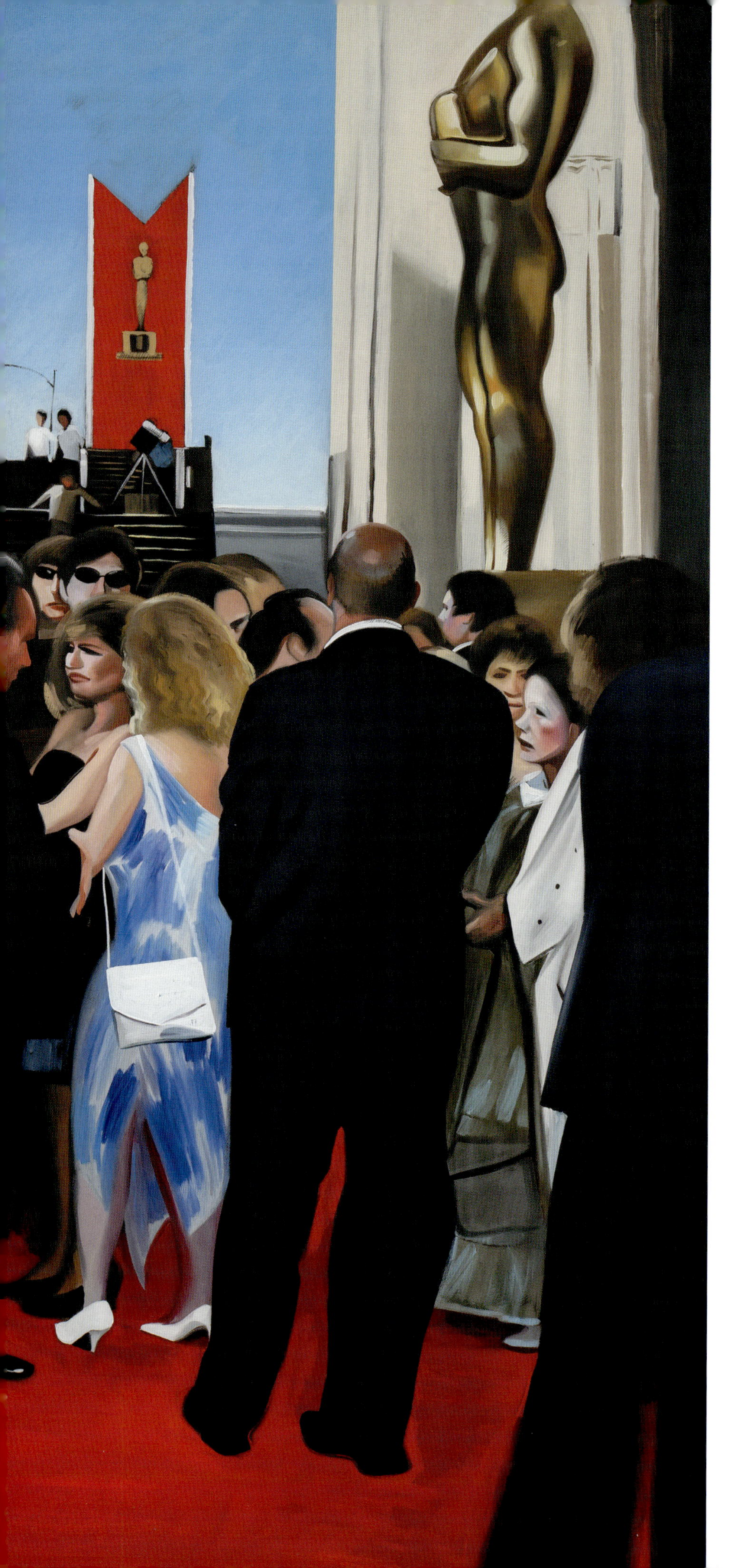

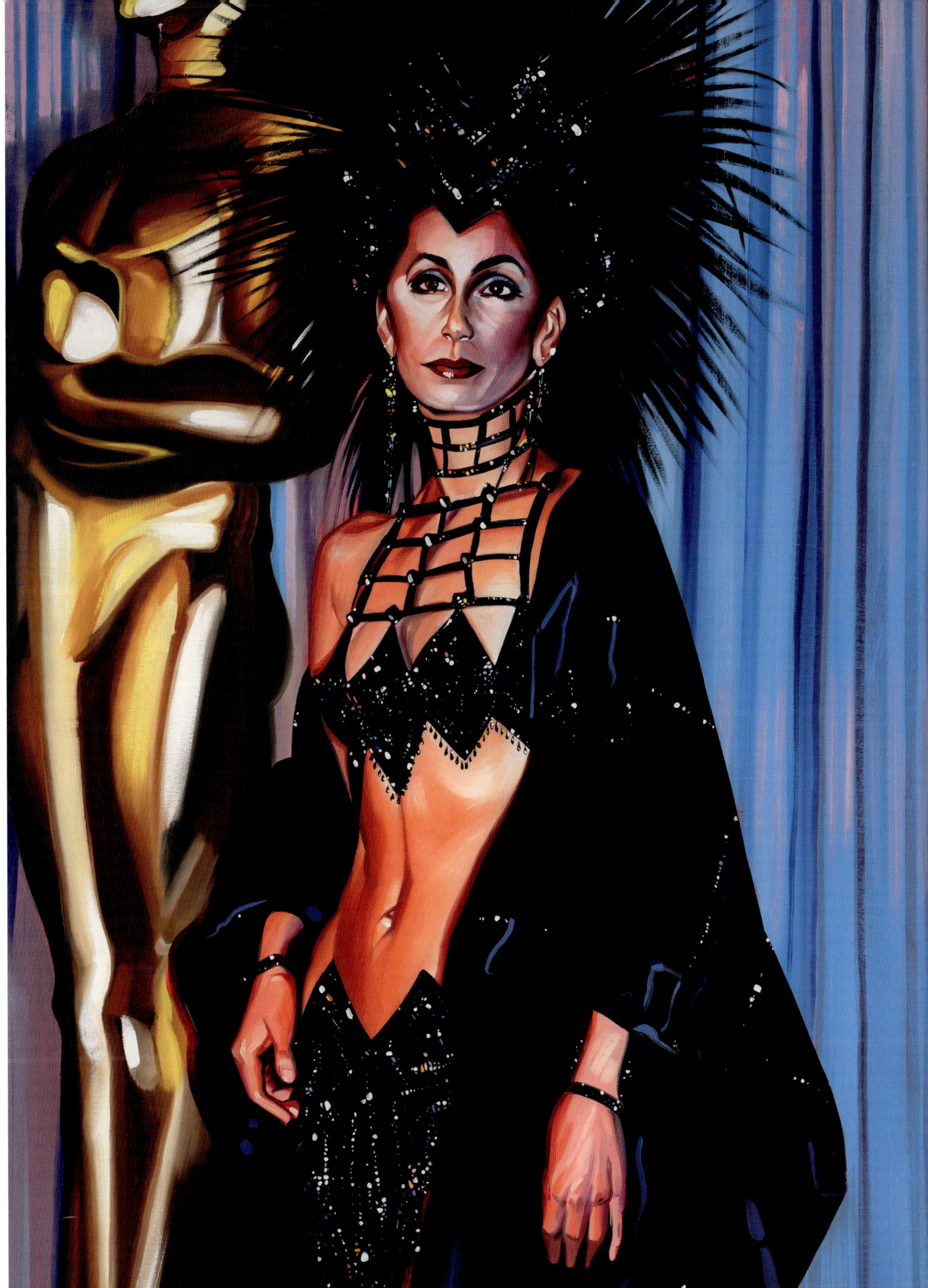

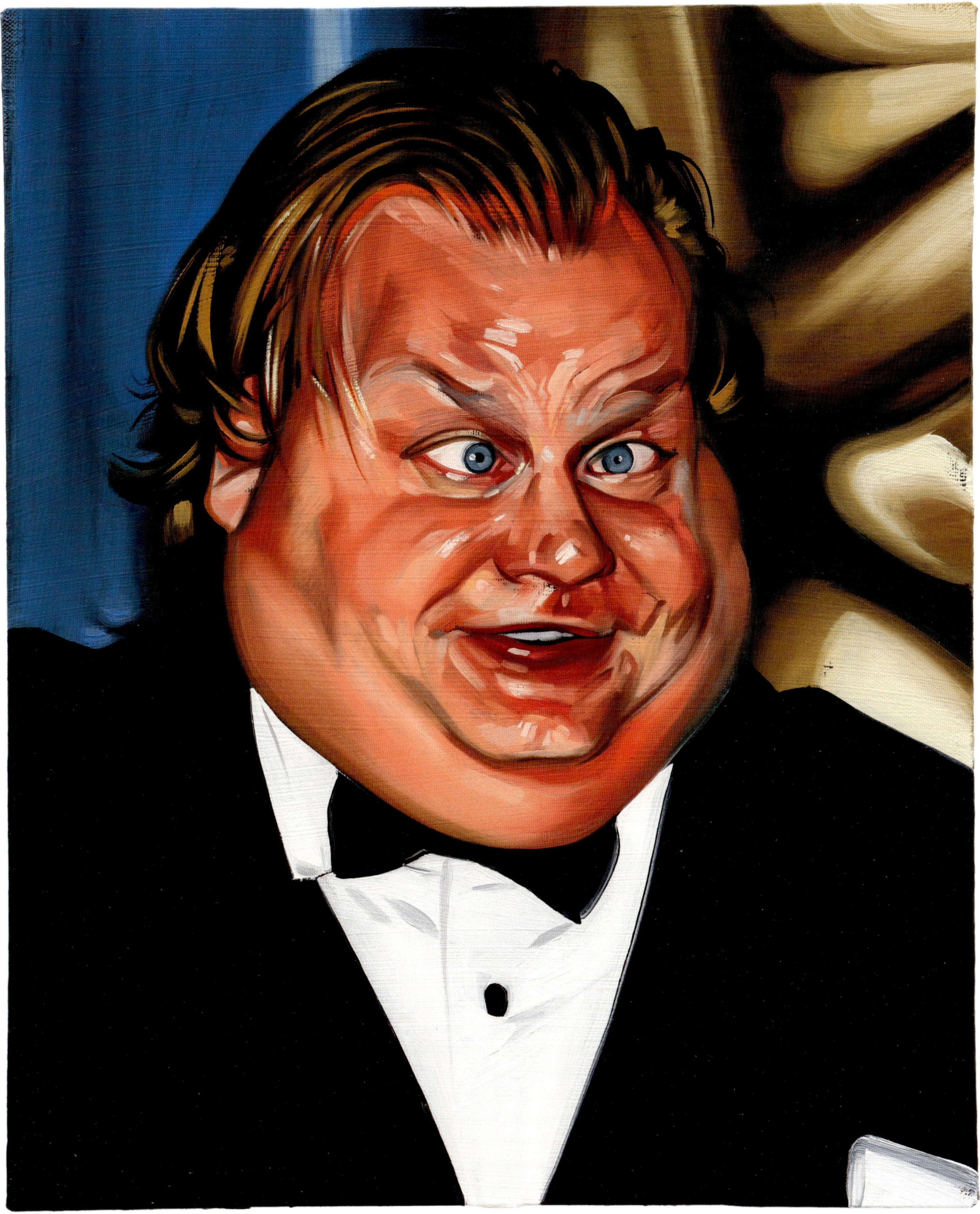

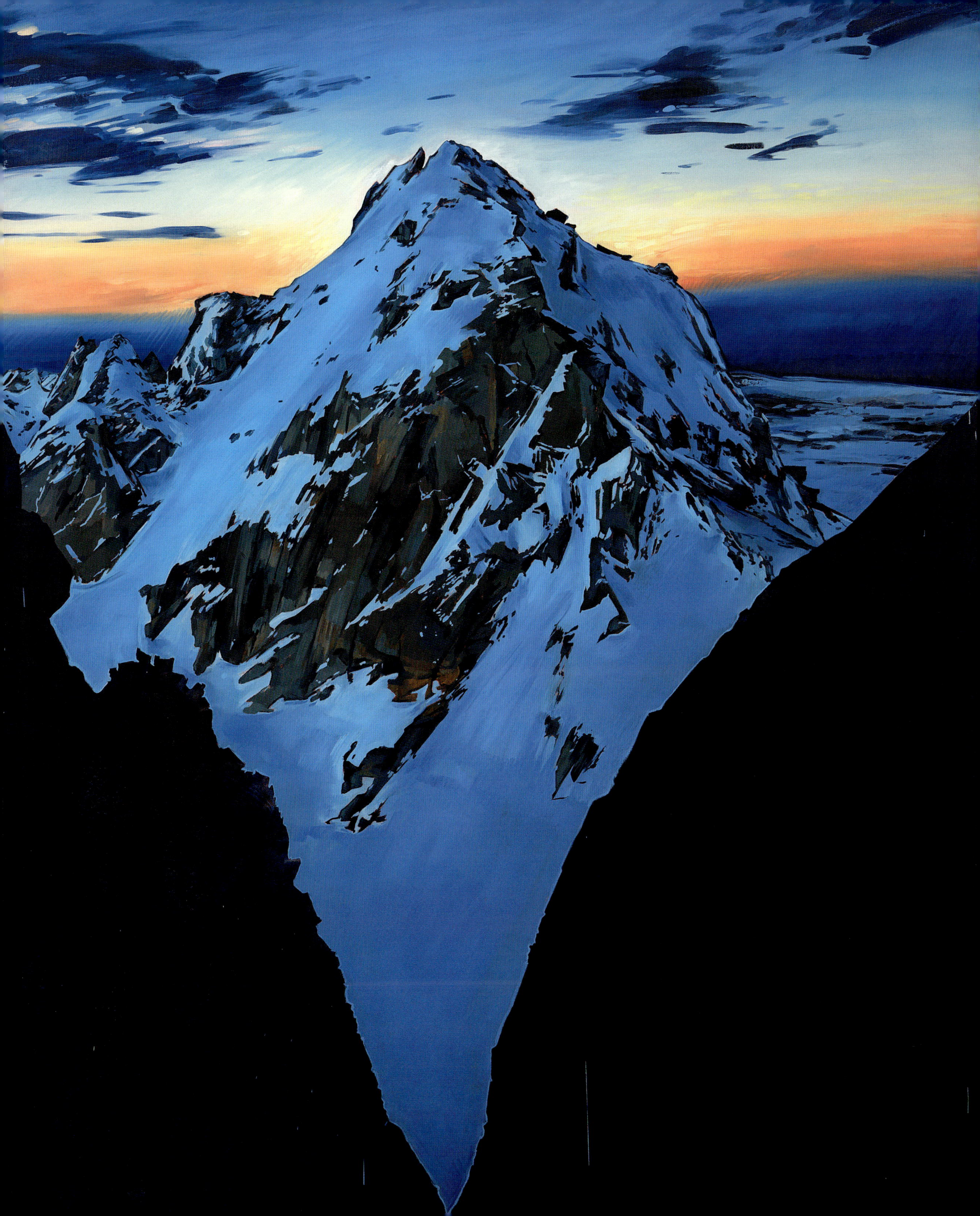

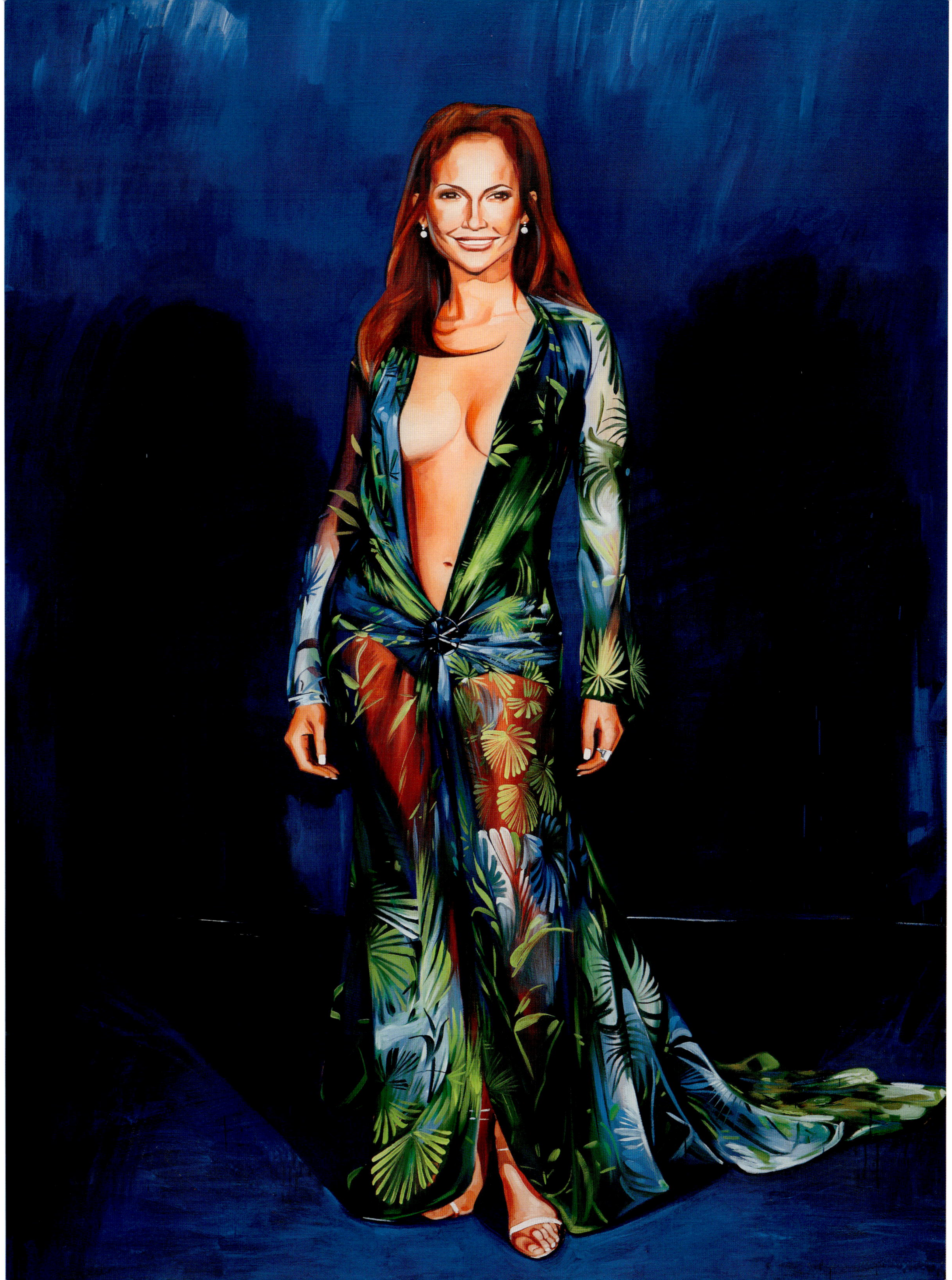

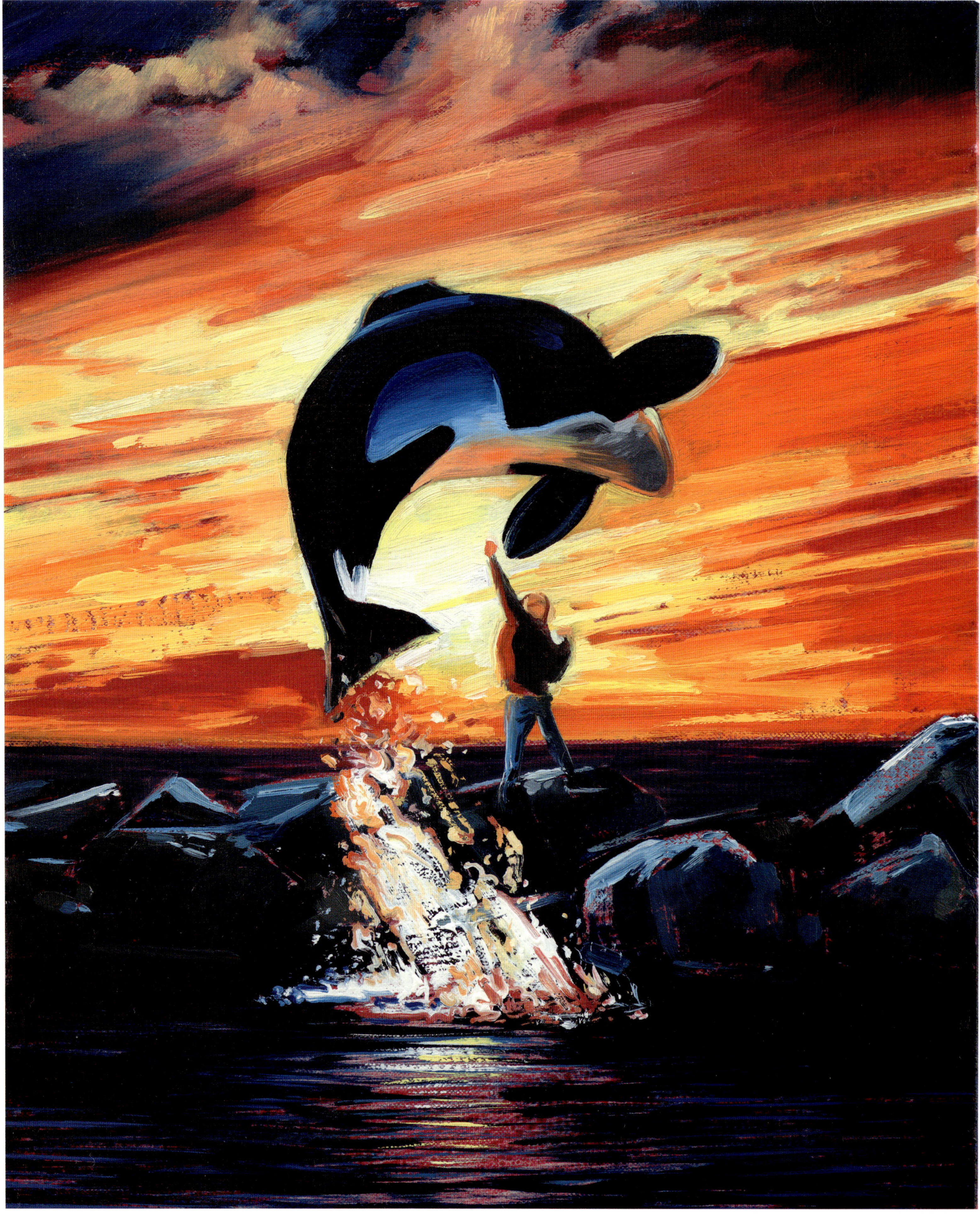

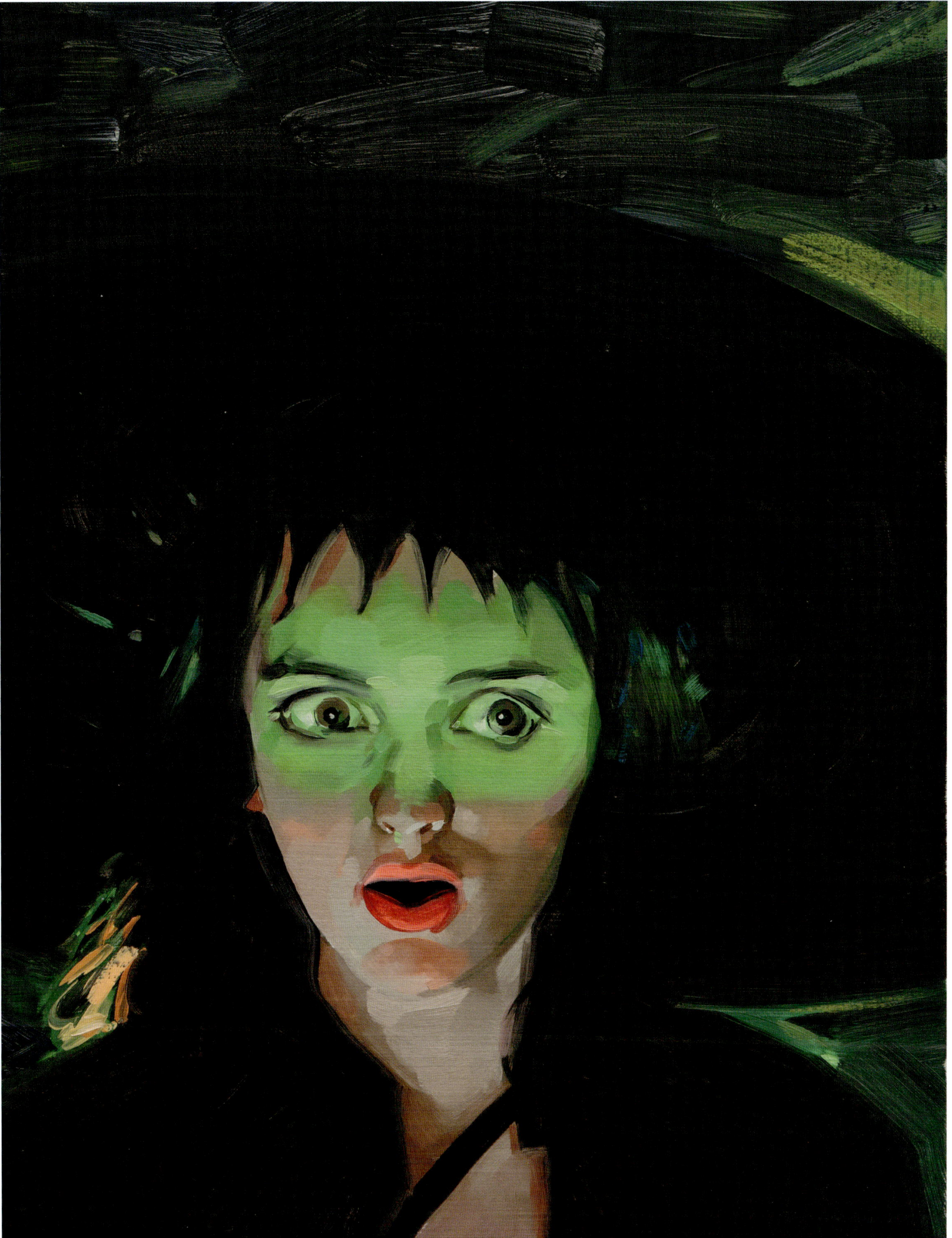

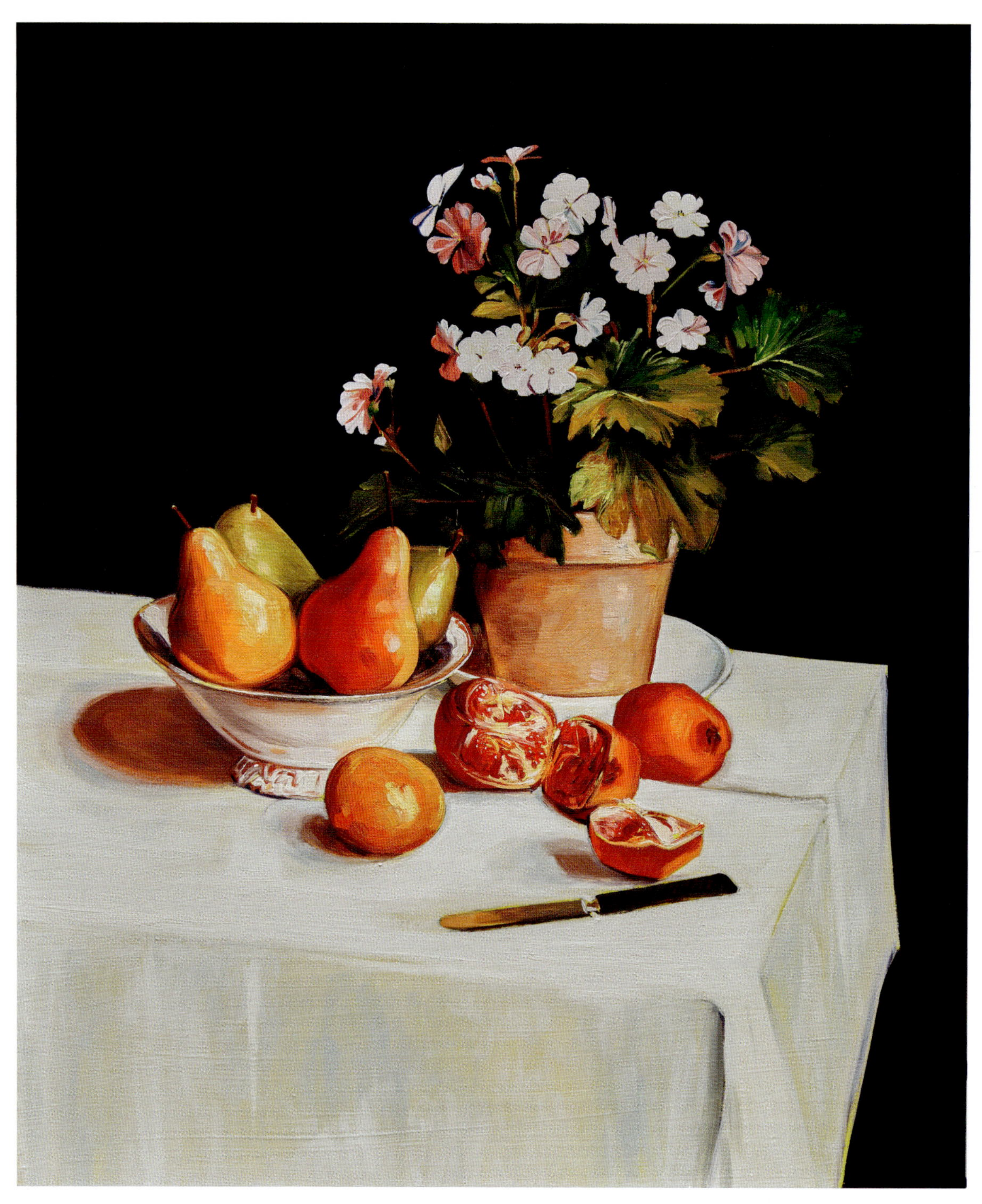

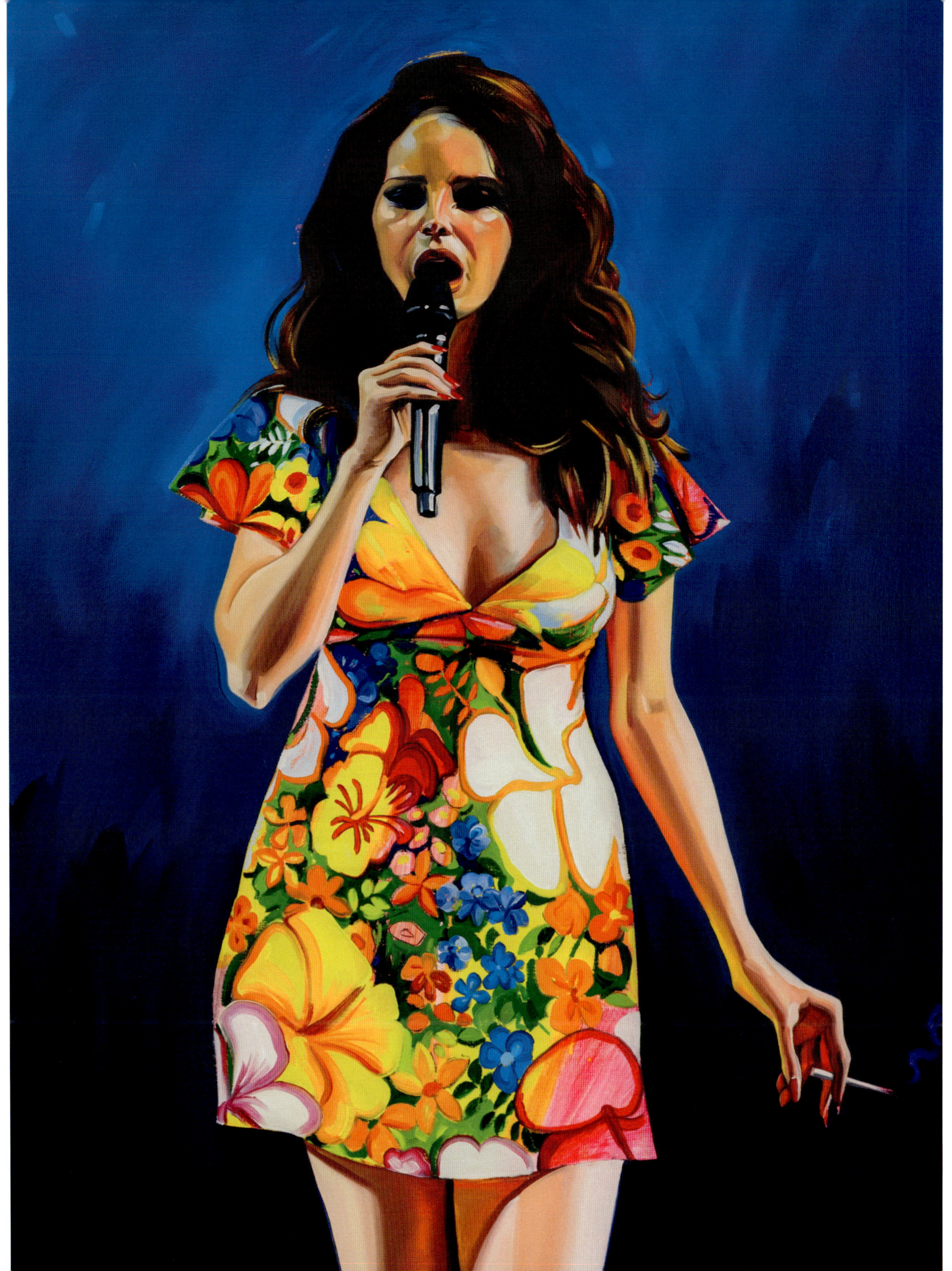

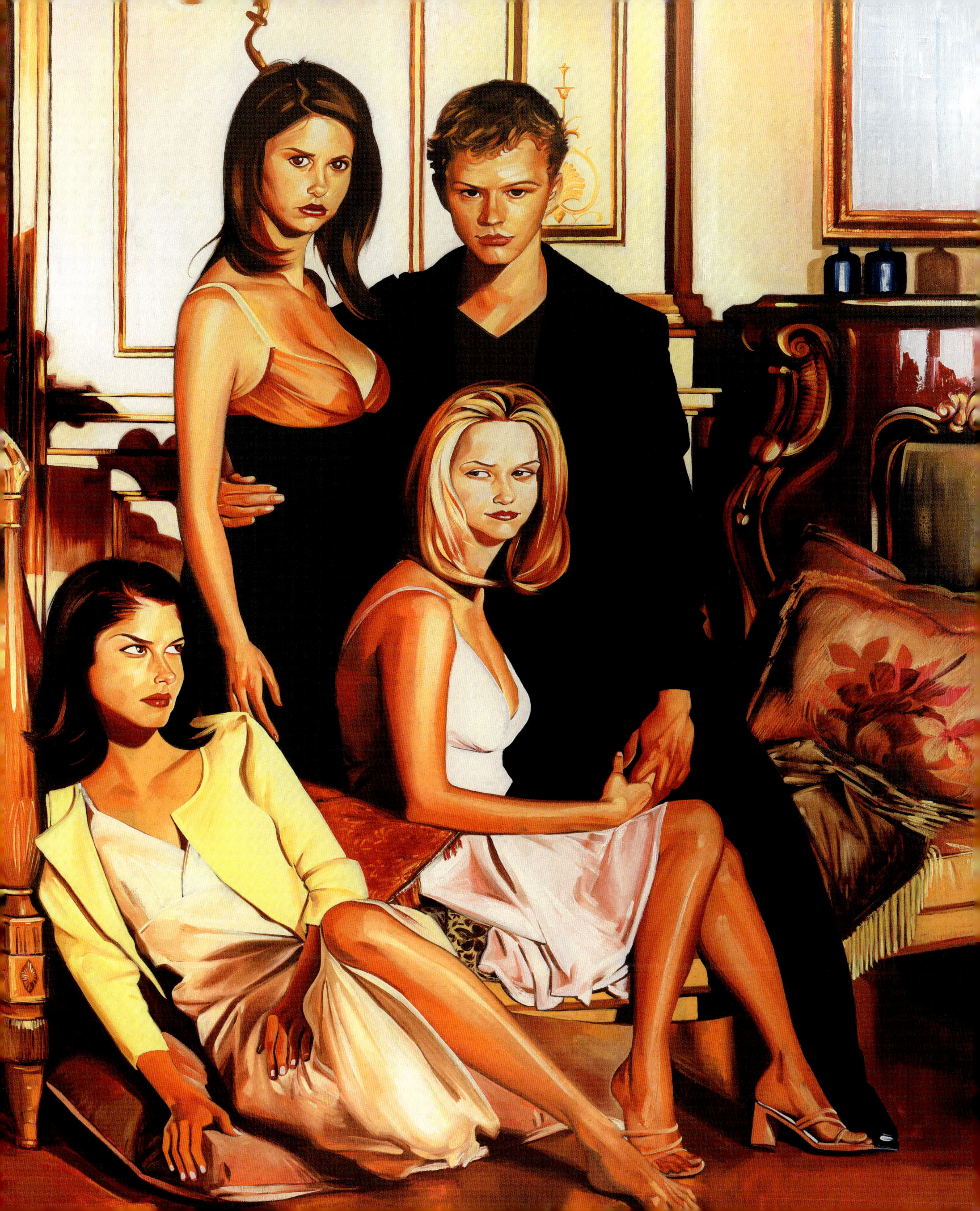

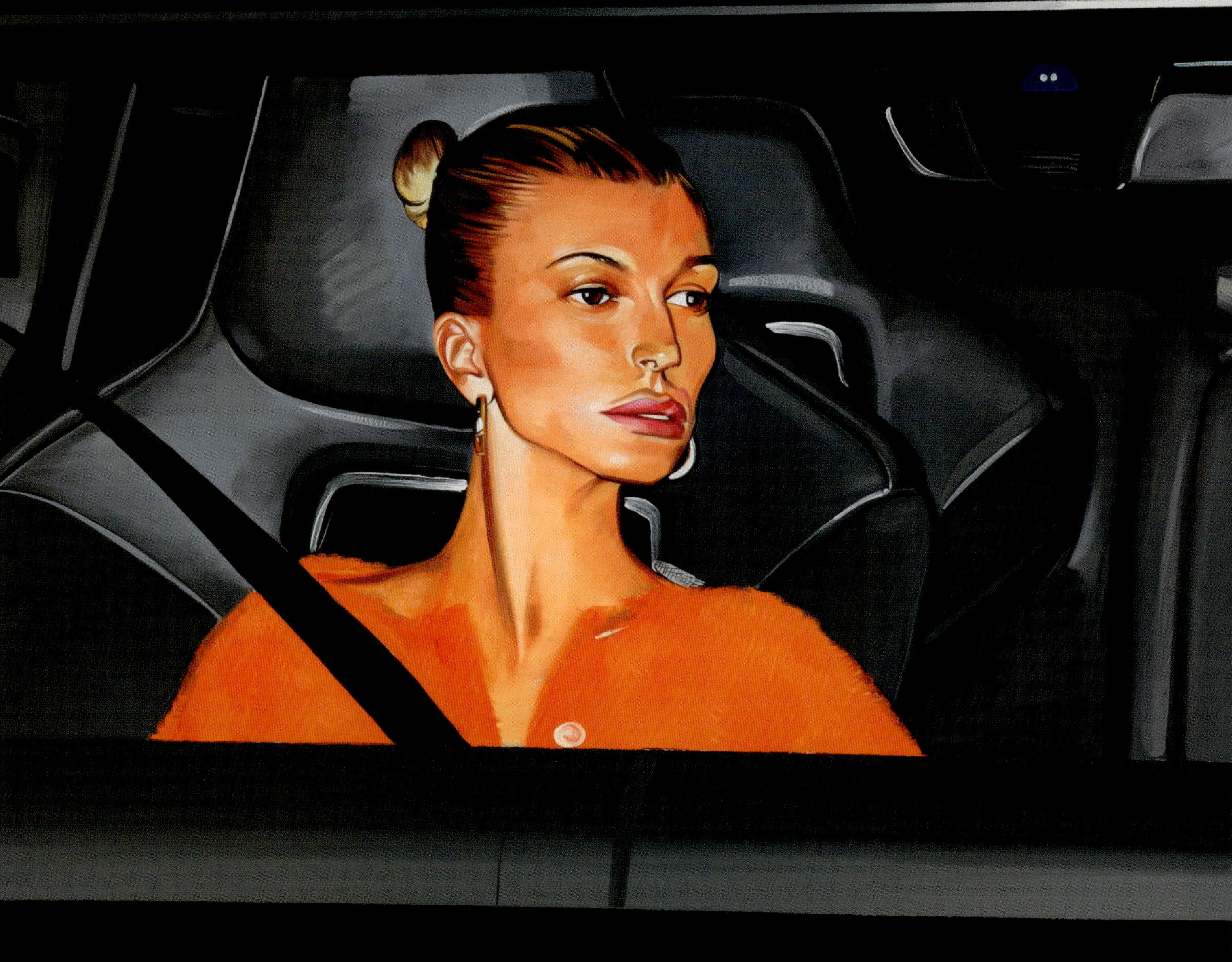

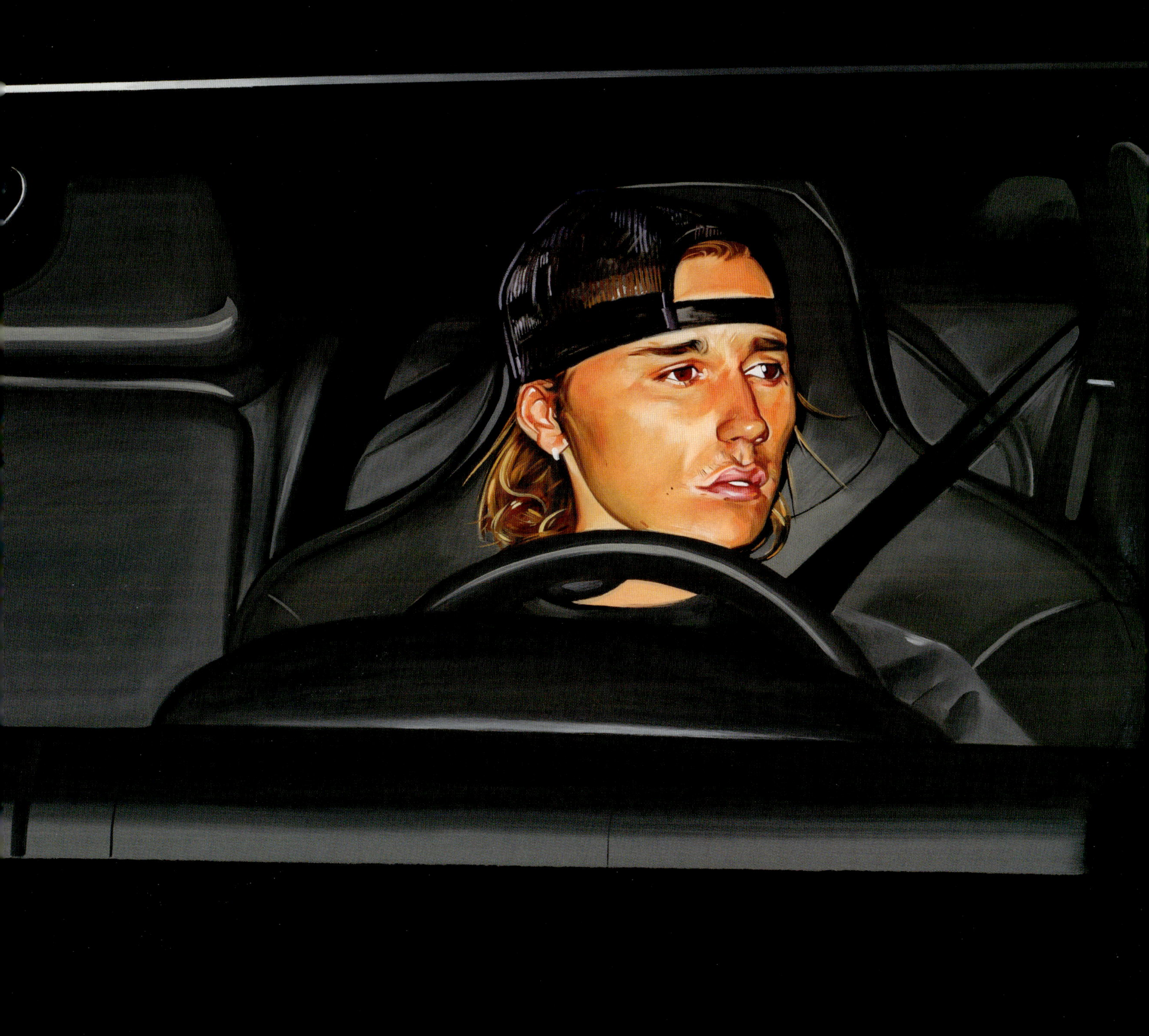

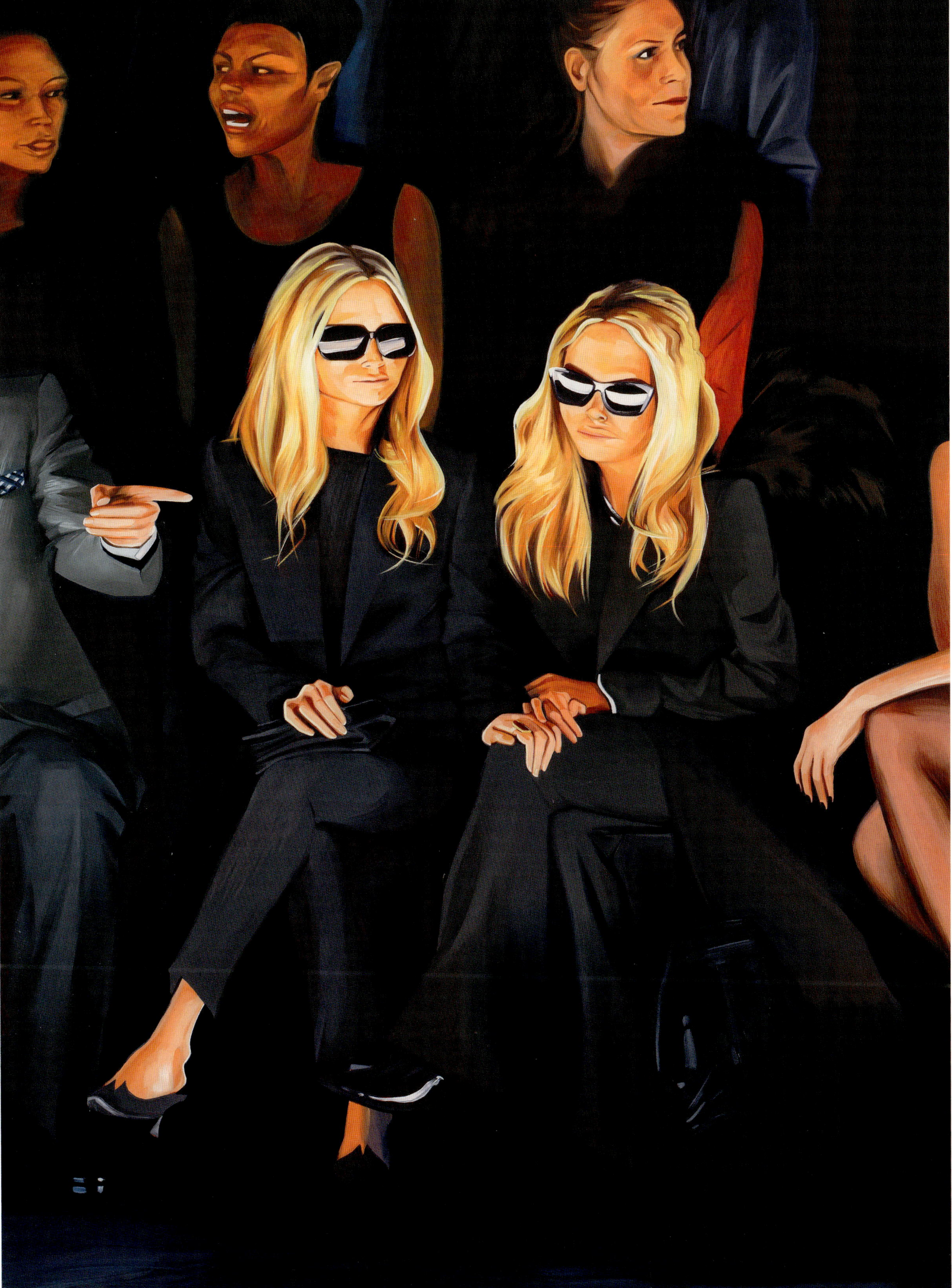

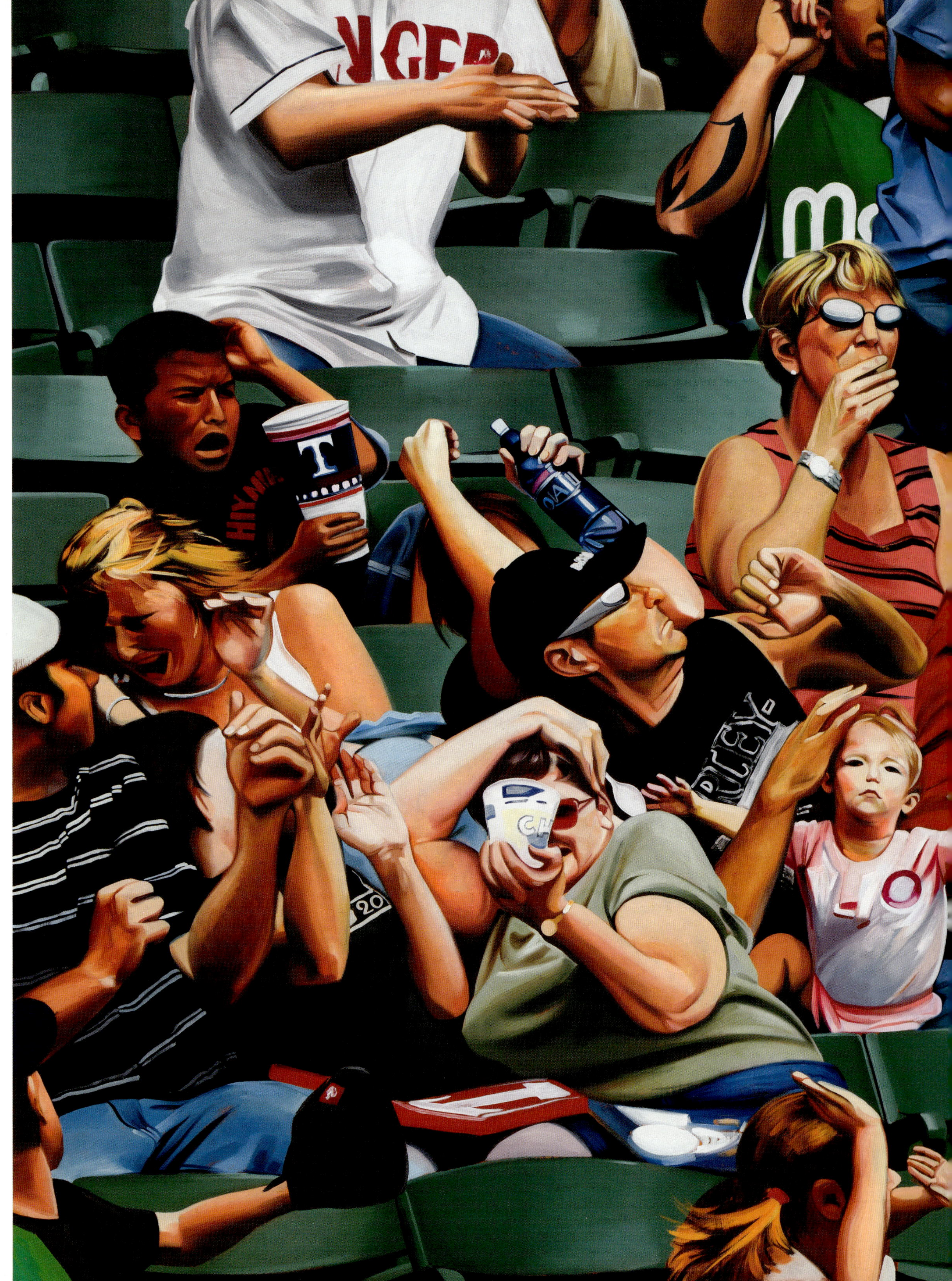

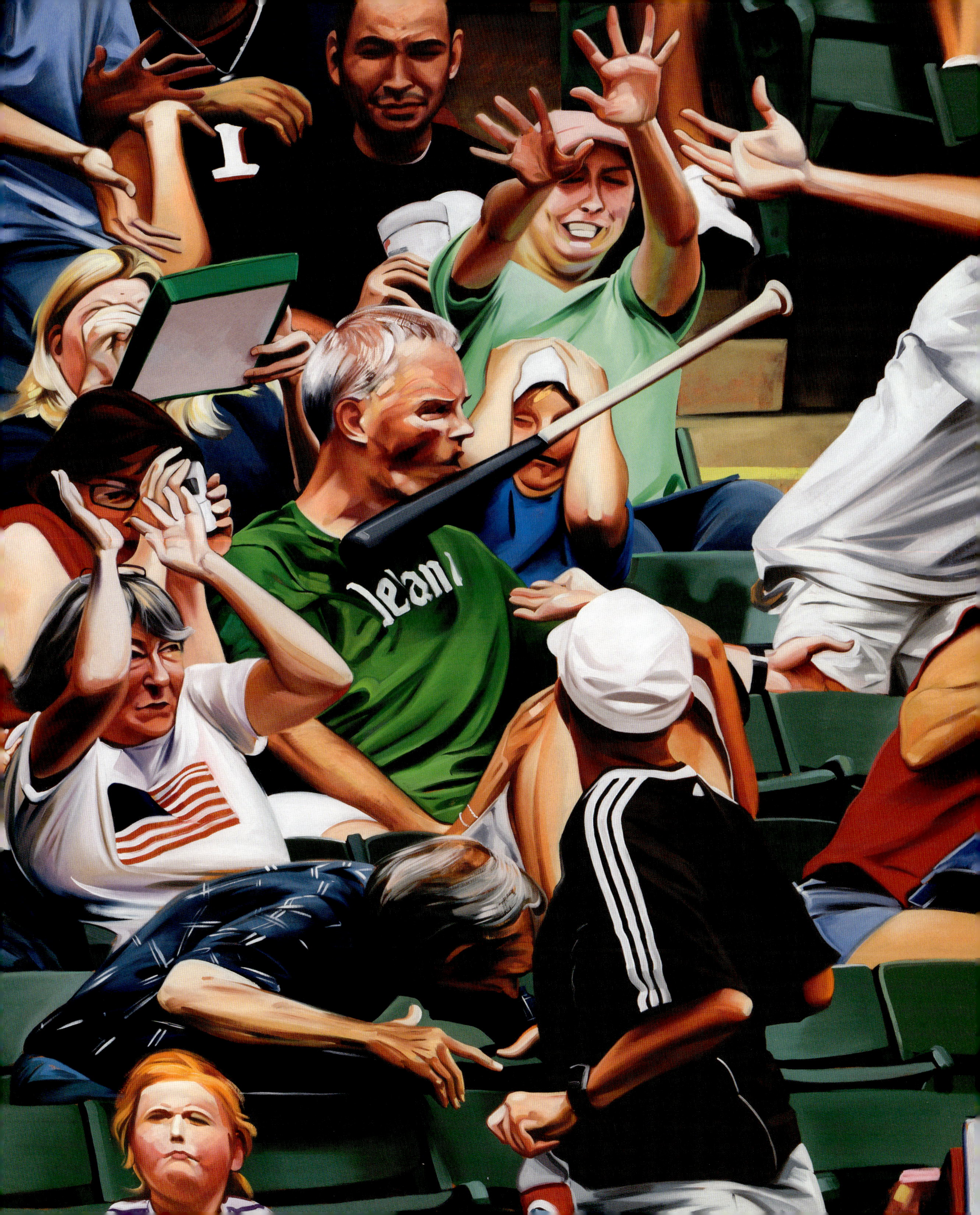

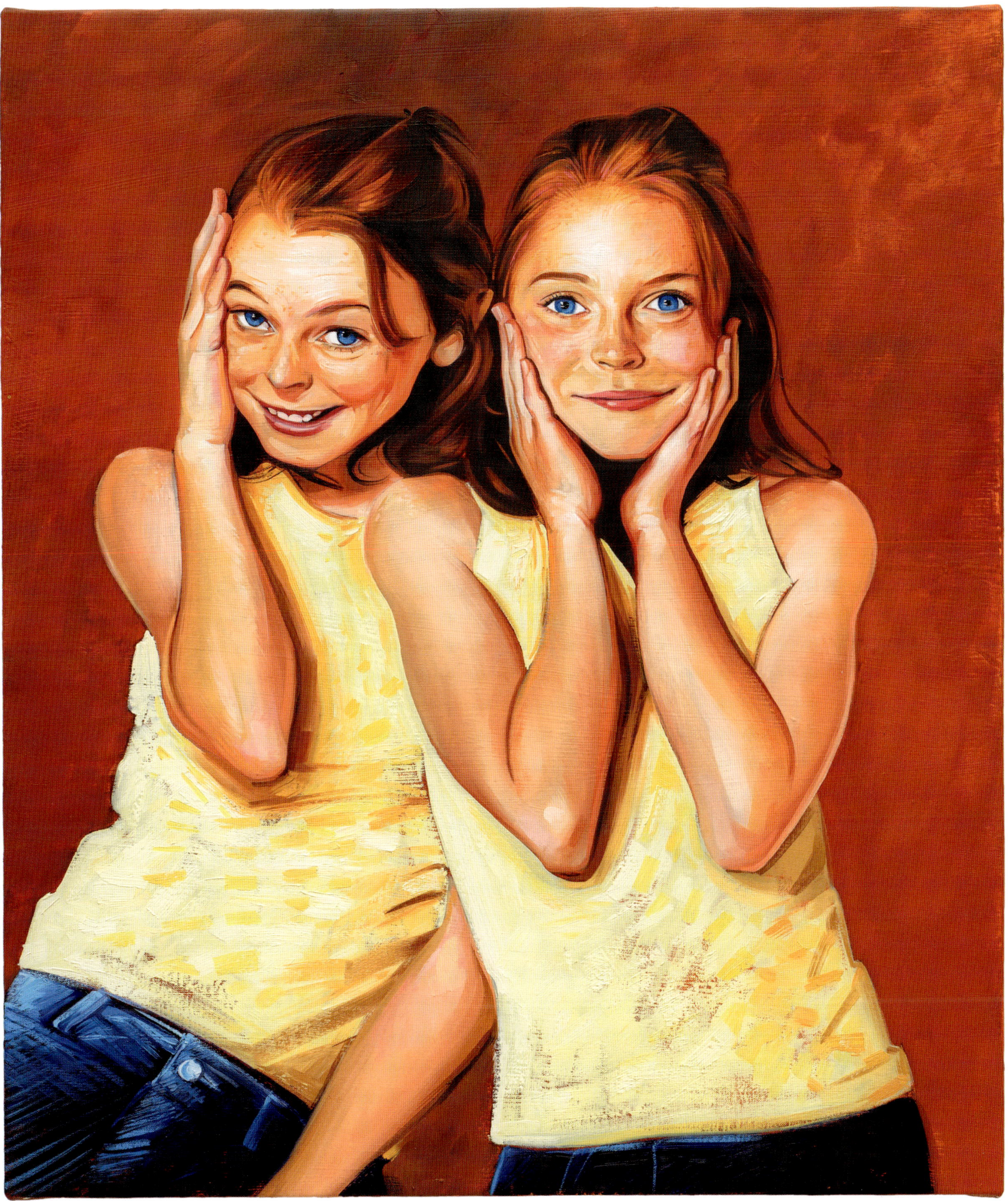

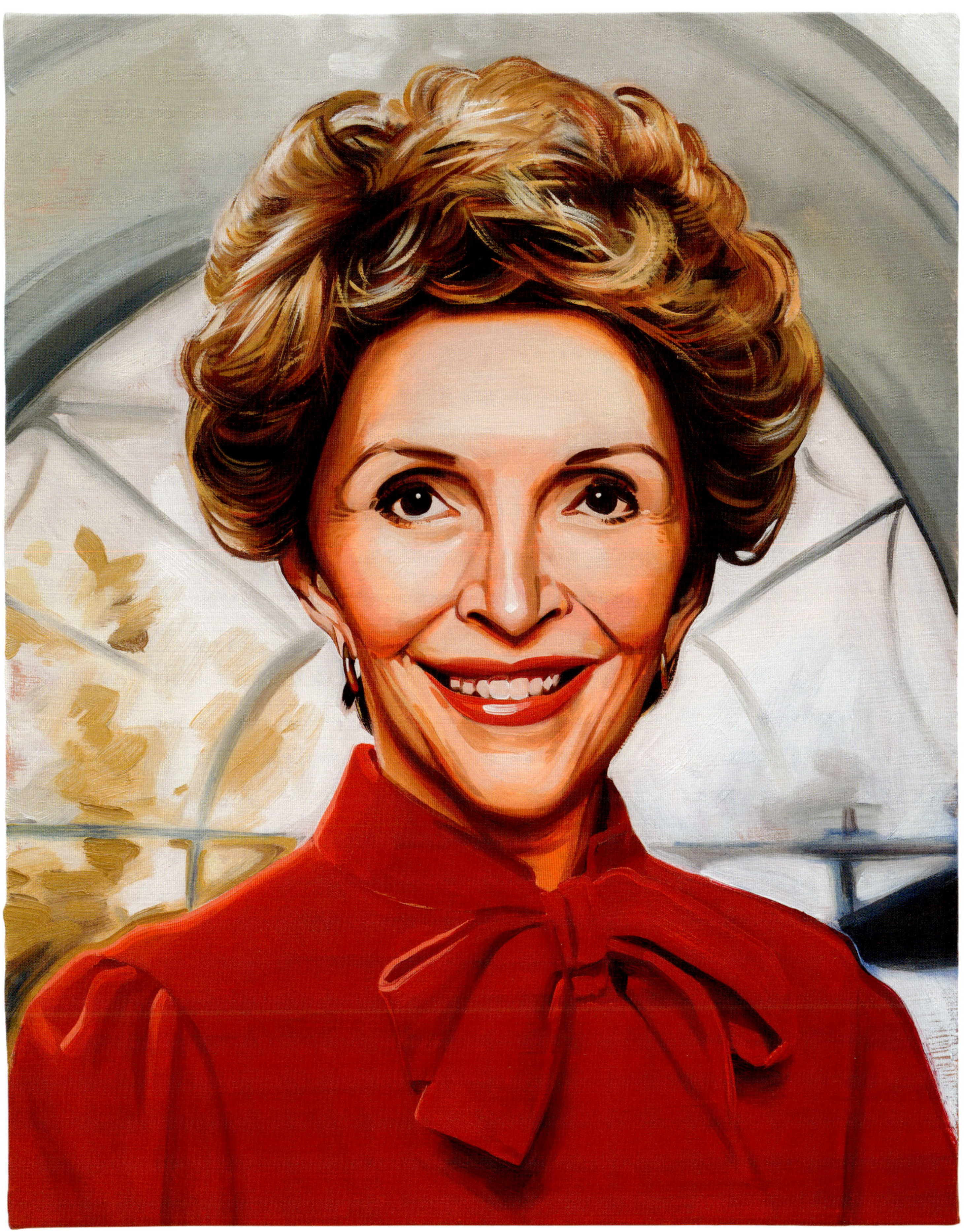

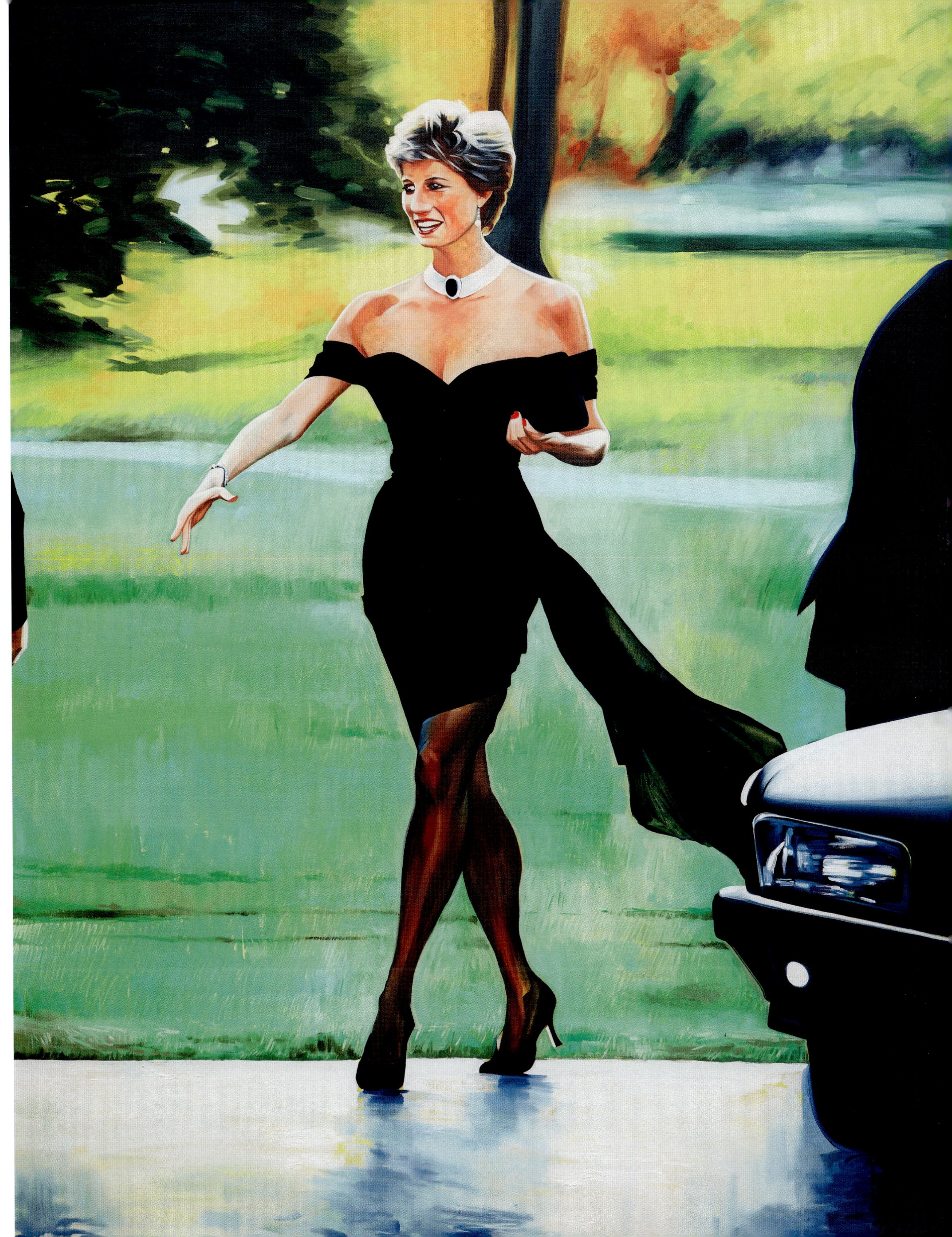

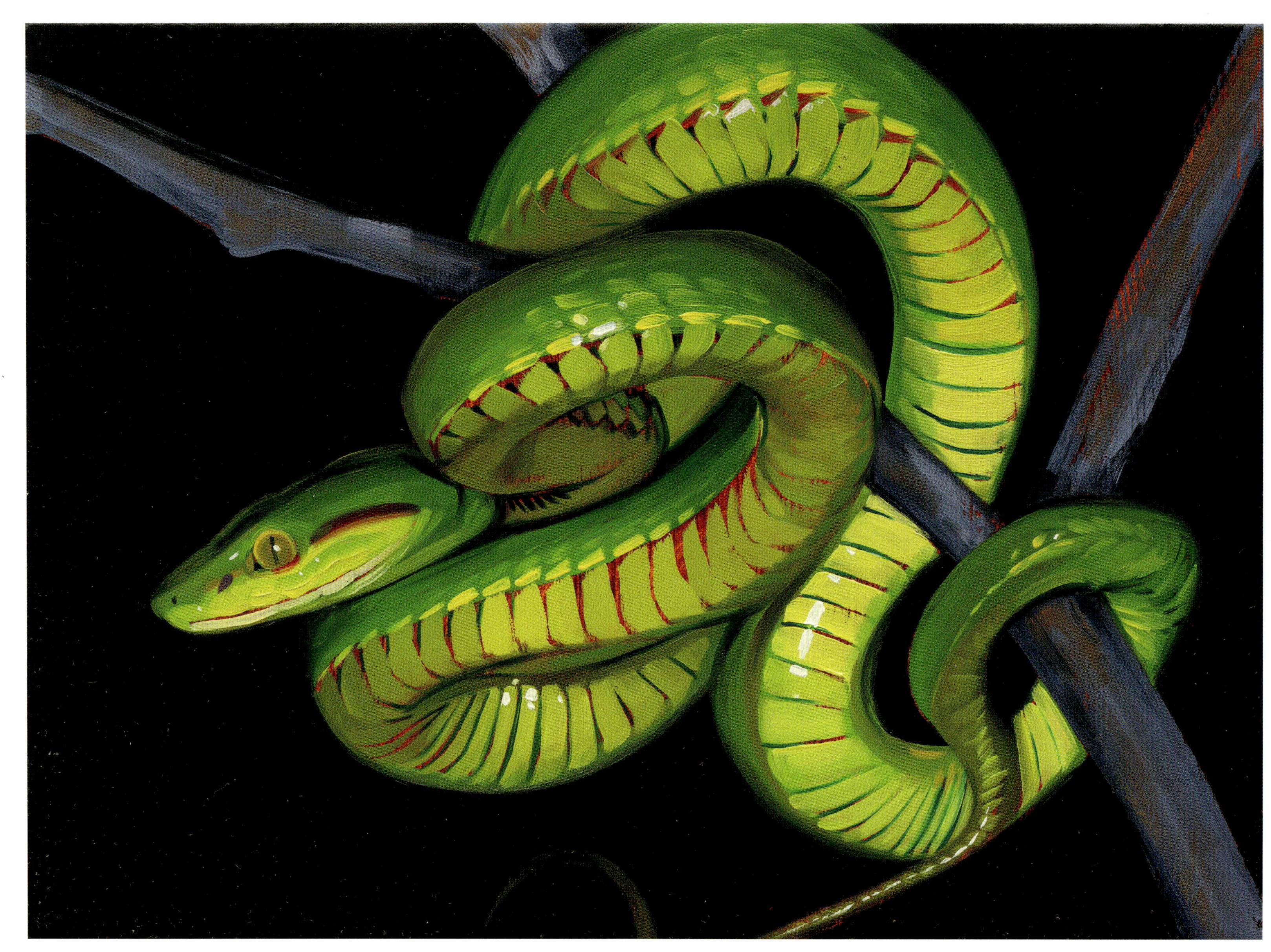

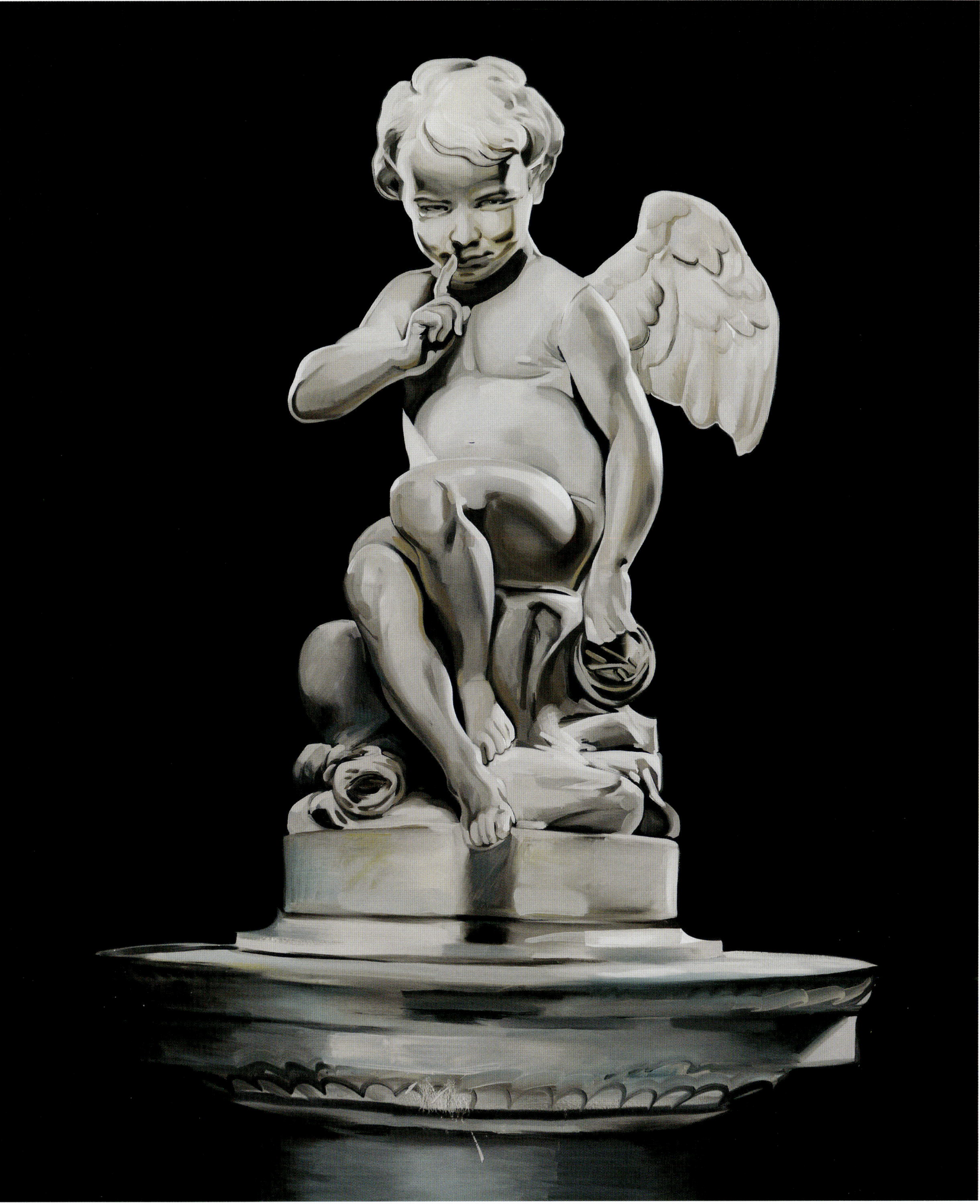

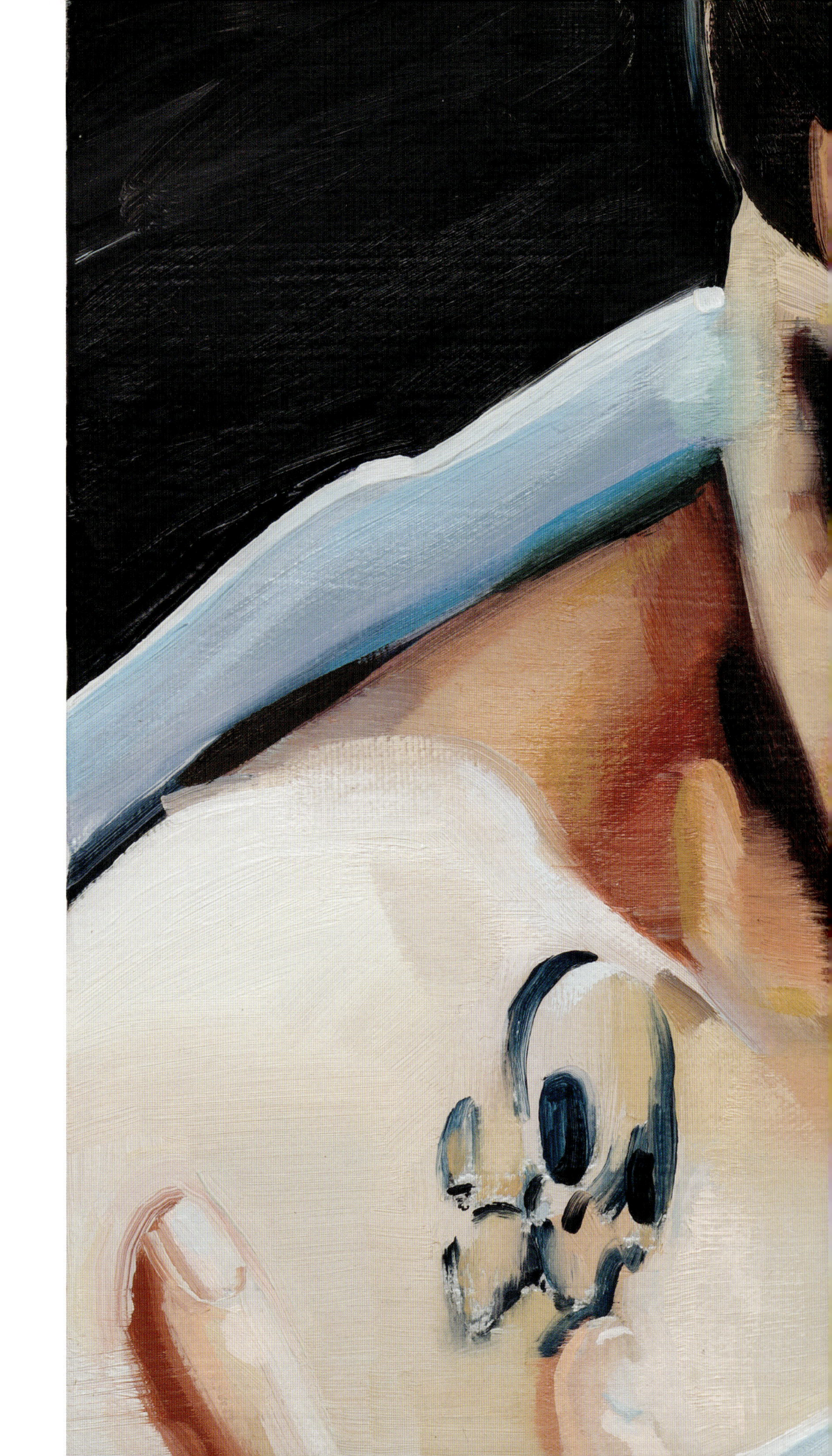

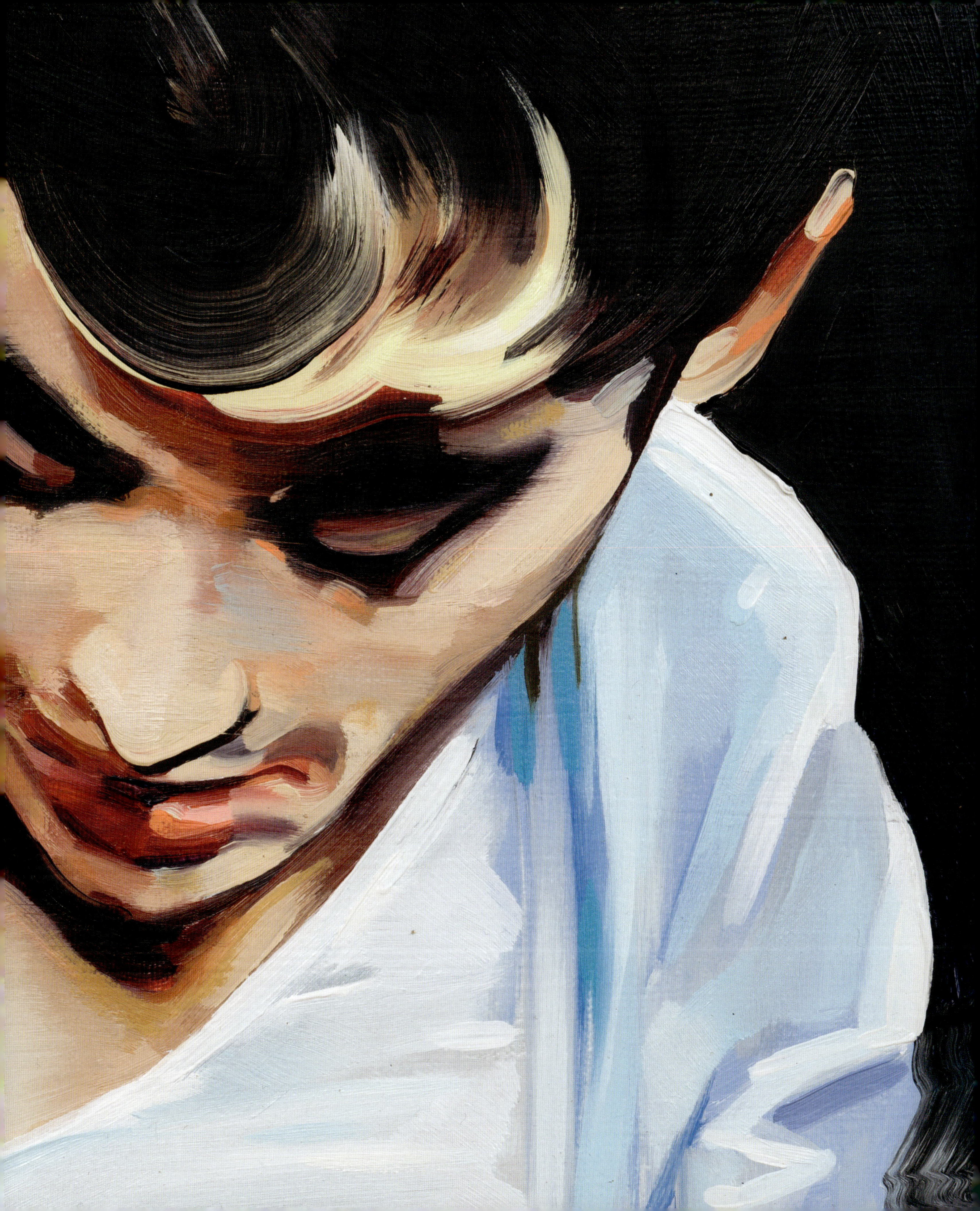

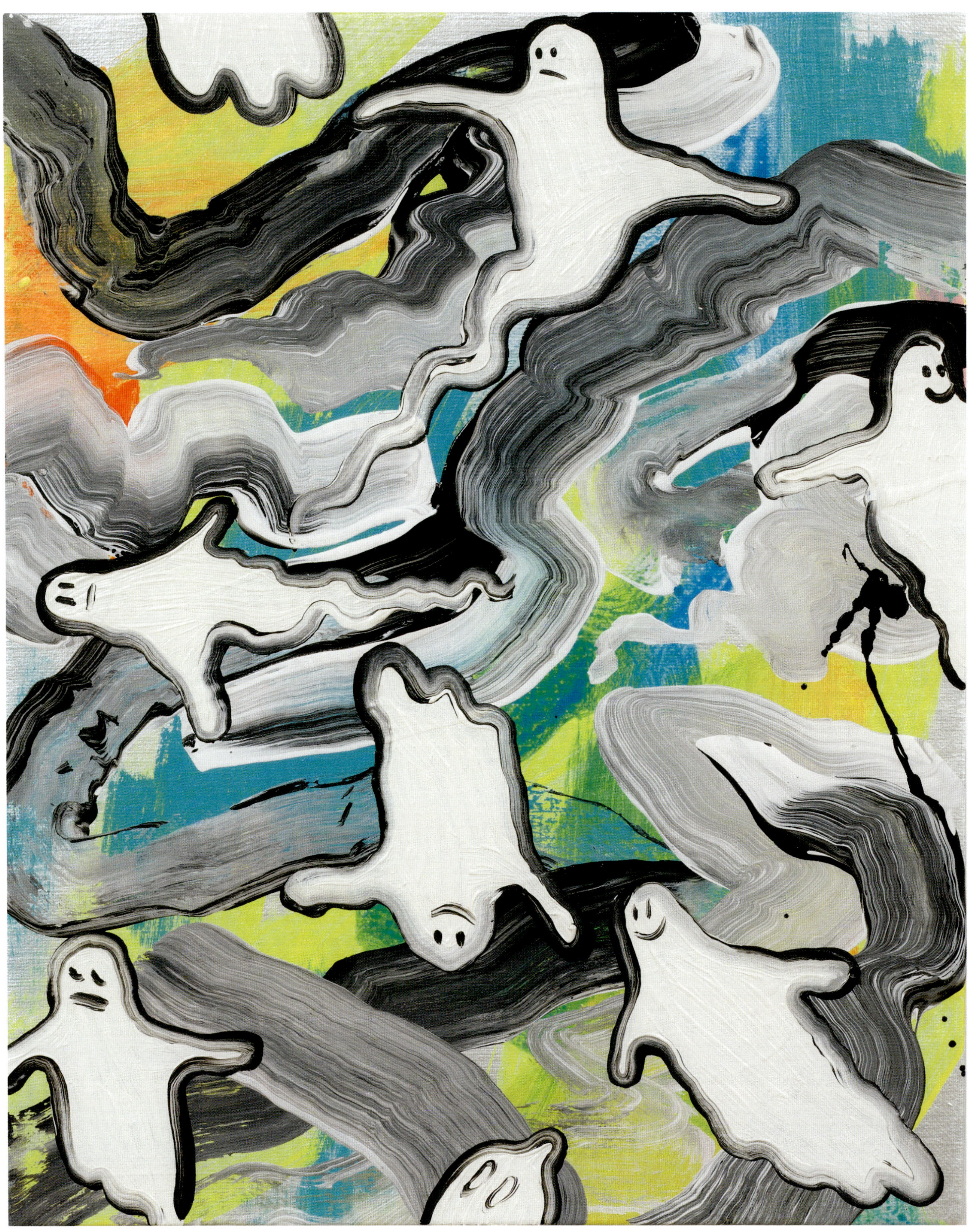

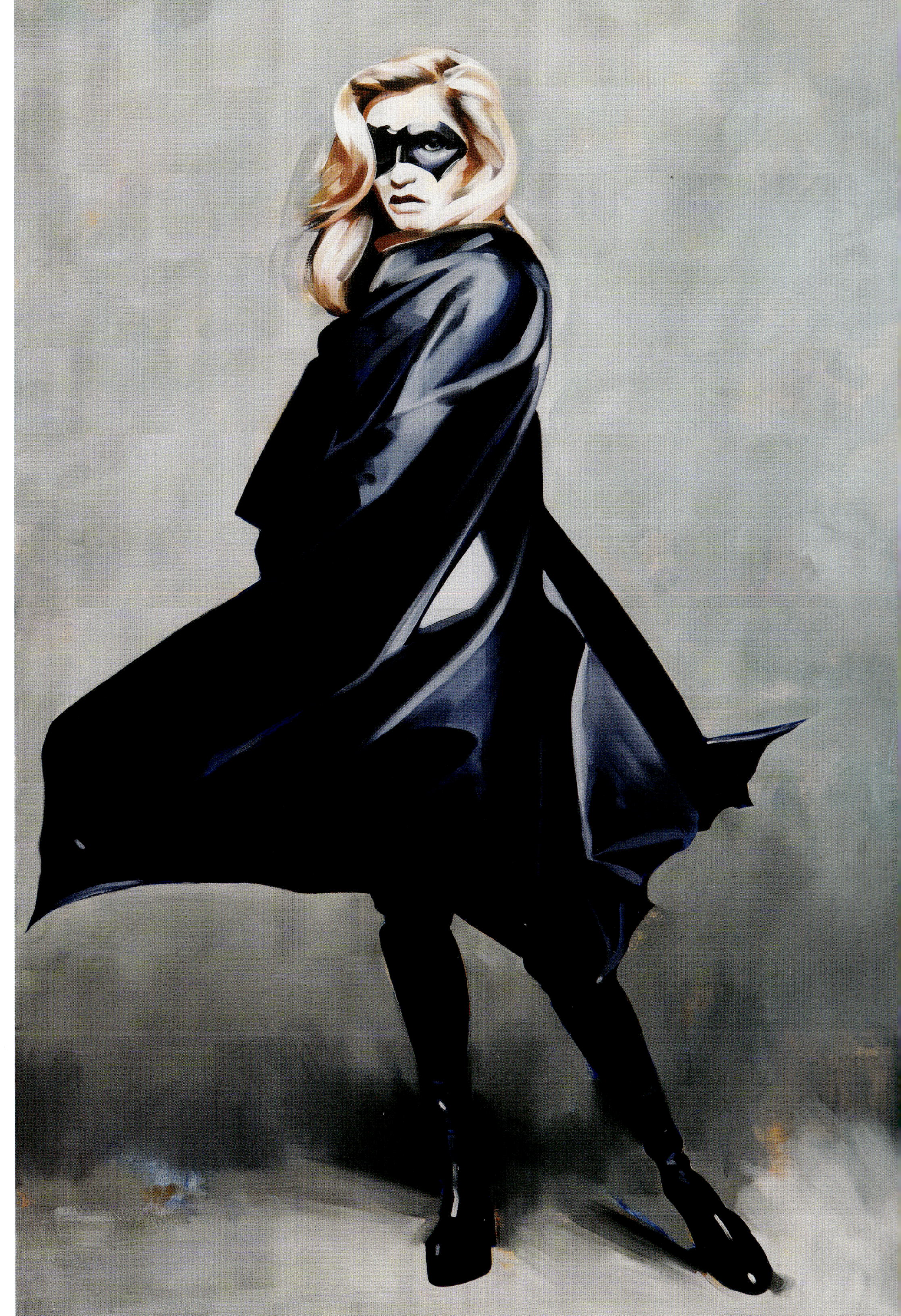

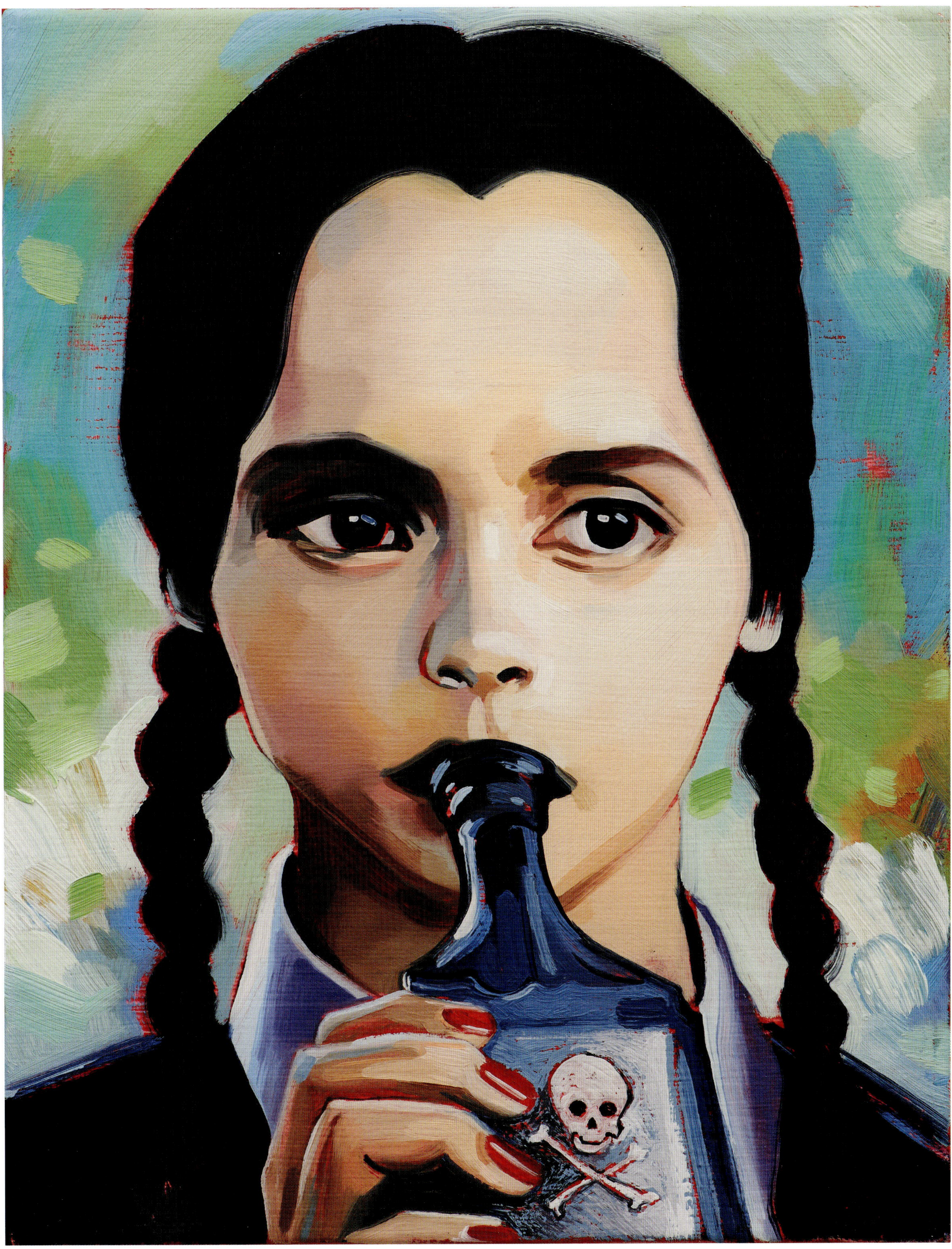

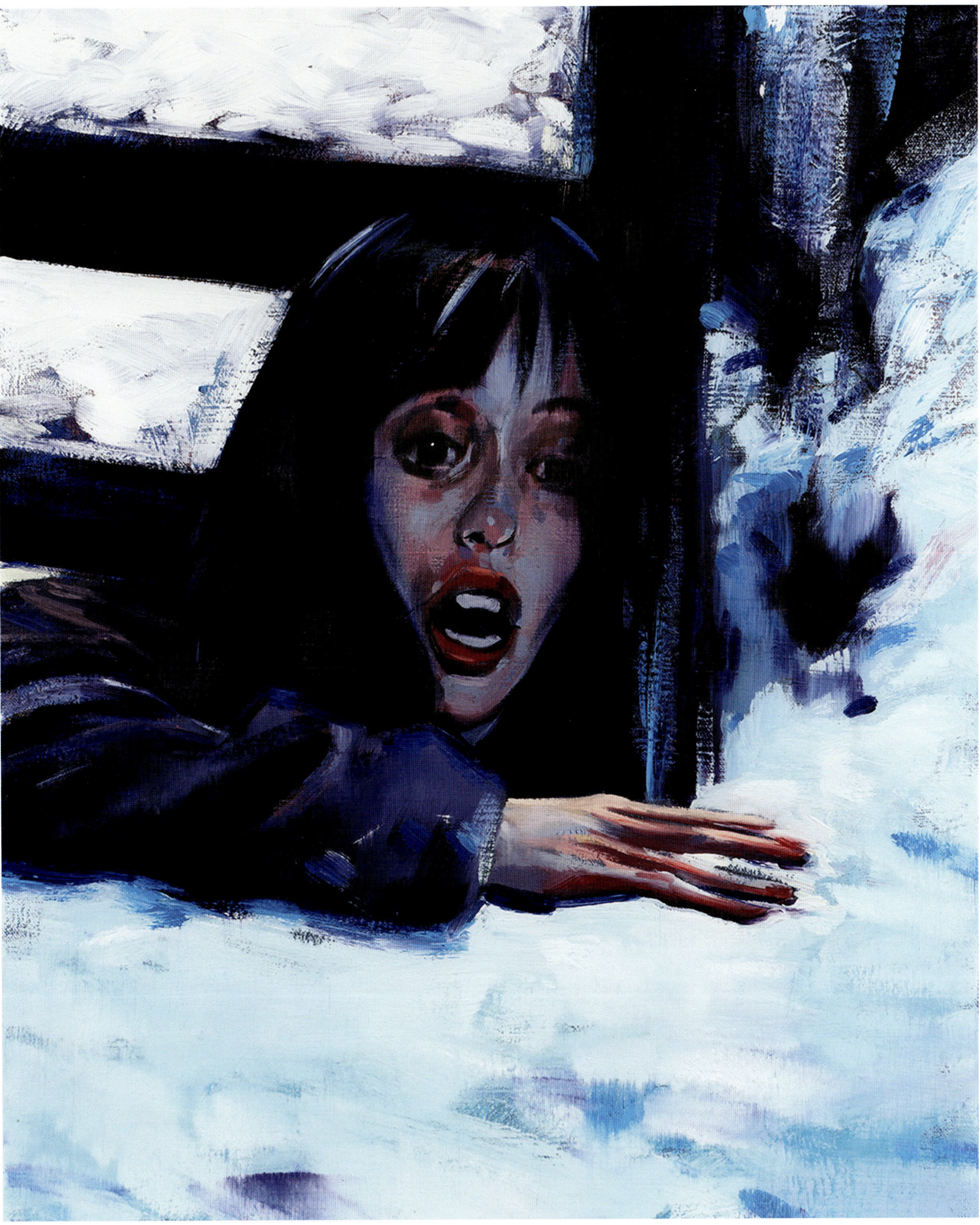

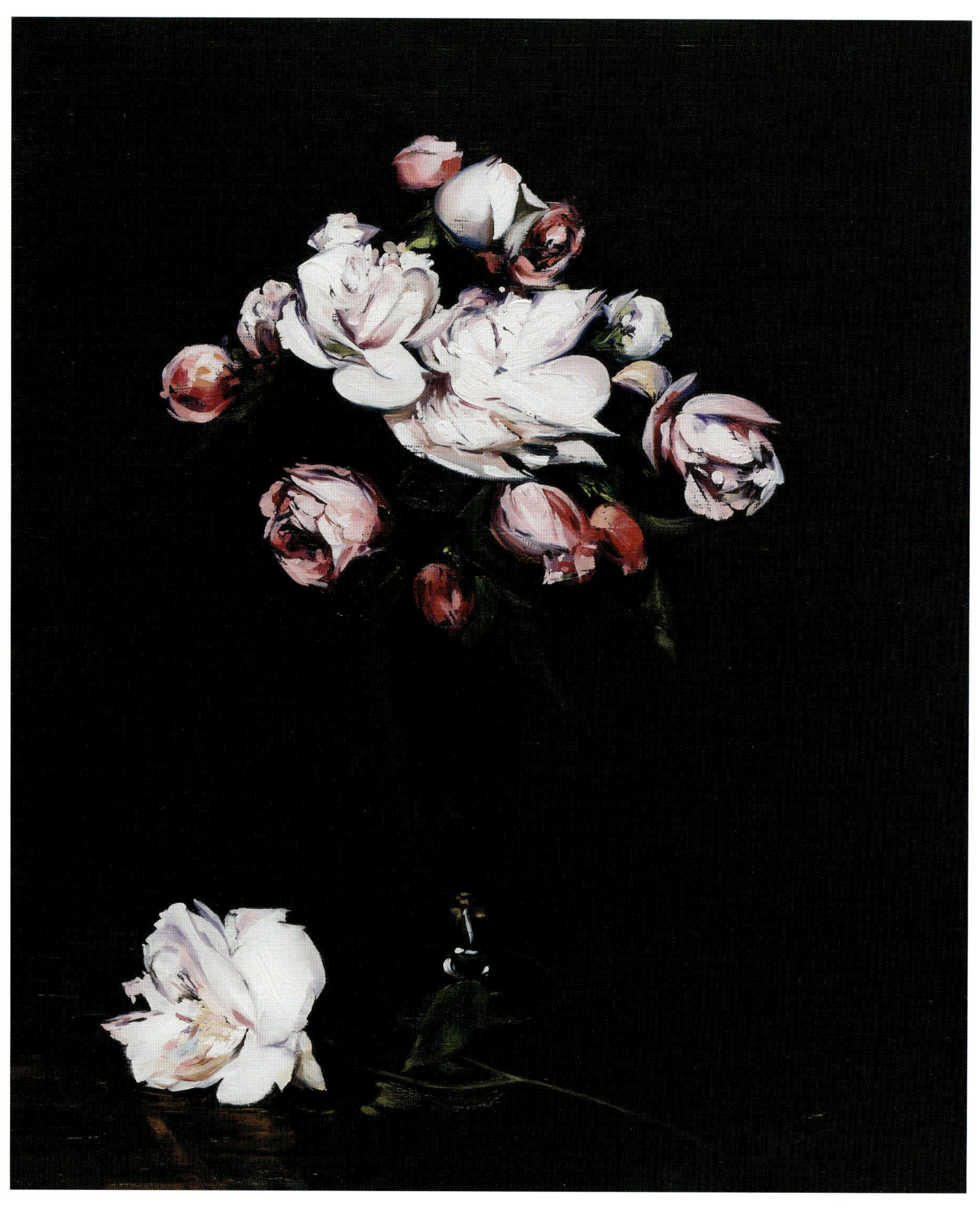

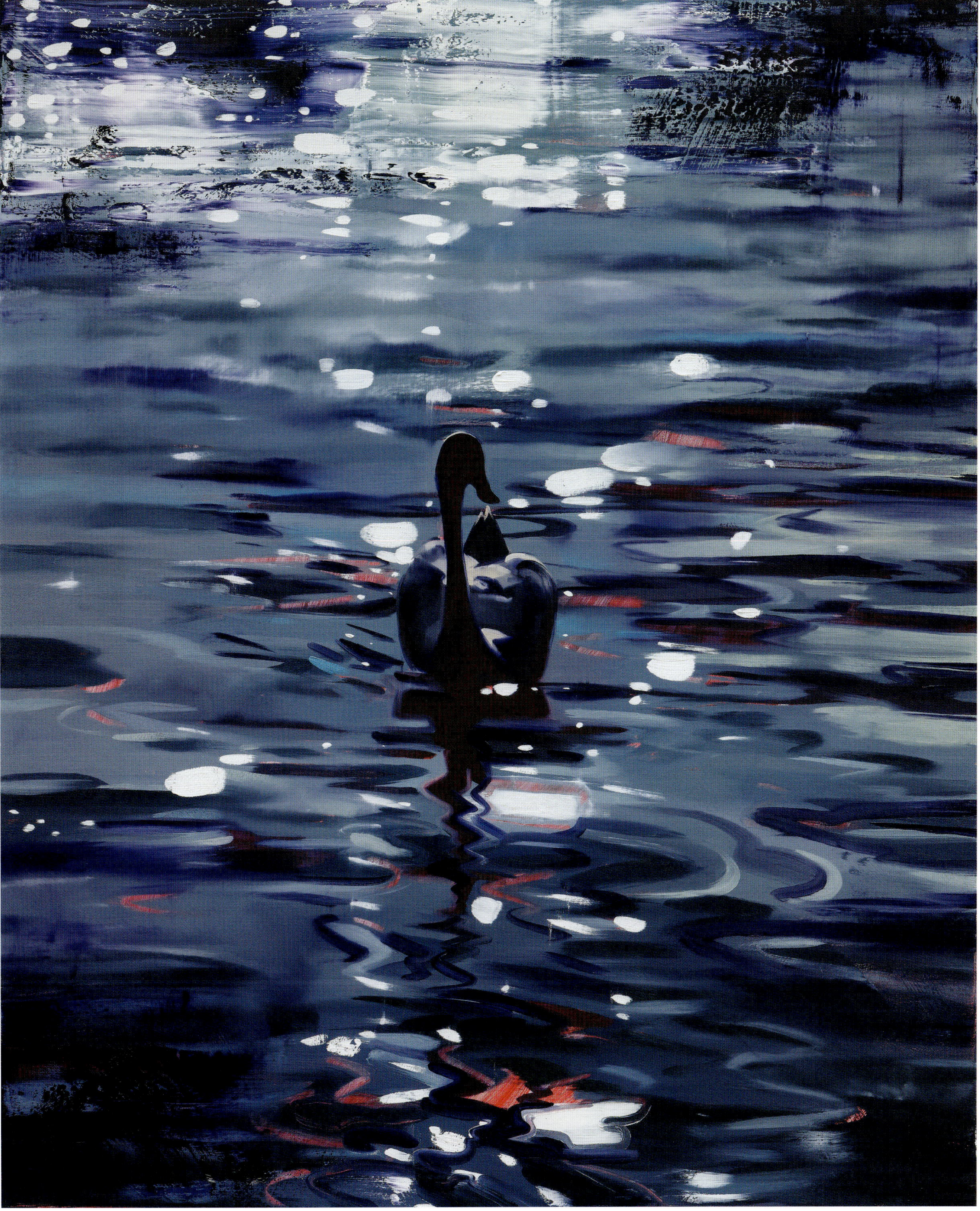

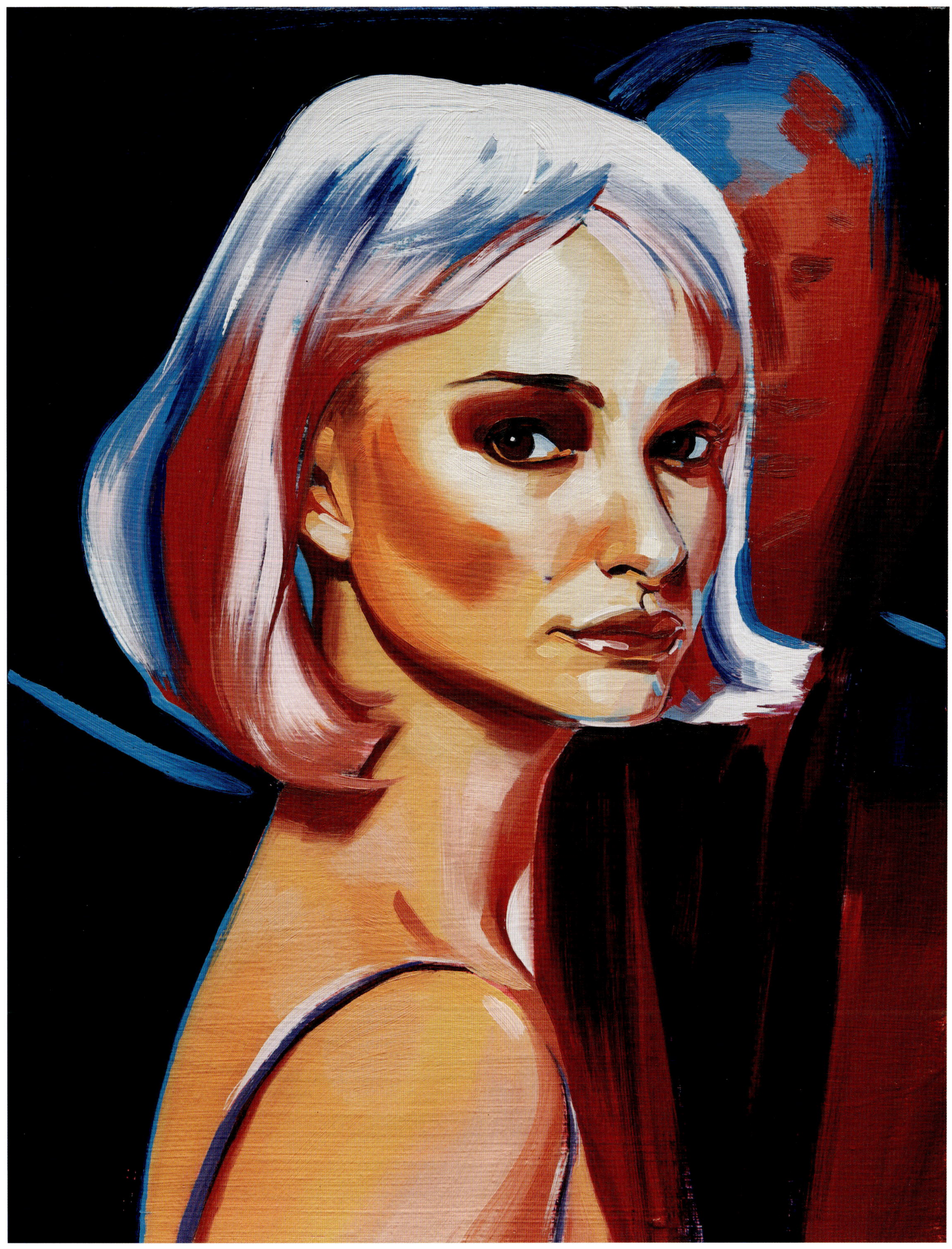

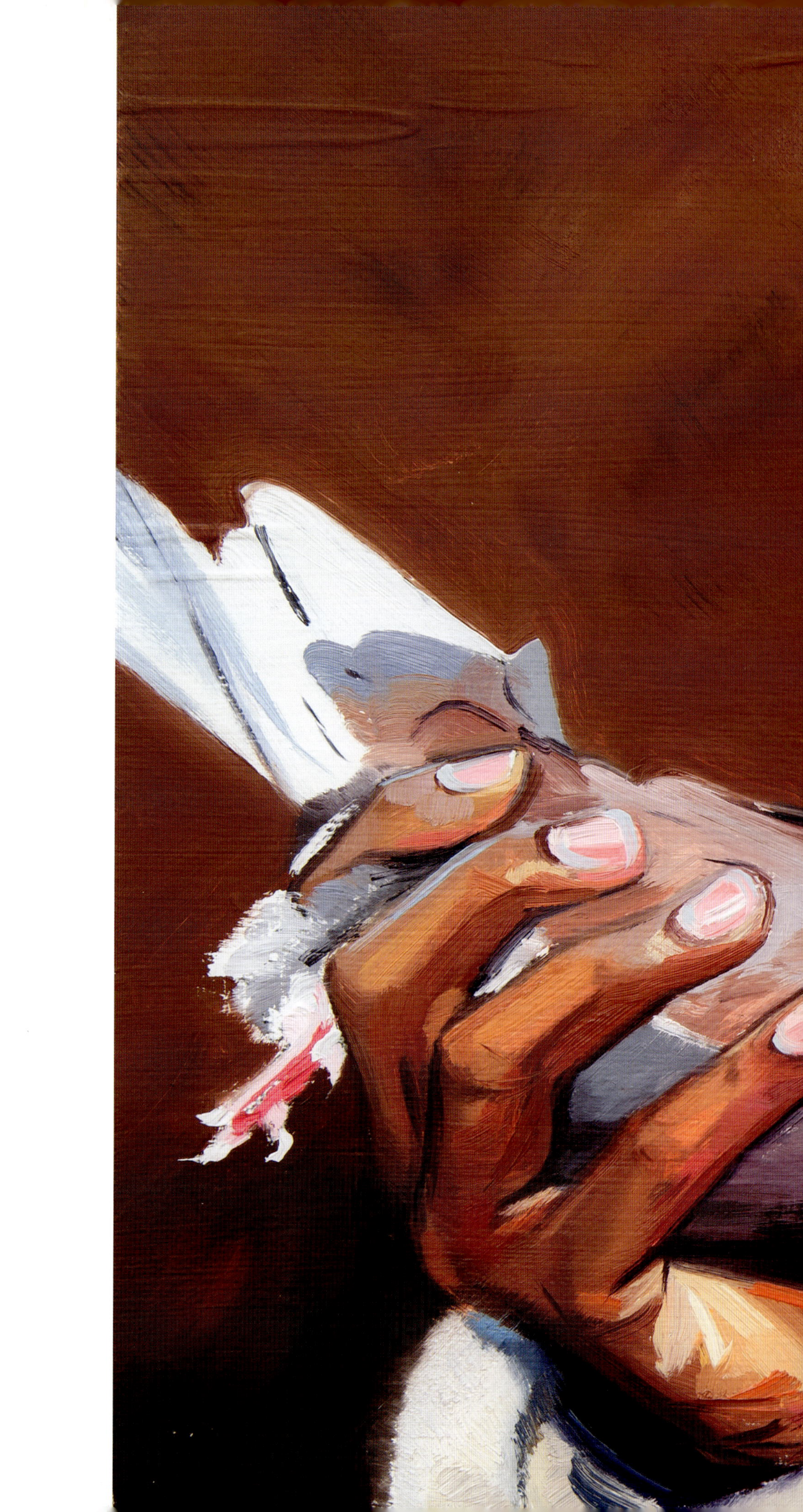

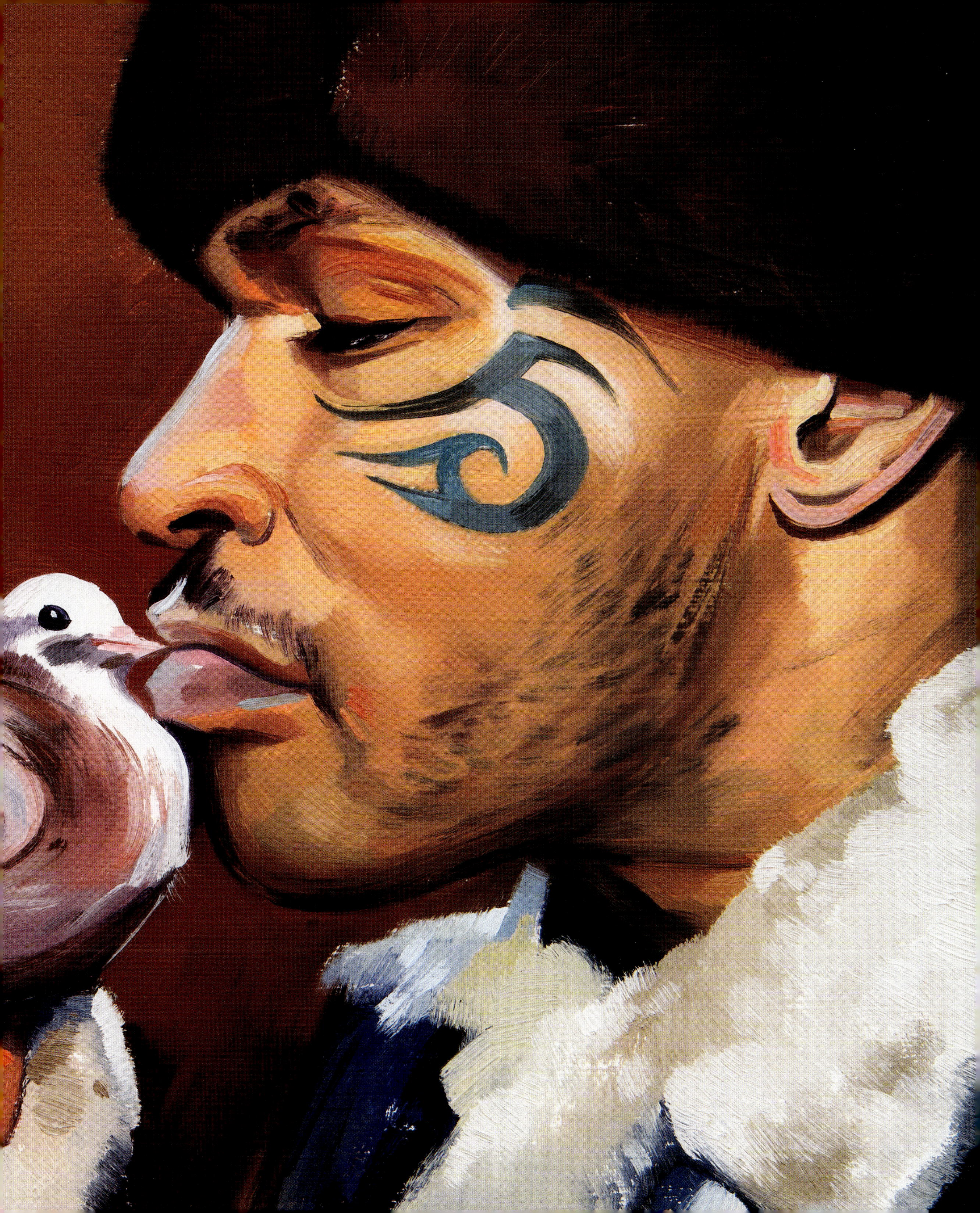

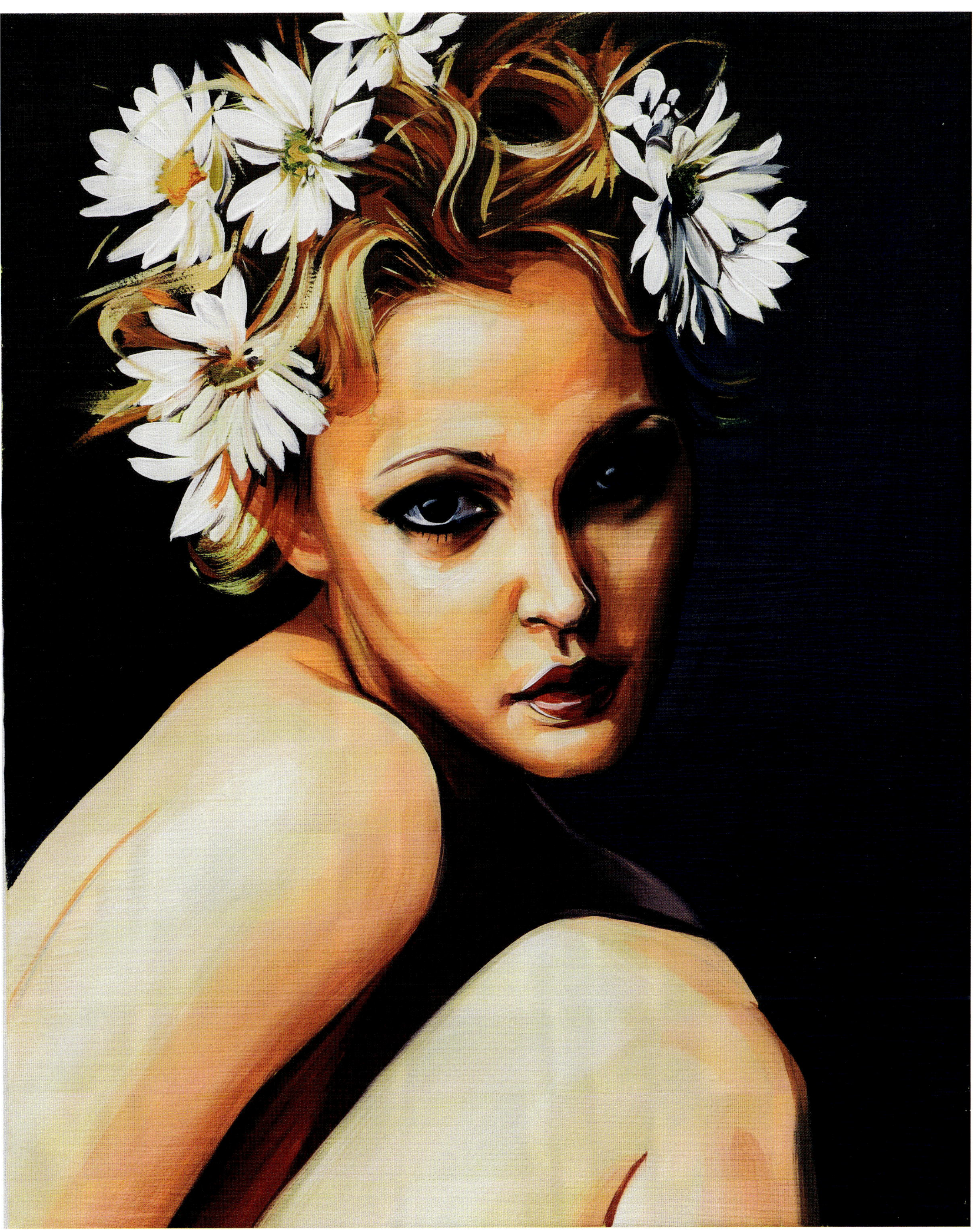

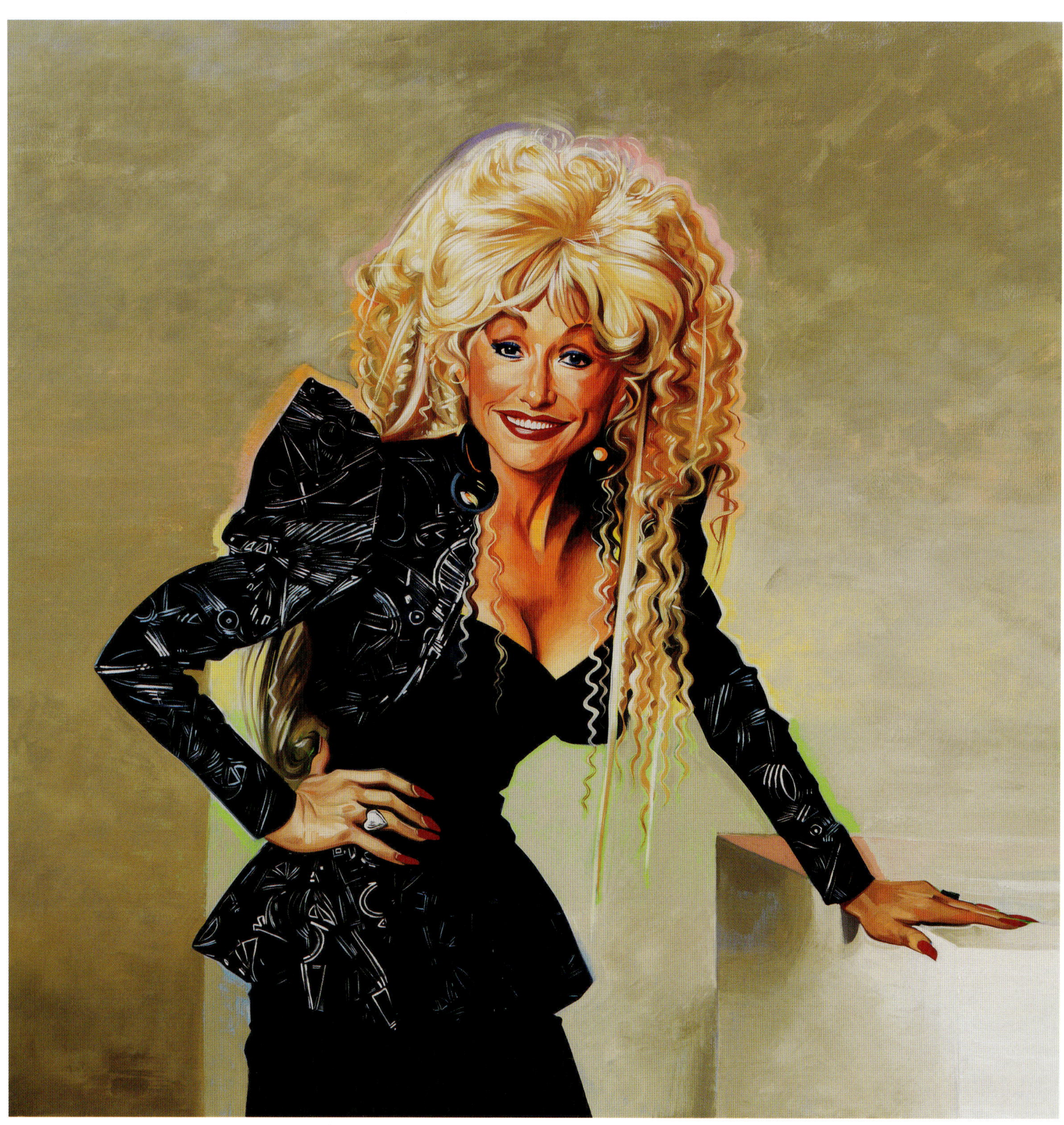

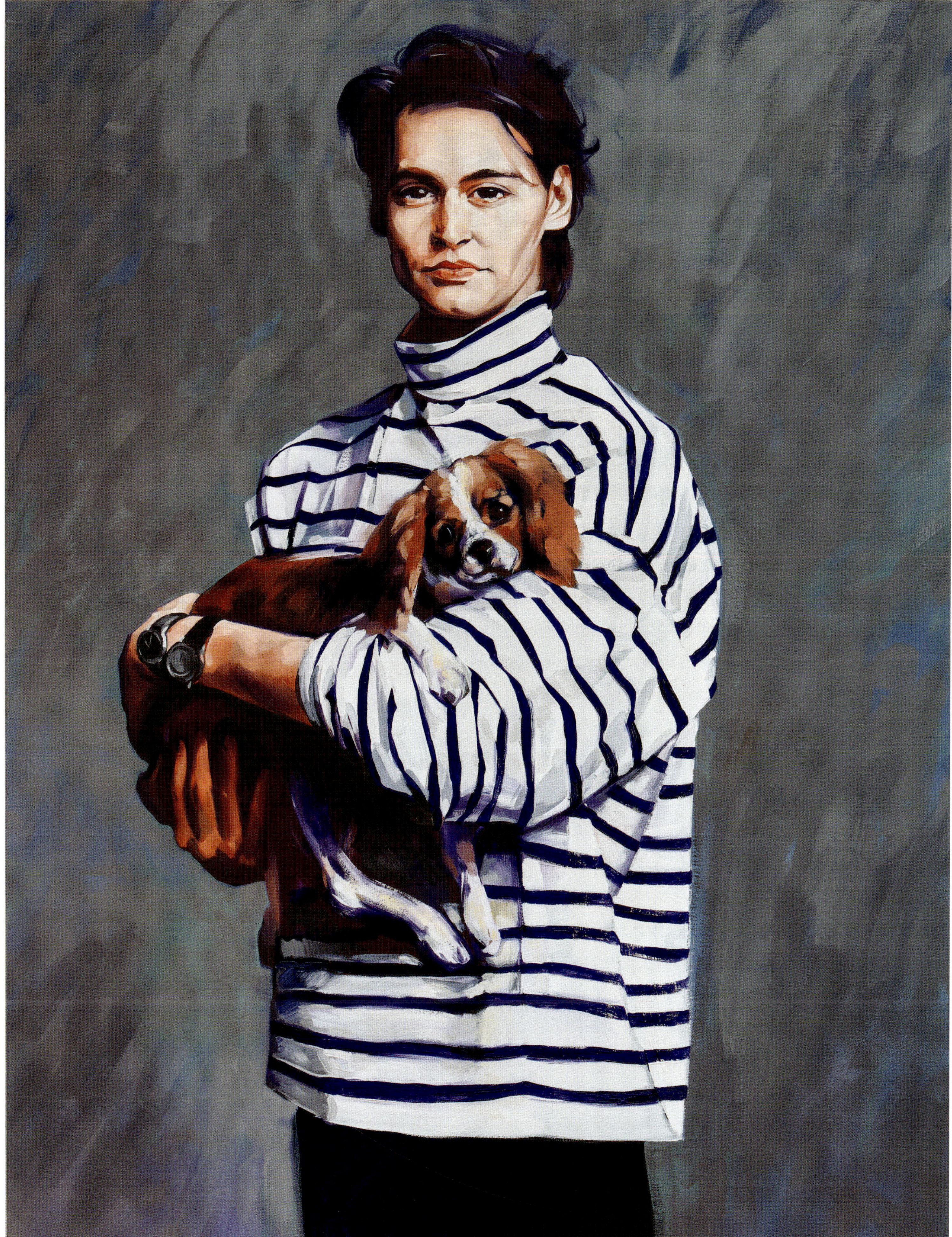

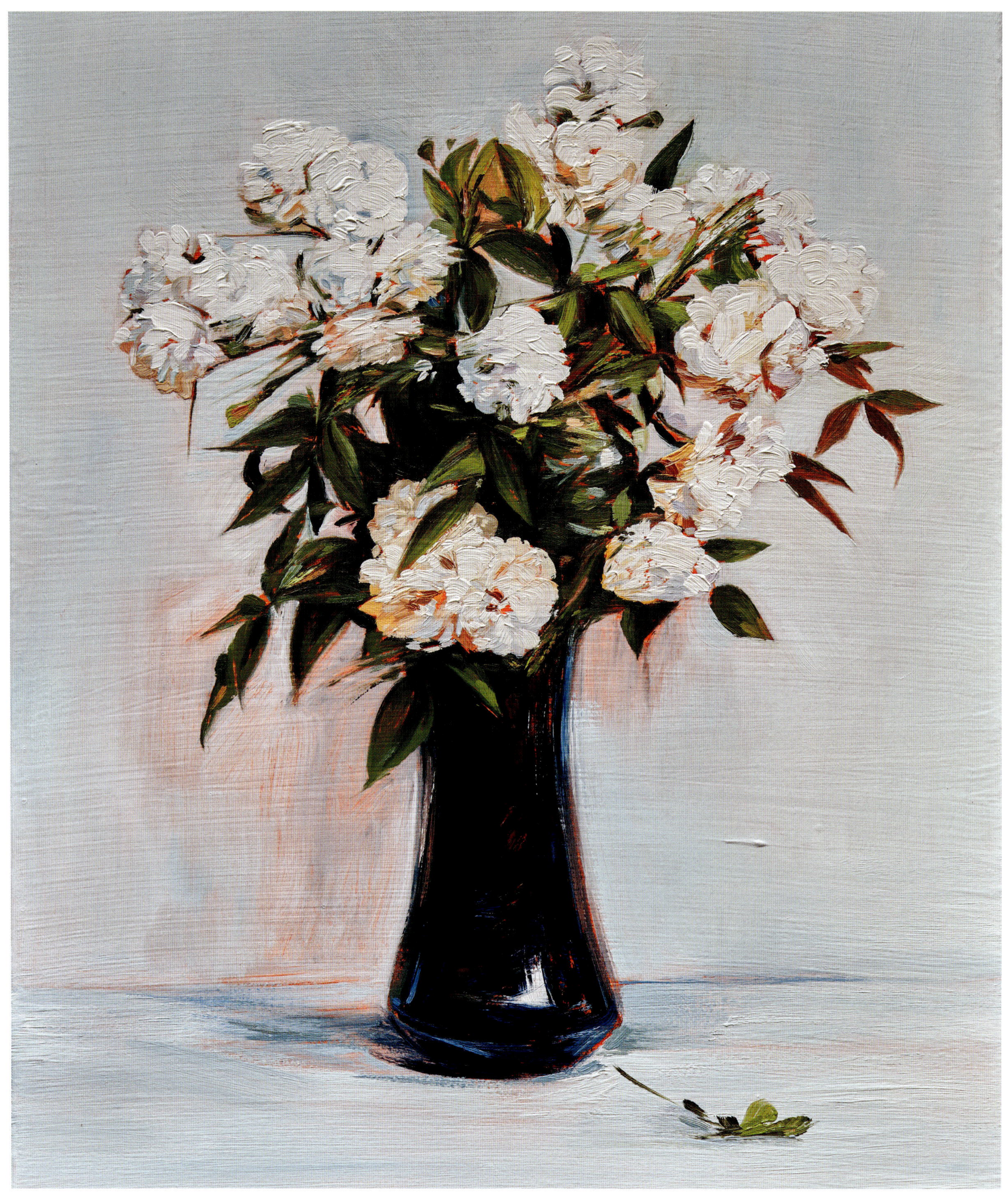

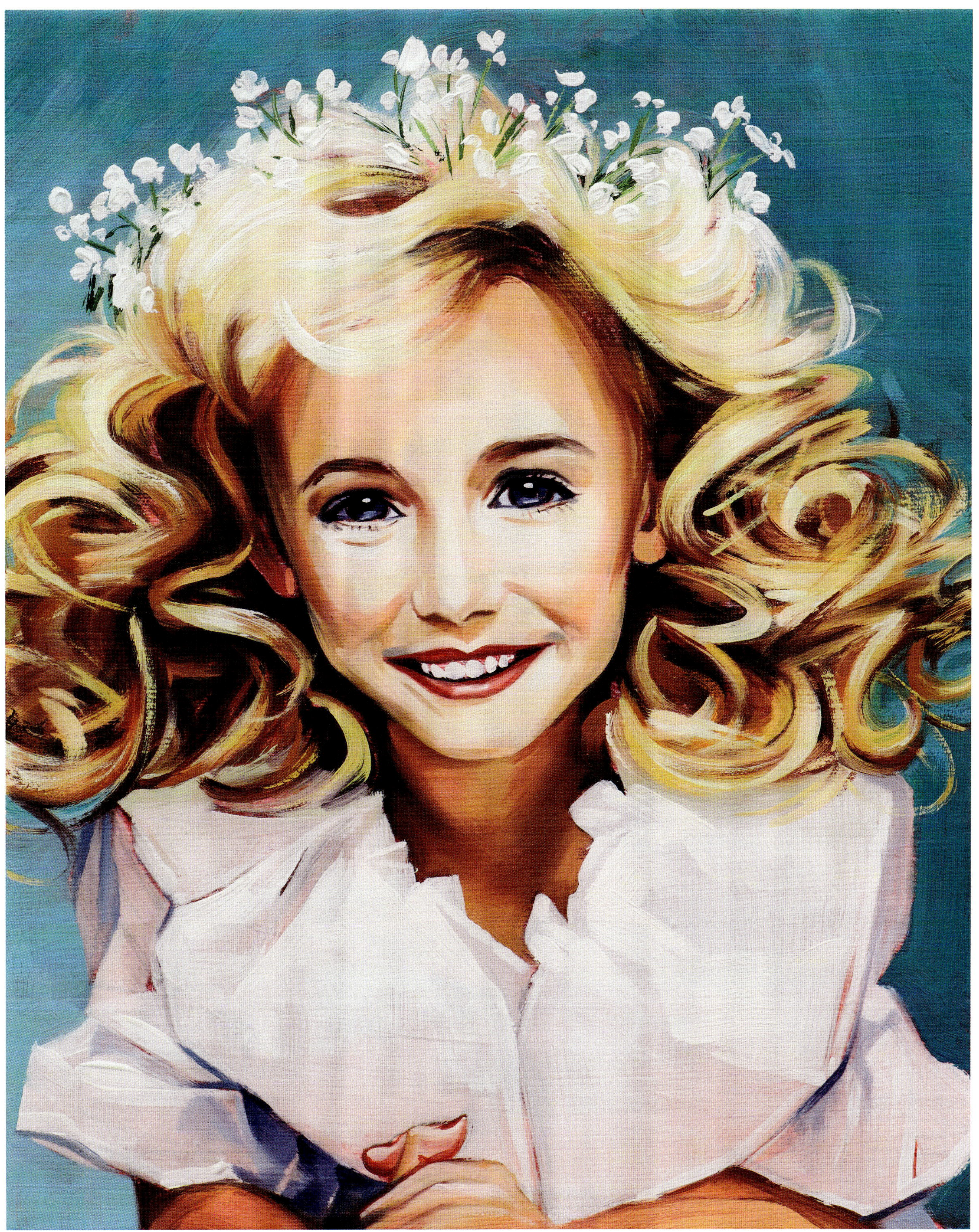

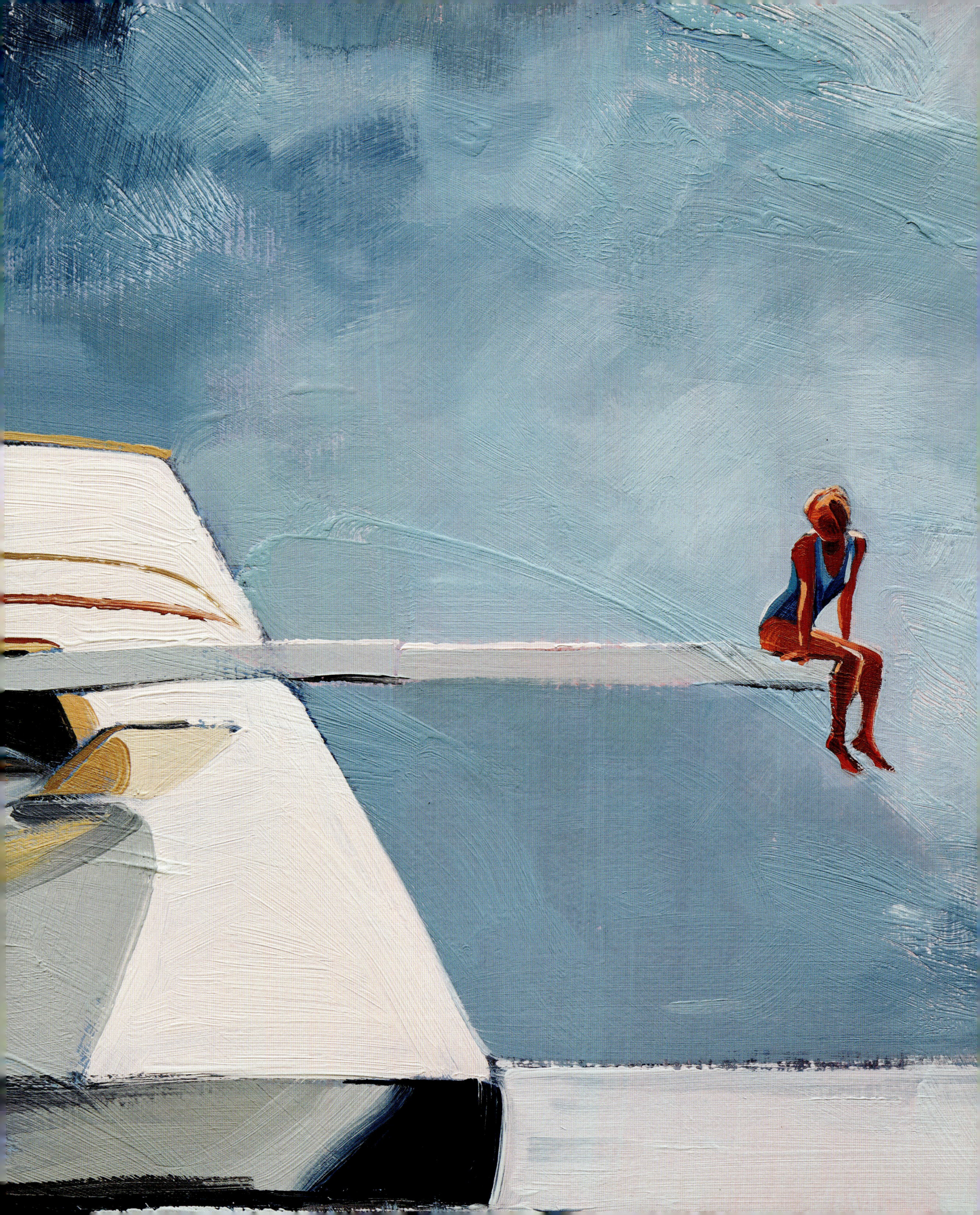

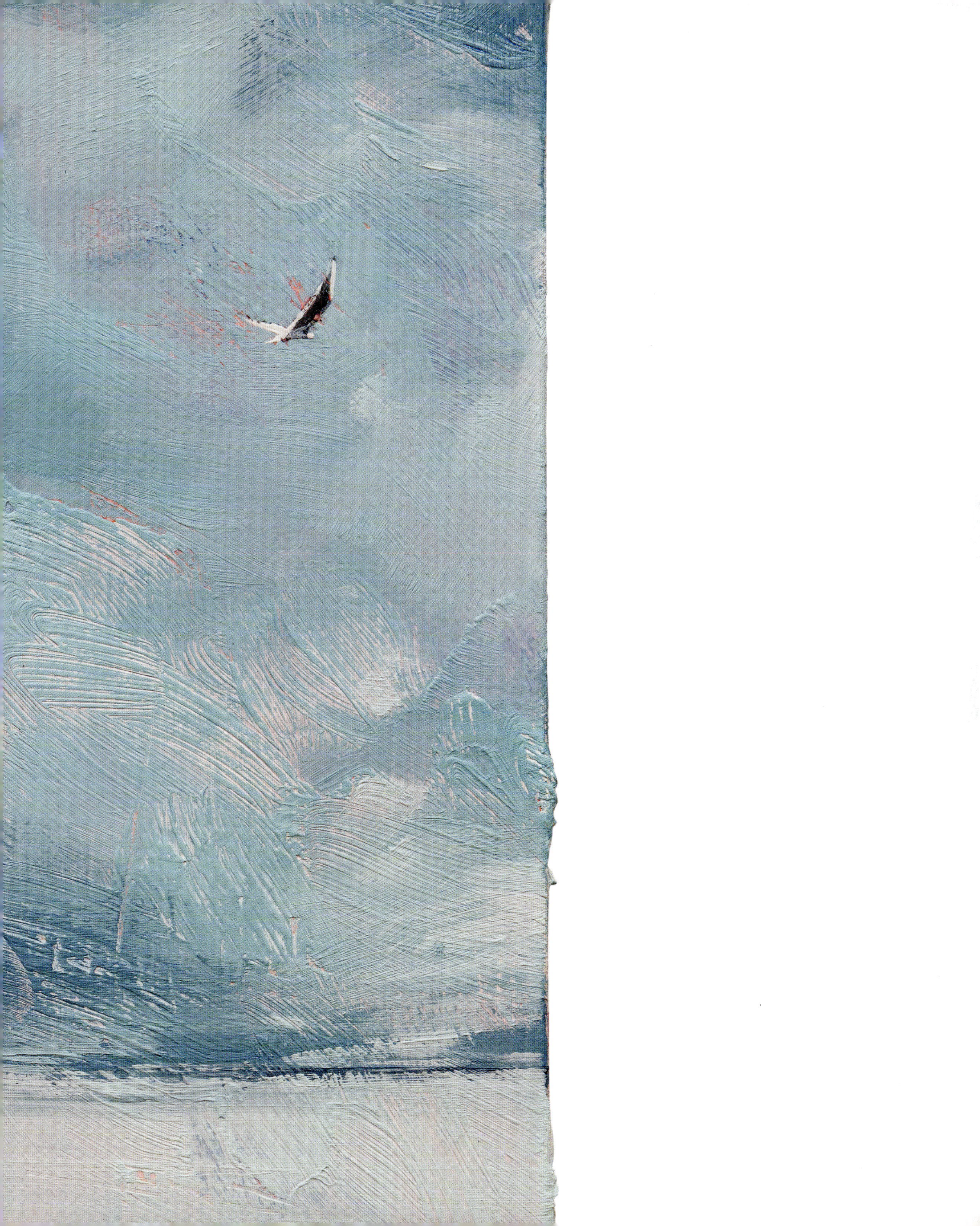

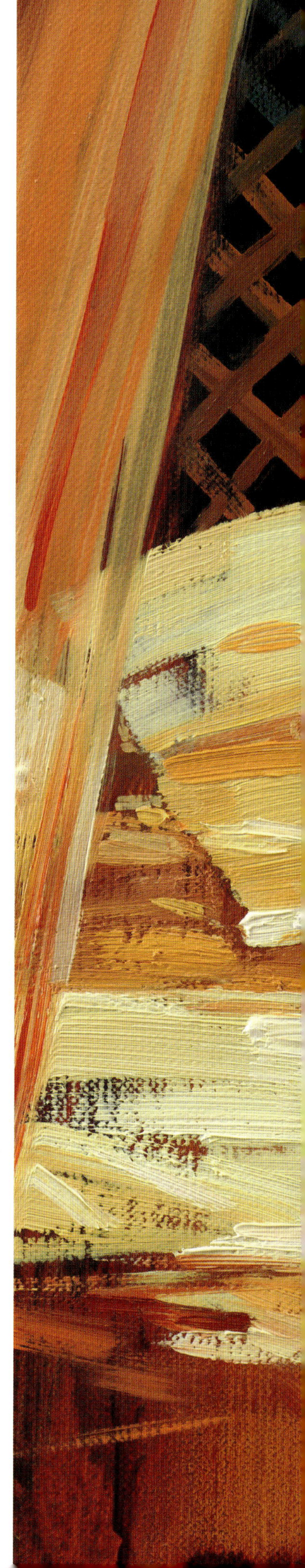

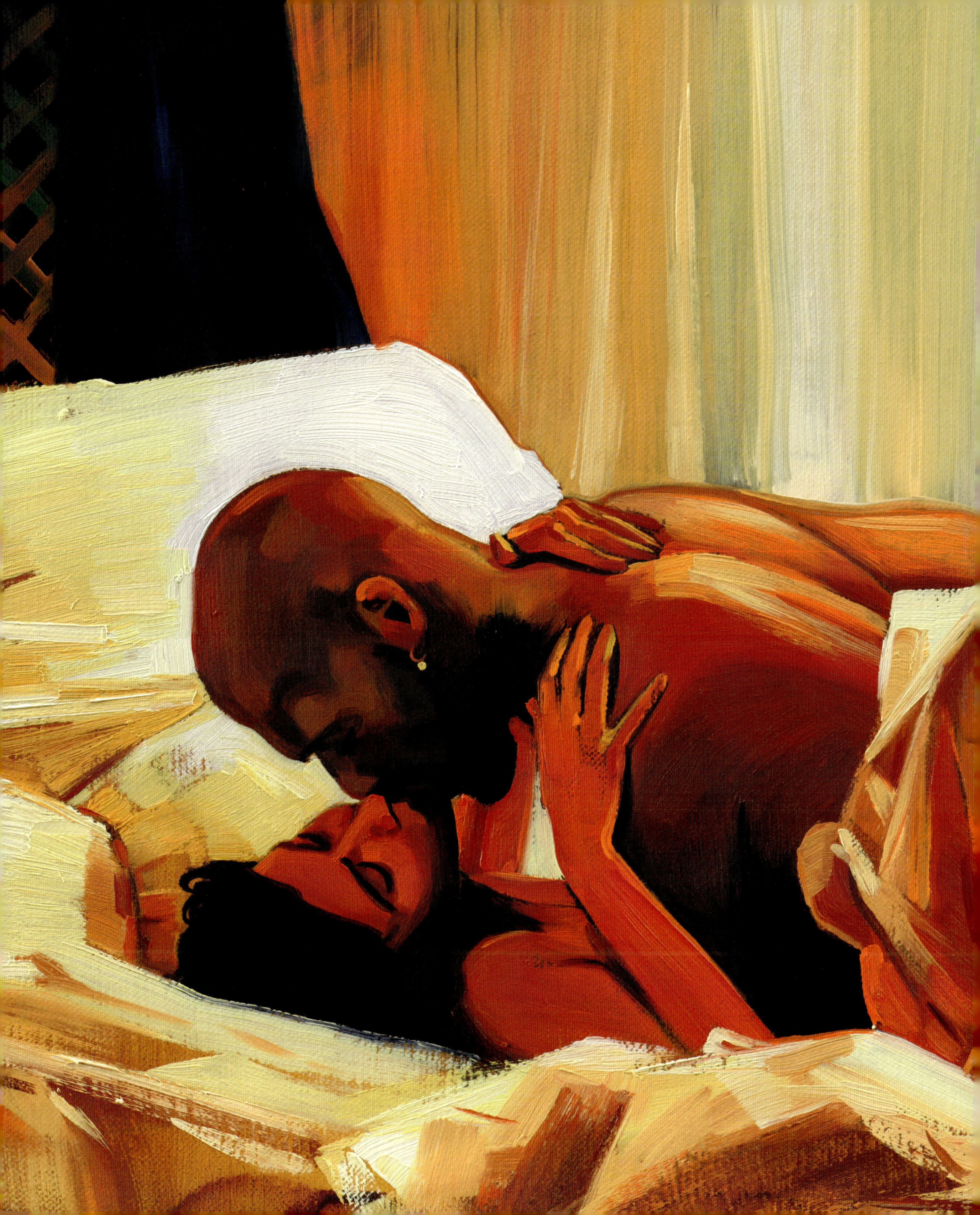

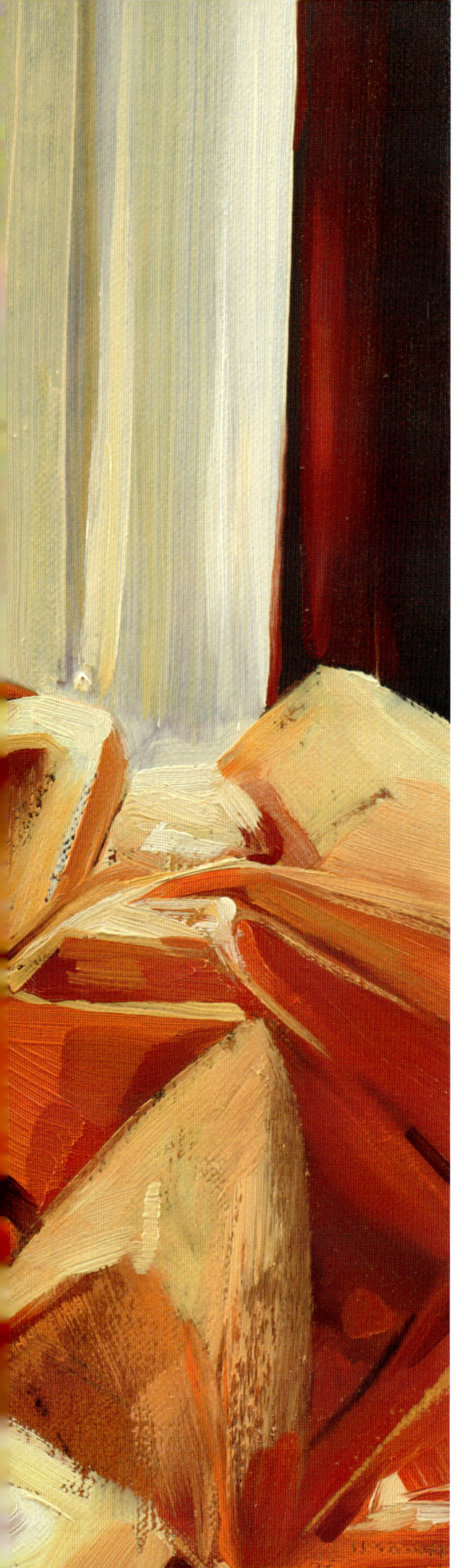

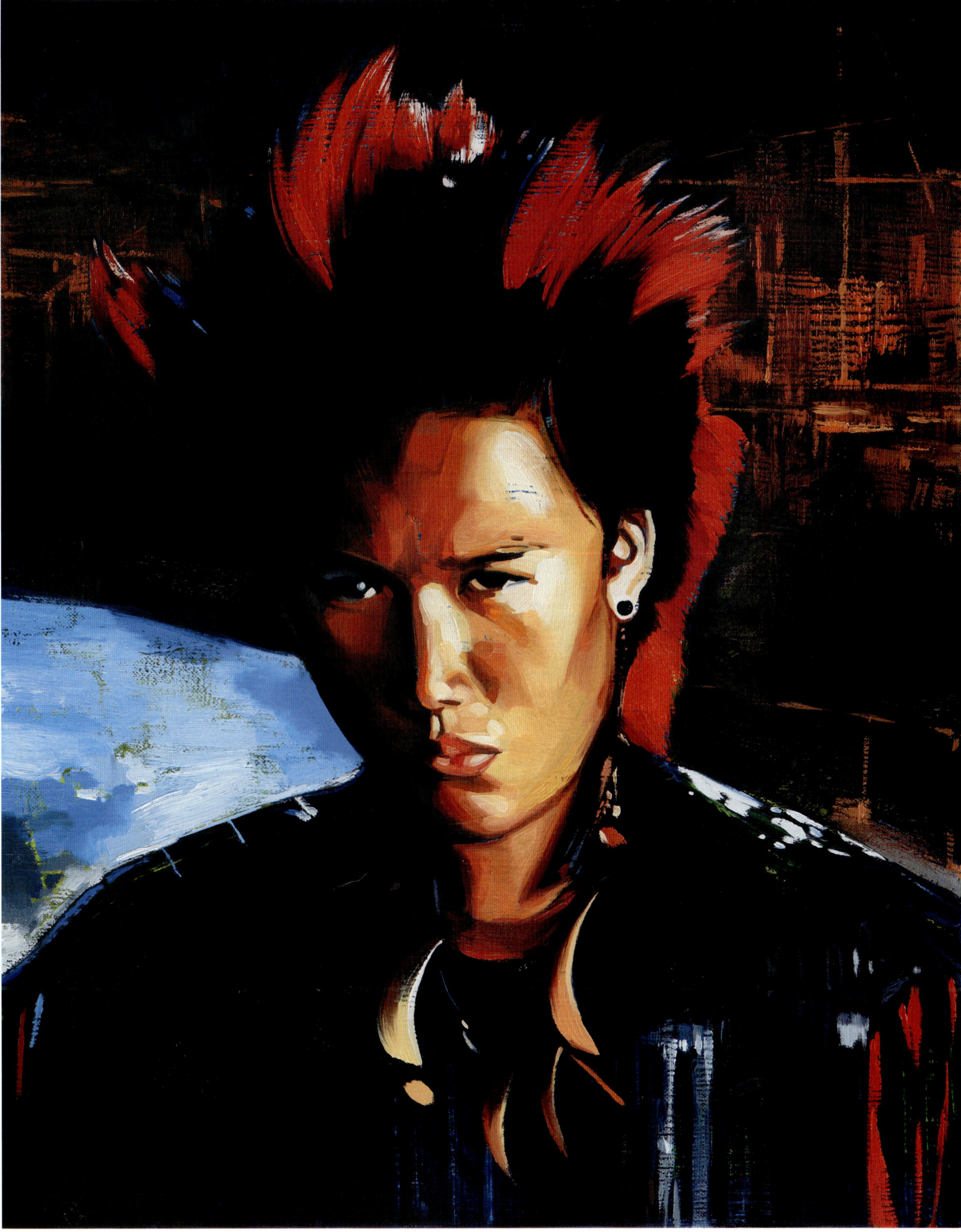

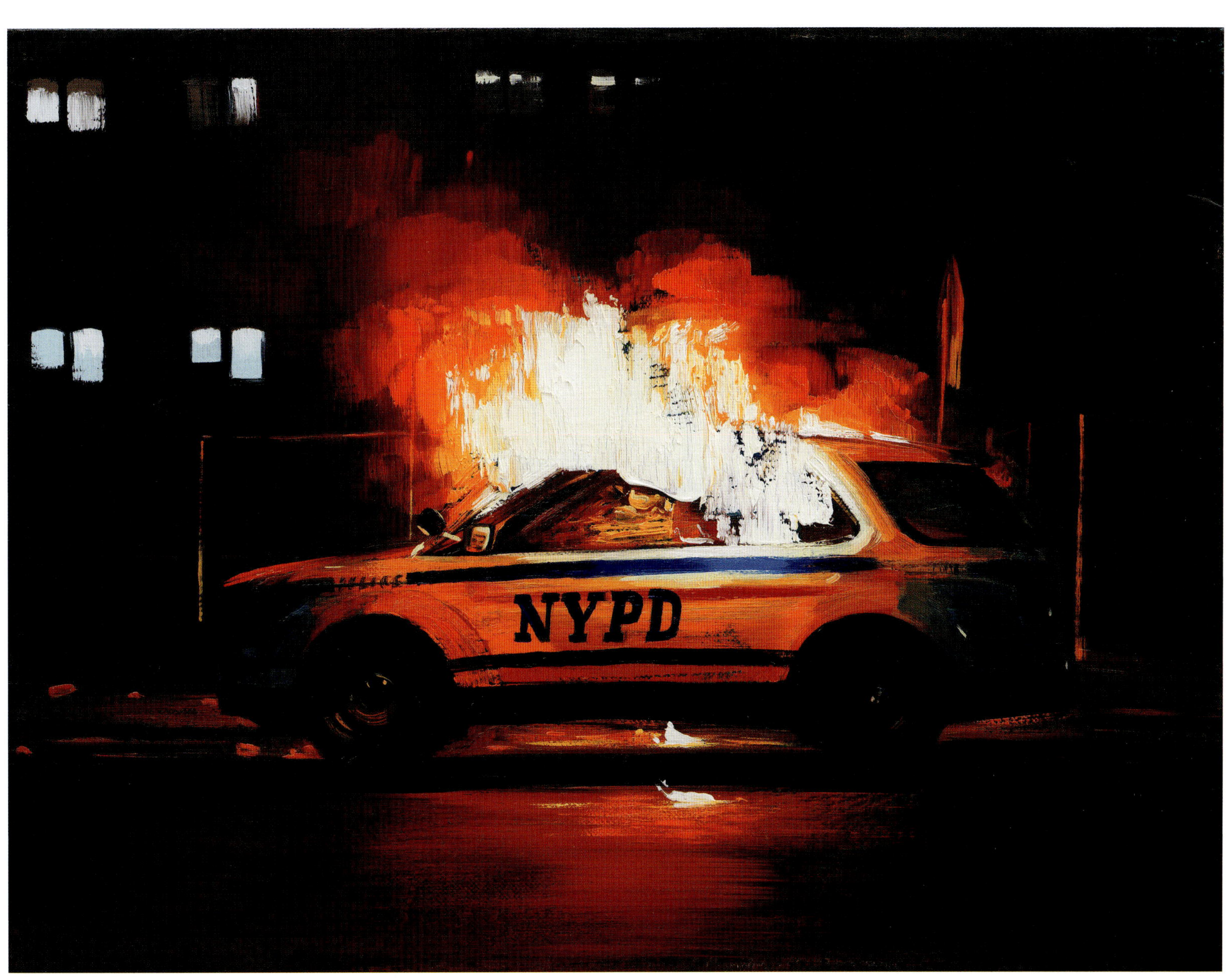
NYPD

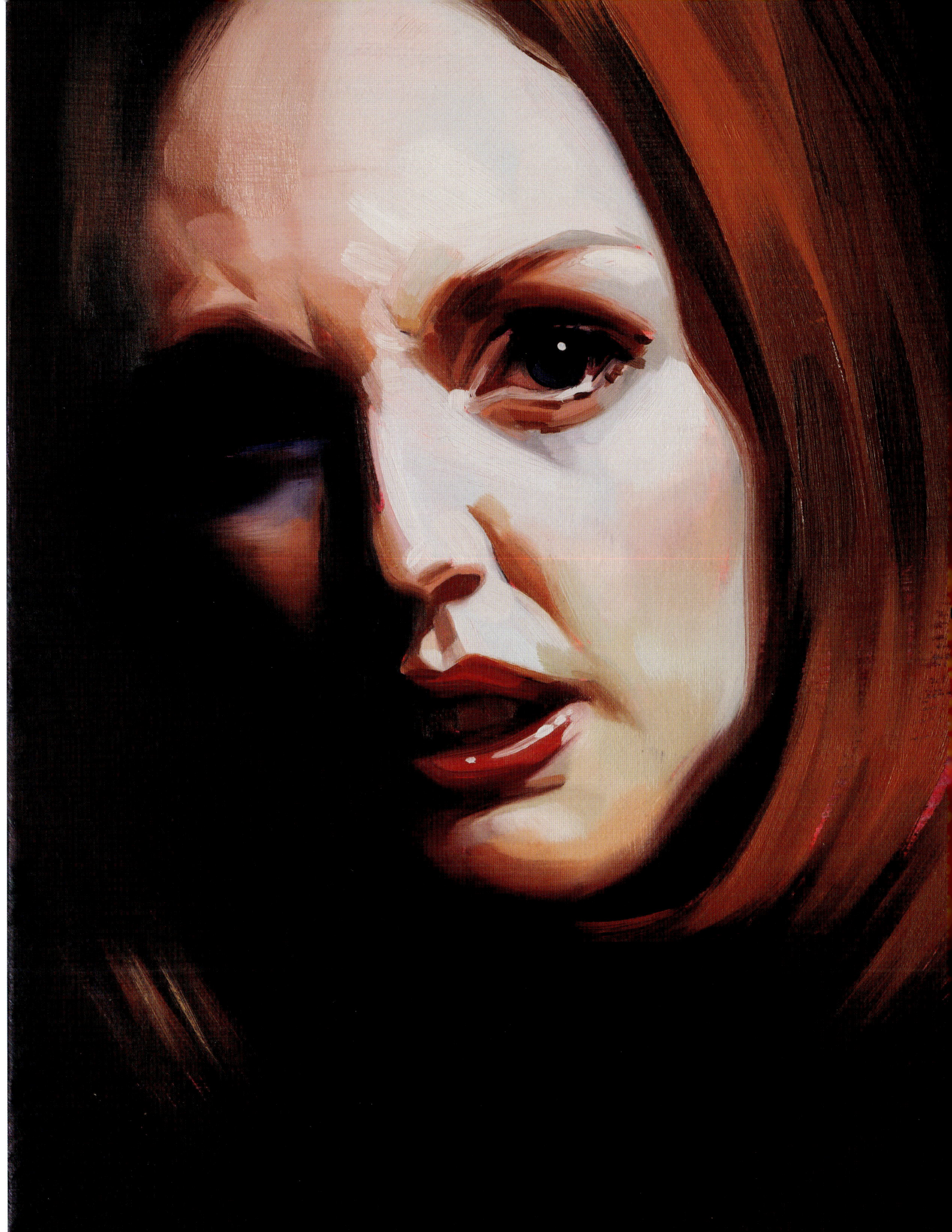

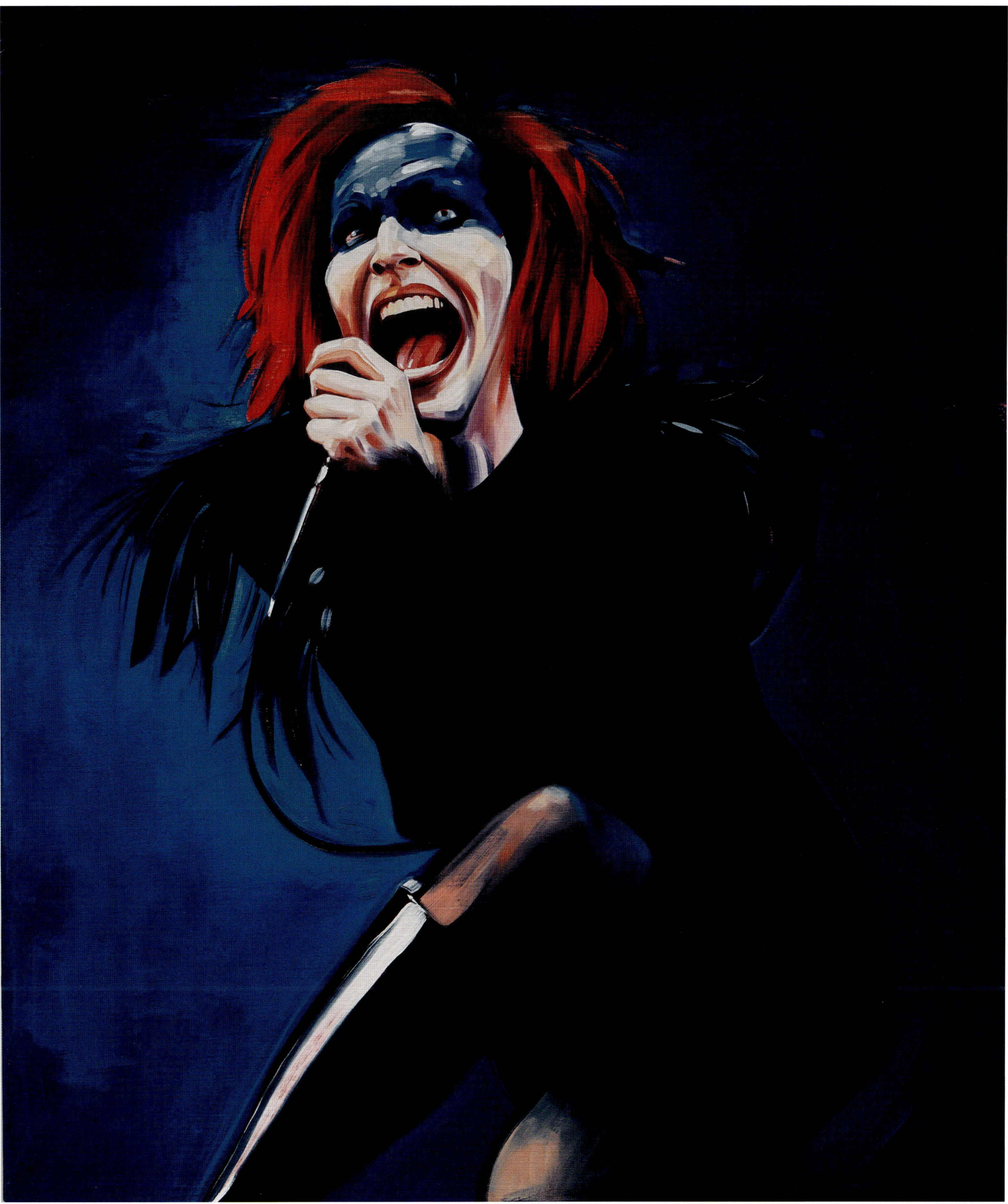

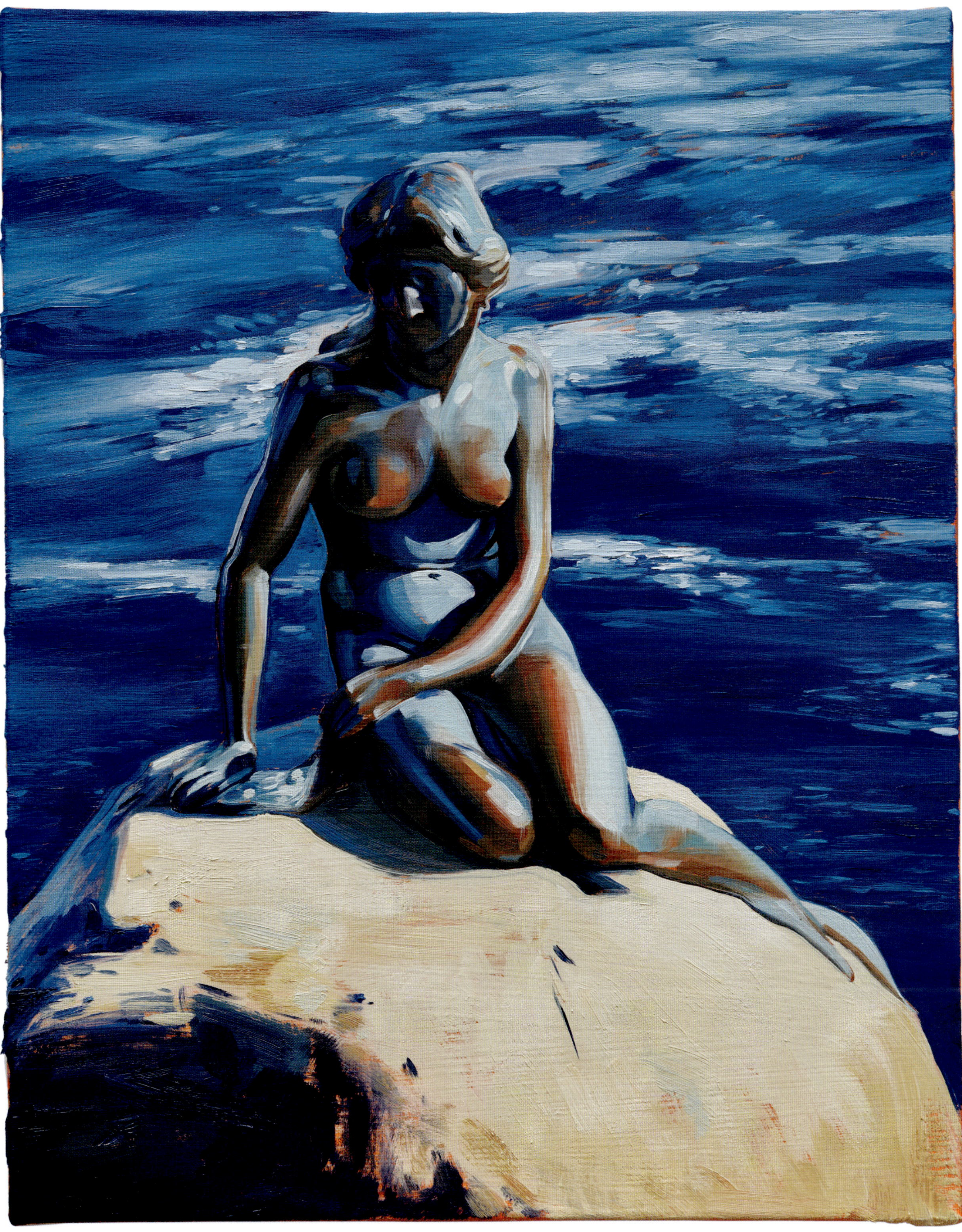

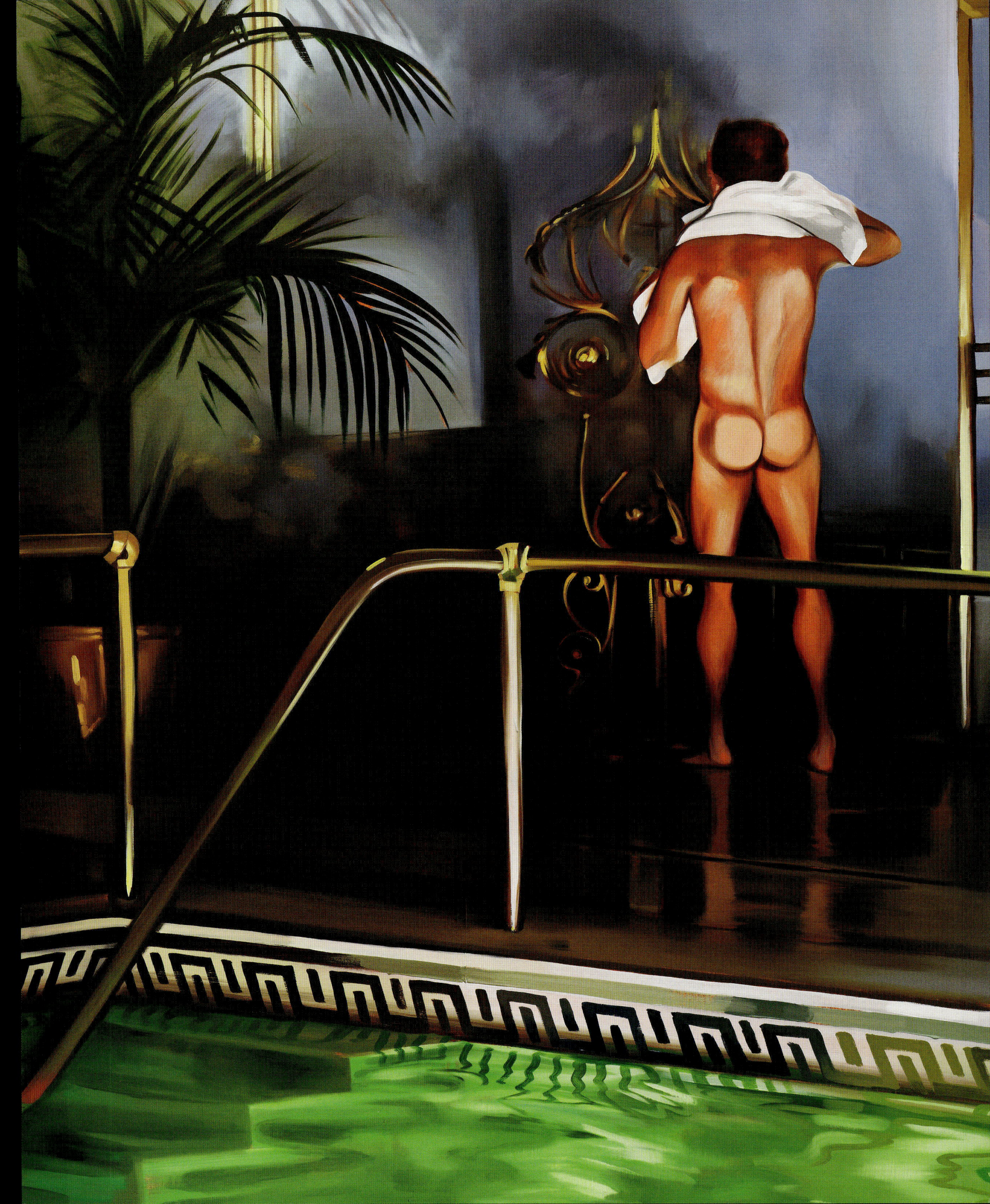

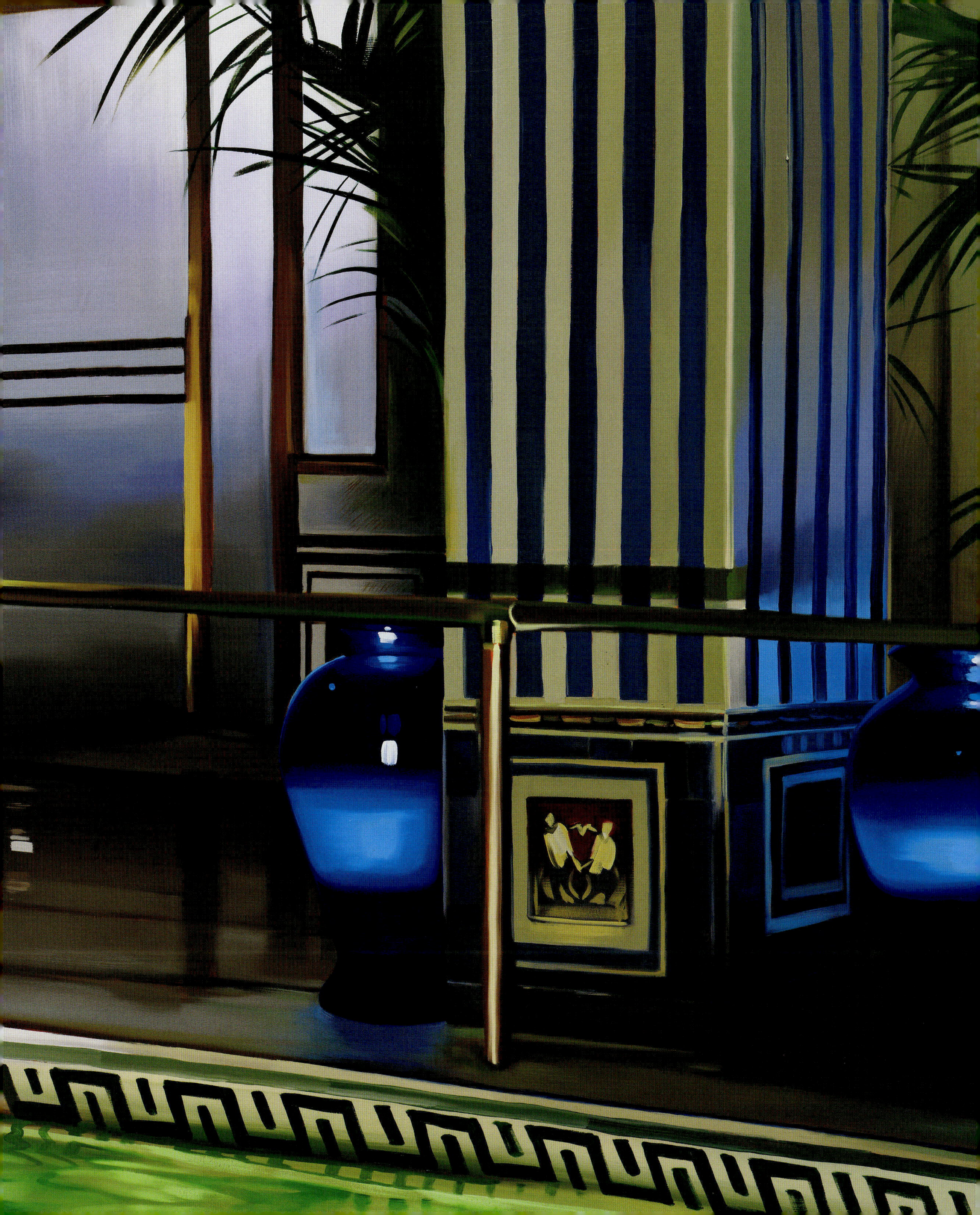

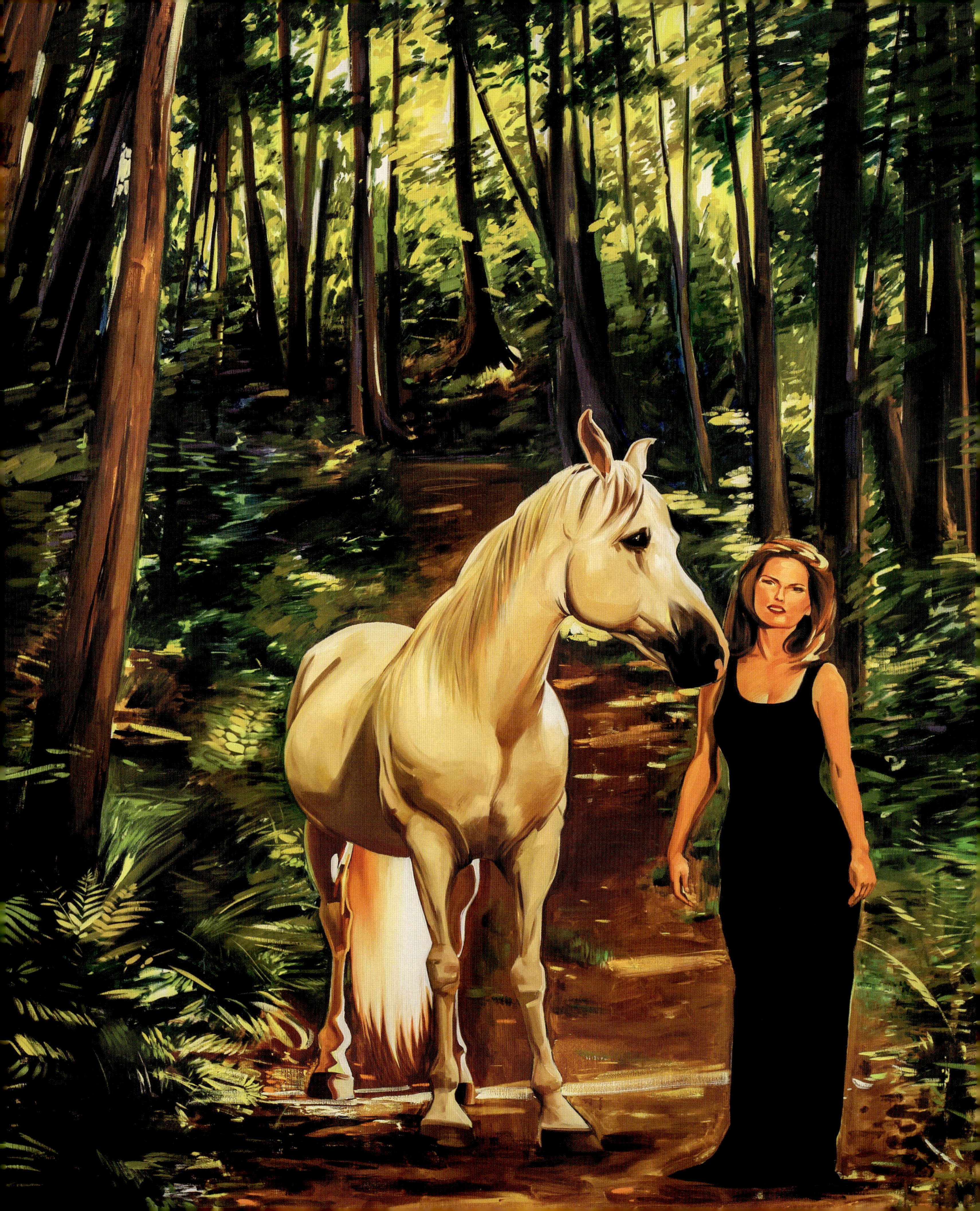

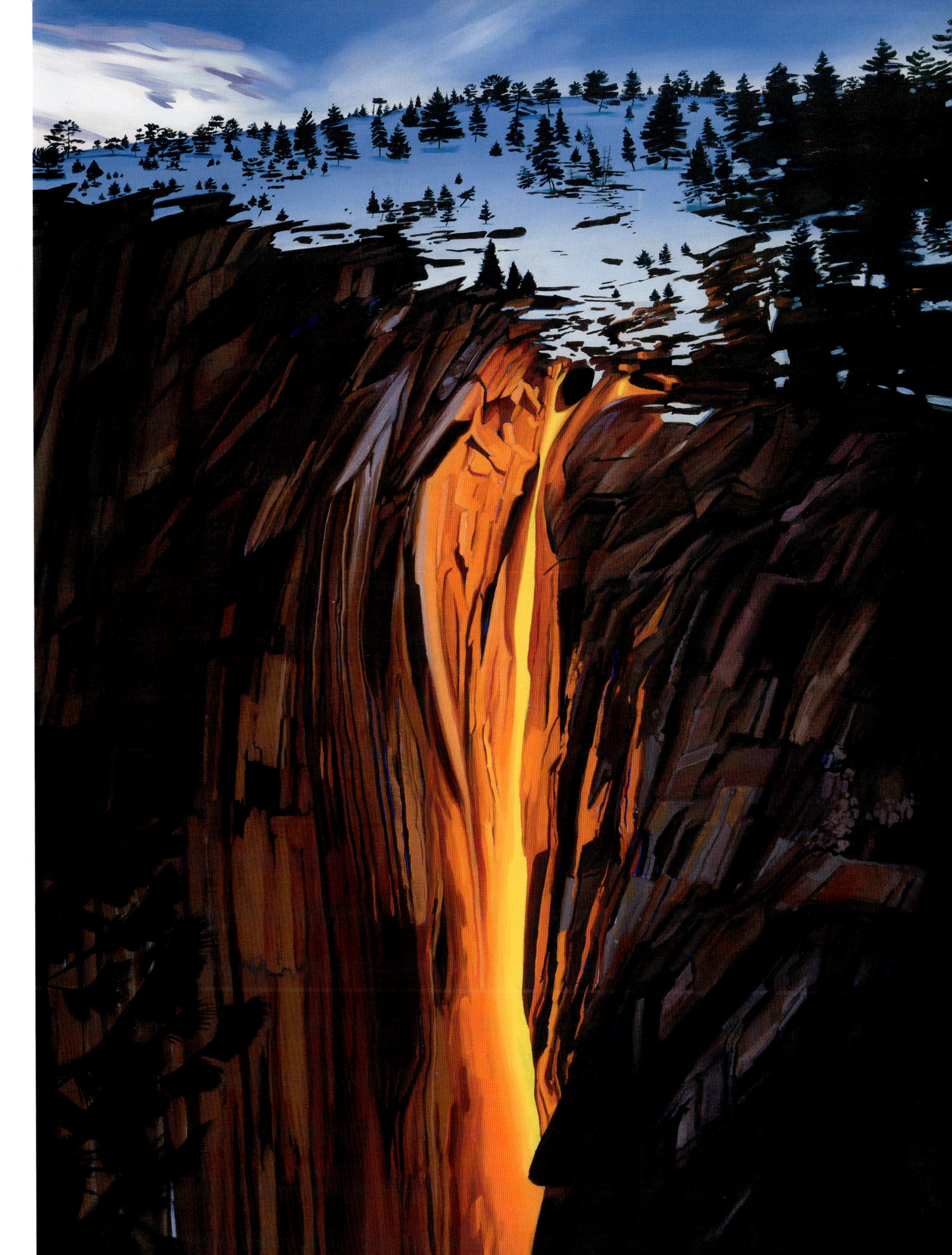

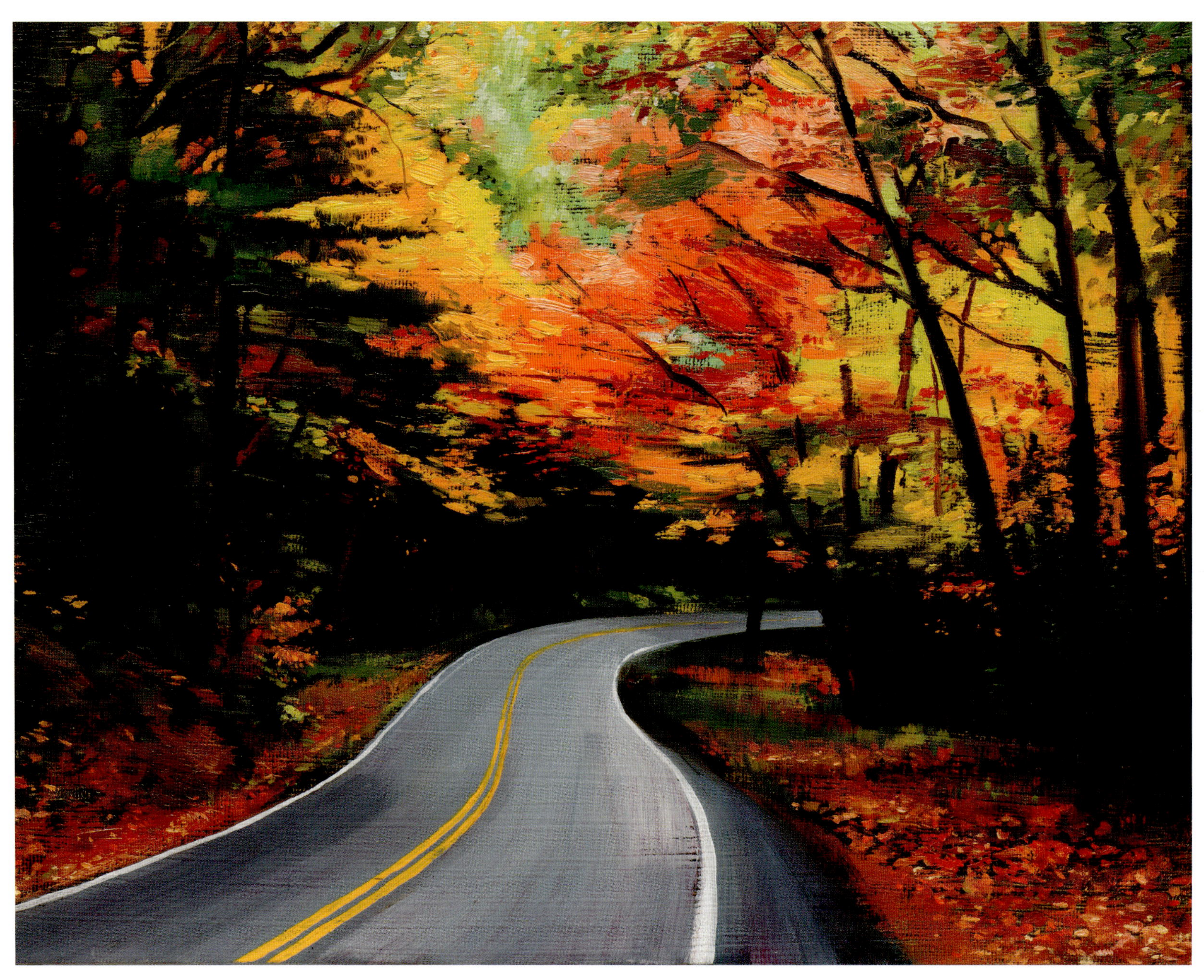

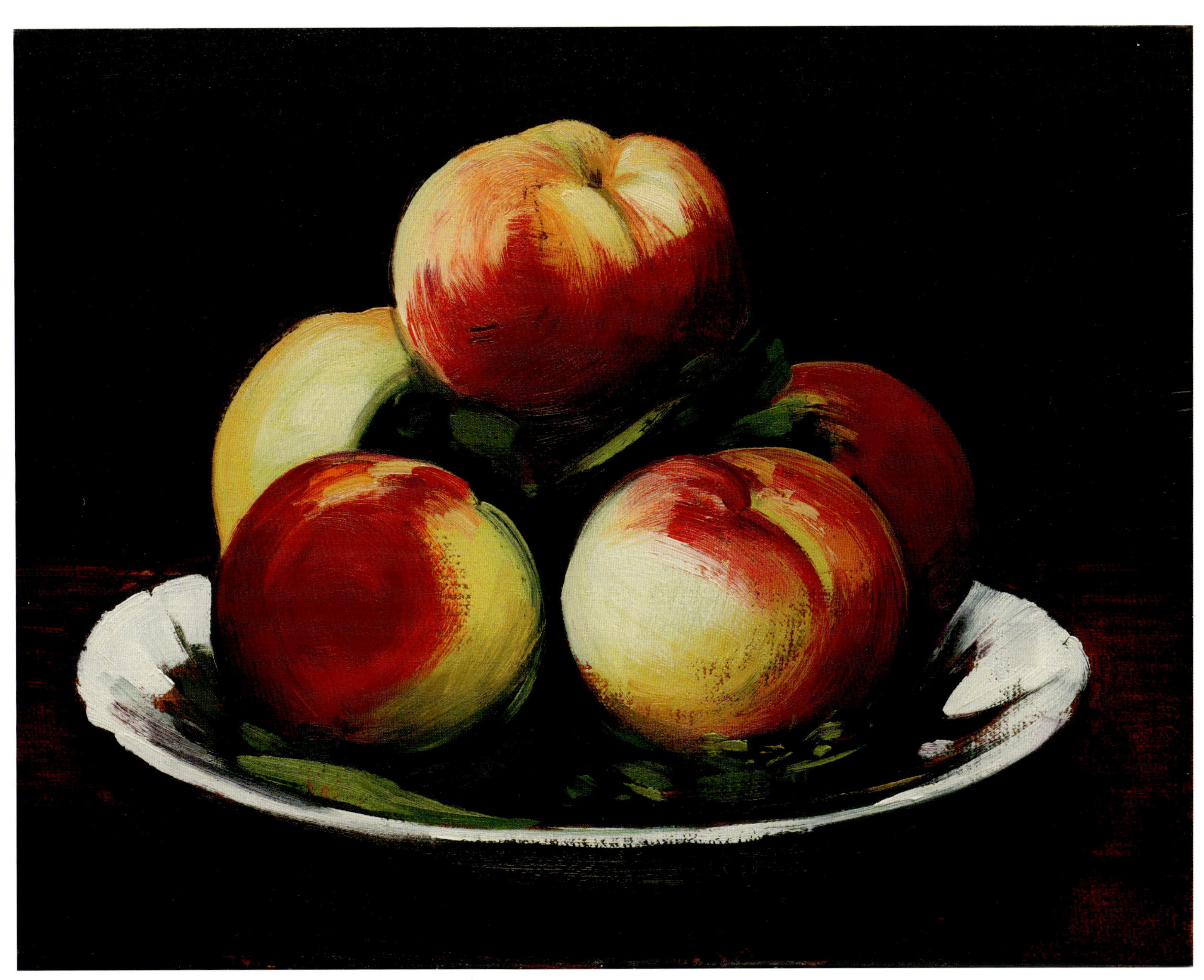

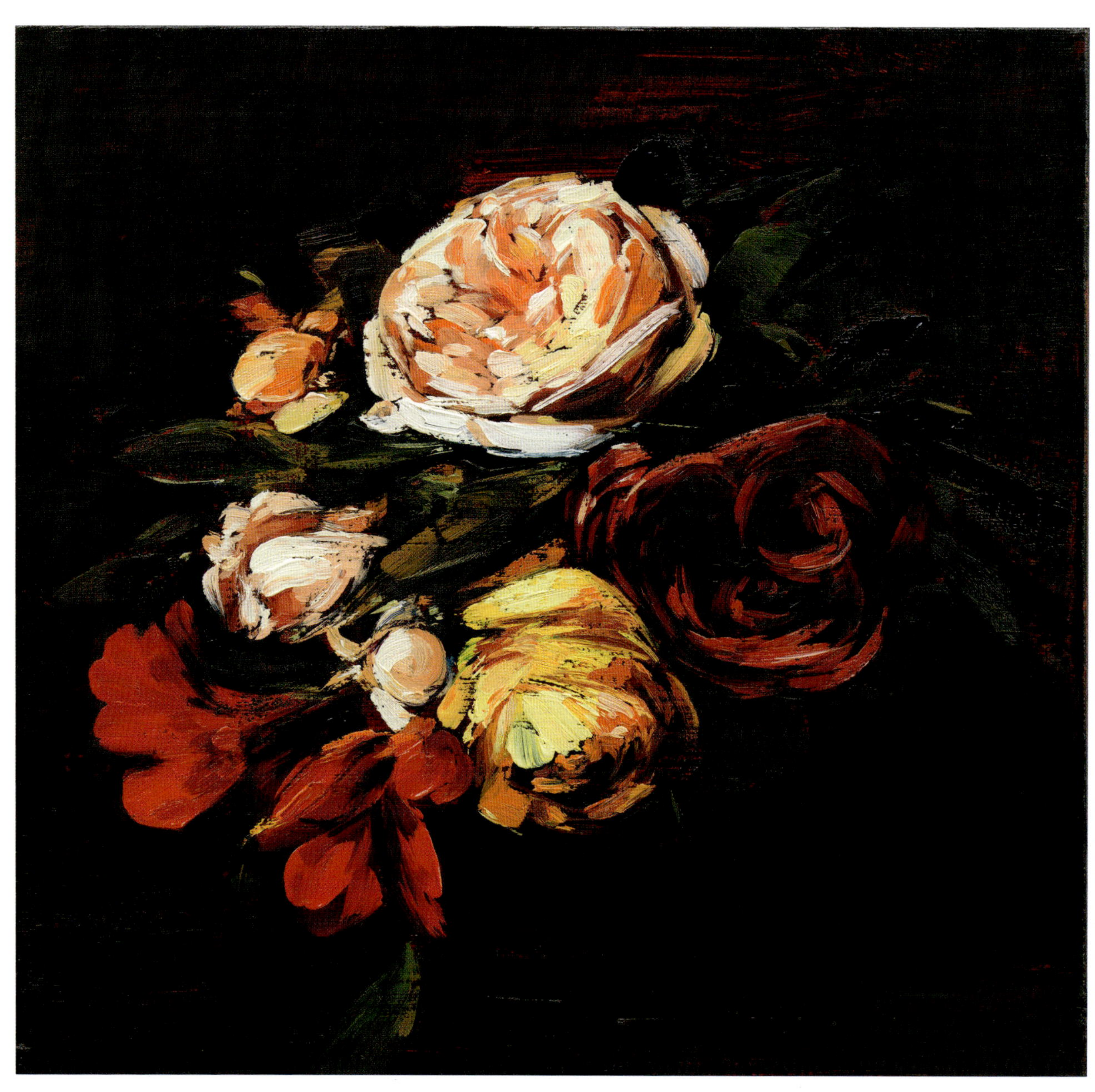

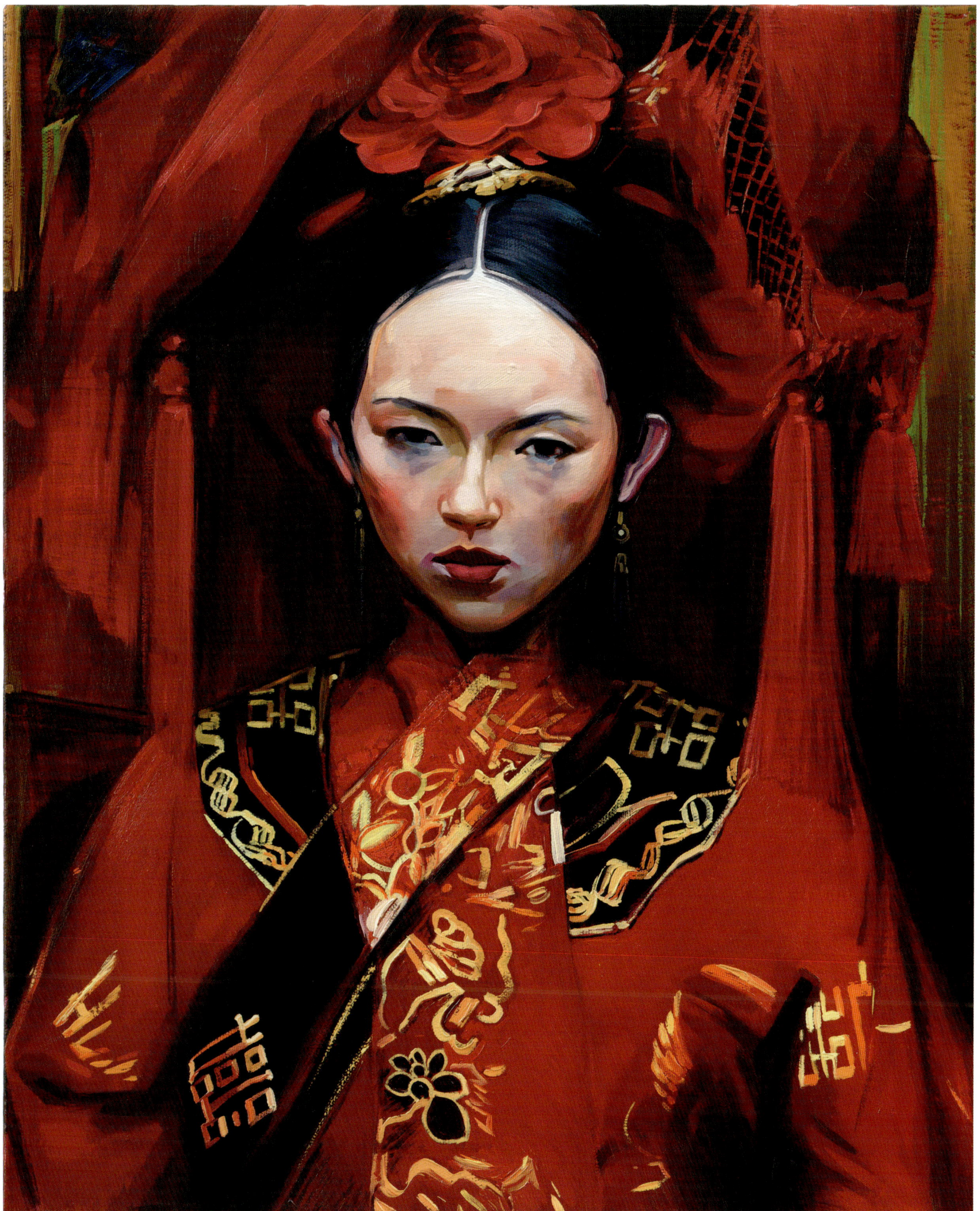

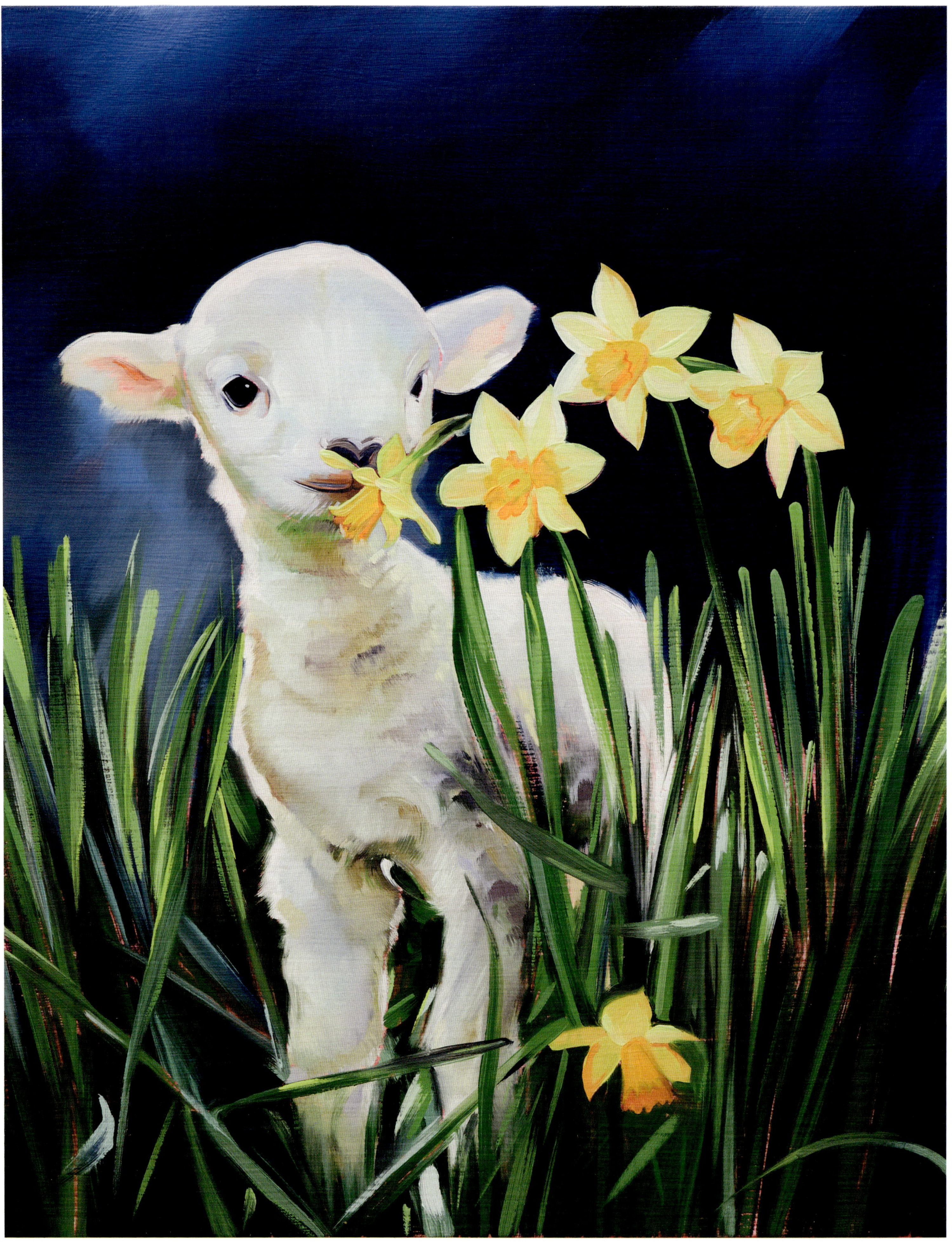

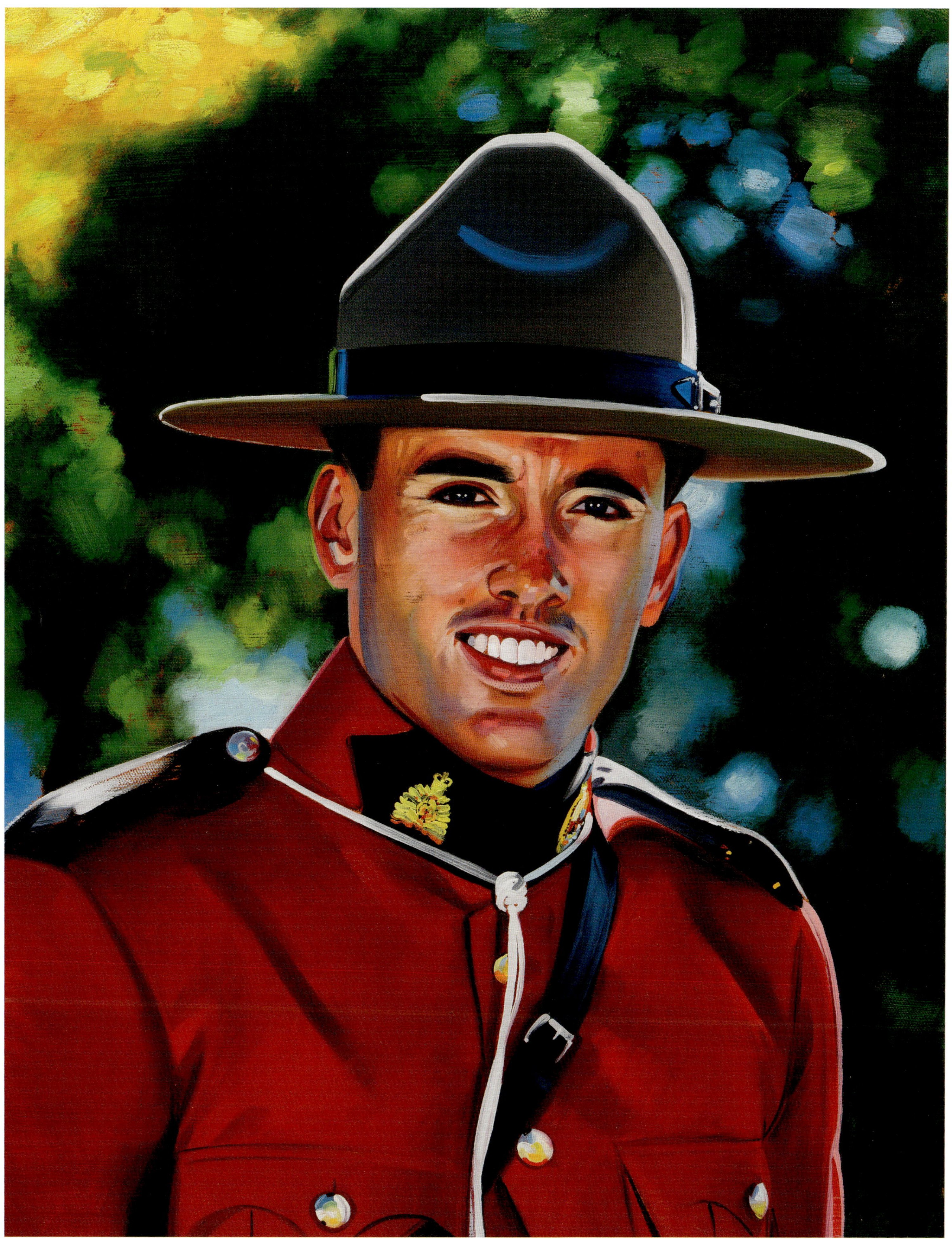

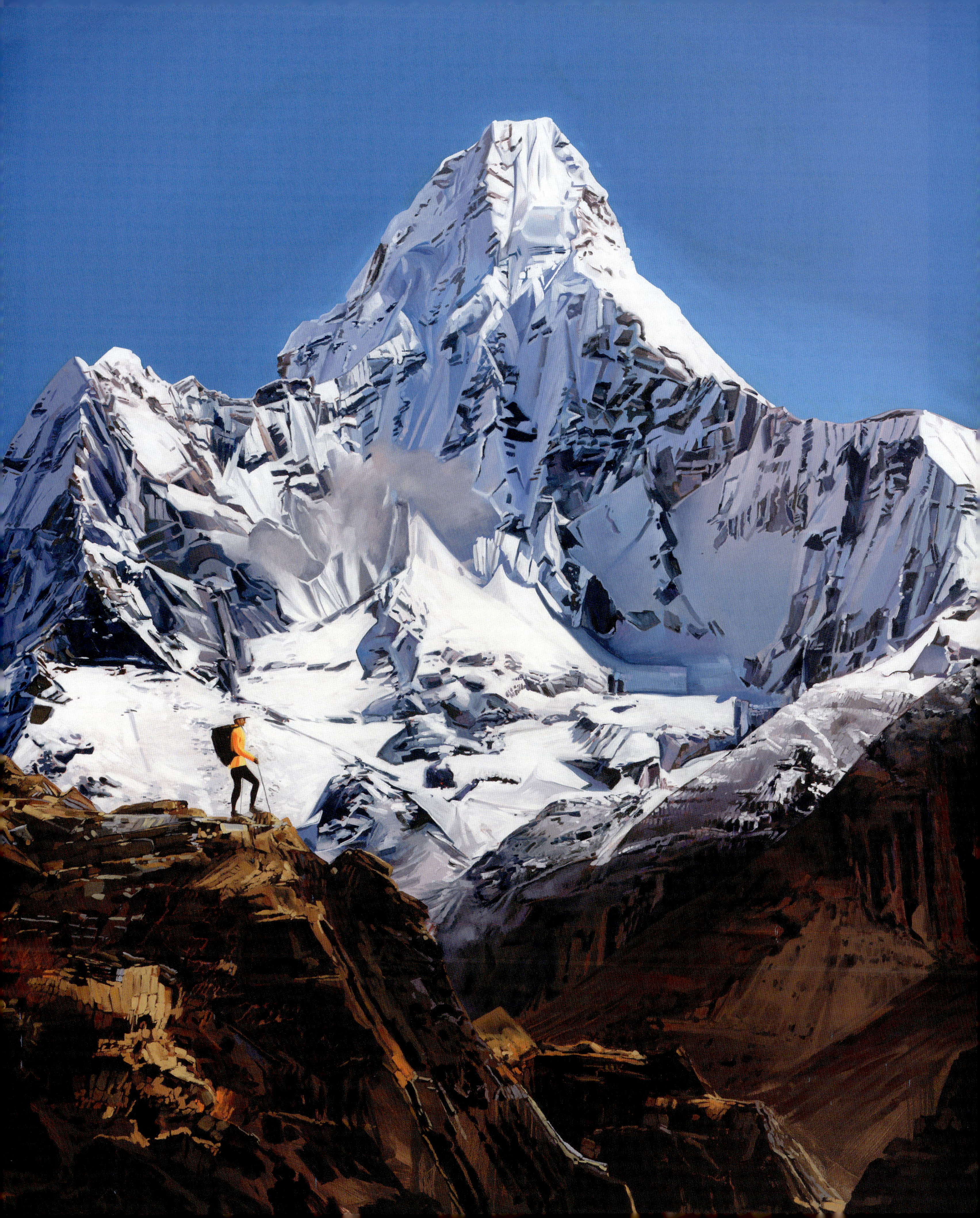

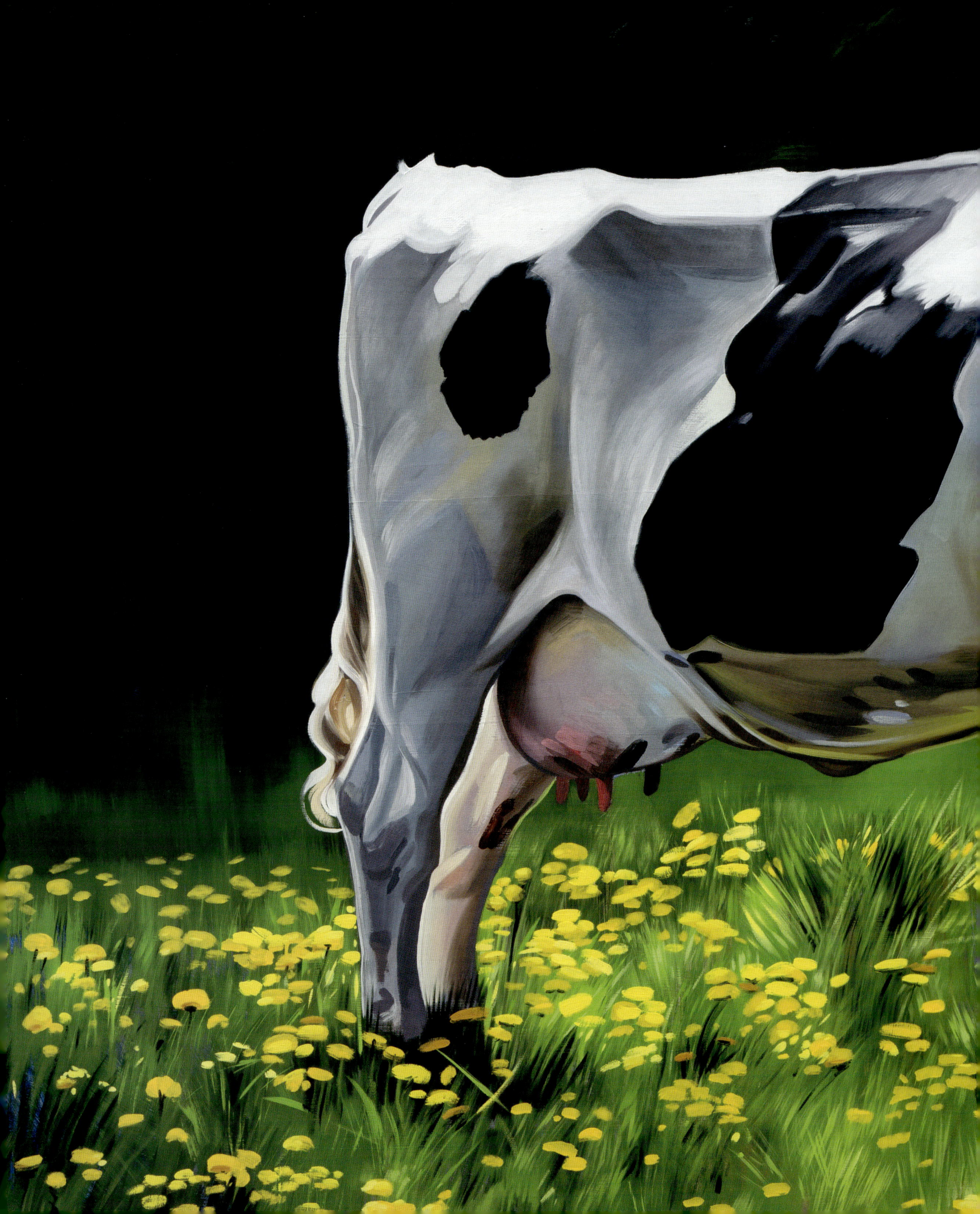

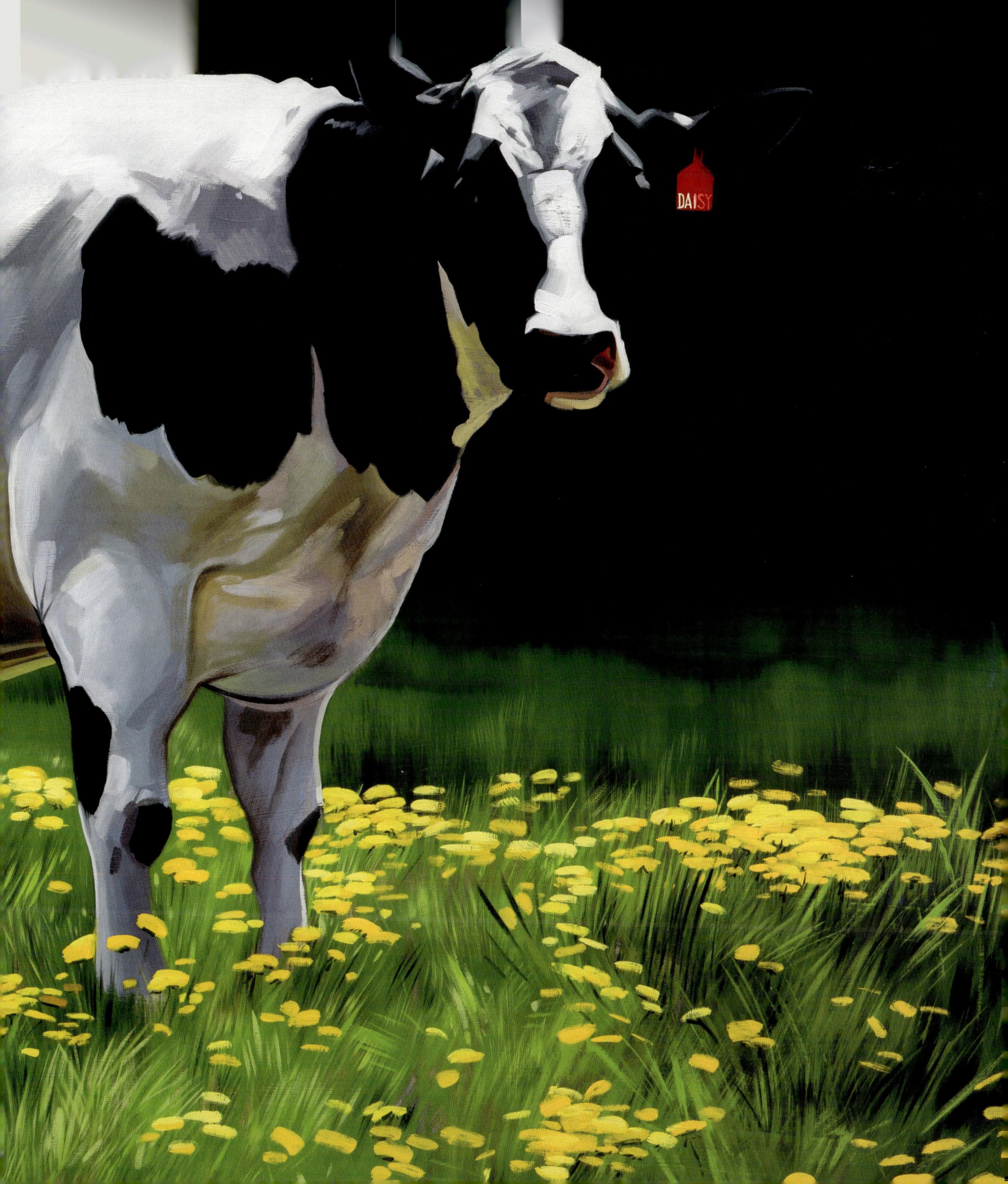
DAISY

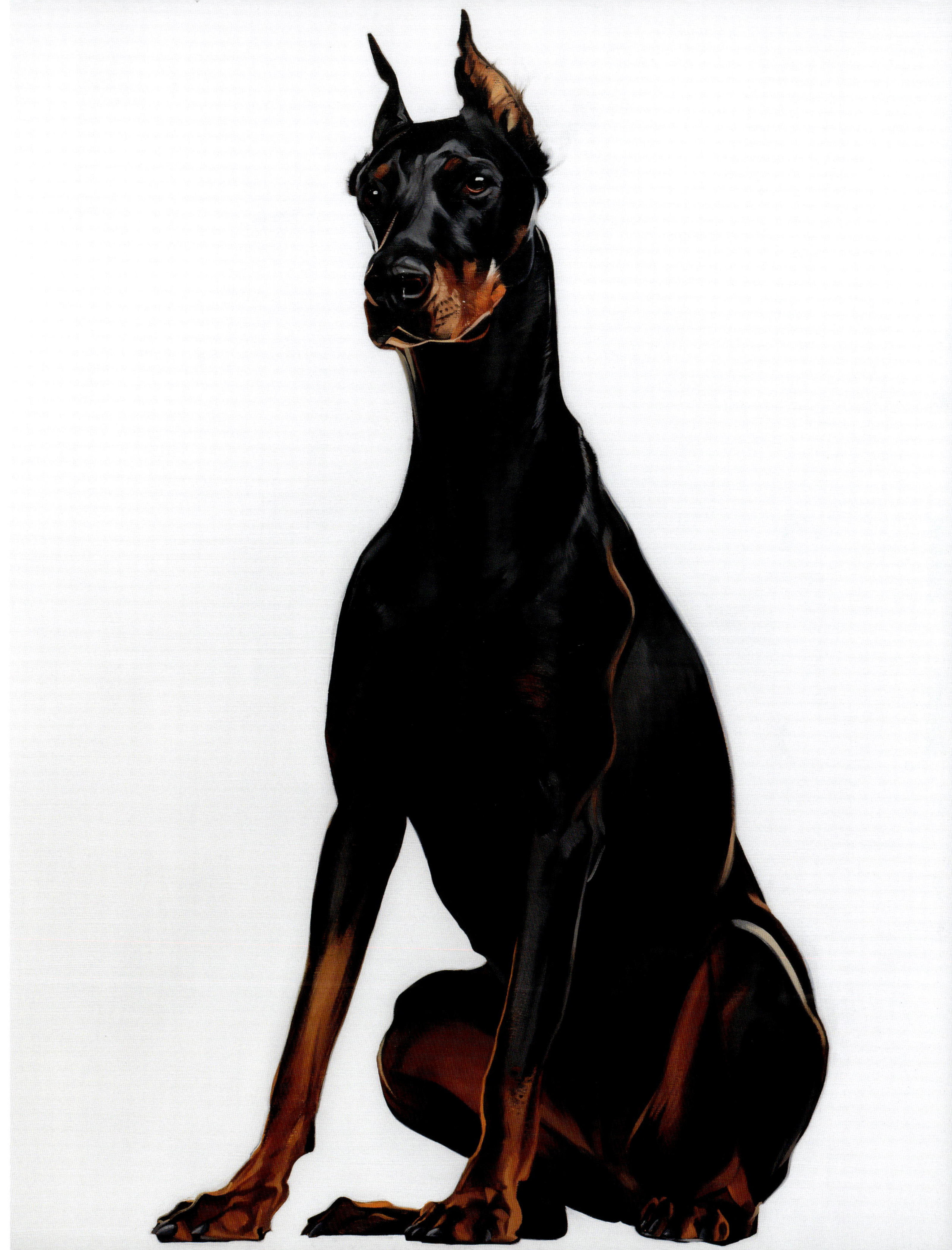

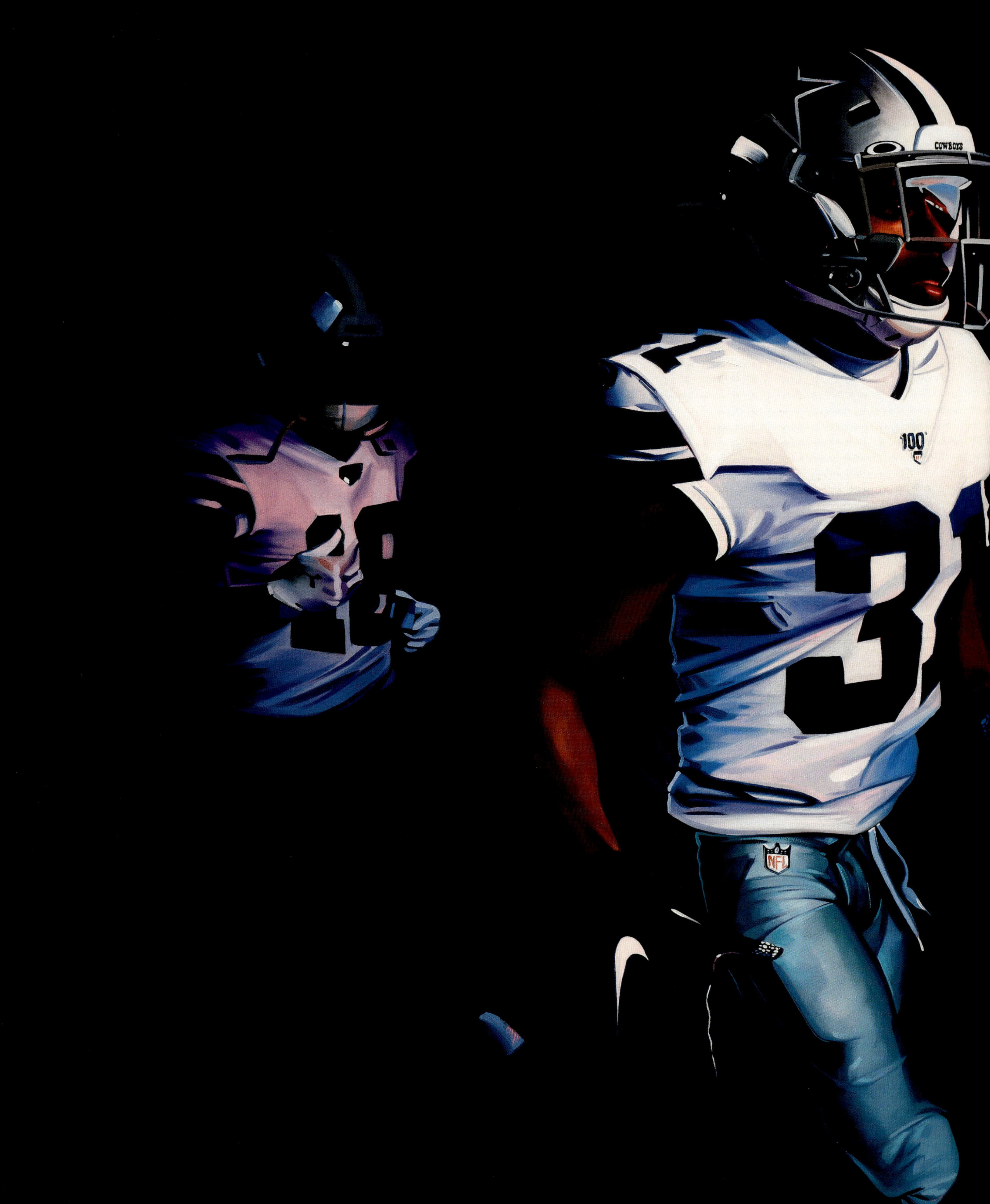
COWBOYS
100
NFL

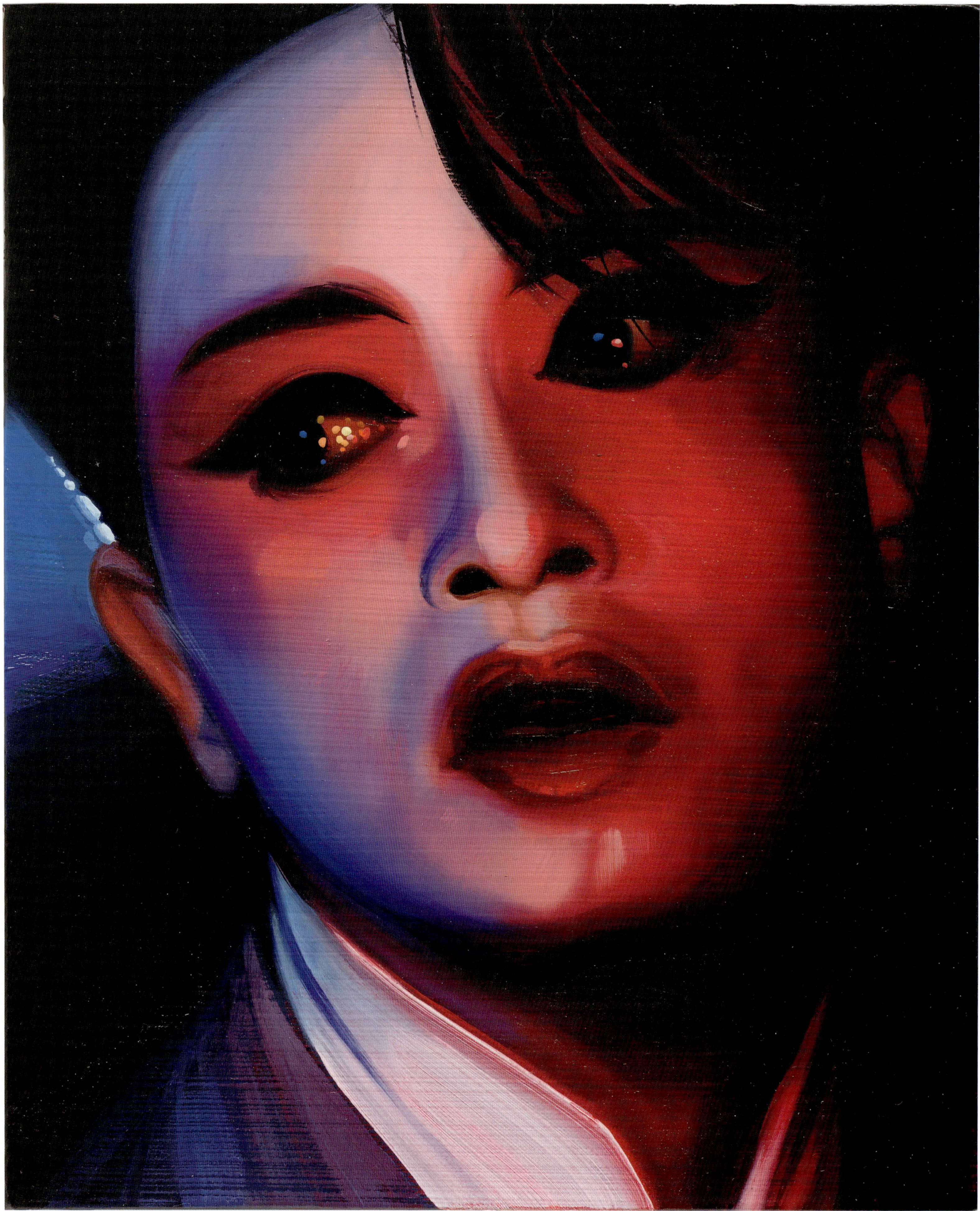

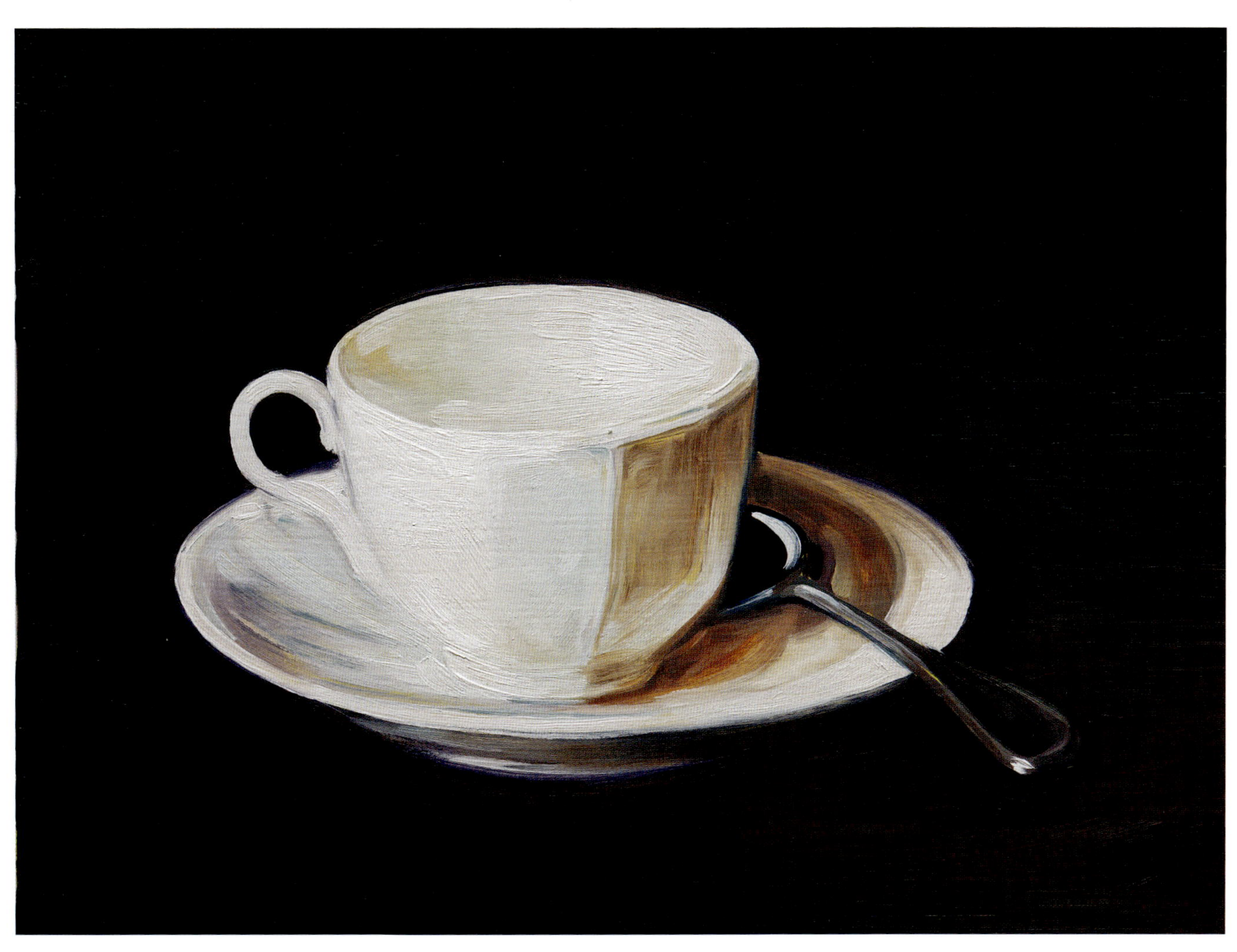

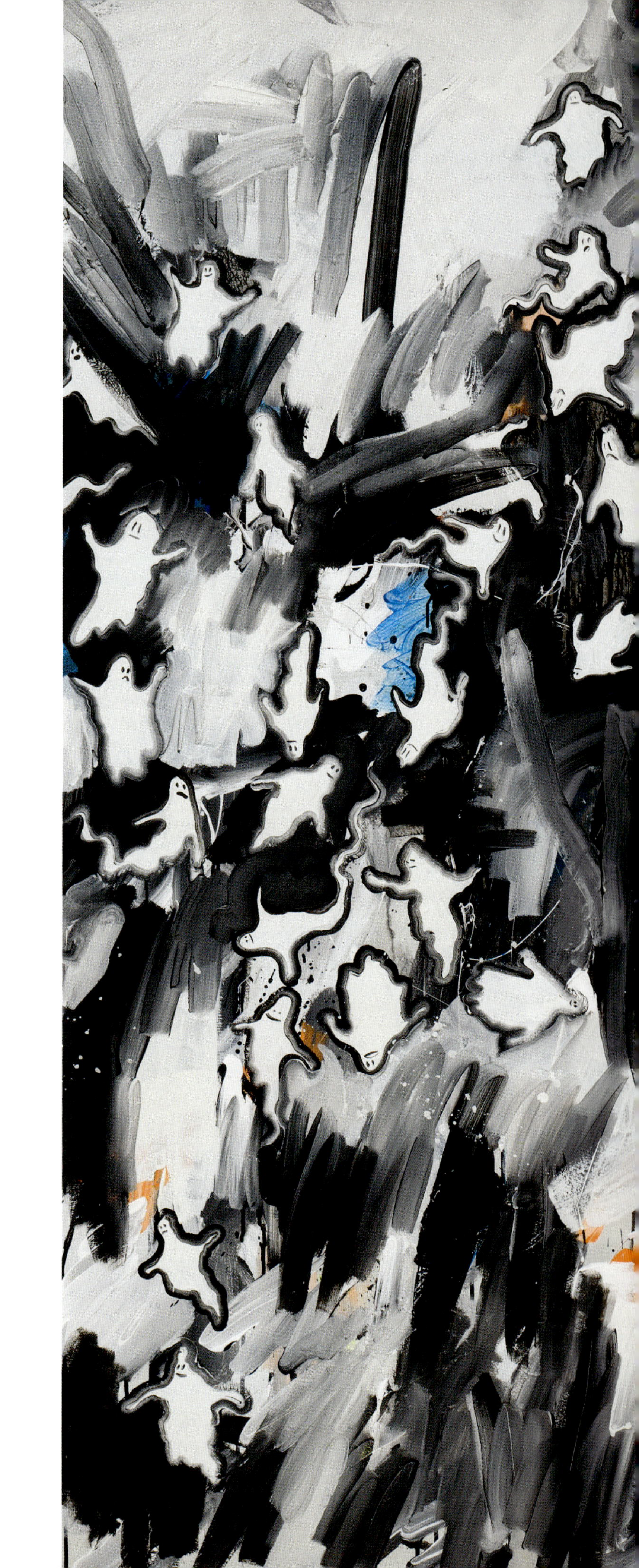

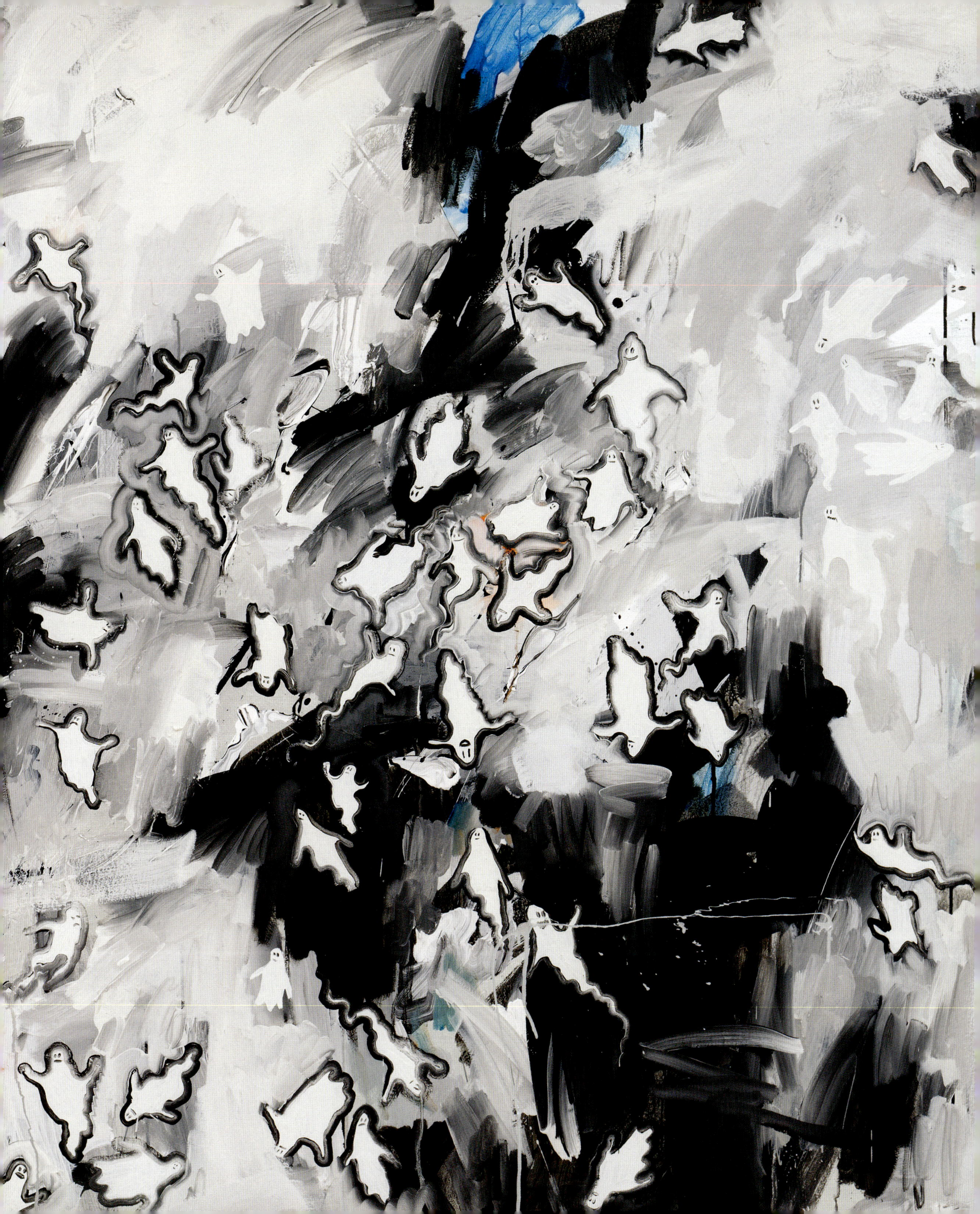

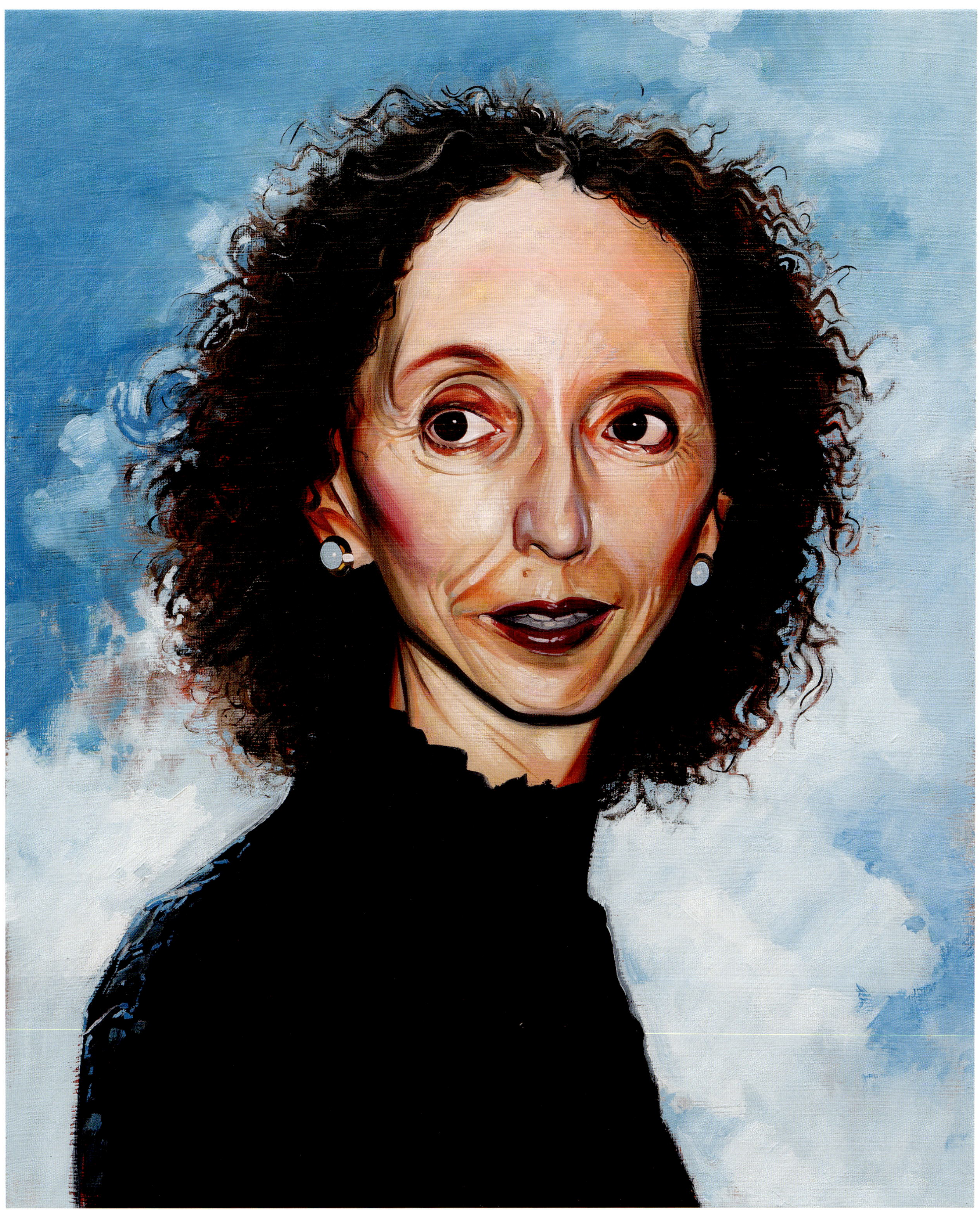

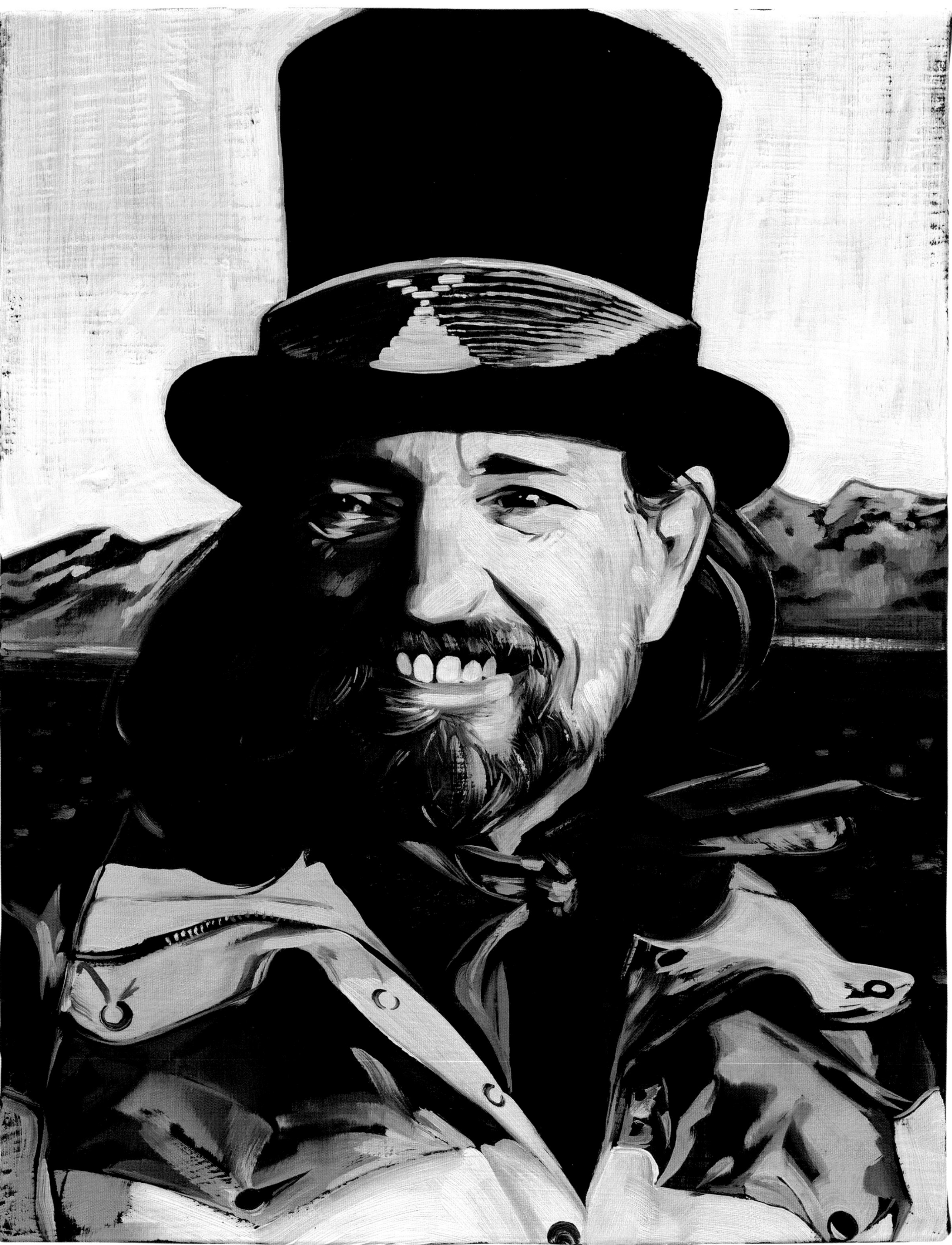

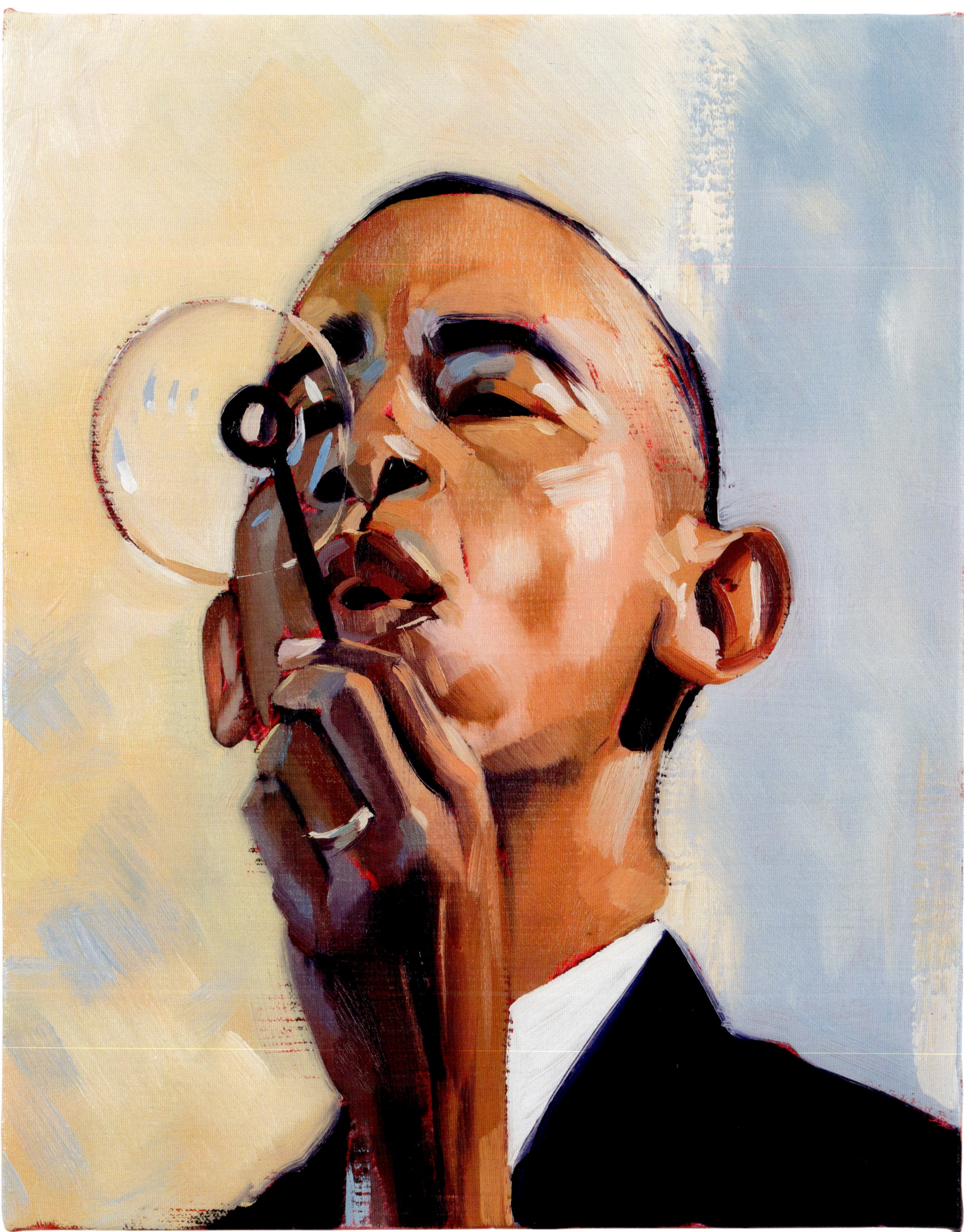

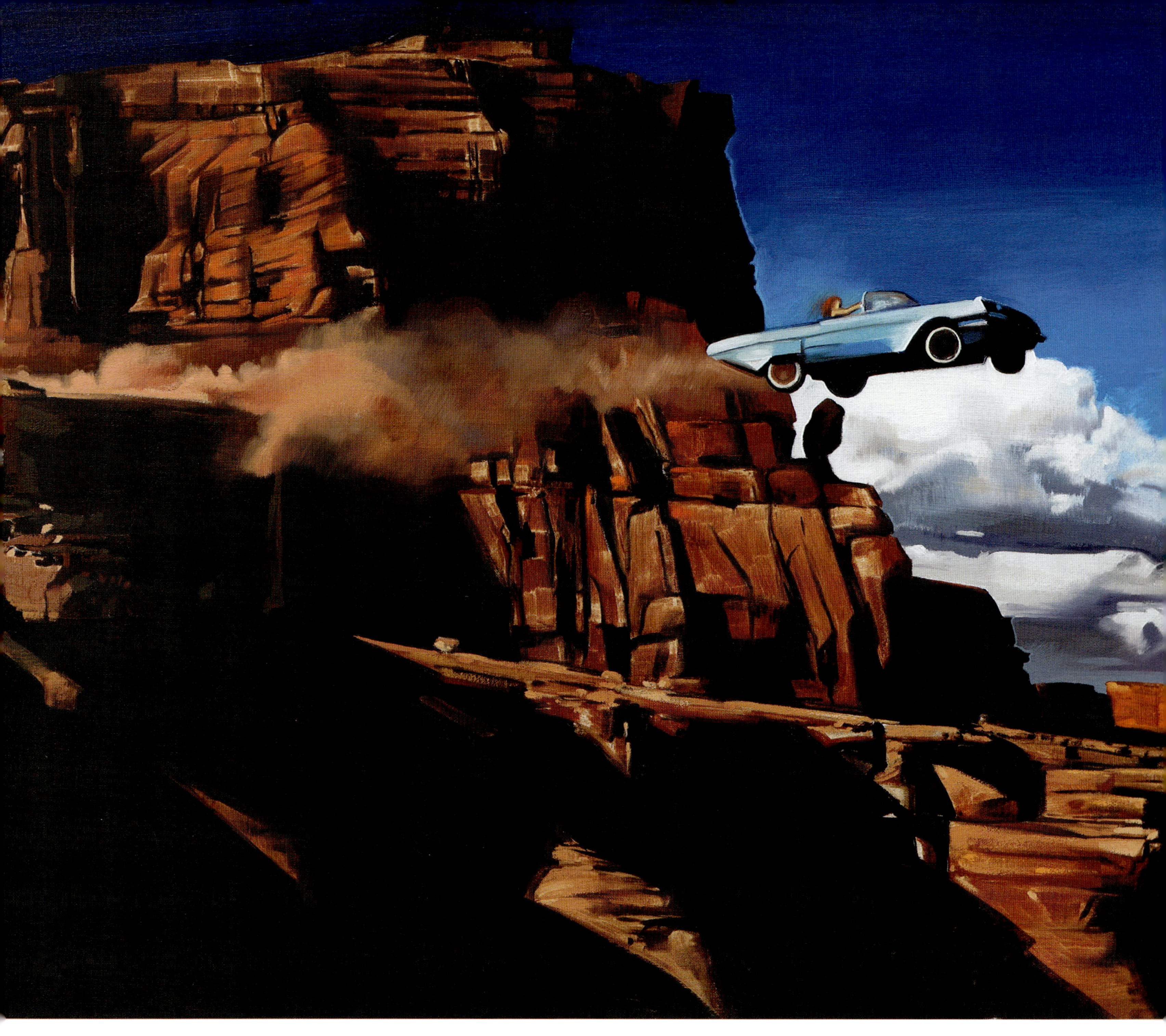

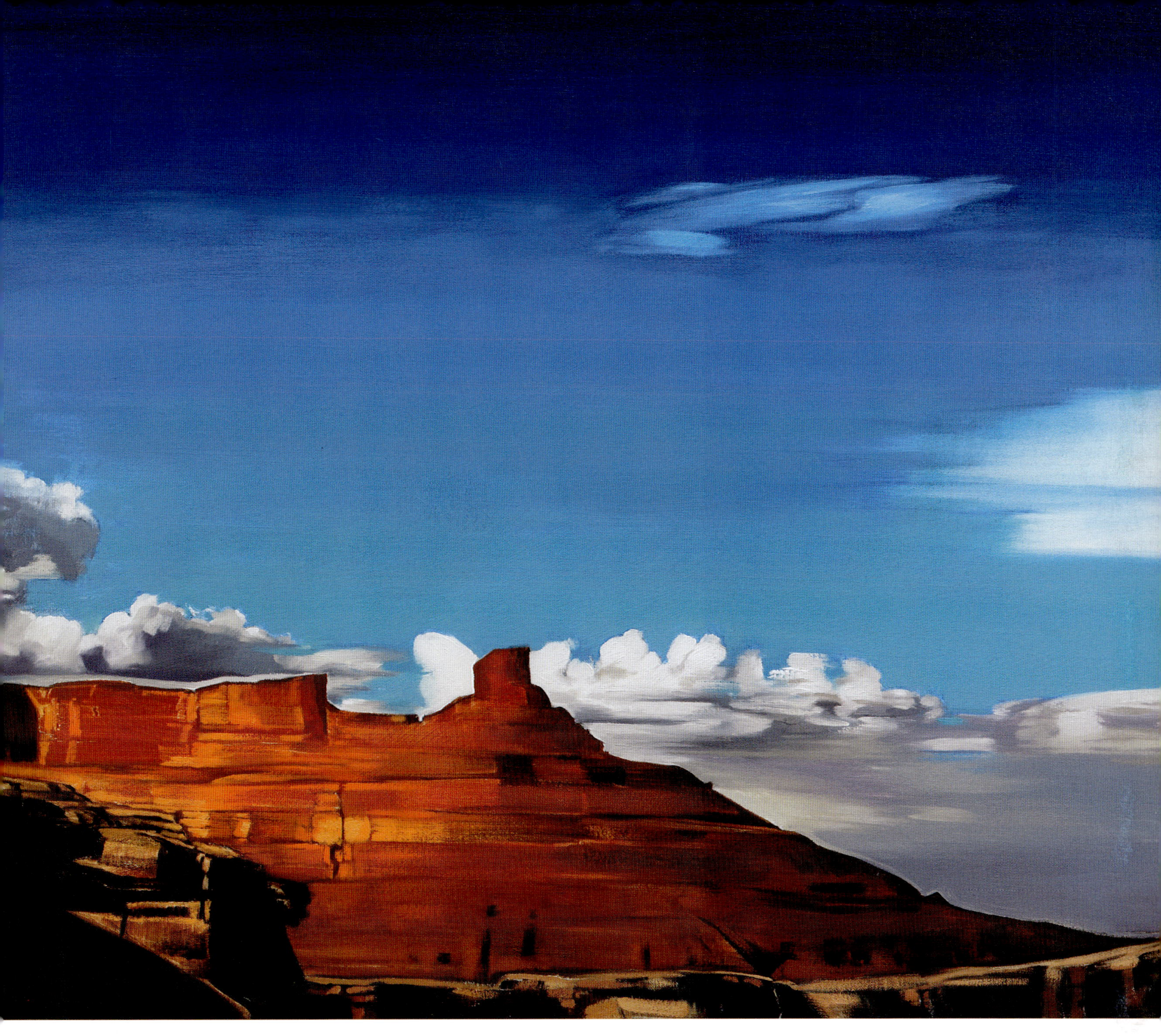

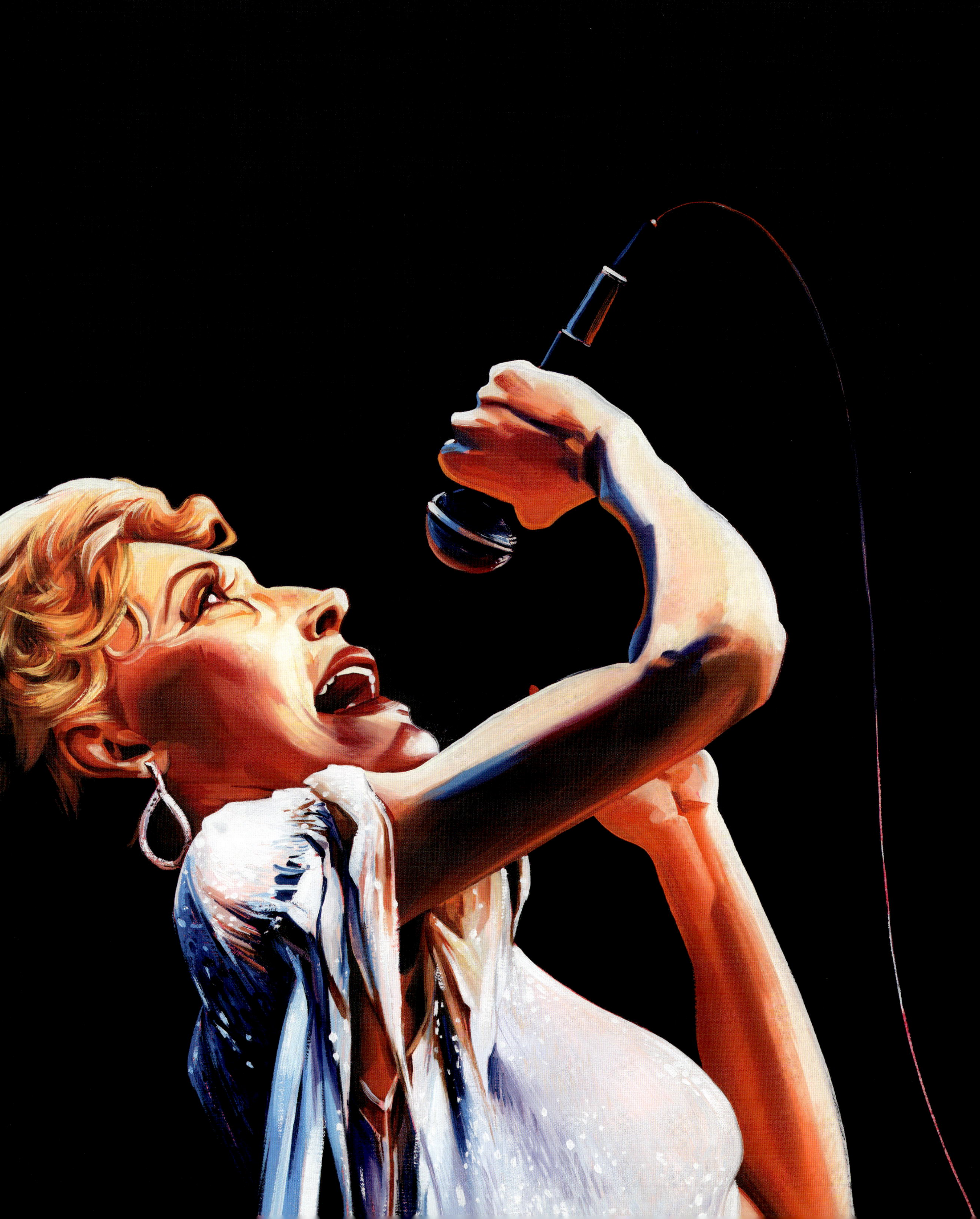

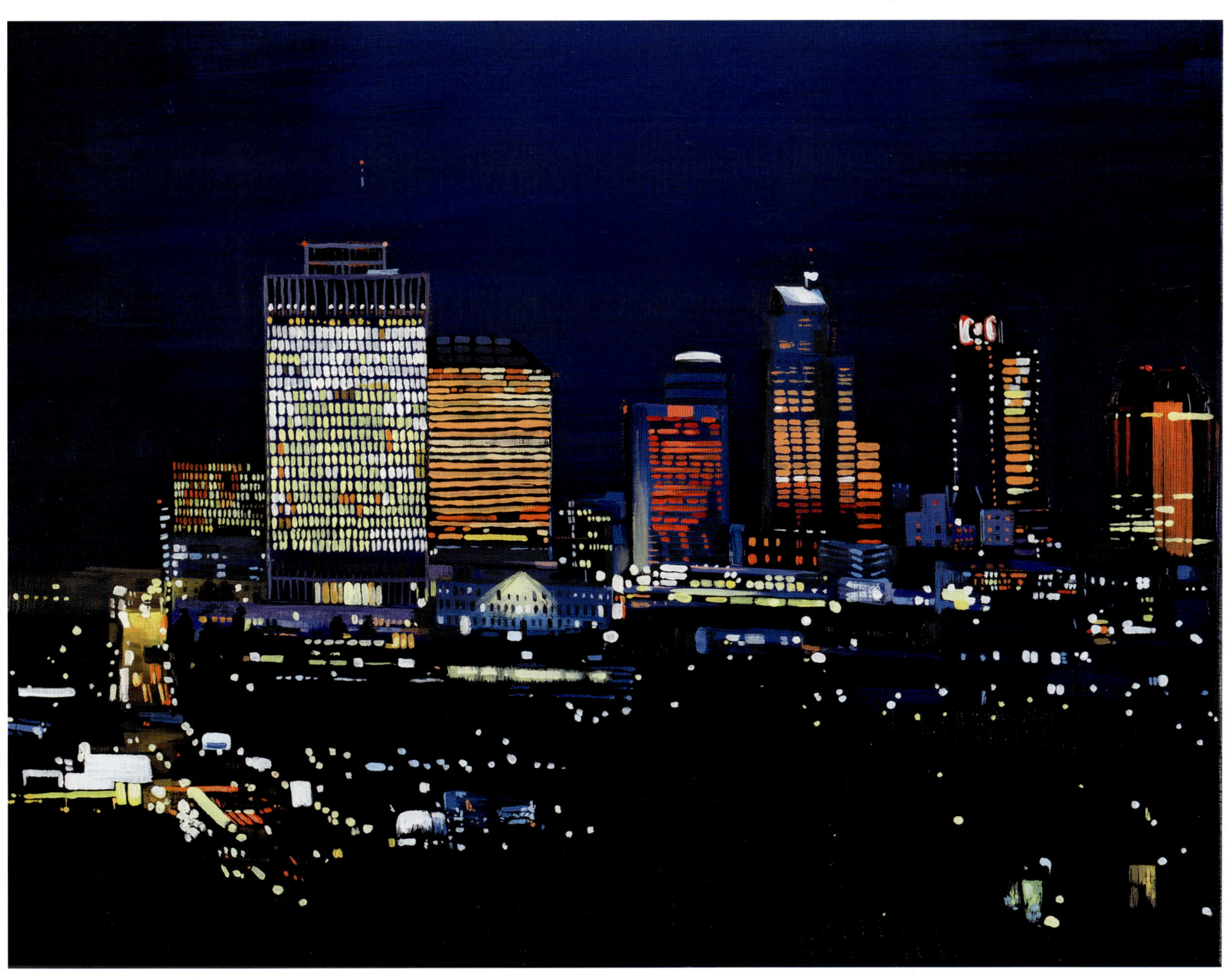

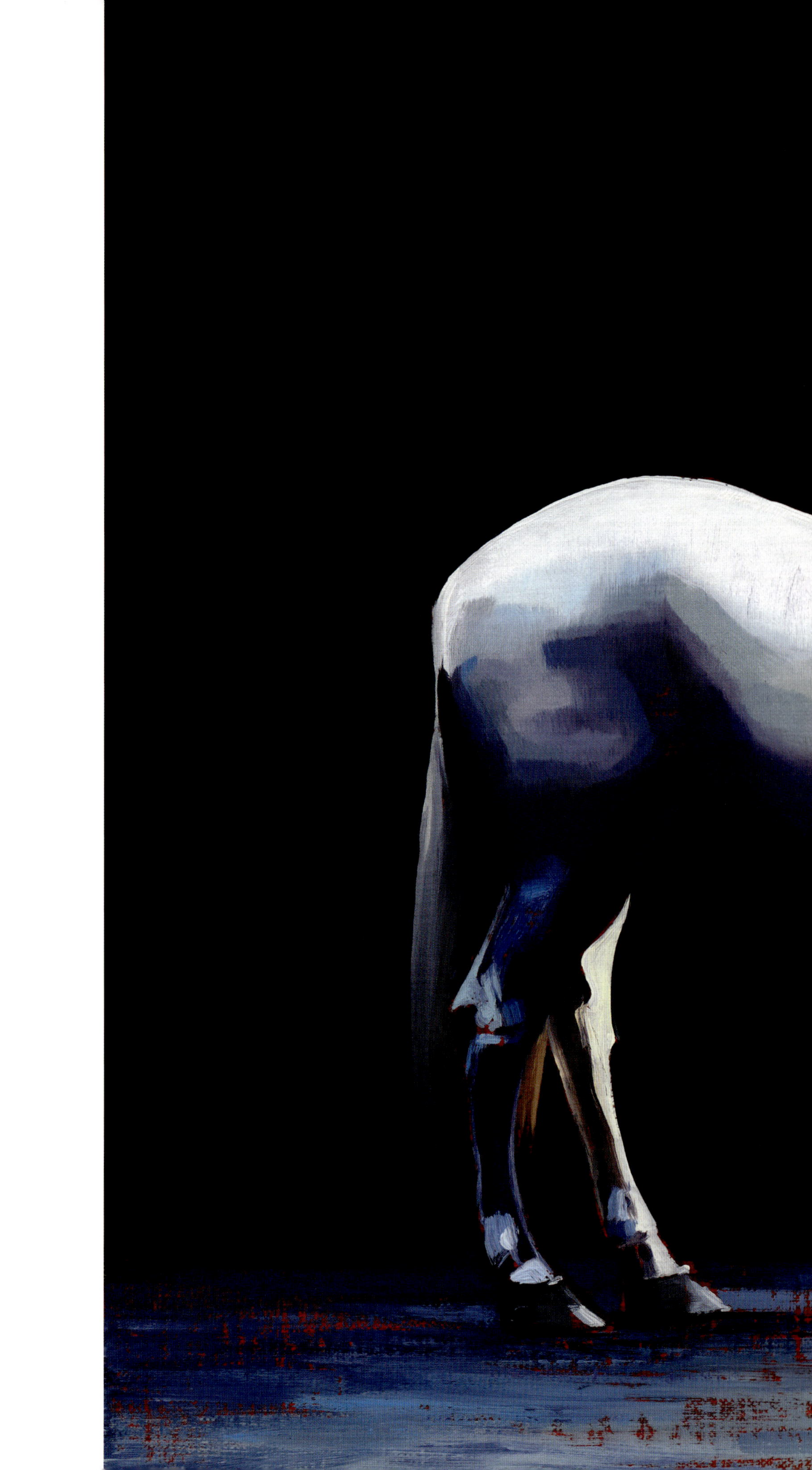

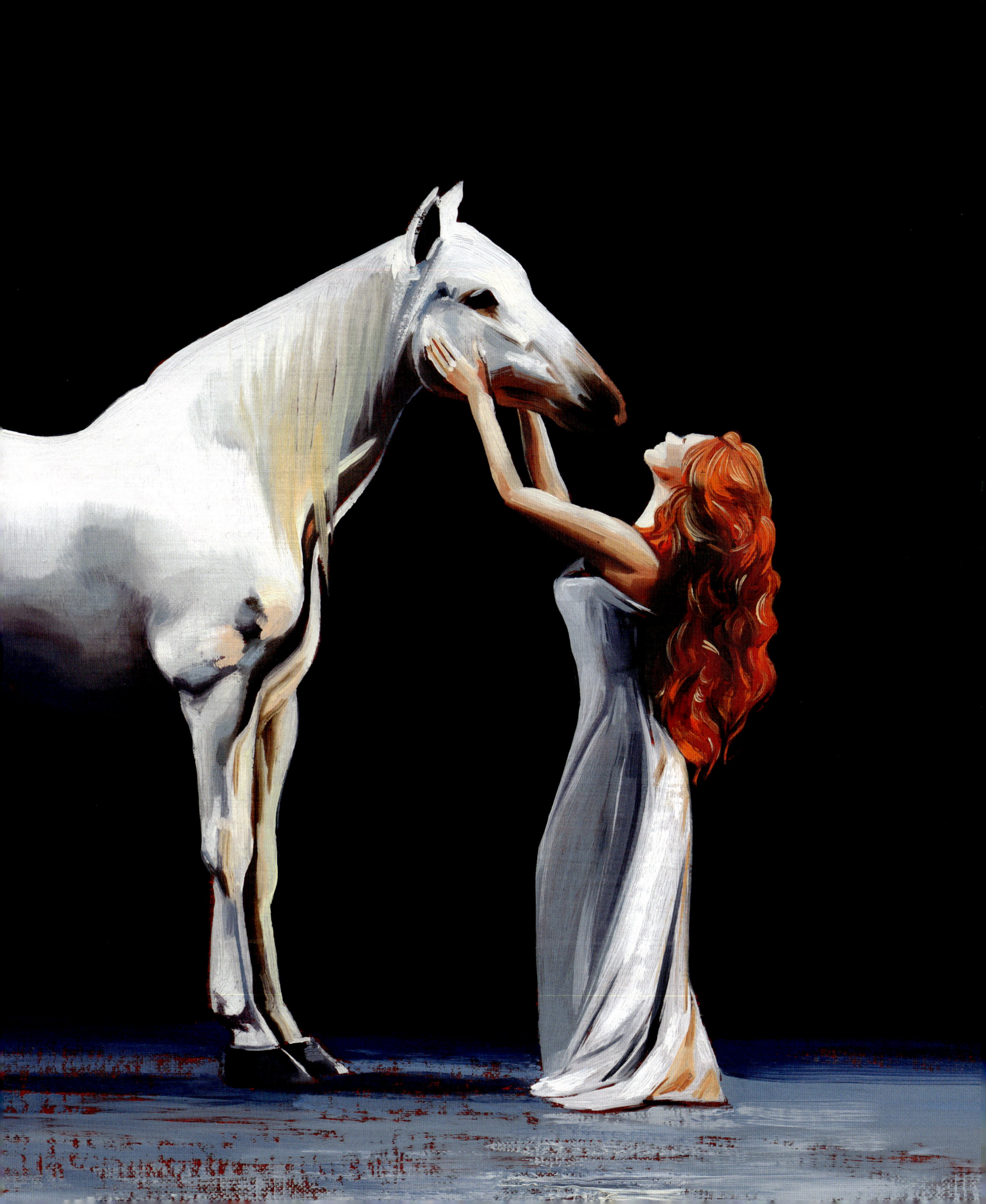

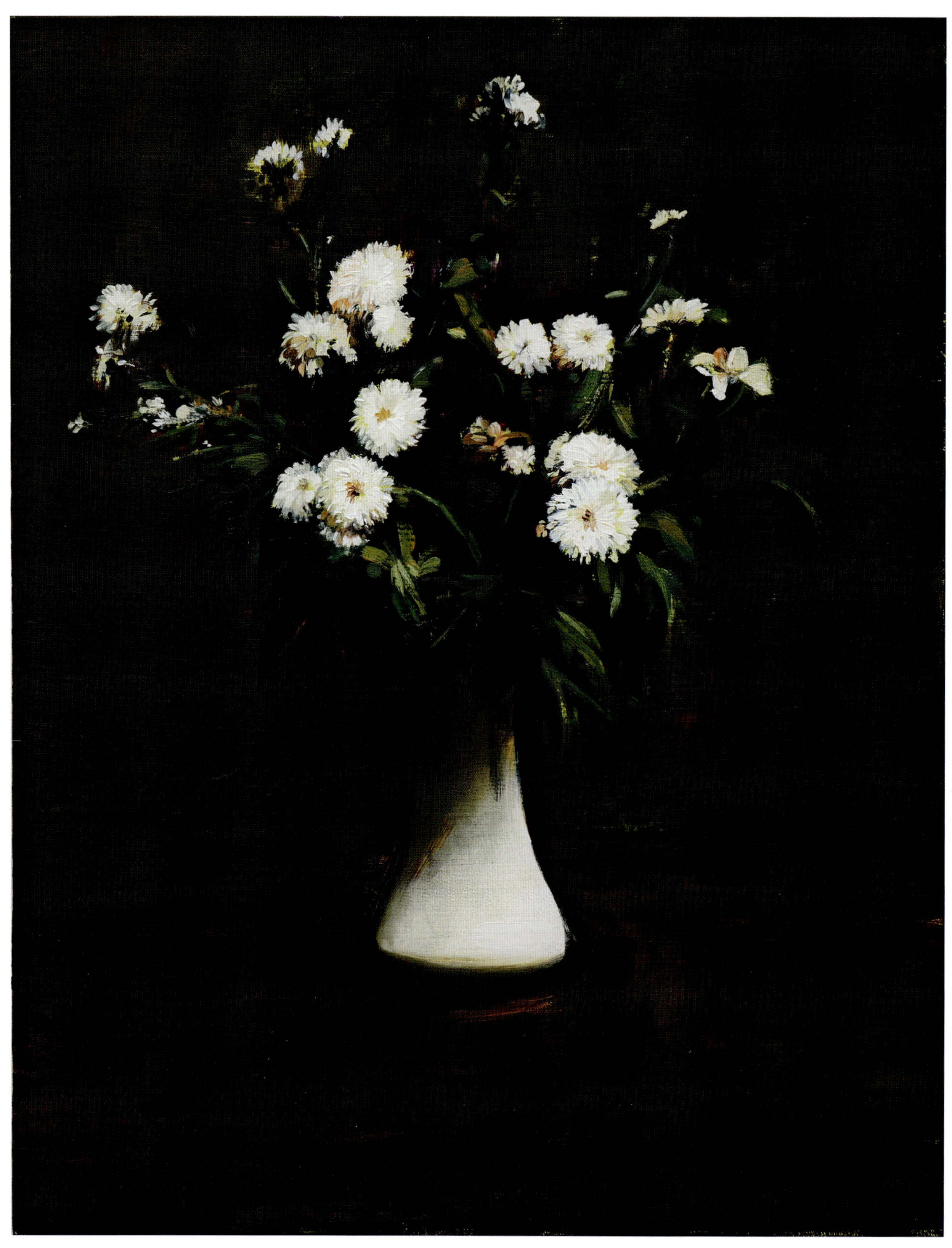

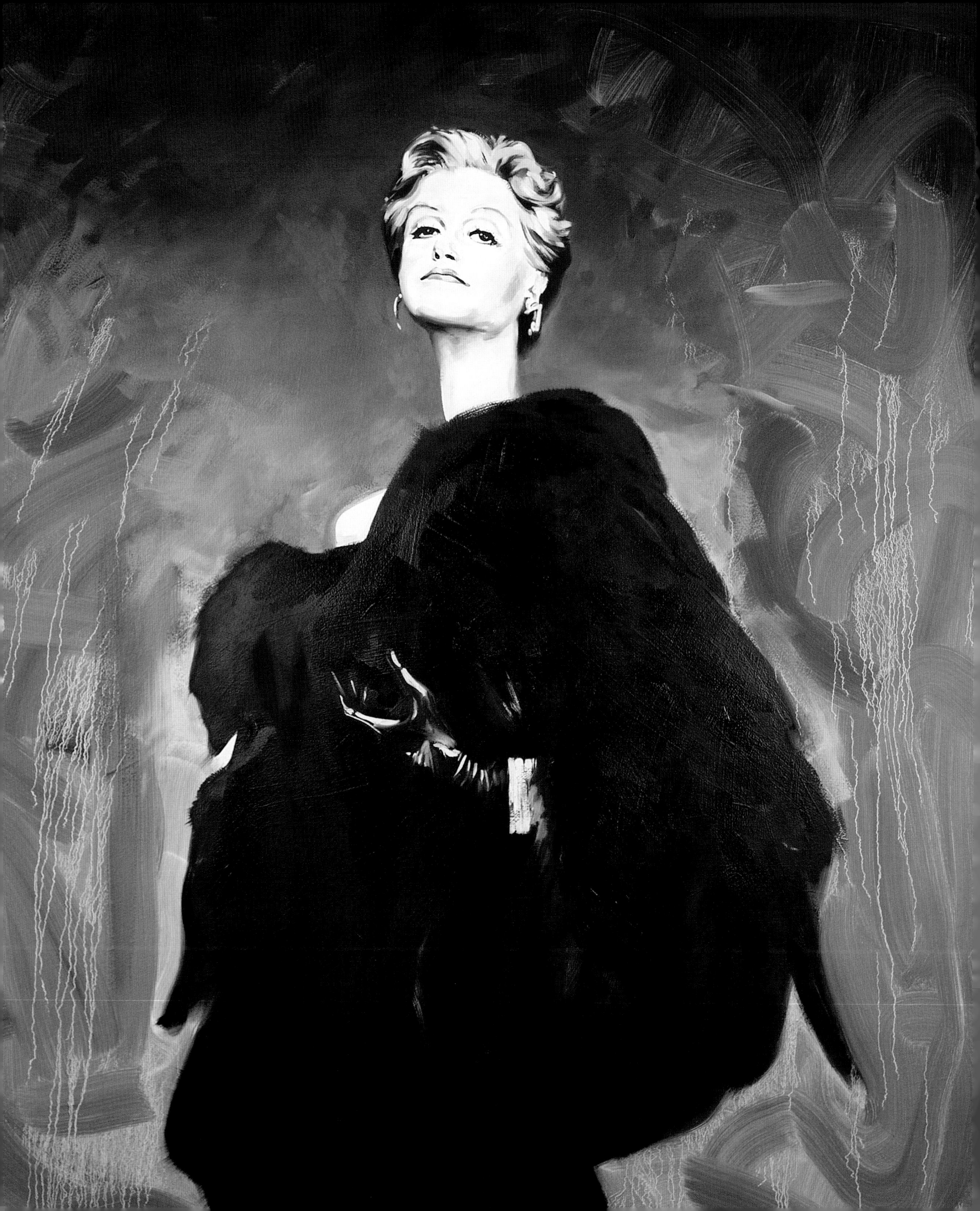

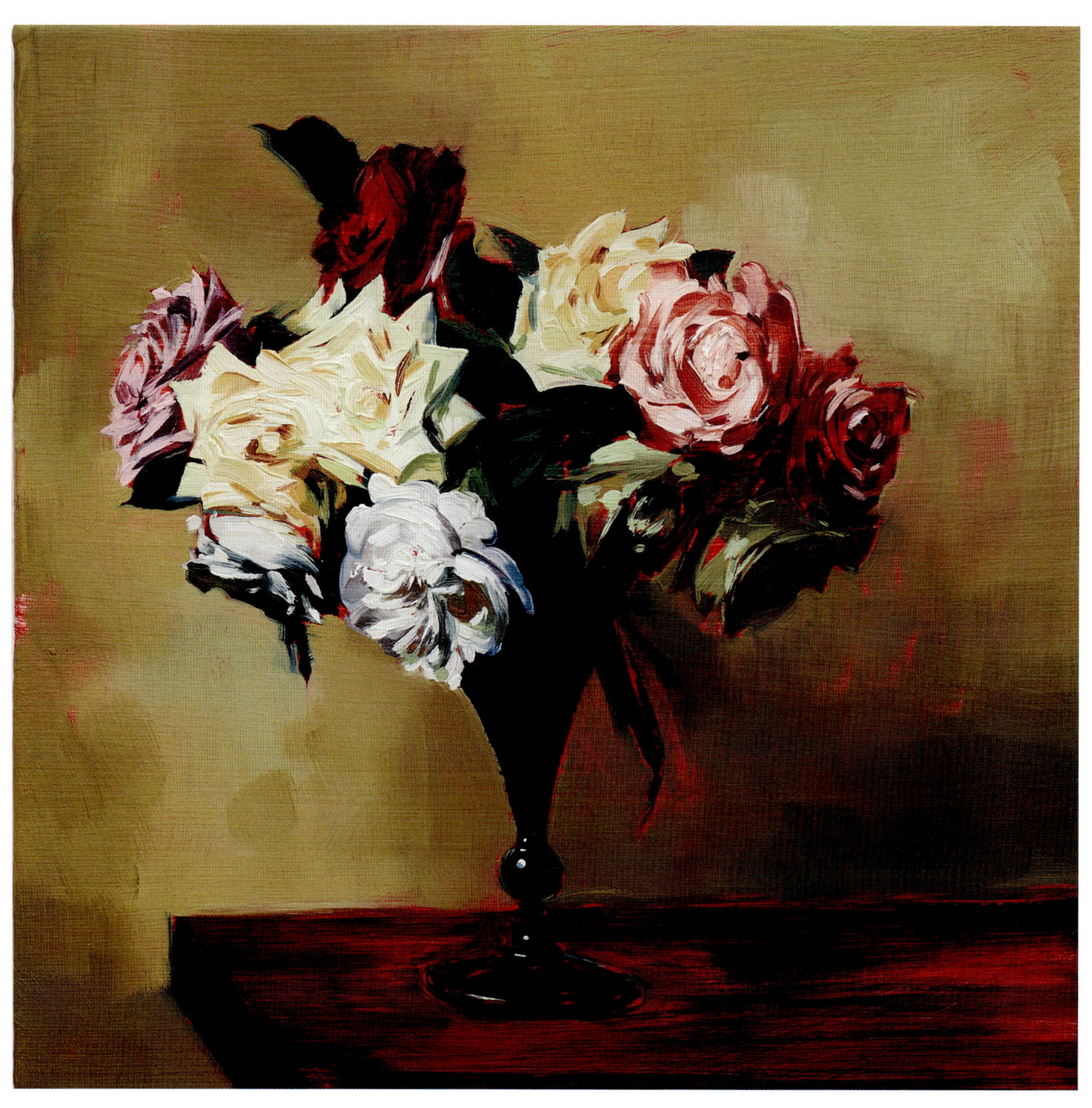

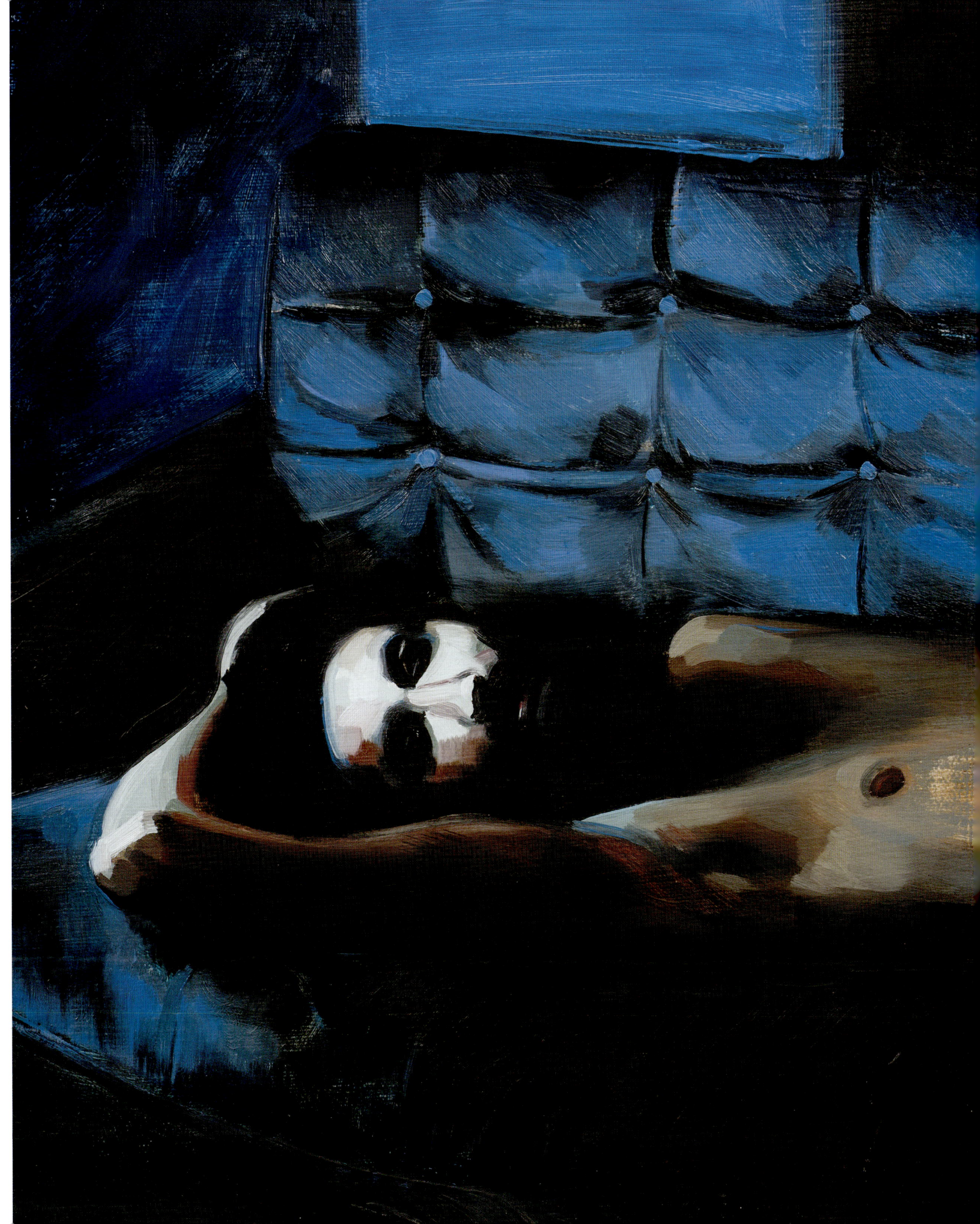

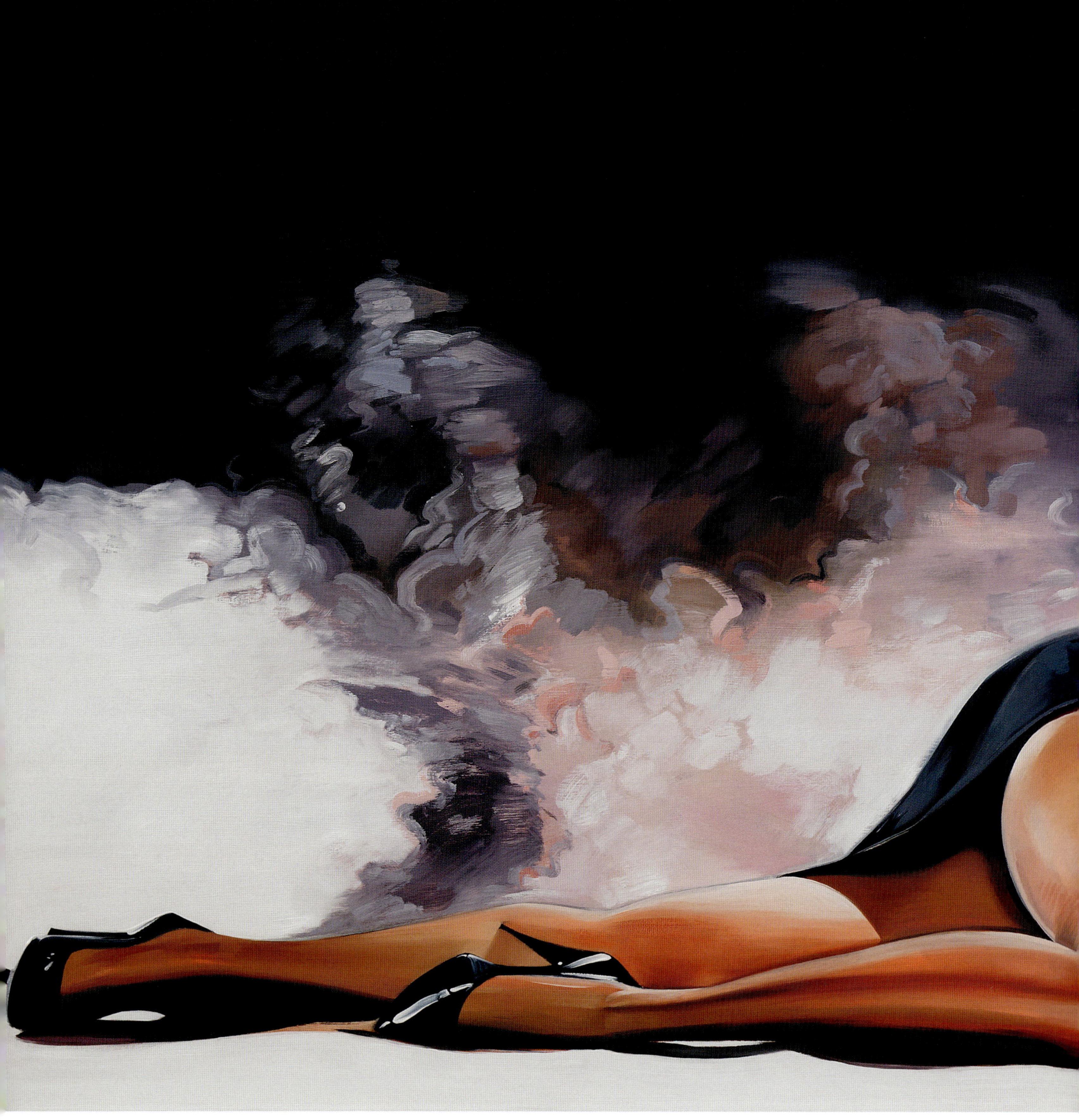

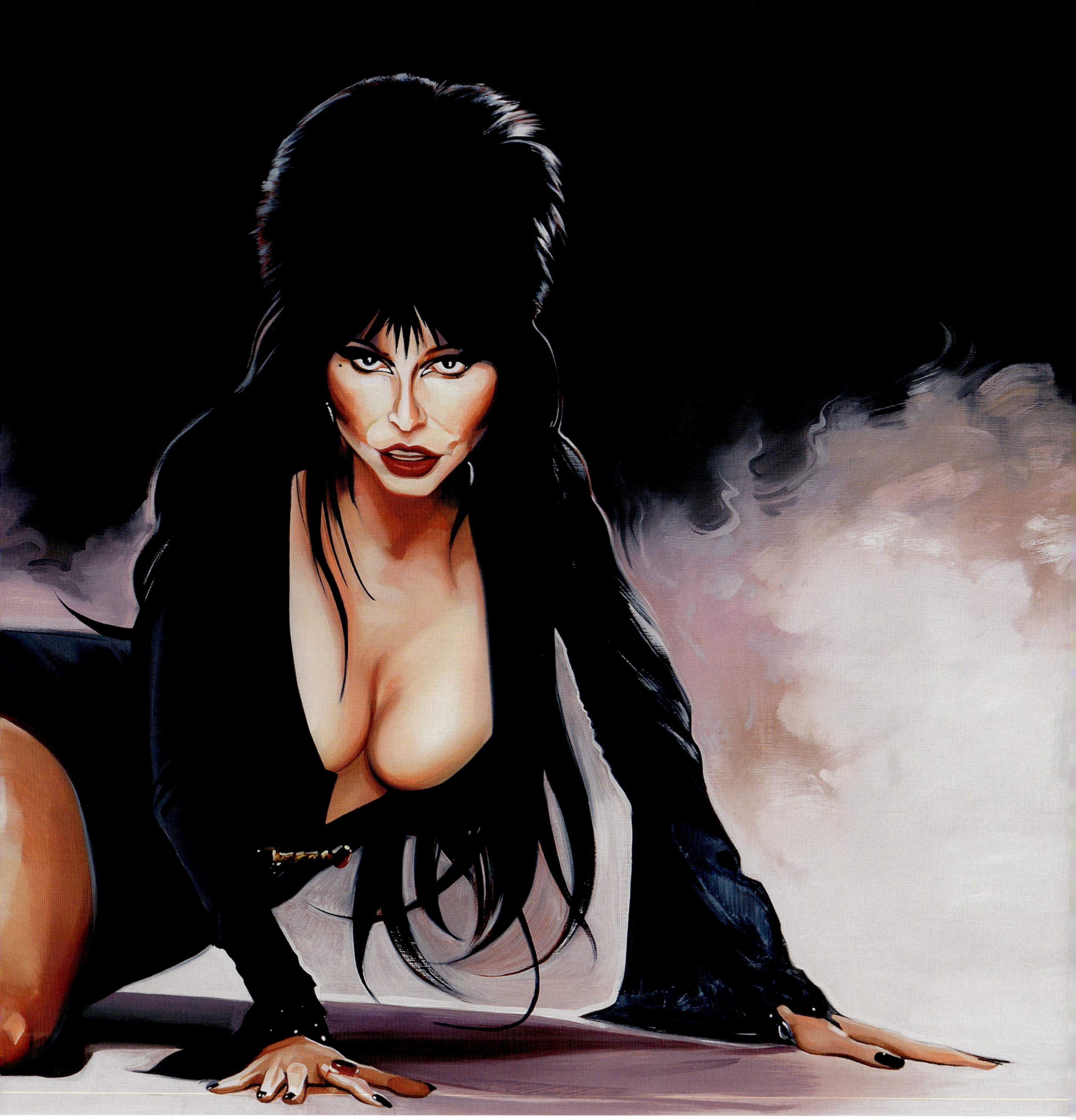

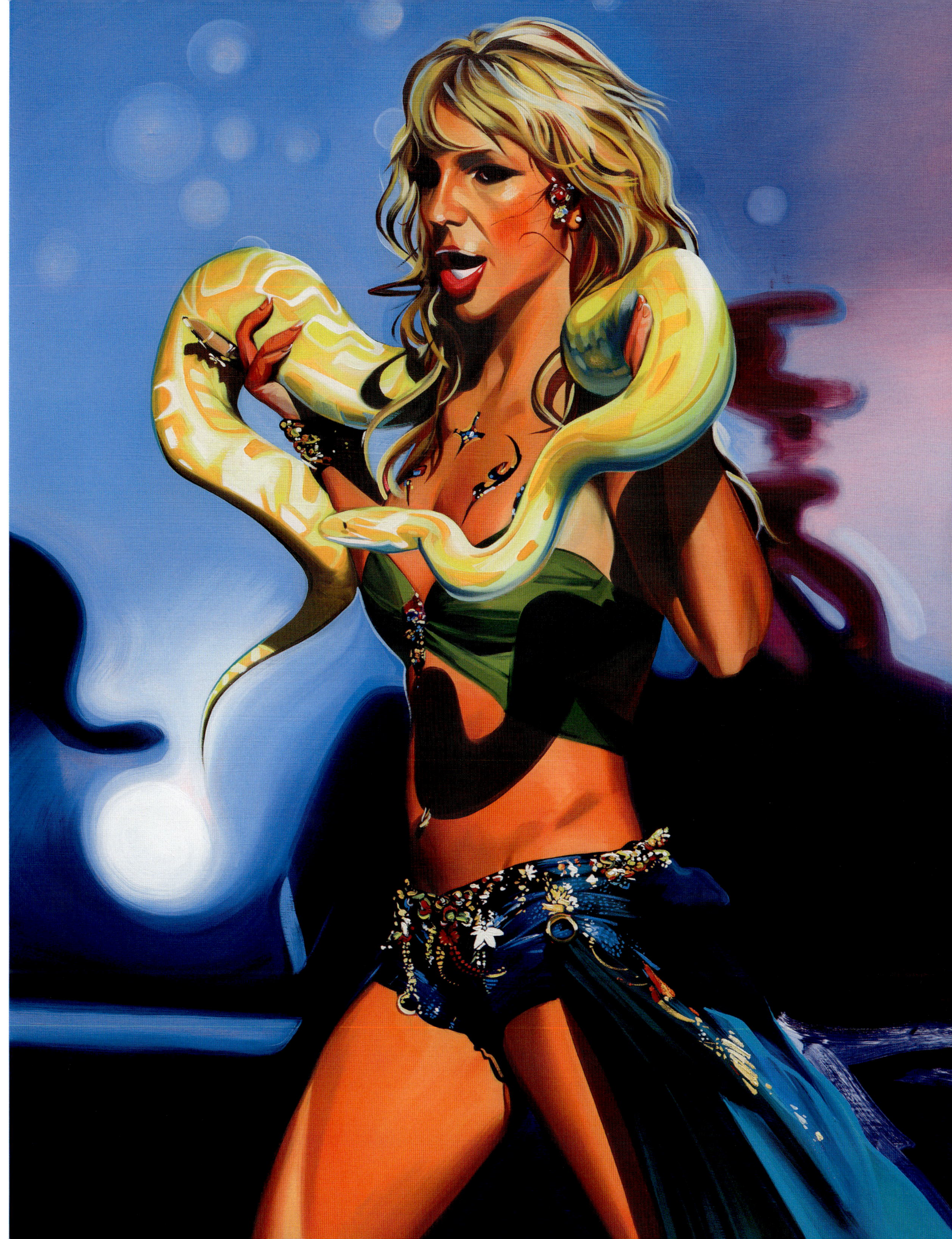

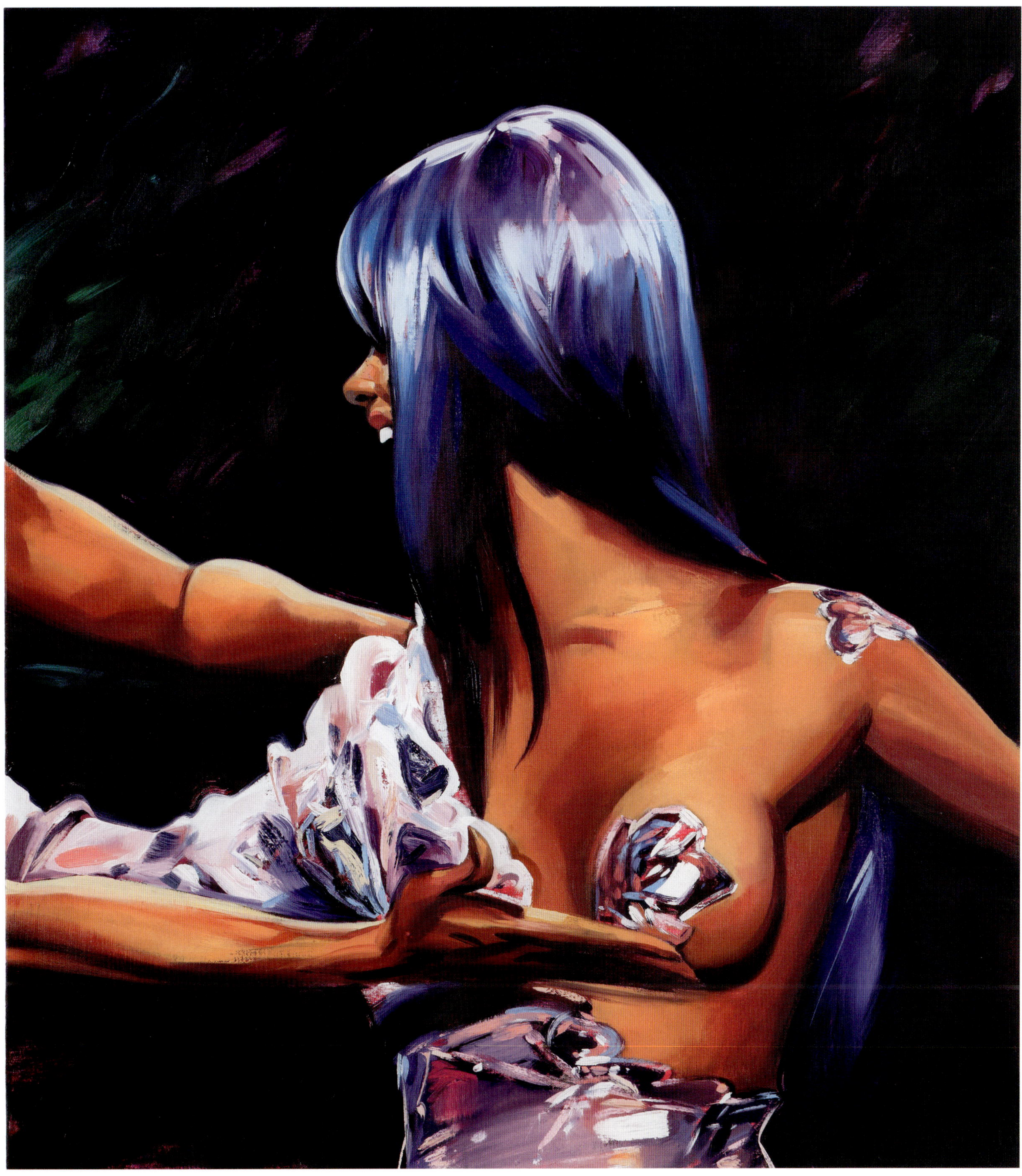

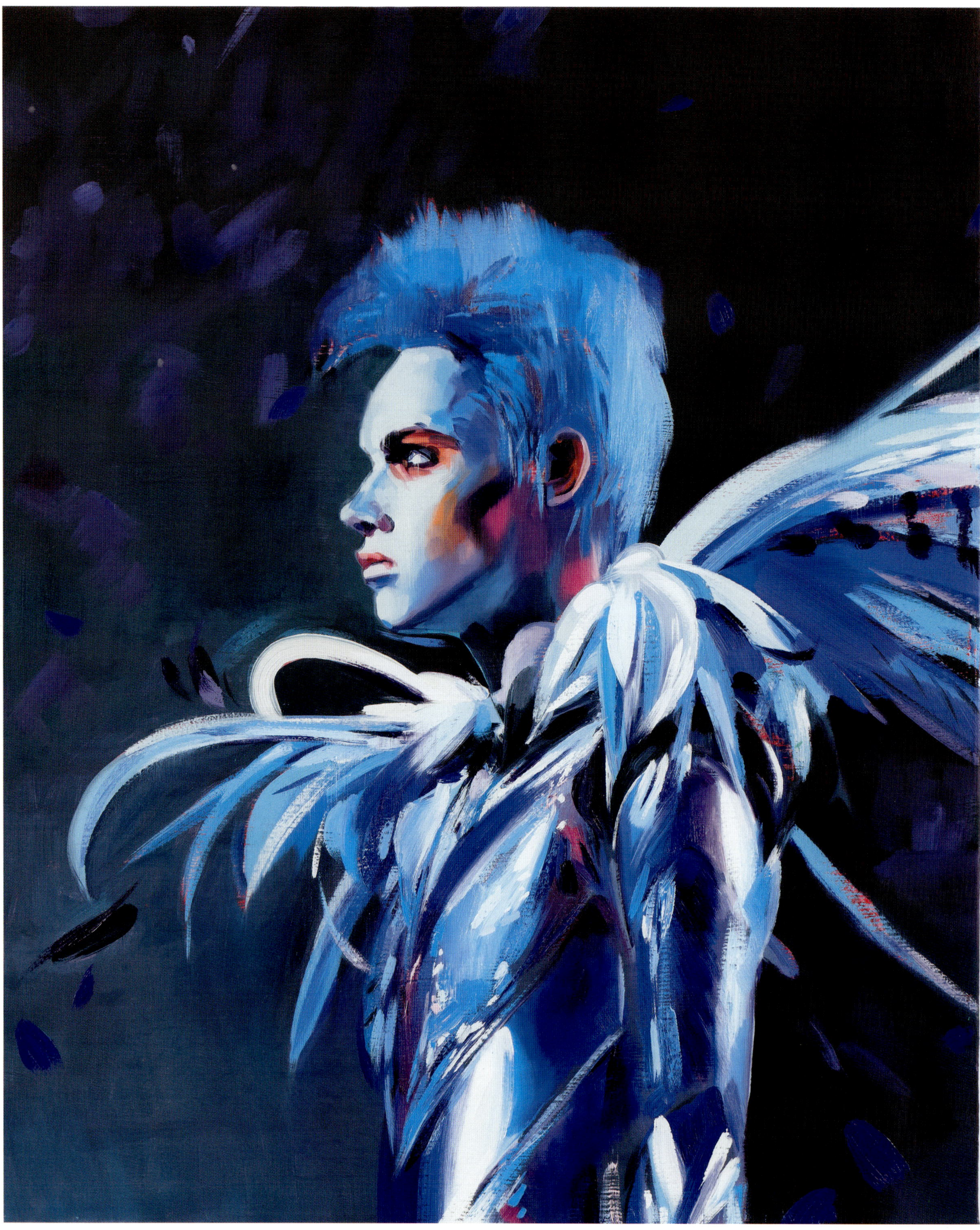

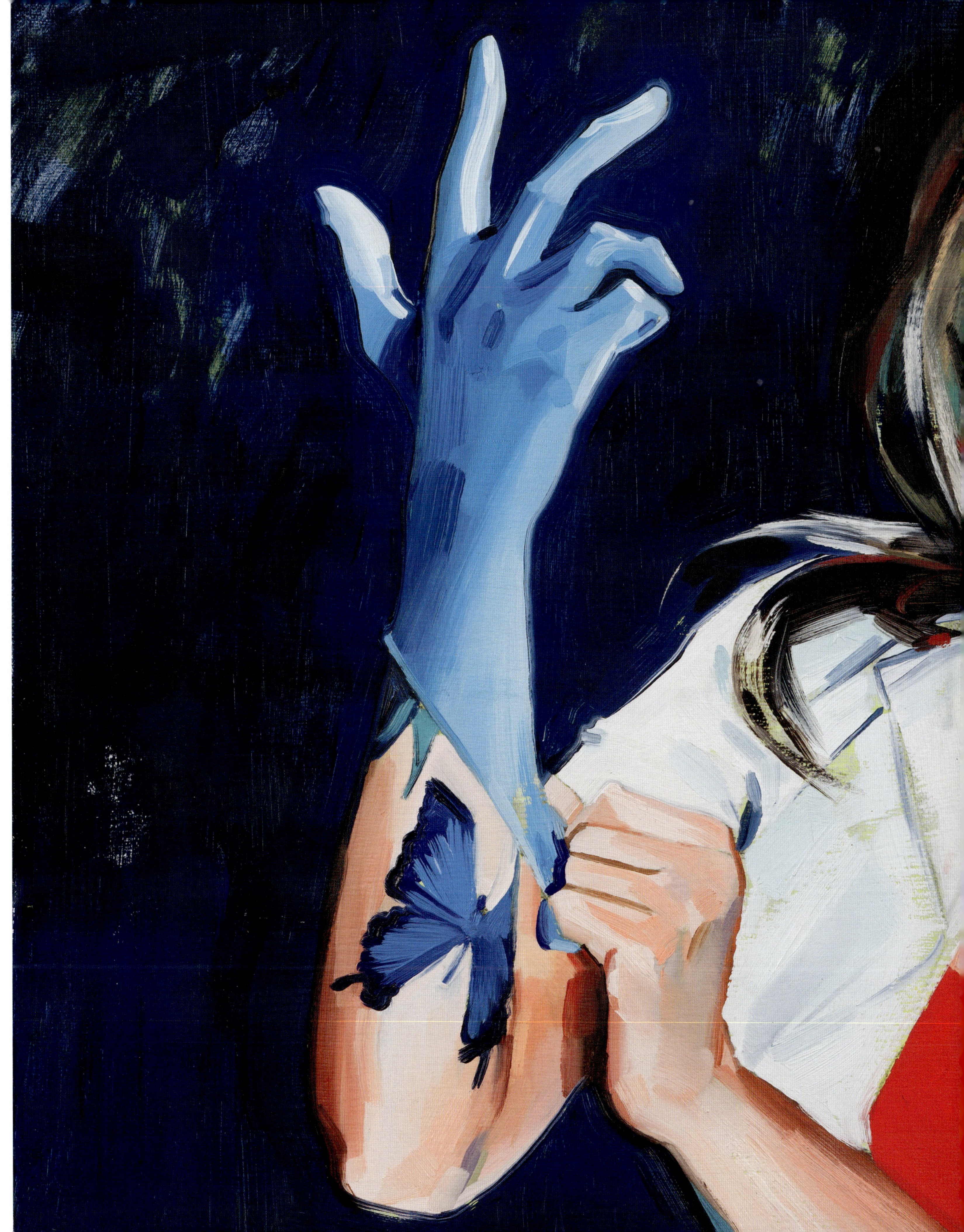

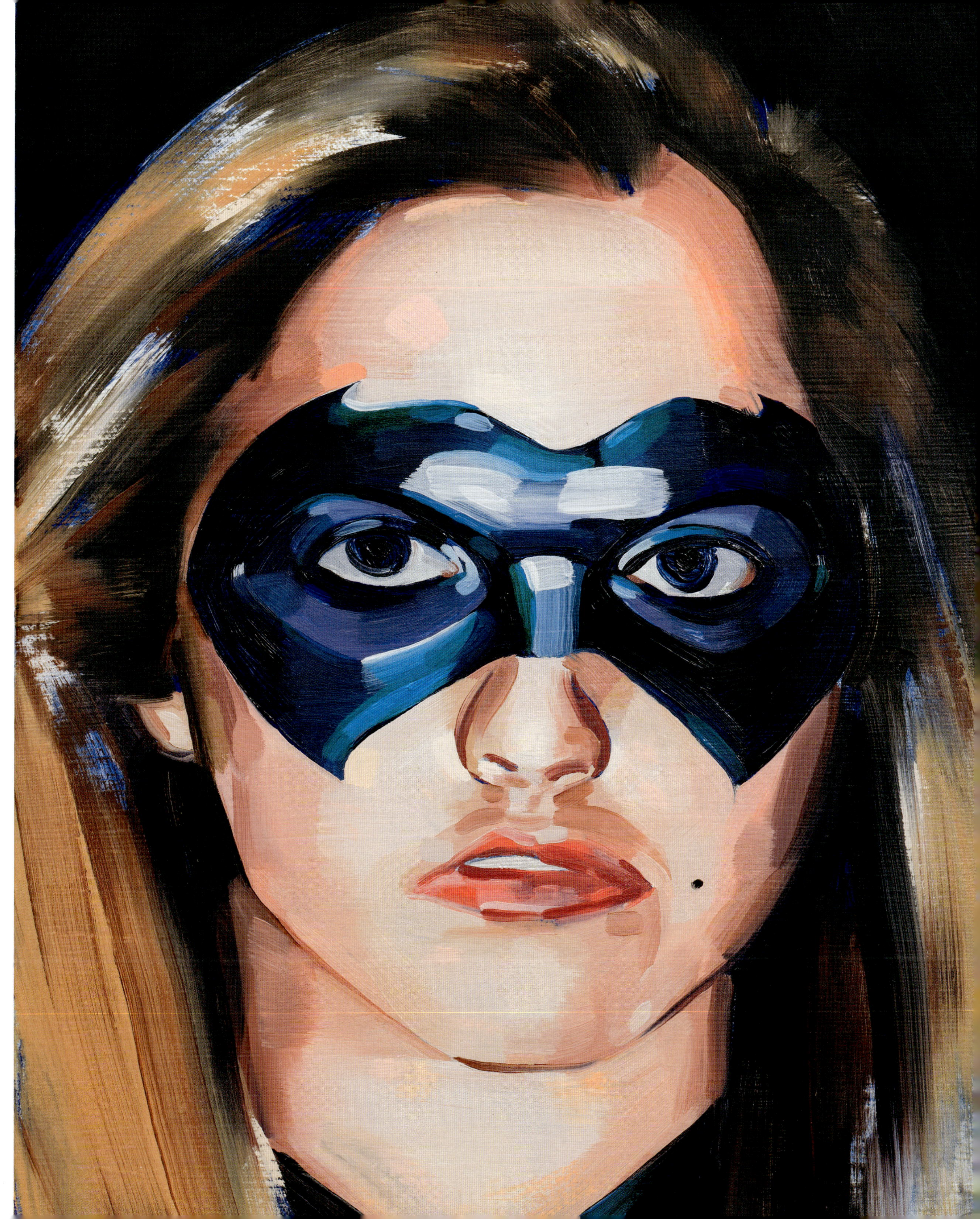

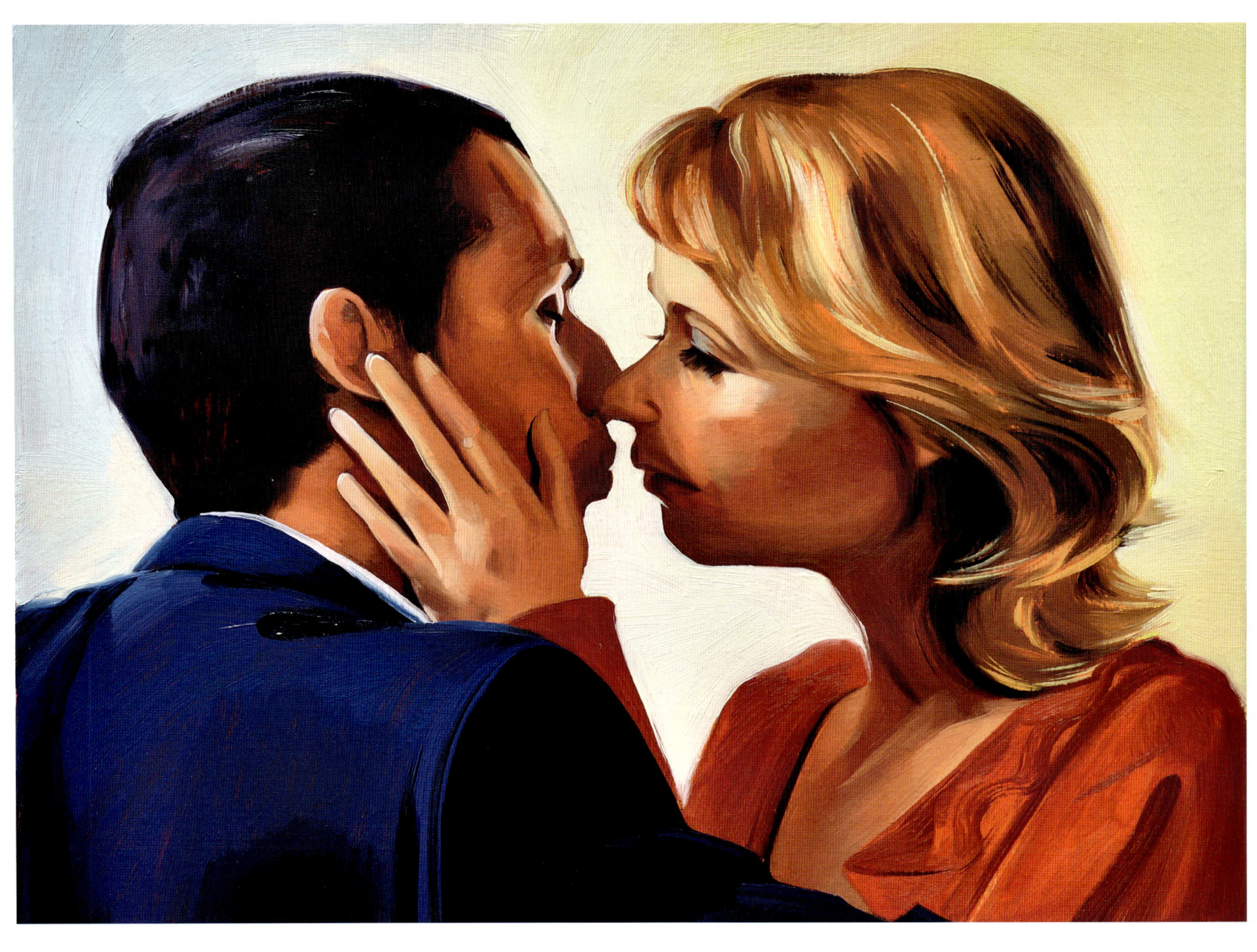

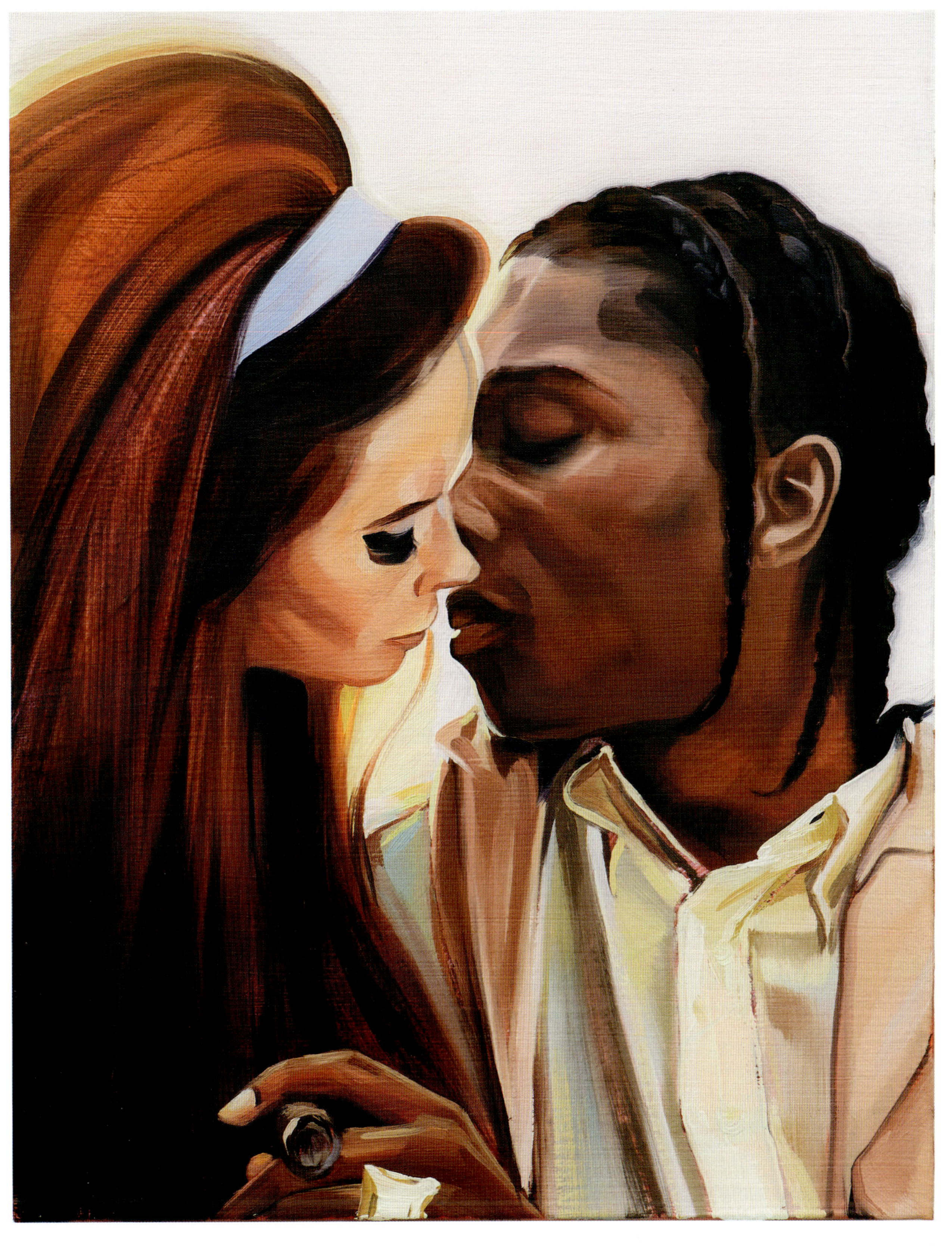

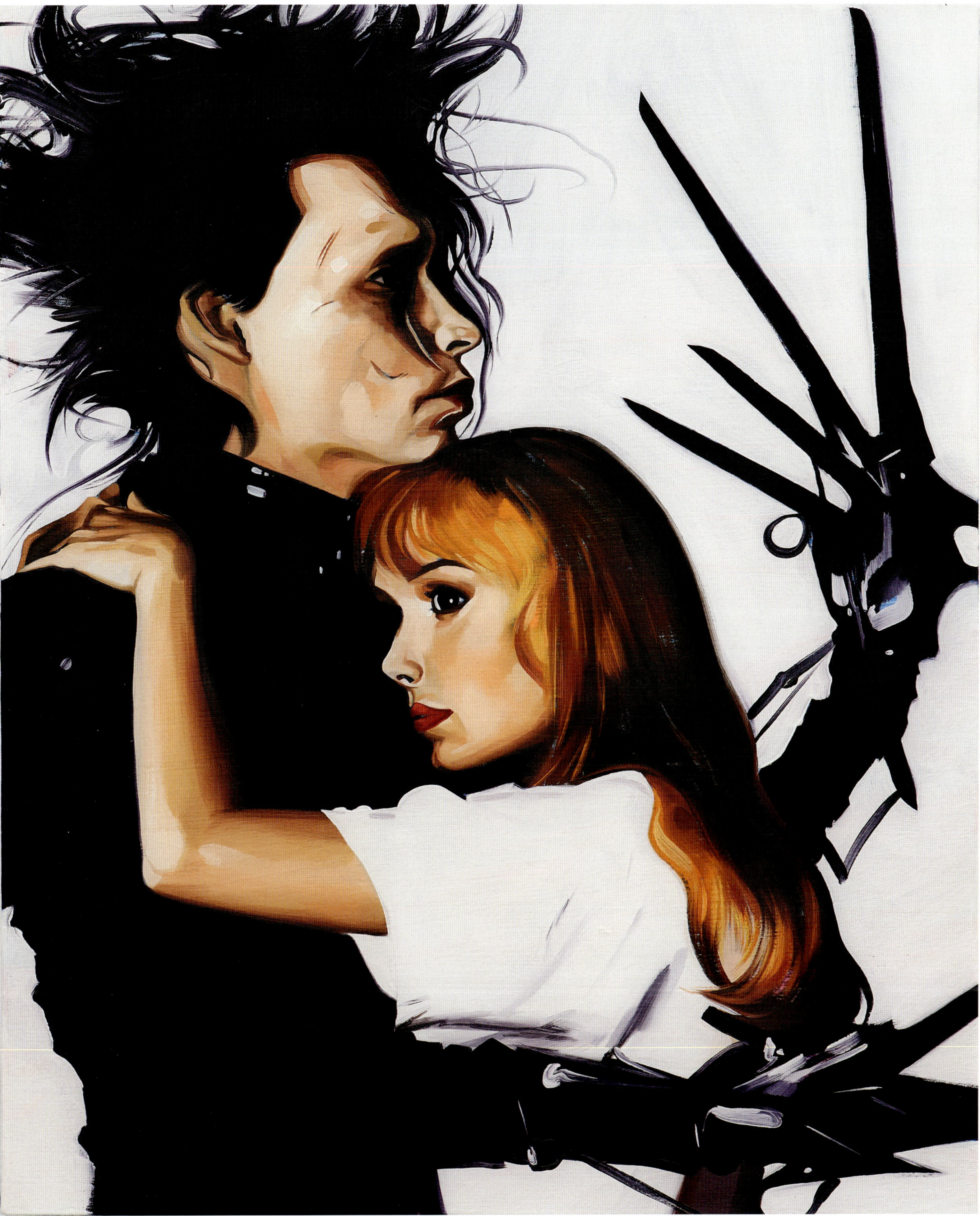

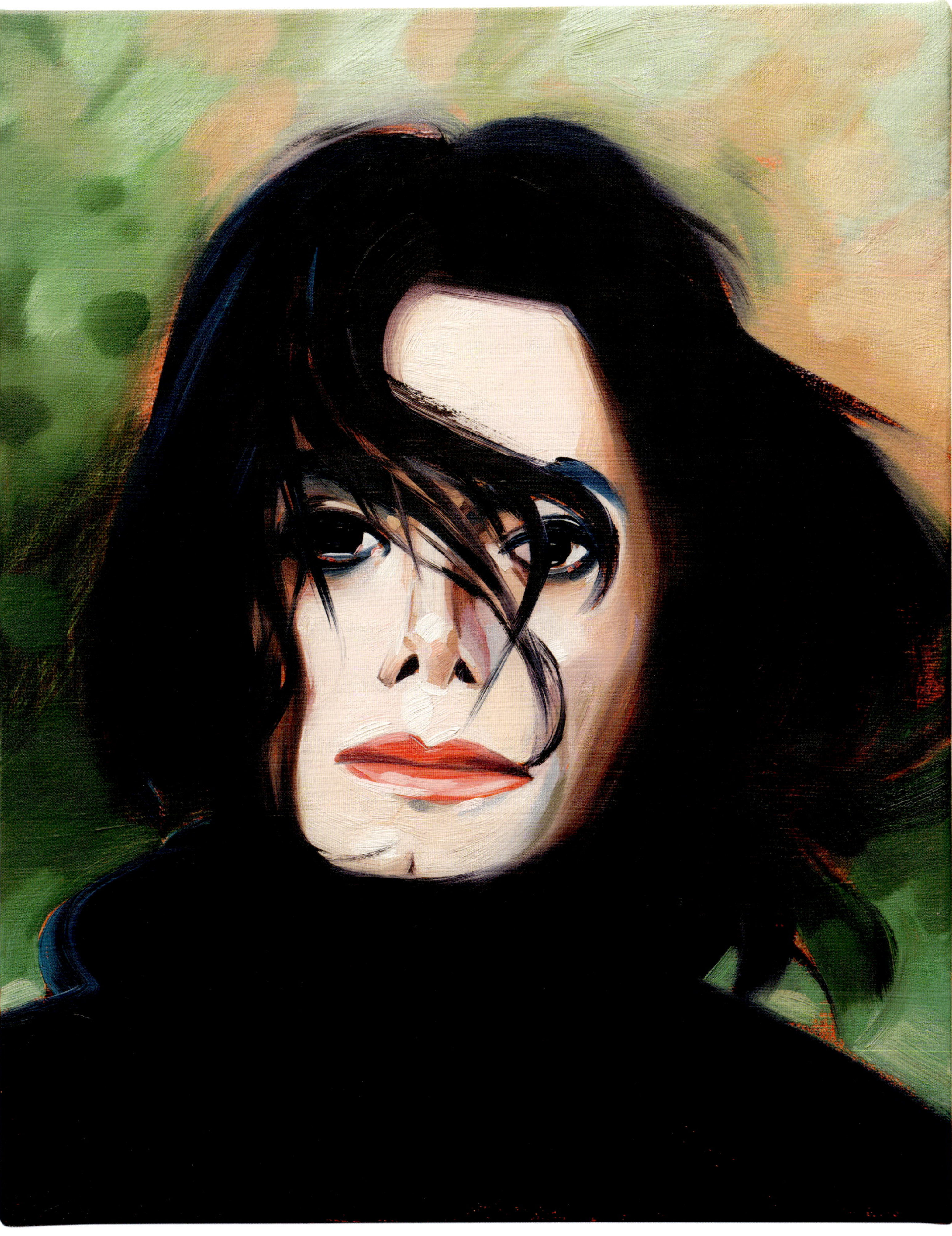

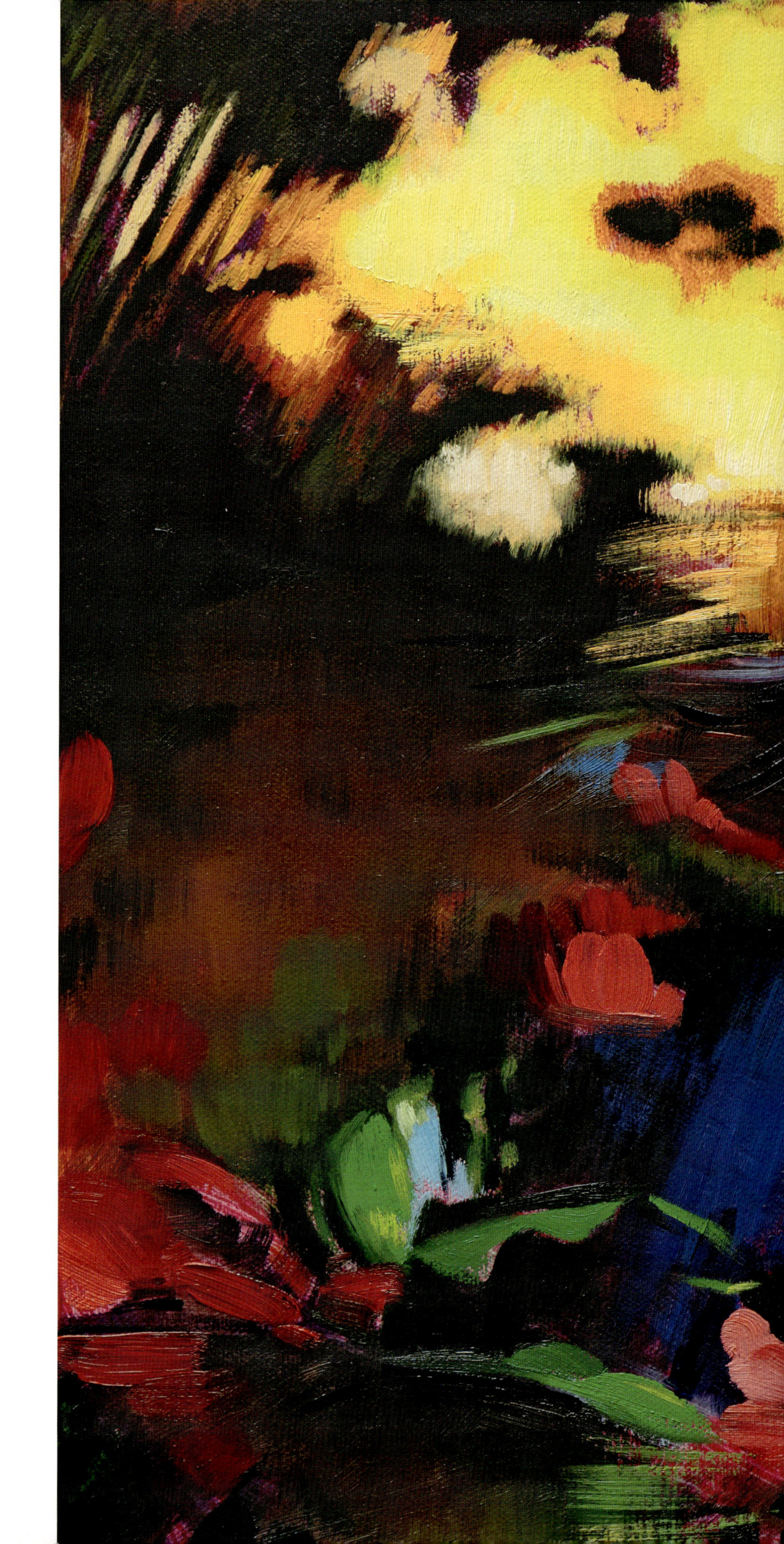

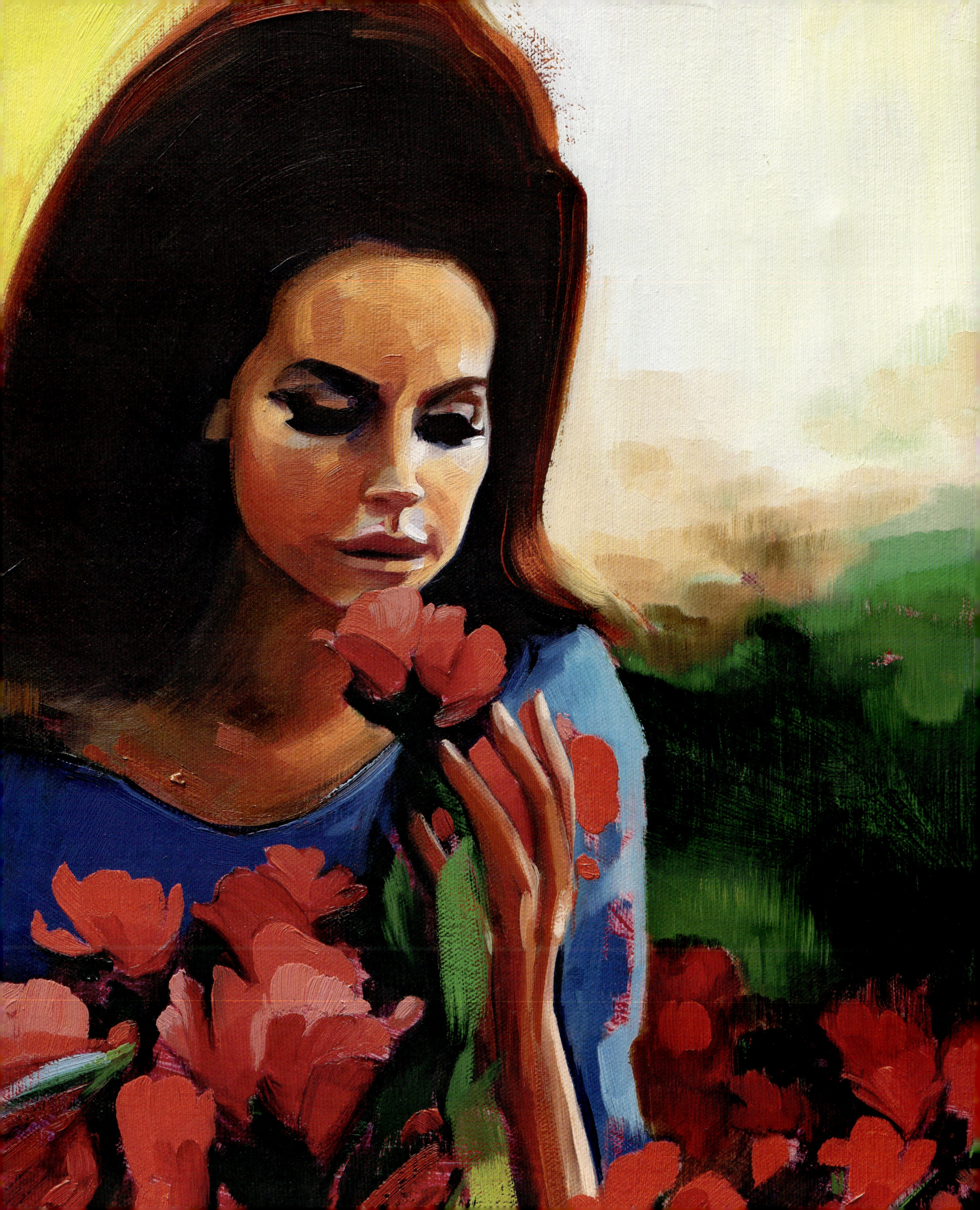

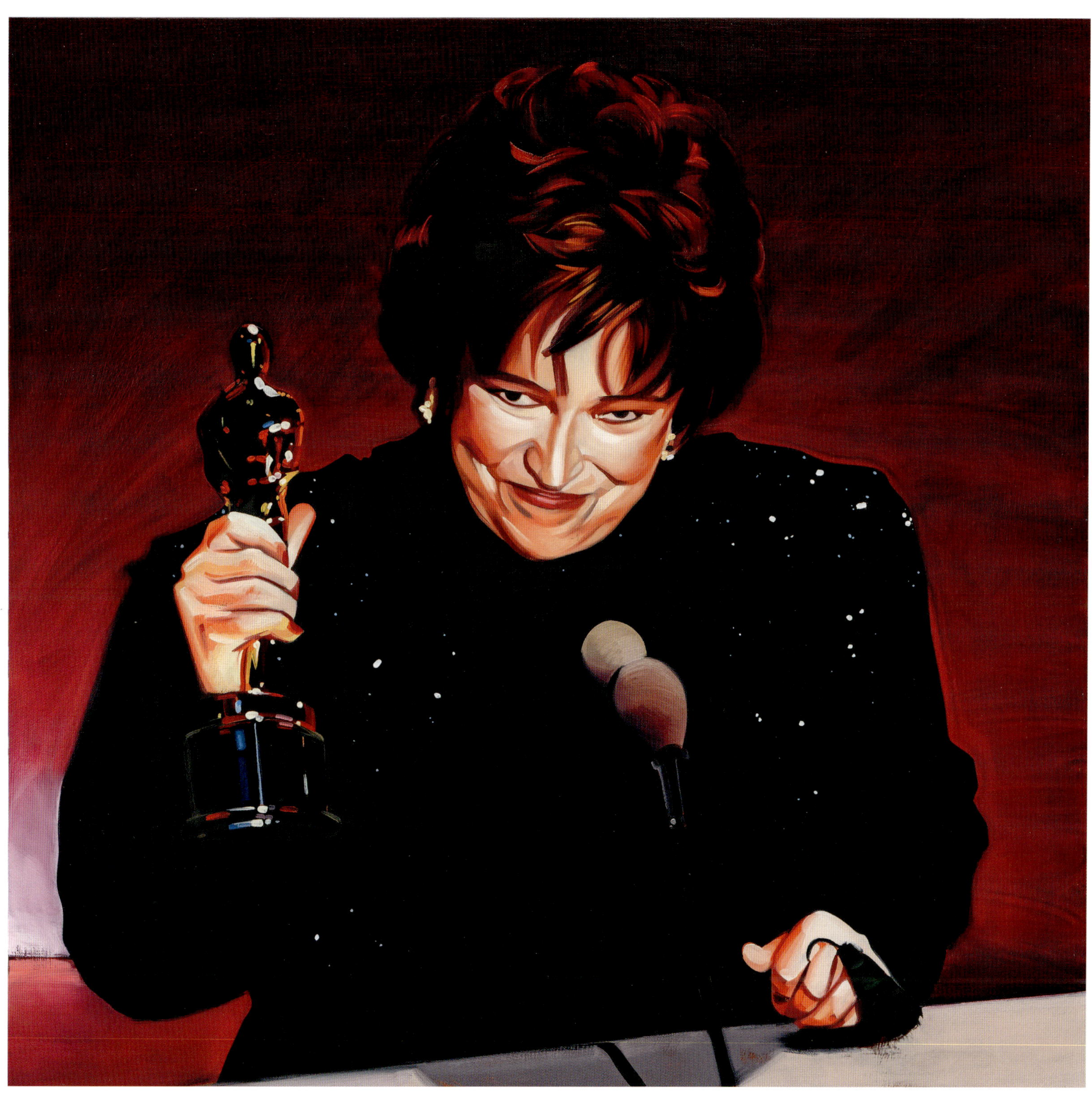

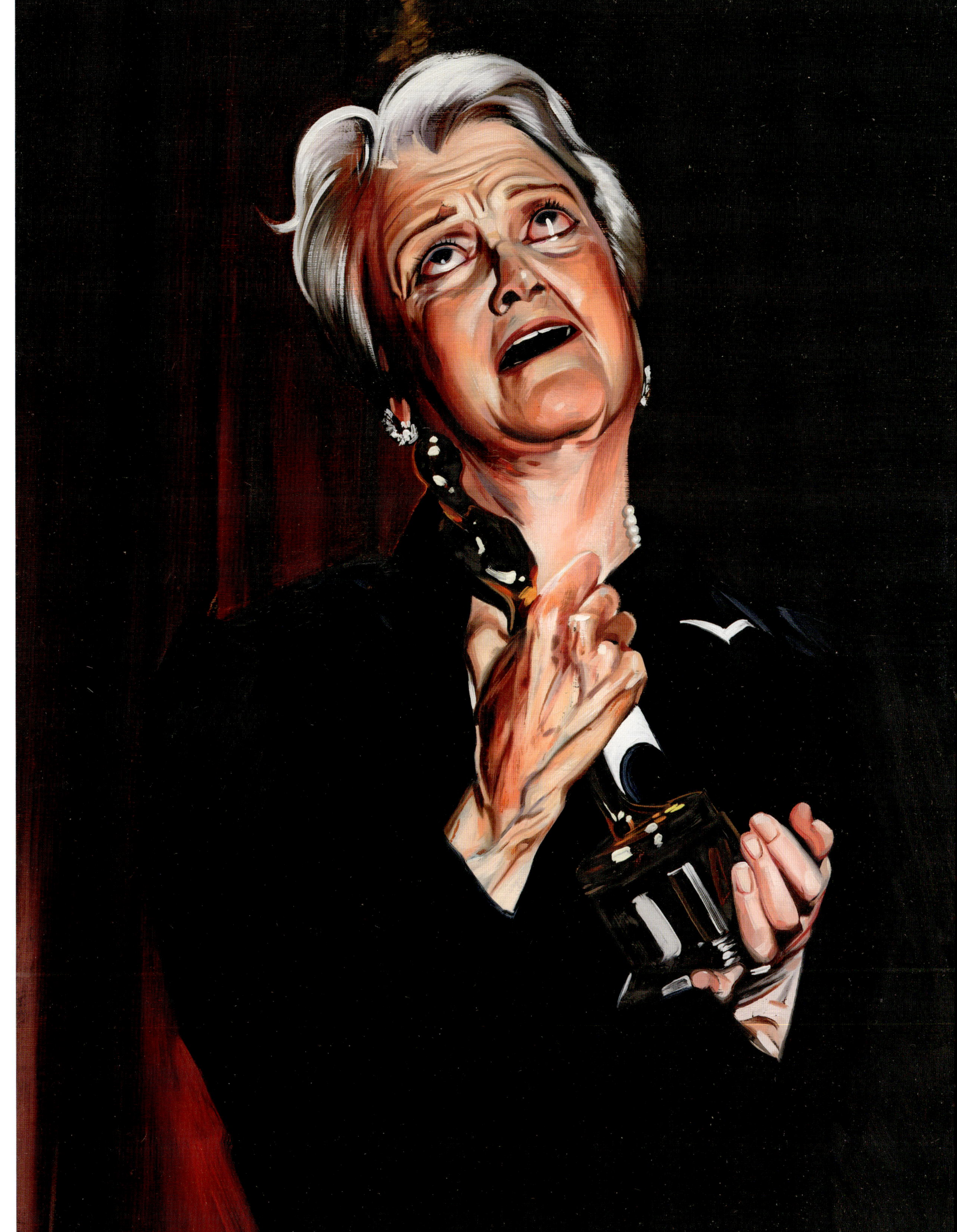

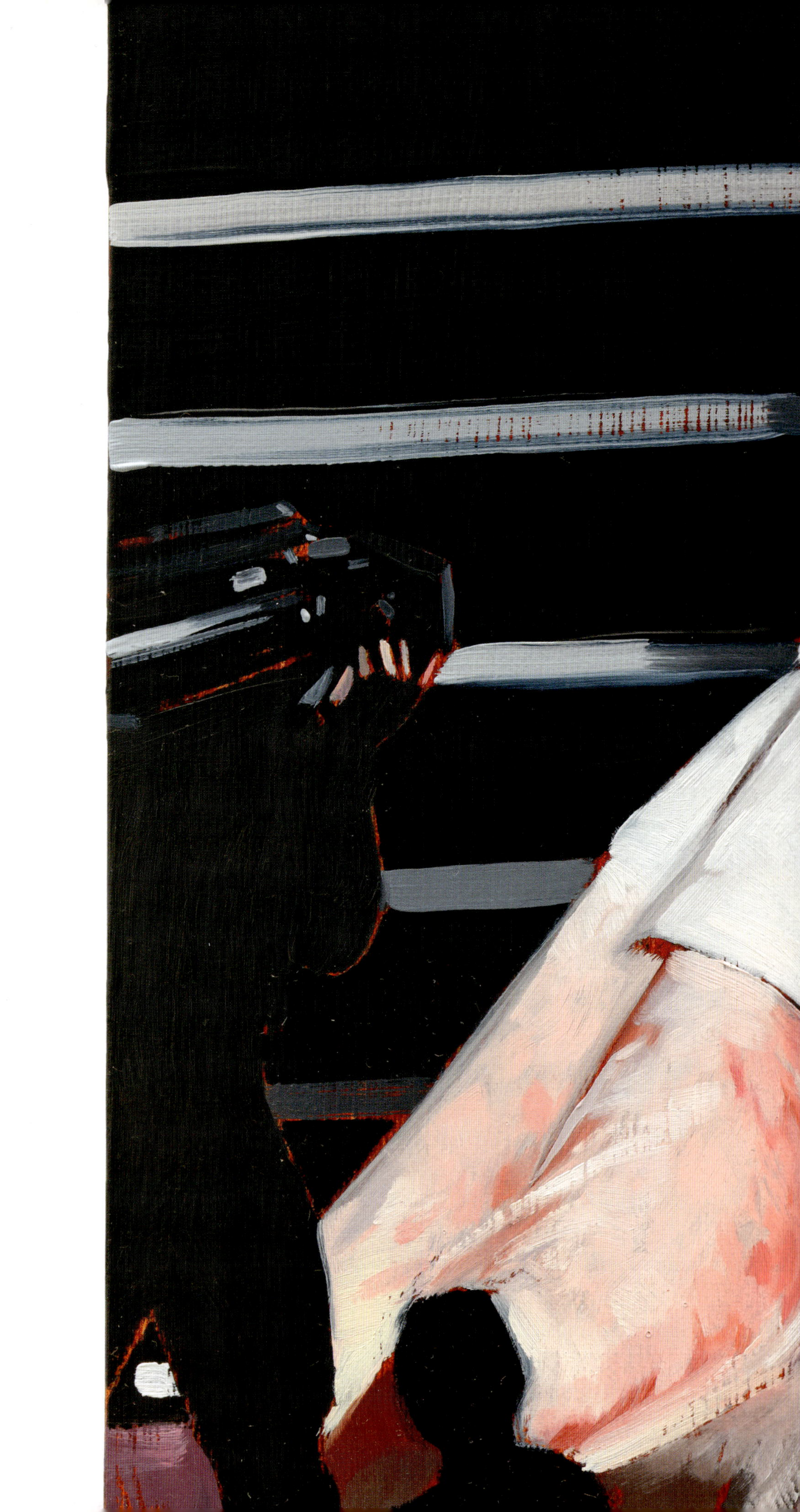

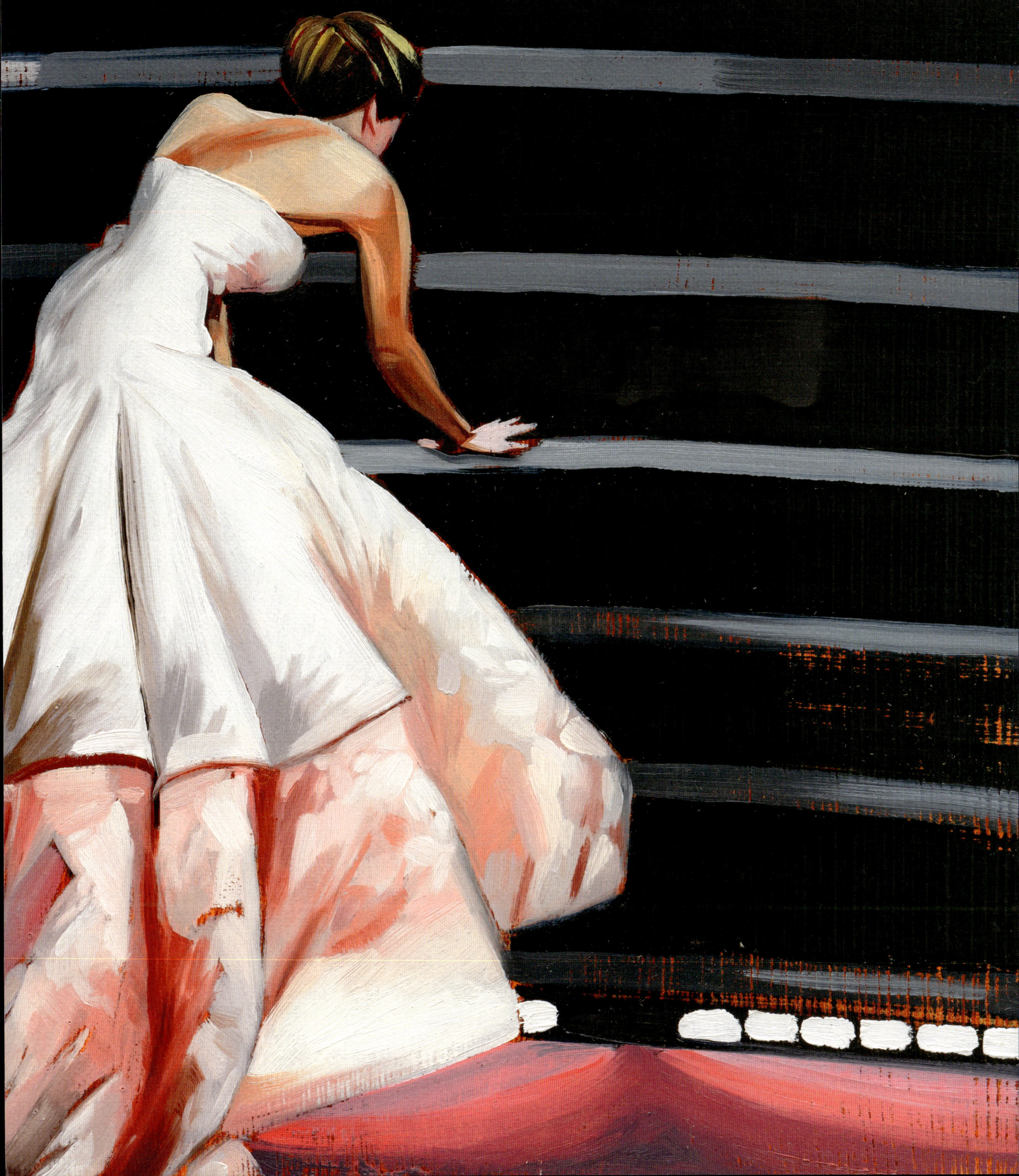

End

Index

p. 61
J. Crew Model (self-portrait), 2023
Oil on linen
$44^{3/4}$ x $33^{1/2}$ x $1^{1/4}$ inches
(113.7 x 85.1 x 3.2 cm)
Courtesy of the artist and
David Kordansky Gallery

pp. 63–64
Saturday Night Live, 2017
Oil and acrylic on canvas
14 x 18 inches (35.6 x 45.7 cm)

pp. 66–67
Nude Study (Rose & Jack), 2020
Oil on linen
15 x 21 inches (38.1 x 53.3 cm)

p. 69
Abigail Williams, 2023
Oil on linen
$14^{1/8}$ x $10^{7/8}$ x $1^{3/8}$ inches
(35.9 x 27.5 x 3.3 cm)
Framed: $15^{5/8}$ x $12^{3/8}$ x 2 inches
(39.7 x 31.3 x 5.1 cm)
Courtesy of David Kordansky Gallery

p. 70
Junior, 2022
Oil on linen
12 x 9 inches (30.5 x 22.9 cm)

p. 71
Will Smith, 2022
Oil on linen
14 x 11 inches (35.6 x 27.9 cm)

p. 73
Merry Christmas, Mariah Carey, 2021
Oil on linen
10 x 8 inches (25.4 x 20.3 cm)

p. 74
Sunset over Penobscot Bay, 2023
Oil on linen
16 x 20 x $1^{3/8}$ inches
(40.6 x 50.8 x 3.5 cm)
Courtesy of the artist and
David Kordansky Gallery

p. 75
Threesome
(Xavier, Amy, and Jordan), 2018
Oil and acrylic on canvas
11 x 14 inches (27.9 x 35.6 cm)

p. 77
Mason
(at Walmart with Grandma), 2020
Acrylic and oil on canvas
12 x 9 inches (30.5 x 22.9 cm)

p. 78
Missy Elliott, 2021
Oil on canvas
72 x 48 x 2 inches
(182.9 x 121.9 x 5.1 cm)

p. 79
Ghosts (orange and green), 2015
Oil, acrylic, and aqua-leaf on canvas
72 x 60 inches (182.9 x 152.4 cm)

pp. 80, 82 (detail)
Paris Hilton, 2023
Oil on linen
50 x 33 inches (127 x 83.8 cm)

p. 81
Flipper, 2016
Oil and acrylic on canvas
96 x 72 inches (243.8 x 182.9 cm)

p. 87
The Terminator, 2018
Oil over acrylic on canvas
72 x 60 inches (182.9 x 152.4 cm)

pp. 88–89
Costume Drama, installation view, 2021
The Ovitz Family Collection,
Beverly Hills
Curated by Viet-Nu Nguyen
Courtesy of the Ovitz Family Collection

pp. 88, 133
Kathryn, Sebastian, Cecile, & Annette,
2020
Oil on linen
84 x 72 inches (213.4 x 182.9 cm)

pp. 91
Country Western, installation view, 2021
Almine Rech, London
Courtesy of Almine Rech

pp. 91, 220–21
Elvira, 2021
Oil on linen
44 x 84 inches (111.8 x 213.4 cm)

p. 92
Max in Ecstasy, 2014
Oil on canvas
40 x 60 inches (101.6 x 152.4 cm)

p. 93
BOYTWEETSWORLD, 2013
Oil on canvas
10 x 10 inches (25.4 x 25.4 cm)

p. 94
Black Leather Sectional,
installation views, 2015
Joe Sheftel Gallery, New York
Courtesy of the artist

p. 95
T.J. Lane, 2015 [destroyed 2021]
Oil on canvas
60 x 48 inches (152.4 x 121.9 cm)

p. 96
Black Leather Sectional,
installation view, 2015
Joe Sheftel Gallery, New York
Courtesy of the artist

p. 97
Batgirl (after Joel Schumacher), 2015
Oil on canvas
30 x 24 inches (76.2 x 60.9 cm)

p. 99
Luc Tuymans
The Secretary of State, 2005
Oil on canvas
18 x $24^{3/8}$ inches (45.7 x 61.9 cm)
© Luc Tuymans. The Museum of
Modern Art, New York; Fractional and
promised gift of David and Monica
Zwirner. Image: Art Resource/NY

p. 100
The Star Spangled Banner, 2022
Colored pencil on paper
12 x 9 inches (30.48 x 22.86 cm)

pp. 102–03
SAFE, installation view, 2018
Gladstone64, New York
Featuring ***Linda***, 2018, and ***Philippe Parenno's carpet, 6.00 PM***, 2000–06
Curated by Cooke Maroney
Courtesy of Gladstone Gallery

pp. 103, 177
Linda, 2018
Oil over acrylic on canvas
12 x 9 inches (30.5 x 22.9 cm)
Courtesy of the artist and
Gladstone Gallery

pp. 104–05
Picnic (Cecile and Kathryn), 2021
Oil and acrylic on linen
42 x 77 inches (106.7 x 195.6 cm)

p. 106
Reines marguerites
(after Fantin-Latour), 2024
Oil on linen
14 x 11 inches (35.6 x 27.9 cm)
Framed: $15^{1/2}$ x $12^{1/2}$ inches
(39.4 x 31.8 cm)

p. 107
Blue Morpho
(after Martin Johnson Heade), 2015
Oil and acrylic on canvas
16 x 12 inches (40.6 x 30.5 cm)

p. 109
Serena, 2019
Oil on canvas
84 x 96 inches (213.4 x 243.8 cm)

p. 111
It's not right but it's OK, 2016
Oil and acrylic on canvas
12 x 9 inches (30.5 x 22.9 cm)

p. 112
Beck, 2017
Oil and acrylic on canvas
16 x 12 inches (40.6 x 30.5 cm)

p. 113
Snoop Dogg, 2016
Oil on canvas
16 x 12 inches (40.6 x 30.5 cm)

p. 114
Lyle Lovett, 2021
Oil on linen
14 x 11 inches (35.6 x 27.9 cm)

p. 115
Madonna, 2018
Oil over acrylic on canvas
16 x 12 inches (40.6 x 30.5 cm)

p. 116
Lake McDonald, 2021
Oil and acrylic on linen
96 x 84 inches (244 x 213.5 cm)

p. 117
Han and Leia in Cloud City (with Chewbacca and C-3PO), 2018
Oil and acrylic on canvas
60 x 36 inches (152.4 x 91.4 cm)

p. 121
Cher, 2022
Oil on linen
54 x 38 inches (137.2 x 96.5 cm)

p. 123
Chris Farley, 2022
Oil on linen
20 x 16 inches (50.8 x 40.6 cm)

p. 125
The Middle Teton, 2020
Oil on linen
96 x 84 inches (243.8 x 213.4 cm)

p. 127
Jennifer, 2018
Oil over acrylic on canvas
84 x 60 inches (213.4 x 152.4 cm)

p. 128
Willy & Jesse, 2020
Oil on linen
10 x 8 inches (25.4 x 20.3 cm)

p. 129
Lydia Discovers Hell, 2015
Oil and aqua-leaf on canvas
16 x 12 inches (40.6 x 30.5 cm)

p. 130
Still Life with Primroses, Pears and Pomegranates (after Fantin-Latour), 2018
Oil and acrylic on canvas
30 x 24 inches (76.2 x 61 cm)

p. 131
Coachella (Lana), 2017
Oil and acrylic on canvas
48 x 36 inches (121.9 x 91.4 cm)

pp. 134–35
The Biebers, 2020
Oil and acrylic on canvas
50 x 72 inches (127 x 182.9 cm)

p. 137
The Olsens, 2019
Oil on canvas
84 x 60 inches (213.4 x 152.4 cm)

pp. 138–39
Ameriquest Field in Arlington, TX, Sept. 3, 2006, 2022
Oil on linen
70 x 108 inches (177.8 x 274.3 cm)

p. 141
Hallie and Annie, 2020
Oil on canvas
24 x 20 inches (61 x 50.8 cm)

p. 143
Nancy Reagan, 2022
Oil on linen
18 x 14 inches (45.5 x 35.5 cm)

p. 145
Diana, 2018
Oil over acrylic on canvas
96 x 72 inches (243.8 x 182.9 cm)

p. 146
Salazar's Pit Viper, 2022
Oil on linen
9 x 12 inches (22.9 x 30.5 cm)

p. 147
l'amour menaçant (after Etienne-Maurice Falconet), 2015
Oil on canvas
72 x 60 inches (182.9 x 152.4 cm)

p. 150
Ghosts (Little Metal Spectrum), 2015
Oil, acrylic, and aqua-leaf on canvas
14 x 11 inches (35.6 x 27.9 cm)

p. 151
Batgirl (Leather Cape), 2015
Oil on canvas
72 x 48 inches (182.9 x 121.9 cm)

p. 153
Wednesday, 2017
Oil and acrylic on canvas
12 x 9 inches (30.5 x 22.9 cm)

p. 155
Wendy, 2016
Oil and acrylic on canvas
20 x 16 inches (50.8 x 40.6 cm)
Courtesy of the artist and Almine Rech

p. 156
White Roses and Pink Roses in a Footed Glass (after Fantin-Latour), 2023
Oil on linen
$20^{1/8}$ x $16^{1/8}$ x $1^{3/8}$ inches
(51 x 41 x 3.5 cm)
Framed: $21^{5/8}$ x $17^{5/8}$ x 2 inches
(54.8 x 44.8 x 5.1 cm)
Courtesy of David Kordansky Gallery

p. 157
Swan II, 2016
Oil and acrylic on canvas
60 x 48 inches
(152.4 x 121.9 cm)

p. 159
Alice, 2018
Oil and acrylic on canvas
16 x 12 inches (40.6 x 30.5 cm)

pp. 160–61
Mike Tyson and his pigeon, 2017
Oil on canvas
11 x 14 inches (27.9 x 35.6 cm)

p. 163
Drew, 2017
Oil and acrylic on canvas
14 x 11 inches (35.6 x 27.9 cm)

p. 164
Dolly Parton, 2021
Oil on linen
50 x 48 inches (127 x 122 cm)

p. 165
Johnny's Puppy, 2015
Oil on canvas
48 x 36 inches (121.9 x 91.4 cm)

p. 166
Fairy Roses (after Fantin-Latour), 2018
Oil and acrylic on canvas
20 x 16 inches (50.8 x 40.6 cm)

p. 167
JonBenet, 2017
Oil and acrylic on canvas
14 x 12 inches (35.5 x 30.5 cm)

pp. 168–69
Diana (on Jonikal), 2018
Oil over acrylic on canvas
11 x 14 inches (27.9 x 35.6 cm)

pp. 170–72
Othello & Desdemona, 2020
Oil on linen
11 x 14 inches (27.9 x 35.6 cm)

p. 173
Rufio, 2020
Oil on linen
18 x 14 inches (45.7 x 35.6 cm)

p. 175
Cop Car in Brooklyn, 2020
Oil on linen
11 x 14 inches (27.9 x 35.6 cm)

p. 179
Marilyn, 2018
Oil over acrylic on canvas
36 x 30 inches (91.4 x 76.2 cm)

p. 181
The Little Mermaid, 2018
Oil and acrylic on canvas
18 x 14 inches (45.7 x 35.6 cm)

pp. 182–83
Bather (Sebastian), 2021
Oil on linen
54 x 99 inches (137.2 x 251.5 cm)

p. 184
Shania Twain's Horse 2, 2021
Oil on linen
84 x 72 inches (213.4 x 182.9 cm)

p. 185
Horsetail Fall, El Capitan, 2022
Oil on linen
84 x 60 inches (213.5 x 152.5 cm)

p. 186
Shenandoah, 2023
Oil on linen
$11\frac{1}{8}$ x $14\frac{1}{8}$ x $1\frac{3}{8}$ inches
(28.3 x 35.9 x 3.3 cm)
Framed: $12\frac{5}{8}$ x $15\frac{5}{8}$ x 2 inches
(32.1 x 39.7 x 5.1 cm)
Courtesy of the artist and
David Kordansky Gallery

p. 187
Peaches (after Fantin-Latour), 2021
Oil on linen
8 x 10 inches (20.3 x 25.4 cm)

p. 188
Roses & Nasturtiums (after Fantin-Latour), 2020
Oil on canvas
12 x 12 inches (30.5 x 30.5 cm)

p. 189
Jen Yu, 2020
Oil on linen
20 x 16 inches (50.8 x 40.6 cm)

p. 190
Lamb, 2017
Oil and acrylic on canvas
18 x 14 inches (45.7 x 35.6 cm)

p. 191
Mountie, 2023
Oil on linen
24 x 18 x 2 inches (61 x 45.7 x 5.1 cm)
Courtesy of the artist and
David Kordansky Gallery

p. 193
Climber on Ama Dablam, 2023
Oil on linen
96 x 84 inches (243.8 x 213.4 cm)

p. 197
Doberman Pinscher, 2023
Oil on linen
$44\frac{1}{4}$ x $33\frac{1}{8}$ x $1\frac{3}{8}$ inches
(112.4 x 84.1 x 3.5 cm)
Framed: $45\frac{3}{4}$ x $34\frac{5}{8}$ x 2 inches
(116.2 x 87.9 x 5.1 cm)
Courtesy of the artist and
David Kordansky Gallery

pp. 198–99
Three Cowboys (Randall Cobb, Byron Jones, Jeff Heath), 2023
Oil and acrylic on linen
56 x $86\frac{1}{8}$ x $1\frac{1}{4}$ inches (142.1 x 218.6 x 3.2 cm) Framed: 59 x 88 x 2 inches
(149.9 x 223.5 x 5.1 cm)
Courtesy of David Kordansky Gallery

p. 200
Cheng Dieyi, 2024
Oil on linen
10 x 8 inches (25.2 x 20.3 cm)
Framed: $11\frac{1}{2}$ x $9\frac{1}{2}$ inches
(29.1 x 24.1 cm)

p. 201
White Cup and Saucer (after Fantin-Latour), 2018
Oil and acrylic on canvas
9 x 12 inches (22.9 x 30.5 cm)

pp. 202–03
Ghosts (Orange and Blue), 2015
Oil, acrylic, and aqua-leaf on canvas
60 x 72 inches (152.4 x 182.9 cm)
Courtesy of the artist and
David Kordansky Gallery

p. 205
Joyce Carol Oates, 2023
Oil on linen
20 x 16 inches (50.8 x 40.6 cm)

p. 207
Willie Nelson, 2021
Oil on linen
16 x 12 inches (40.6 x 30.5 cm)

p. 209
Obama (bubble), 2016
Oil and acrylic on canvas
14 x 11 inches (35.5 x 27.9 cm)

pp. 210–11
Grand Canyon, 2021
Oil on linen
23 x 54 x 1 inches
(58.4 x 137.2 x 2.5 cm)
Courtesy of the artist and Almine Rech

p. 212
Tammy Wynette, 2021
Oil on linen
30 x 24 inches (76.2 x 61 cm)

p. 213
Nashville, 2021
Oil and acrylic on linen
11 x 14 inches (28 x 35.5 cm)

p. 214–15
Shania Twain's Horse 1, 2021
Oil on linen
14 x 18 inches
(35.6 x 45.7 cm)

p. 216
Chrysanthemums (after Fantin-Latour), 2017
Oil and acrylic on canvas
24 x 18 inches (61 x 45.7 cm)

p. 217
Angela Lansbury, 2014
Oil on canvas
58 x 44 inches (147.3 x 111.7 cm)

p. 218
Roses (after Fantin-Latour), 2018
Oil and acrylic on canvas
12 x 12 inches (30.5 x 30.5 cm)

p. 219
Blue Chris, 2015
Oil and aqua-leaf on canvas
14 x 11 inches (35.5 x 27.9 cm)

p. 225
Lil' Kim (with Diana Ross), 2016
Oil and acrylic on canvas
30 x 26 inches
(76.2 x 66 cm)

p. 226
Brian Slade, 2016
Oil and acrylic on linen
30 x 24 inches (76.2 x 60.9 cm)

p. 227
Janice (enema), 2016
Oil and acrylic on canvas
16 x 12 inches (40.6 x 30.5 cm)

p. 229
Batgirl (Pap Shot), 2015
Oil and acrylic and aqua-leaf on canvas
14 x 11 inches (35.5 x 27.9 cm)

p. 230
Barry and Lena, 2019
Oil over acrylic on linen
12 x 16 inches (30.5 x 40.6 cm)

p. 231
Lana and Rocky, 2017
Oil and acrylic on canvas
16 x 12 inches (40.6 x 30.5 cm)

p. 233
Edward and Kim, 2018
Oil and acrylic on canvas
30 x 24 inches (76.2 x 61 cm)

p. 235
Michael Jackson, 2017
Oil and acrylic on canvas
14 x 11 inches (35.6 x 27.9 cm)

p. 236–37
Lana Del Rey in a Rose Garden,
2018–20
Oil and acrylic on canvas
14 x 18 inches (35.6 x 45.7 cm)

p. 239
Kathy Bates, 2022
Oil on linen
33 x 33 inches (83.8 x 83.8 cm)

p. 241
Angela Lansbury, 2022
Oil on linen
24 x 18 inches
(61 x 45.7 cm)

pp. 242–43
Jennifer Lawrence, 2022
Oil on linen
11 x 14 inches (27.9 x 35.6 cm)

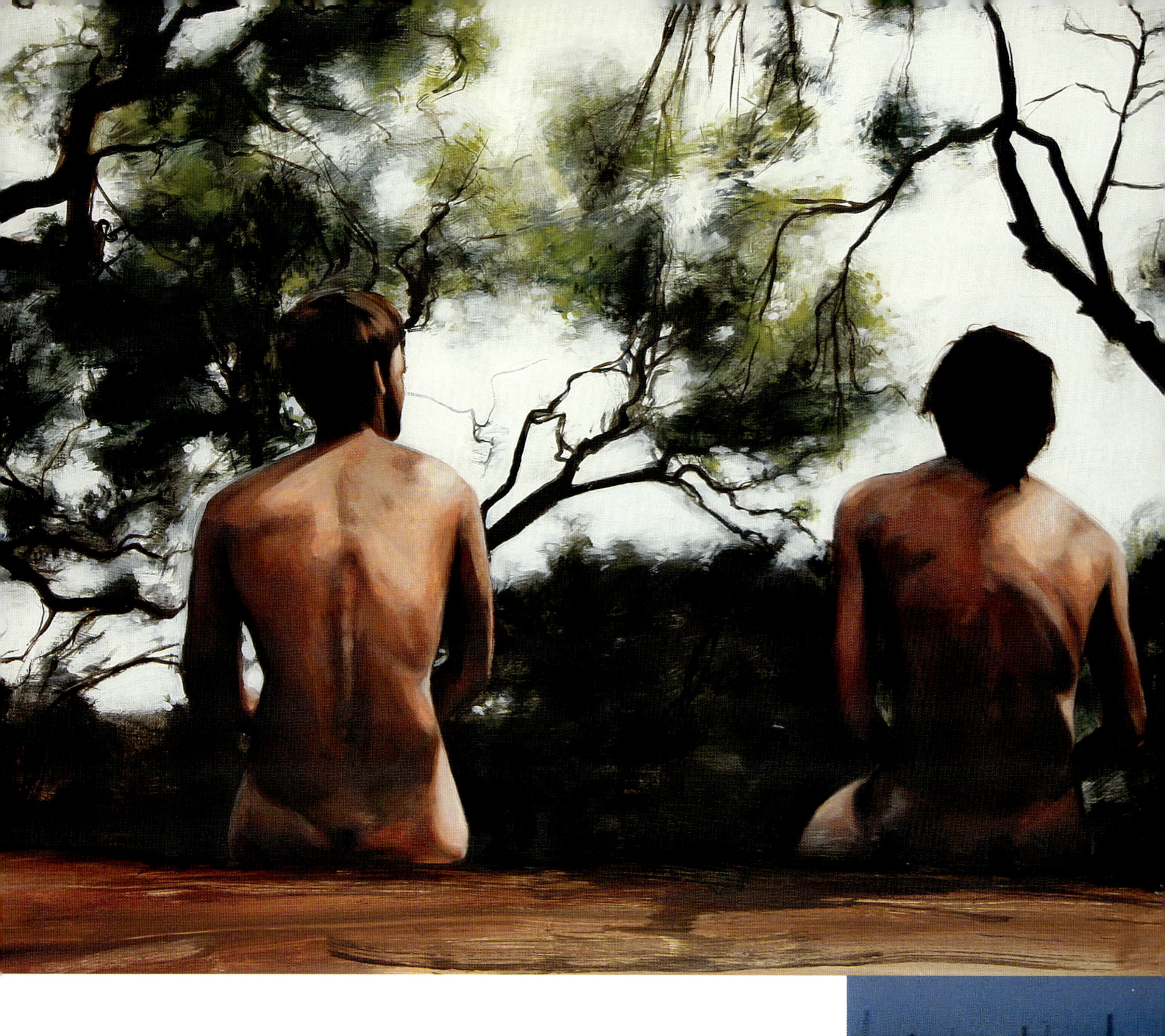

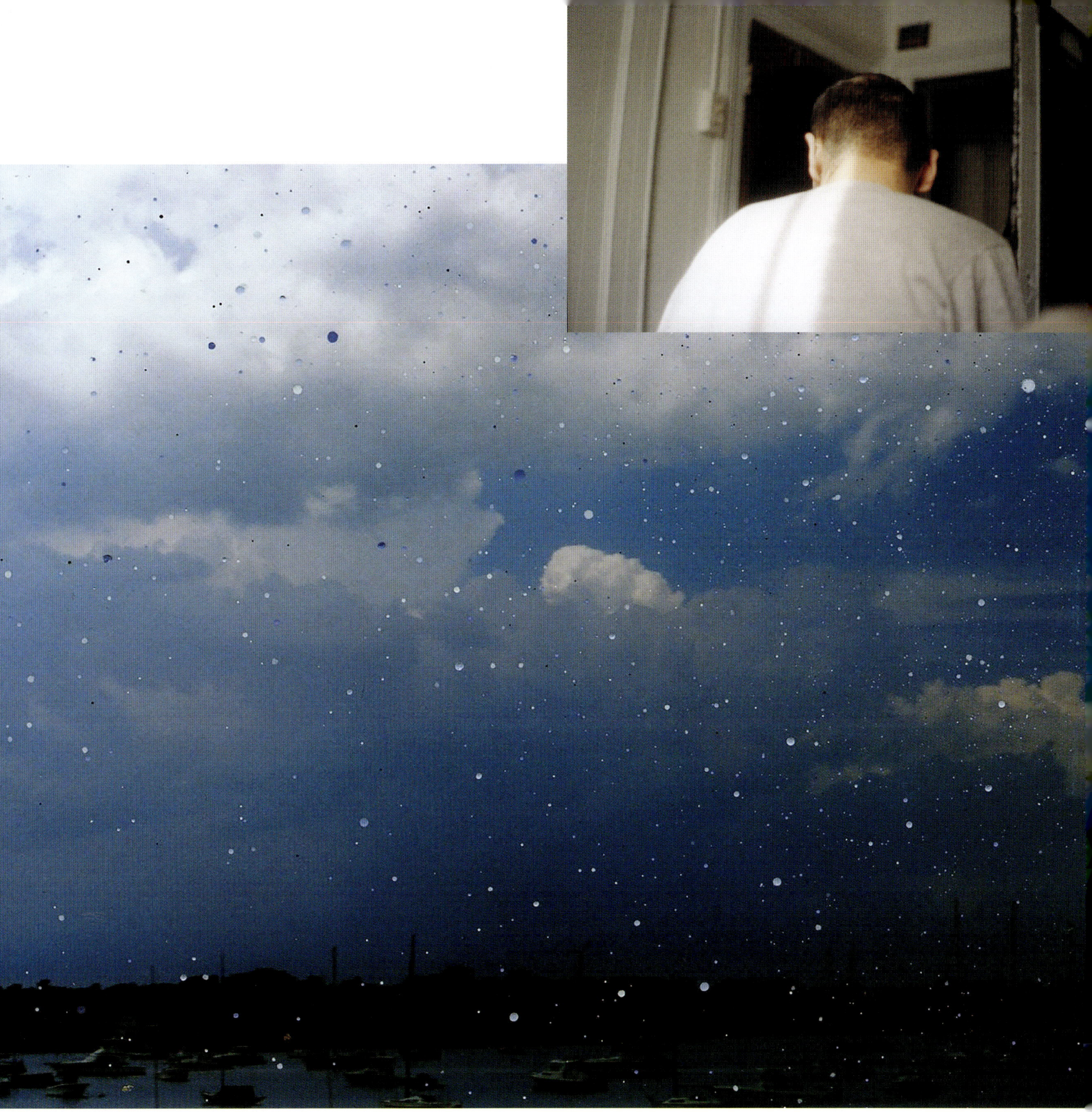

ART

MUSEUMS AND LIBRARIES

Museum of Modern Art
"Insecurities: Tracing Displacement and Shelter"
No word but "disgrace" can describe our passivity in the face of the current displacement of more than sixty-five million people. This grave, accusatory exhibition evokes the transit, and the intermittent protection, of refugees through photographs, artists' projects, water-purification tablets, and a steel-frame tent from the United Nations Refugee Agency: temporary shelter that, for too many people, has now become permanent housing. Photographs appropriated by Xaviera Simmons consider the near-daily deaths in the Mediterranean, and are accompanied by a list of the drowned. Refugee camps from Lebanon to Kenya are among the world's fastest growing; while this show fails to acknowledge the experiences of people trapped in Lesbos or Calais, it complements Bouchra Khalili's videos, recently on view at the museum, that gave voice to refugees who risked their lives to reach Europe. The most shattering object here is the smallest: a color-coded plastic bracelet, used by Doctors Without Borders to measure arm circumference and gauge malnutrition. It rests on a pedestal near a Dorothea Lange photograph of a migrant mother outside a tent in Depression-era California—a reminder that Americans have been displaced persons, too. *Through Jan. 22.*

GALLERIES—UPTOWN

Sally Mann
The photographer commemorates her long friendship with Cy Twombly in a series documenting his modest studio in their home town of Lexington, Virginia. (She began the project in 1999; it ended in 2012, a year after his death.) The painter is absent from these pictures, but Mann remains alert to his presence, most obviously in her photographs of his paintings and sculptures, and of their splattered traces. He feels present, too, in the soft glow of light—a flare, an aura, a dotted
wall. The emptiest of t
Barth's equally poetic int
pictures of a room cro
spindly totemic sculptu
cusi's photographs of his
are every bit as unfussy
Oct. 29. (Gagosian, 976 M
212-796-1224.)

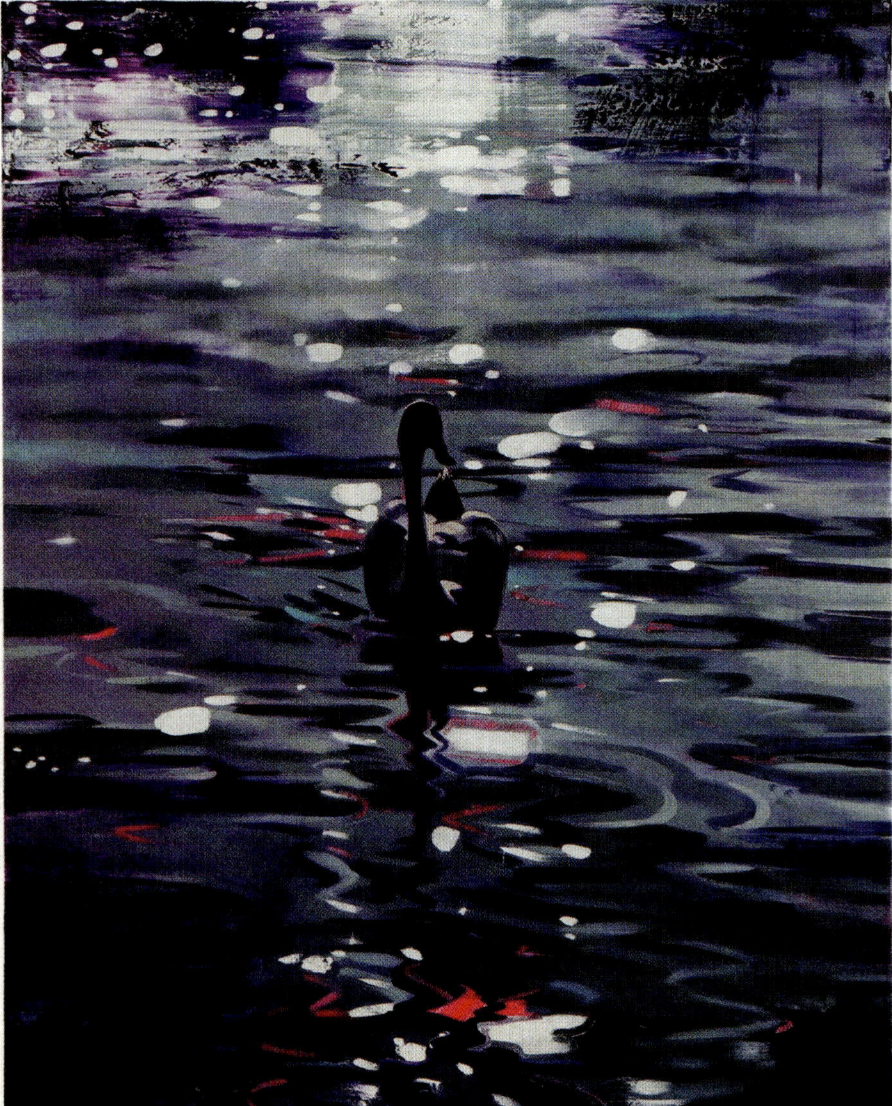

Sam McKinniss's painting "Swan II," in "Egyptian Violet," at the Team gallery, opening Oct. 13. The exhibition title refers to the crepuscular pigment the young artist uses, to striking effect.

GALLERIES-

Ryan Gander
Motion-detector-activ
into the wall, greet visit
ist's strenuously charmi
lashes and waggle their
Further entertainments i
draped with what appea
fact, solid marble, and h
made of gleaming hardw
less, bespeak mopey mo
tures and assemblages (
passport photographs
rated ceramic dildo, am
a conveyor belt behind a
Gander expects you to li
(Lisson, 504 W. 24th St. 2

Meleko Mokgosi
The Botswana-born, N
impresses and tantalize
enigmatic realist paintin
formats. They depict fi
artist's imagination, wh
can citizens or an elegan
or perhaps assaulted, by
a canvas by Bouguereau
two-part exhibition cont
in white on raw linen, in
of southern Africa. (Acc
are tales from an oral tr
provide English transla
nial with a vengeance,
in currents of a powerfu
Through Oct. 22. (Shainm
524 W. 24th St. 212-645-1

Oscar Murillo
At the age of thirty, the
been a market phenom f
may feel that he still ha
In his second solo in Ne
on like a house afire wit
messy but strangely eleg
ture fugitive antique ima
marching band; many ha
ously scribbled drawings
and an immense installat
"A Futile Mercantile Dis
and PVC pipe in framew
shelves or bunks, draped
painted canvas and liner
cial animus. But Murill
to be art about art, with
Imagine a mashup of Be
spun by a d.j. who is high
Oct. 22. (Zwirner, 525 W.

Stephen Shames
The New York photograp
documenting the found
Black Panther Party, in p
substance while admiring
series of Shames's can't a
of radical chic (Angela D

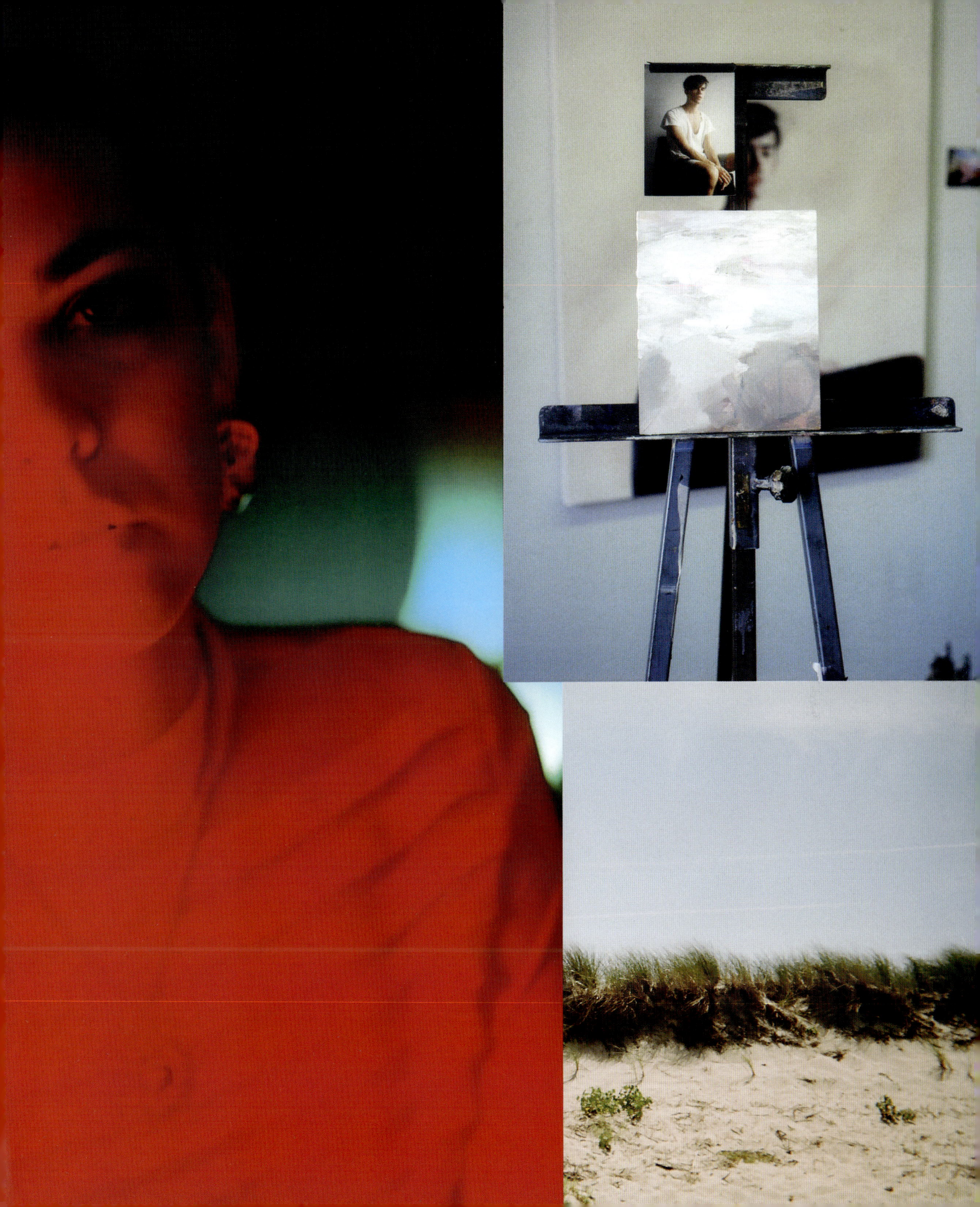

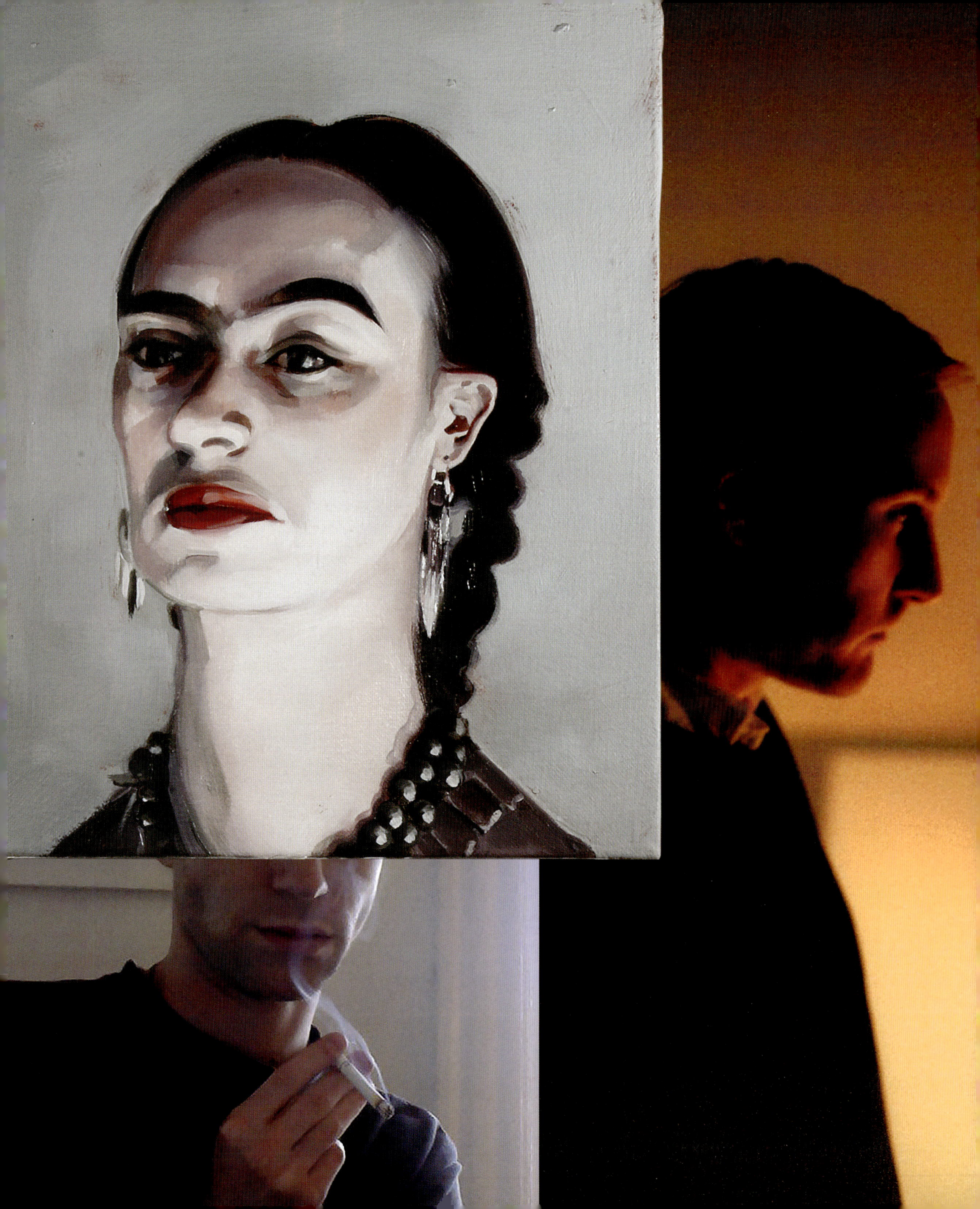

...with the joke.
e paintings clearly mean more than

t some could sneak up and mean
potential is what I'm trying to lever-
variety of sizes and styles into one
by pitting different concerns against
by saying, like, this is sort of loosely
d very loosely organized, but it also
of totality for now.
ality. Yeah, it represents the solip-
ading mind. The totally acceptable,
le kind of solipsism—
hat of having a mind expanded?

t's a nice way of putting it.
anks. [*looks around studio*] Sam, are
ritten on your wall?
ughs] I'm dyslexic for numbers, so I
ber which sizes of paintings I like—
re written next to the prices.
h. I want to buy one of your paint-
n't afford it.
ah, we're close friends. I would just
g for your birthday.
but I'd want to—I'd have to trade
r it.
going to say something really gross.
at? I'm going to lend you my hus-

t's exactly what I was going to say.
atever souls are made of, yours and
f the fucking same.
pe Jesse [Prickett's husband, the writer
esn't read *Interview*. This reminds
ng time ago, I was sleeping with this
e wasn't exactly gay; he was bisexual
just liked it. One time after I fucked
ping there, he was like, "Do you think
m would still go out with me if she
fucking?" [*laughs*] It was one of those
ou have to believe in the joke more
, which was somewhat instructive.
me the wine, I'm going to make a
that time of the afternoon—we've
e lunch wine to the afternoon wine.
our ghosts.
ight. Yeah, the
ng series of semi
ghosts]. They p
they're not repre
y are if you're t
e Snapchat litt
rite a *New York T*
Kinniss's Paint
a Ghost."
me and the Snap
mon, I guess.
also a sense of in
think the ghosts
I think I needed
studio practice.
e, a way that wa

work that so many people have done. But maybe the paintings have something to do with the aftermath. The mess to clean up after furious lovemaking.

PRICKETT: They're also the only paintings of yours that deal in, like, pattern and chaos.

McKINNISS: No, the rest of my paintings are very posed or staged. The figures are aiming for oneness or bodily autonomy. The ghosts try to tear that apart. There's obviously more there than can be said. They are slick; they make fun of painting. They also enjoy everything that painting has to offer. What the figures have going for them in terms of pictorial integrity, they lack in furious loss of control, gestural carelessness, the mess. I describe the ghosts as an alternative means

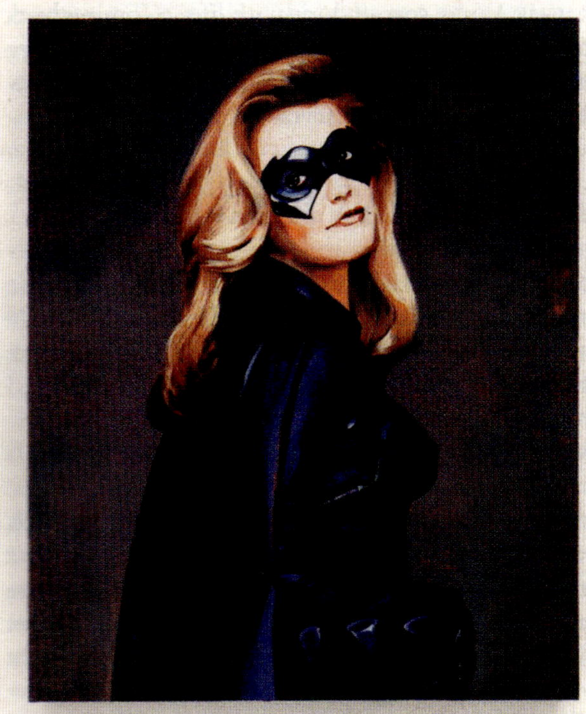

"I RECENTLY ARRIVED SOMEWHERE WHERE I ACTUALLY BELIEVE THAT I KNOW WHAT TO DO. AND I'M GOING TO DO IT."

of approaching a similar erotic or libidinal zone.

PRICKETT: Are they fun to paint?

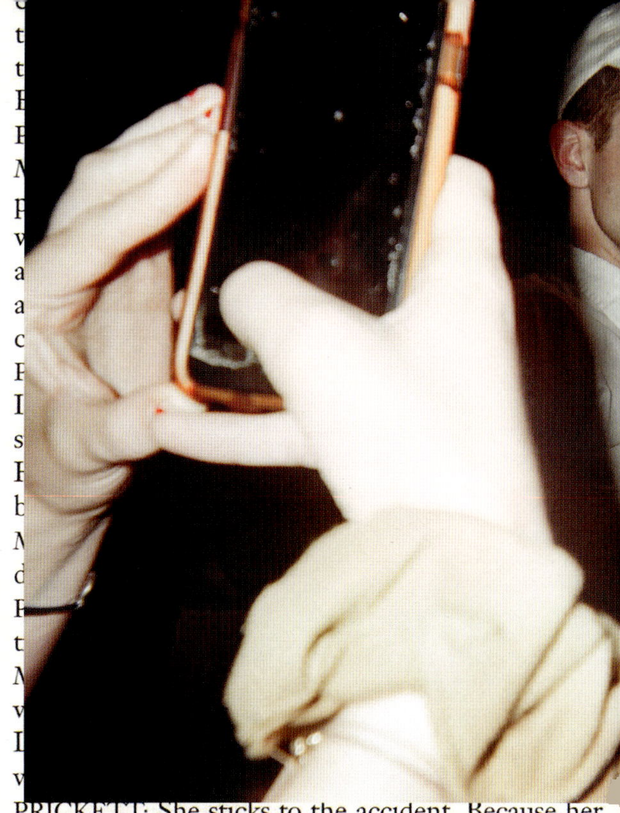

PRICKETT: She sticks to the accident. Because her paintings basically look like, as you say, provincial postage stamps, it seems like she just miscalibrated what painting was supposed to be, or what she was supposed to do as a painter. But she sticks to the accident, which is something Francis Bacon said to Marguerite Duras in an interview once, that you have to integrate the accident into the painting. I wonder if I can explain this more. It has to do with mark-making, but he doesn't refer to marks as marks. He refers to them as spots. So it's kind of like how Koestenbaum, in the Warhol book, talks about the splotches on Warhol's skin.

McKINNISS: Because his body is so compromised, by invasion, or infection, or some kind of incongruity.

PRICKETT: Right. When you talk about the ghosts being slick, it's kind of like that. Like a slick spot on the pavement. You slip on it, you fall, and then you try to understand how it is that you fell, and you repeat the movement until it's graceful. Does that make sense?

McKINNISS: It does make sense. Because if the ghosts resemble a cum stain or something like that, you can also think about how the ghosts resemble midcentury modern New York paintings, and Helen

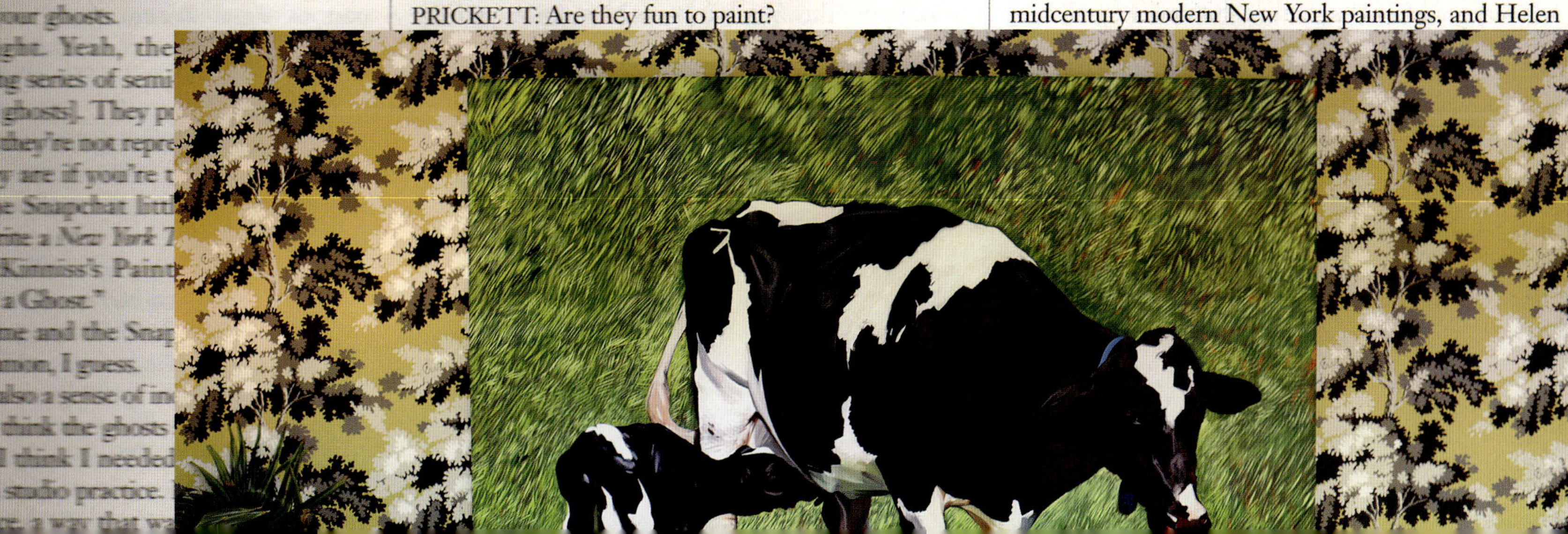

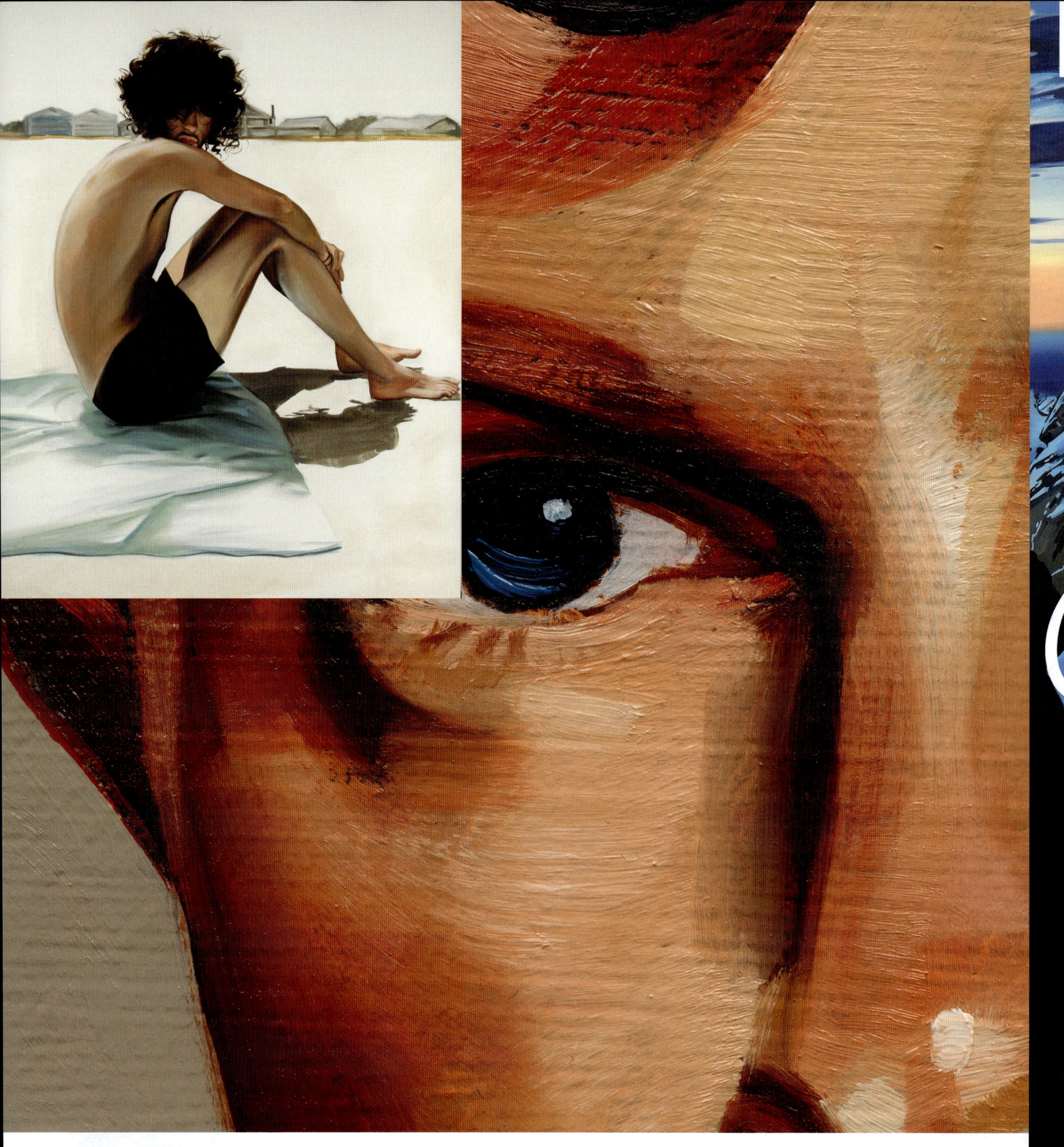

To Painter Sam McKinniss, With Love

GQ's Rachel Tashjian sends a letter of adoration to the New York artist who's turning celebrity fandom on its head.

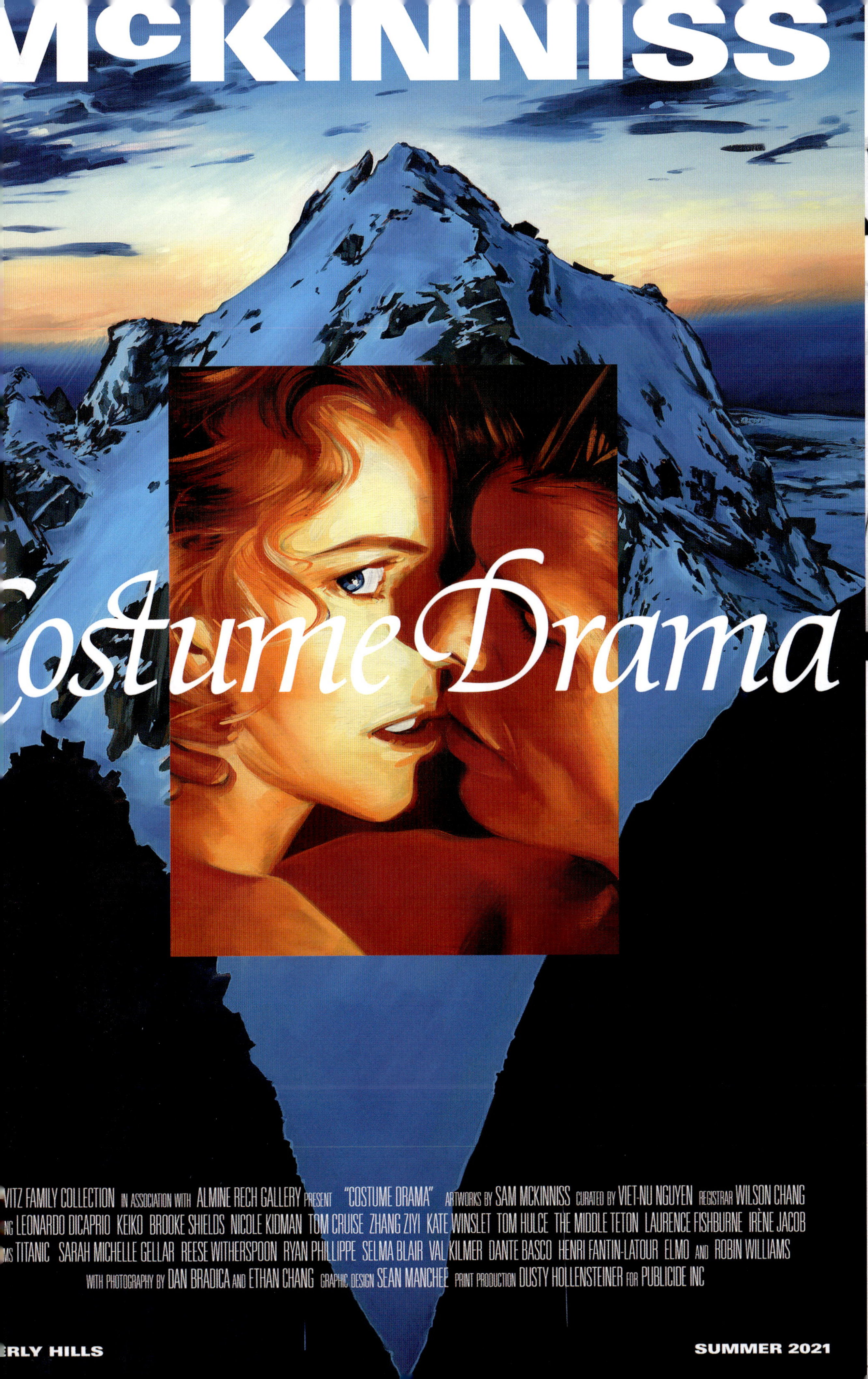

MᶜKINNISS

Costume Drama

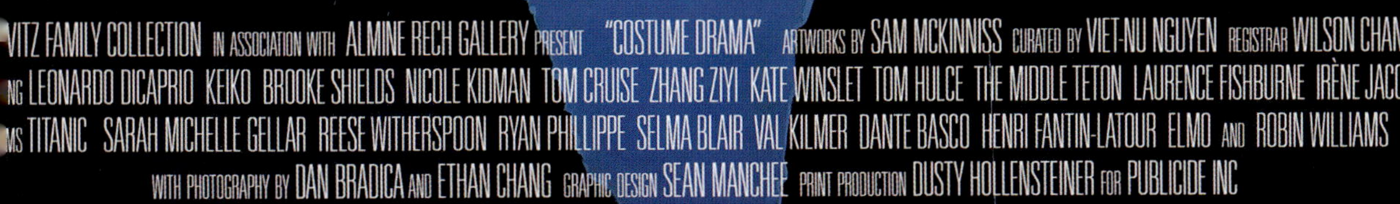

ERLY HILLS

SUMMER 2021

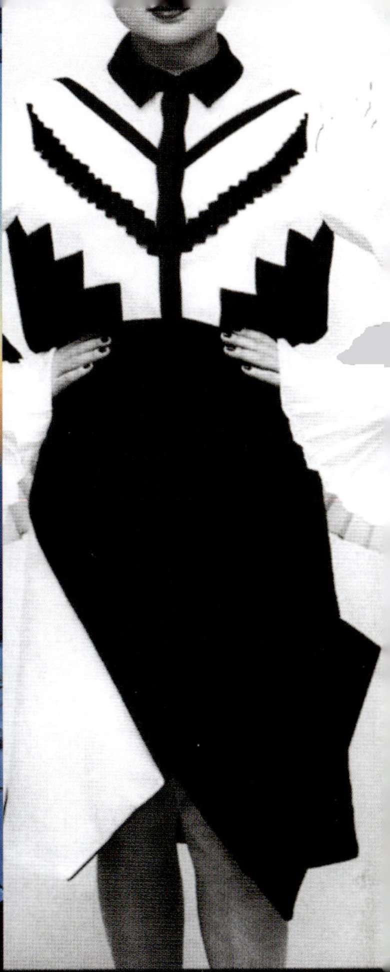

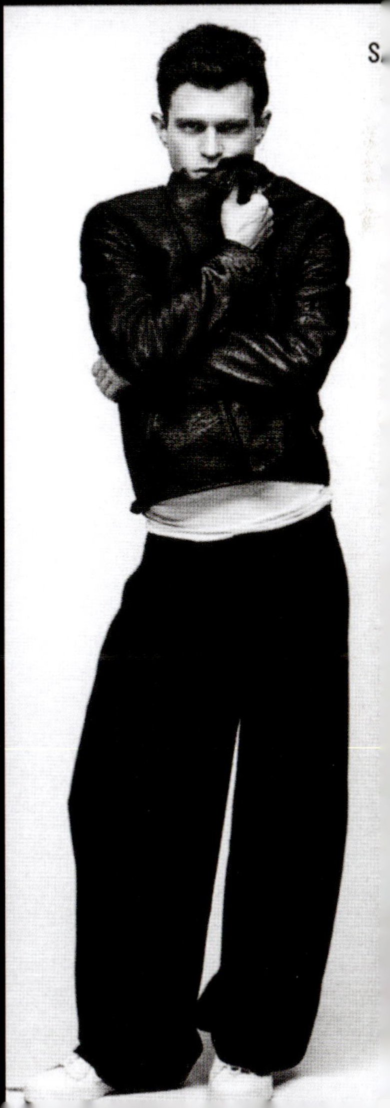

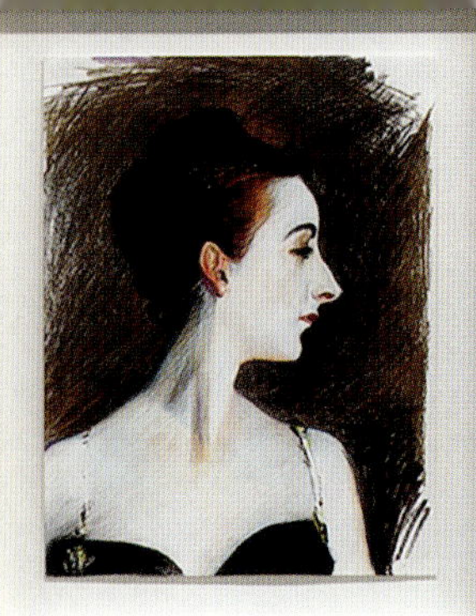
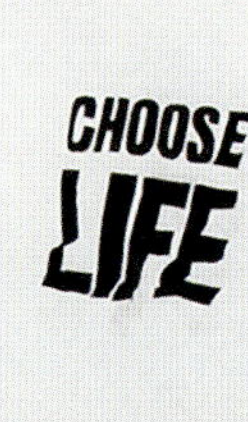
CHOOSE
LIFE
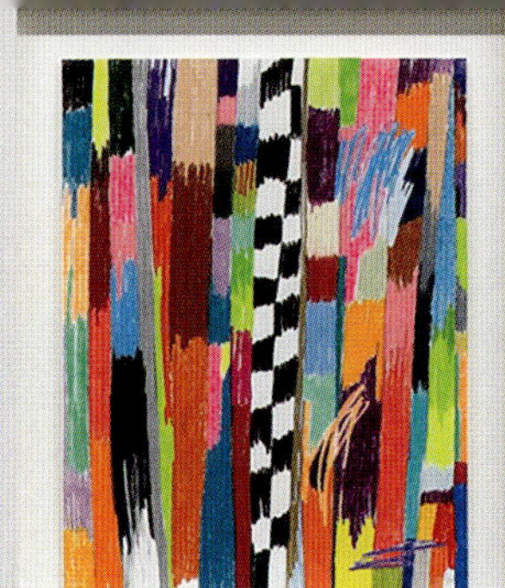
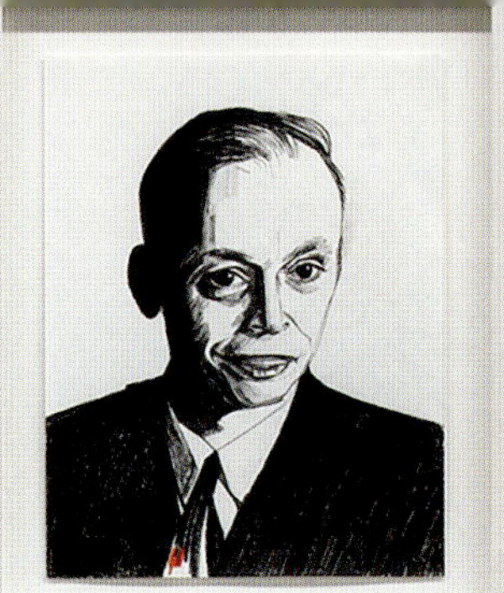
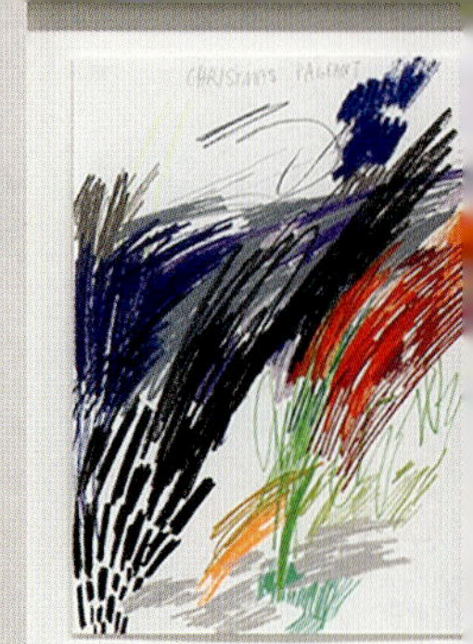
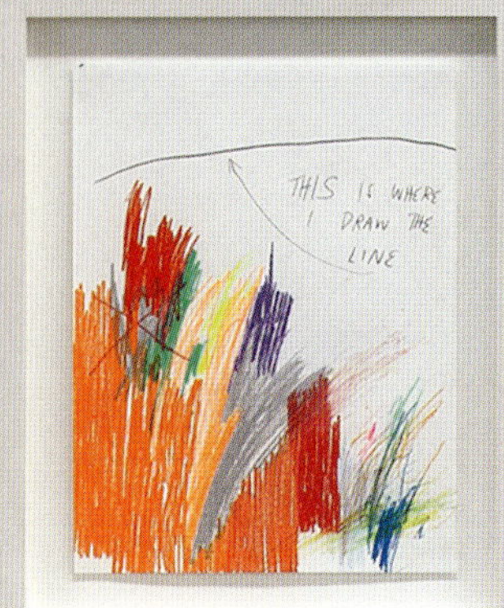
THIS IS WHERE
I DRAW THE
LINE
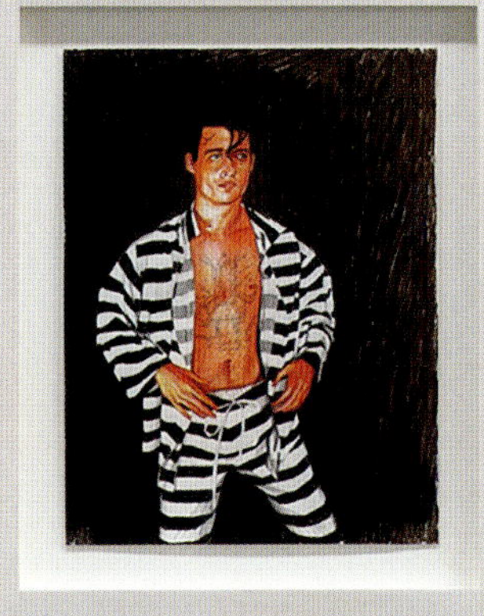
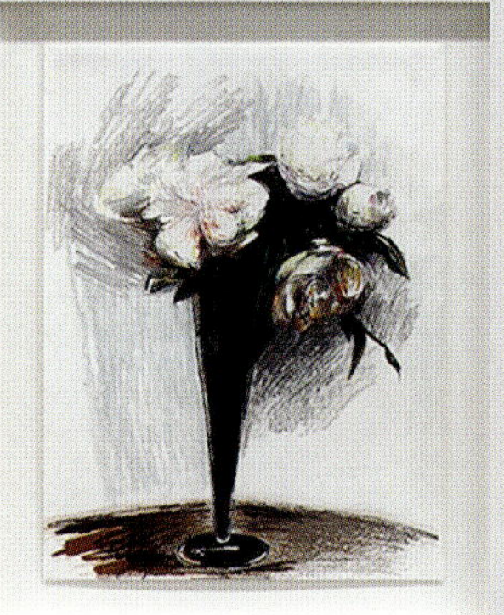
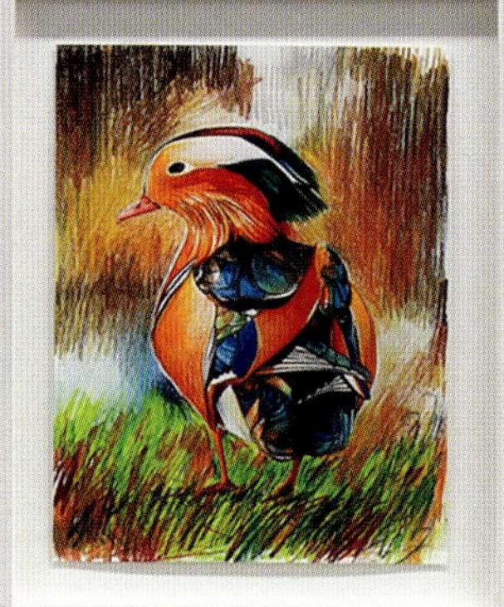
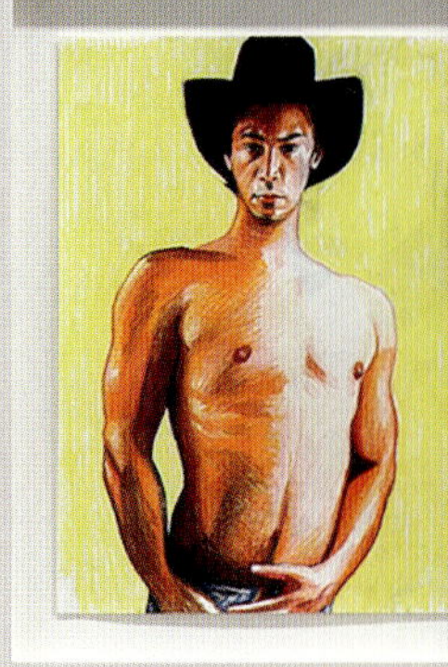
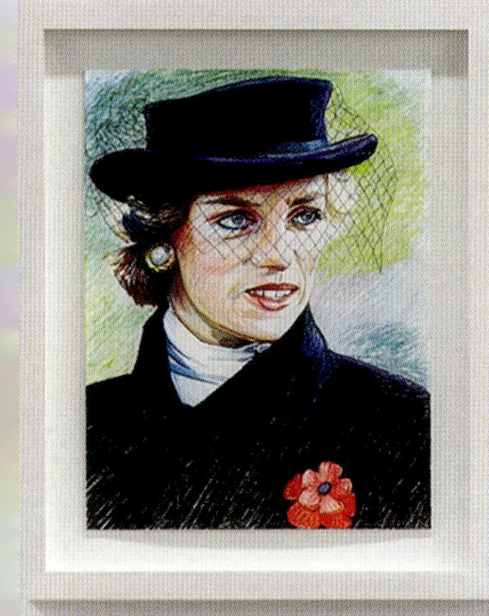
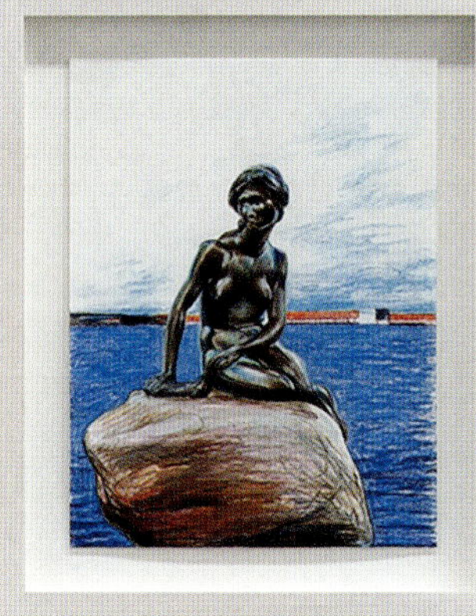
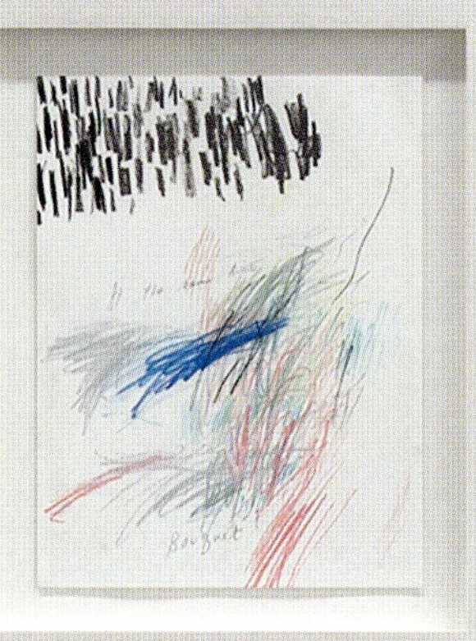
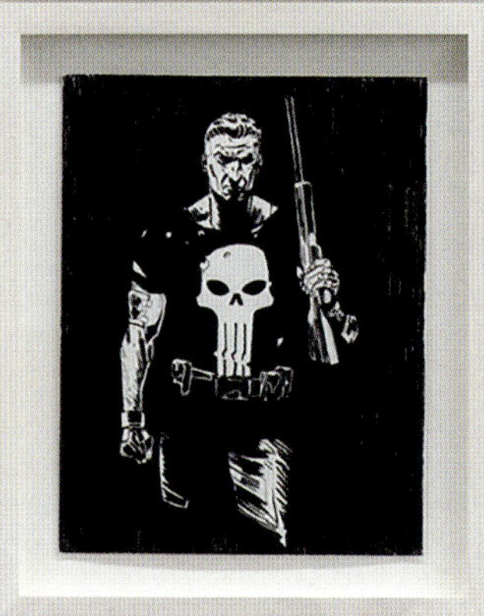
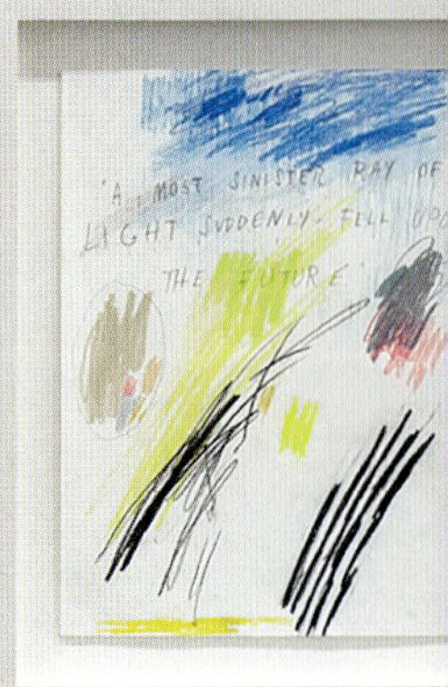
"A MOST SINISTER RAY OF
LIGHT SUDDENLY FELL
THE FUTURE
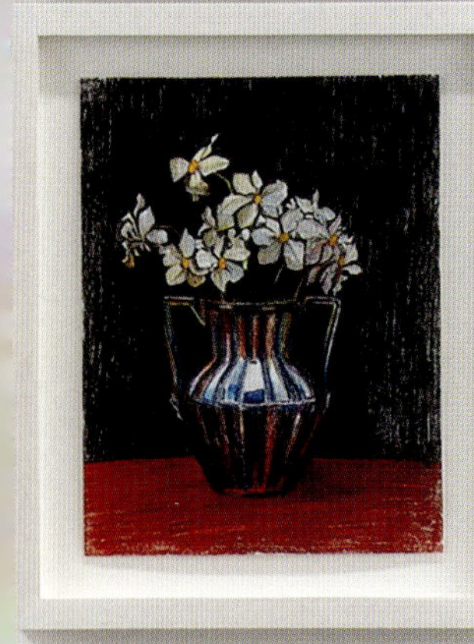
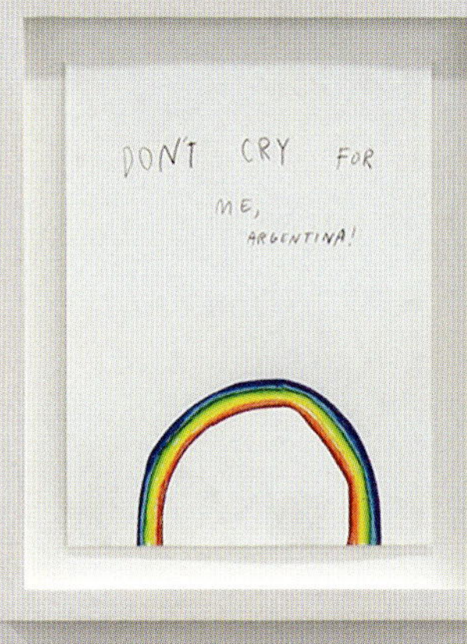
DON'T CRY FOR
ME,
ARGENTINA!
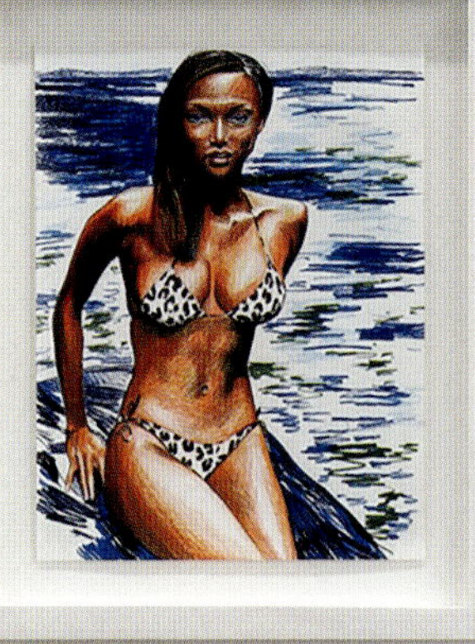
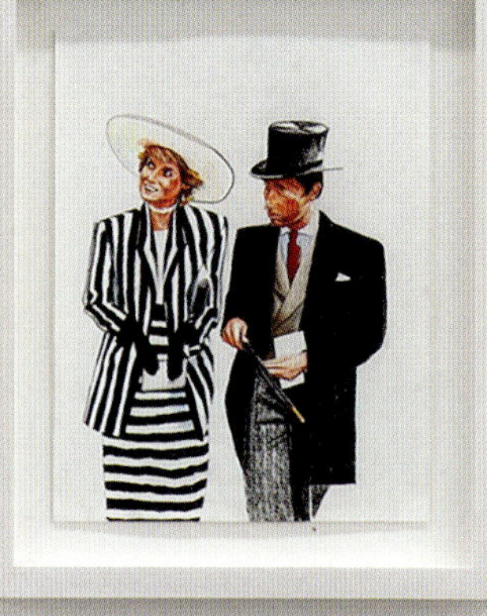
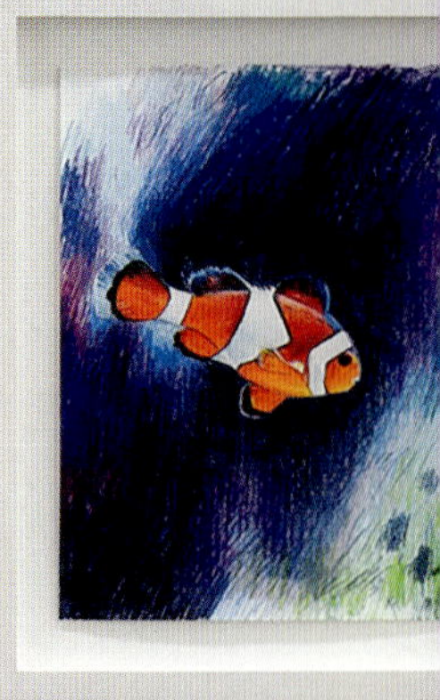
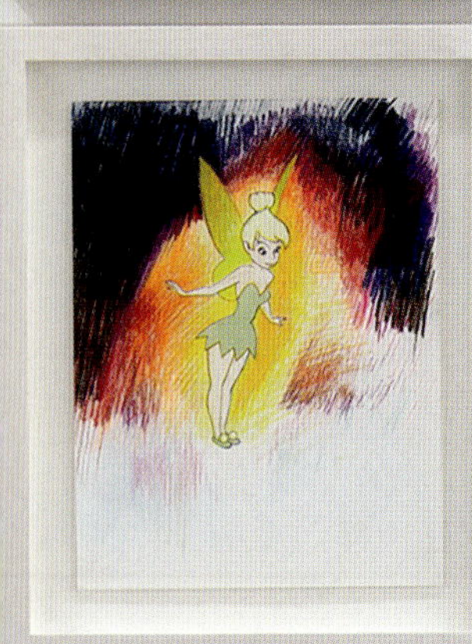
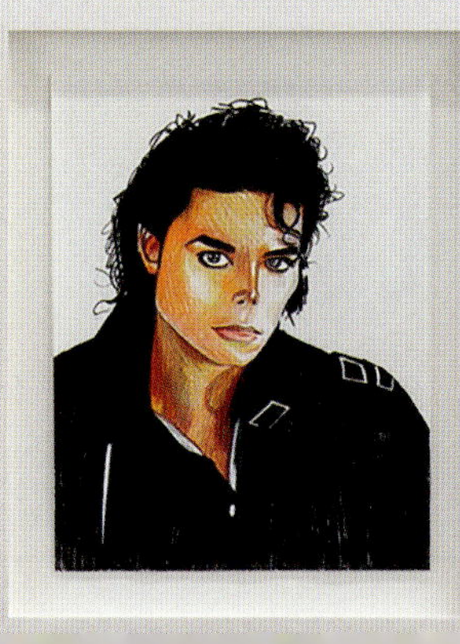
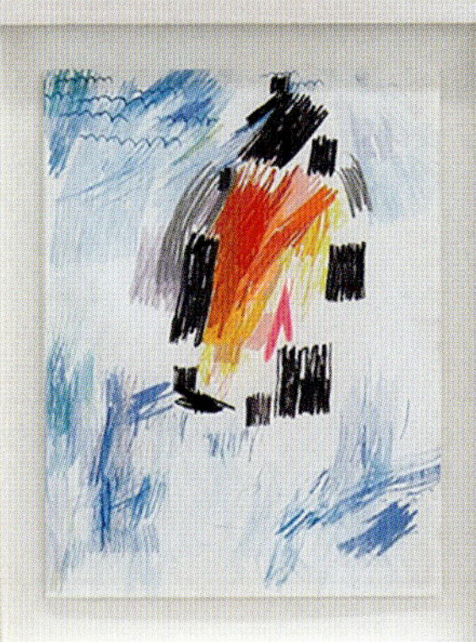
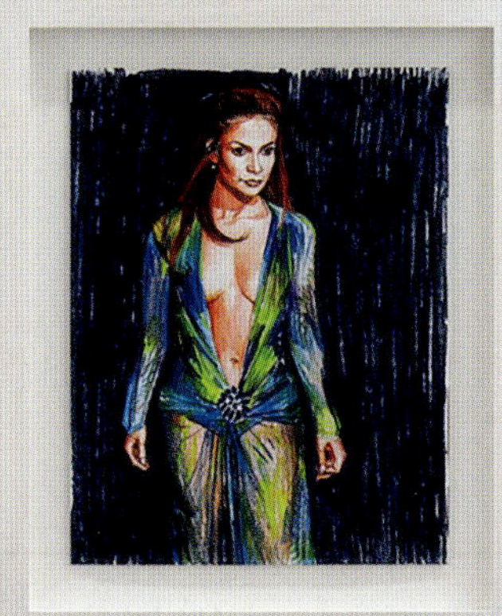

Supreme

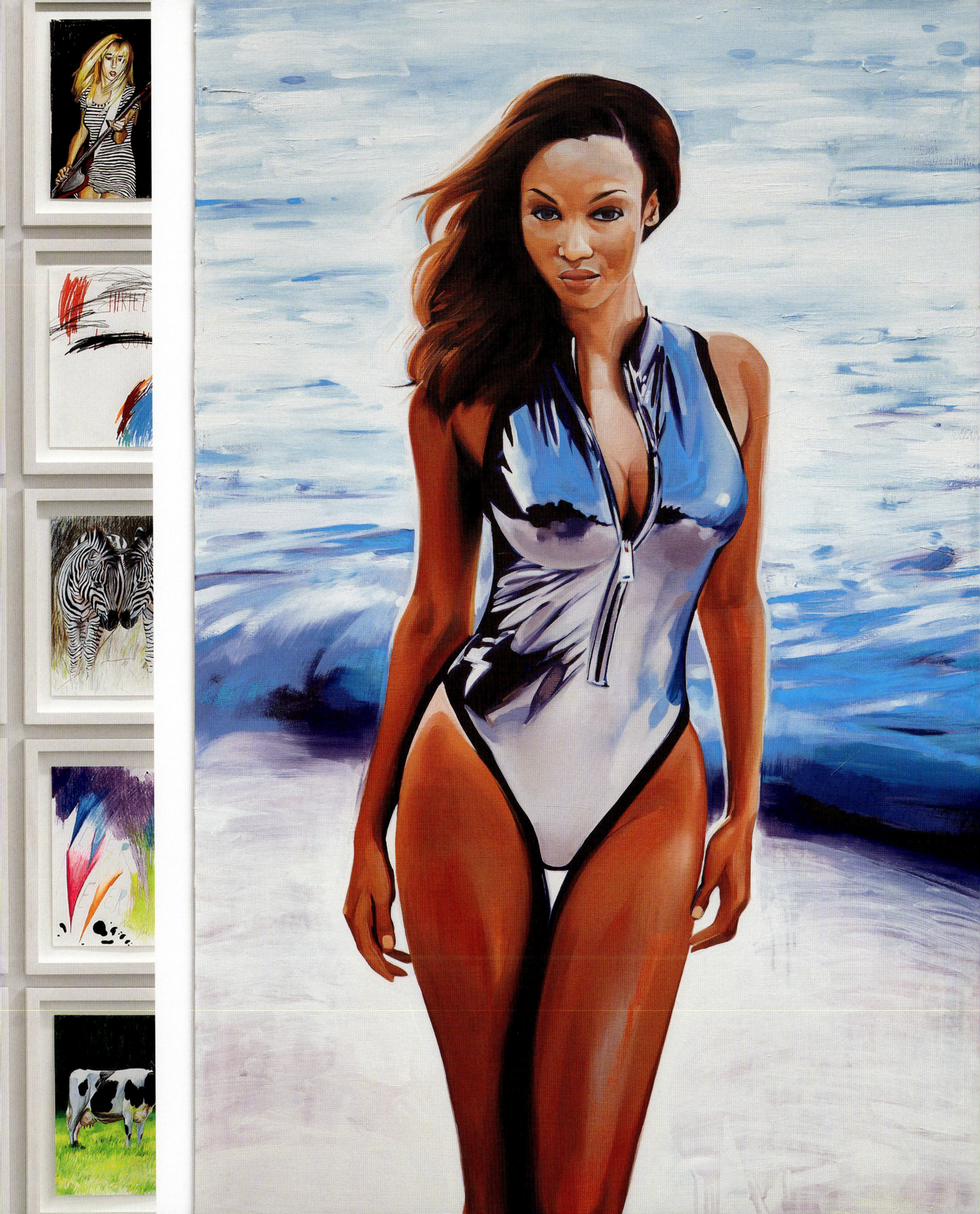

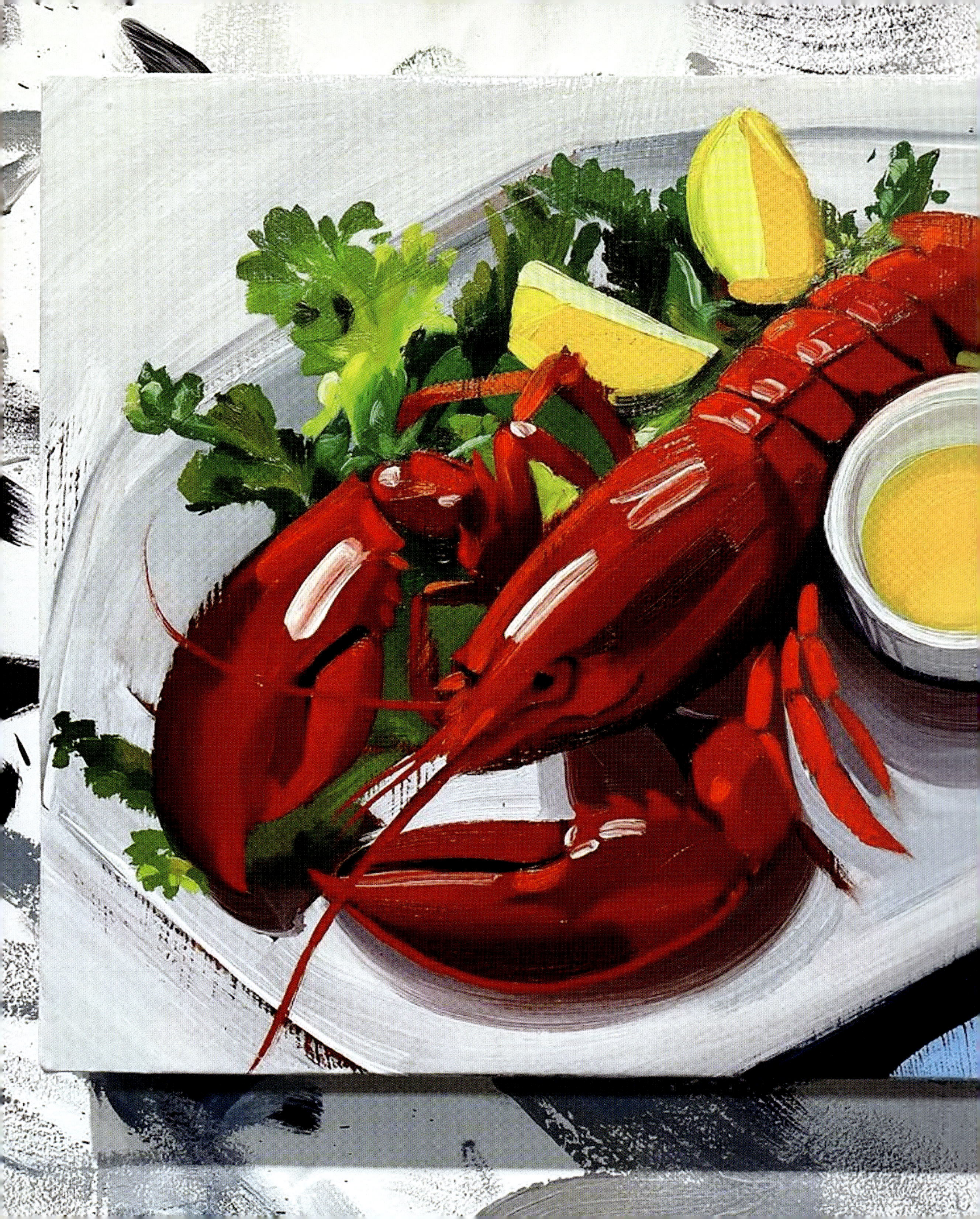

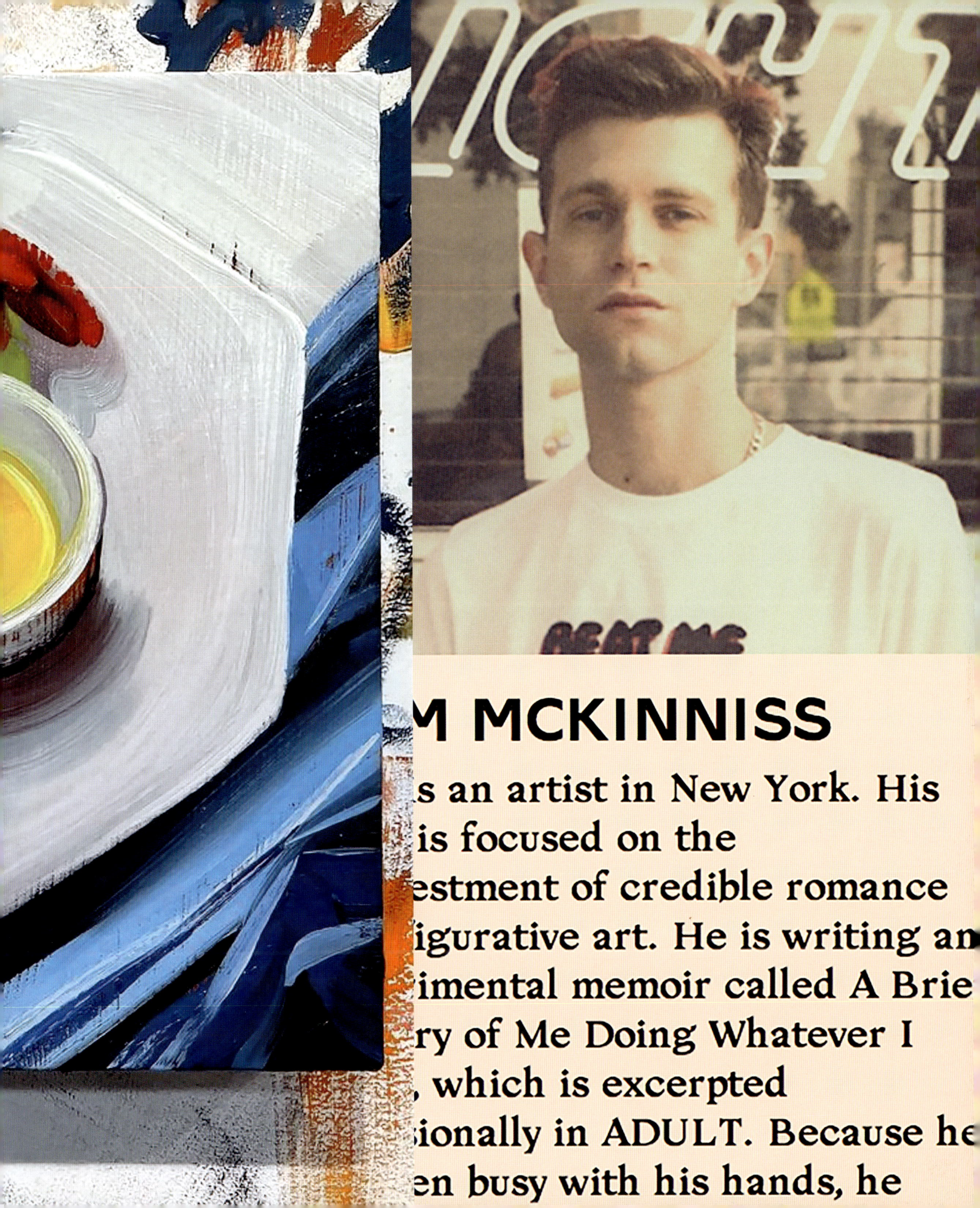
M MCKINNISS
s an artist in New York. His
is focused on the
estment of credible romance
igurative art. He is writing an
imental memoir called A Brie
ry of Me Doing Whatever I
, which is excerpted
sionally in ADULT. Because he
en busy with his hands, he

Afterword

My only wish is to wake up, read the news, then march around my house like a minor patrician espousing fanciful views at an imagined constituency with which I have little to no face time on any day-to-day basis. Assuming their form as my art, these views volunteer the fact that even if I do not know any better, I might. Nearly every painting feels as nostalgic, atomized, and alienated as the times we are living in, and there are a lot of them.

Yet, if a picture is still worth a thousand words, vocabulary suffers inflation. I wonder if the screens—which I take to for source material—are little more than billions of interactive mirrors for billions of inactive narcissists, self included. Thus far, my life's work has held this flagging sense of exasperated wonder in common with any other digital native searching in vain for something worthy of time and attention, for someone to relate to or feel up against, for some call to action or invitation to misbehavior, for reasons to get up and go. In order to say something, I cobble together a visual language picked up from imagery laid to waste by the ongoing explosion in communications technologies. I take them to mean what I want to say.

This long after the graphic revolution, pictures have jumped from the canvas to the page to the screens while carrying almost every bit of information along with them sans aura, detail, or texture. My work guarantees access to a kind of dual citizenship, an expatriation to tangible reality. Paradoxically, my move from the digital to the tangible is advanced in pursuit of pictorial realism by way of quotation—constructed illusions first encountered as online throwbacks, entertainment, or news. Images are stumbled upon, downloaded, printed out, and then rendered again via oleaginous color on a brush held in hand, to be dragged across linen that's been cut, primed, and stretched into shape. The graphic revolution in reverse. The point is that the pictures are fake and often stupid but my hands and the colors are real. This means a lot, to me at least. Incredulity must not always carry the day. And yet suspicions remain with regard to all other conditions, including the health and functioning of my own brain, not to mention the health and functioning of my audience.

Anyway, I want there to be good art. I am in favor of a cooler, more excellent world and I love my friends. I am a sucker for that and I miss them all the time. The paintings keep me away from everybody else (another vexing paradox), but I will see them tonight just as soon as I'm finished.

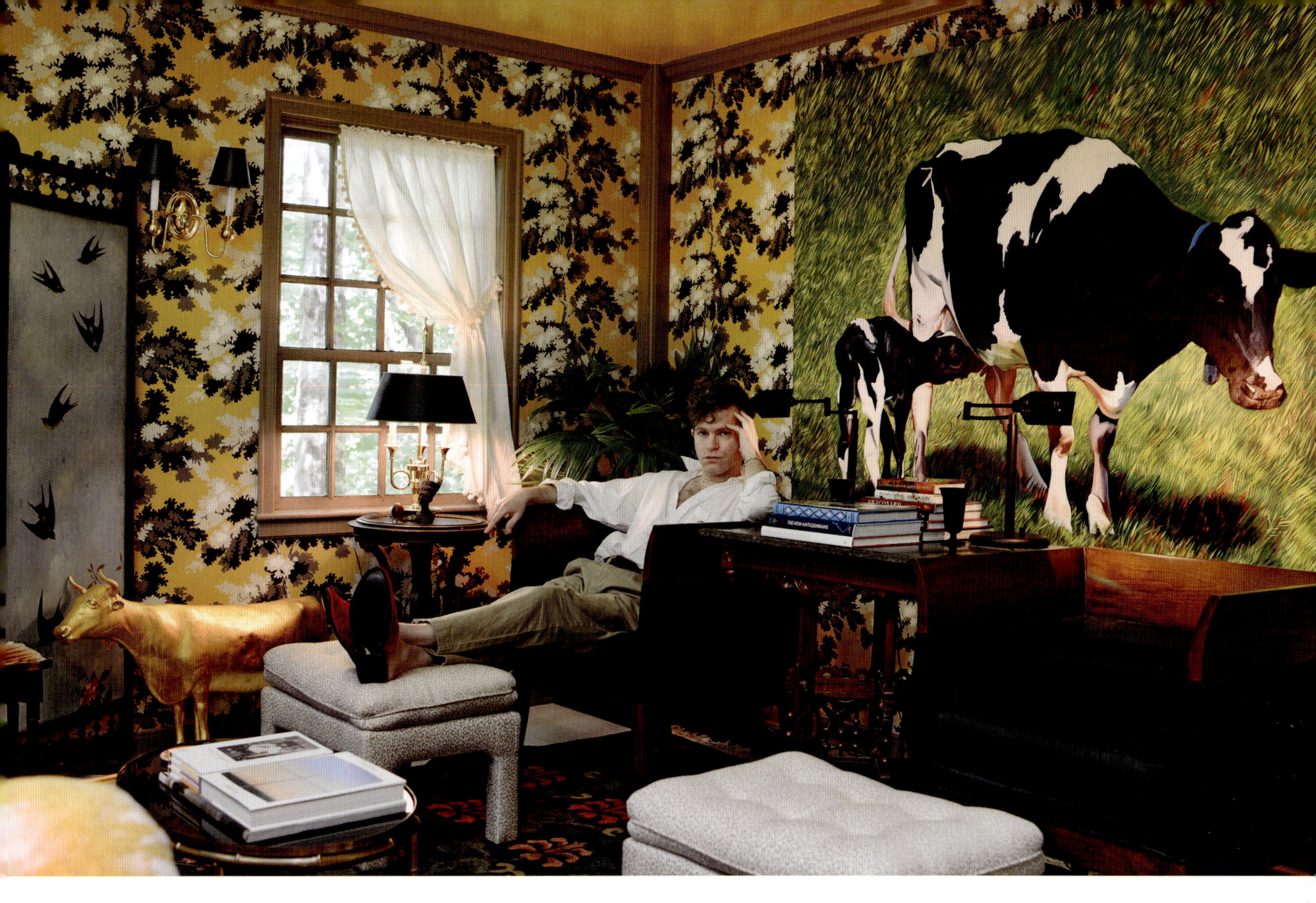
THE NEW ANTIQUARIANS

First published in the United States of America in 2025
by Rizzoli Electa, A Division of
Rizzoli International Publications, Inc.
49 West 27th Street
New York, NY 10001
www.rizzoliusa.com

The publisher would like to thank David Kordansky Gallery and Almine Rech for their generous support of this publication.

Publisher: Charles Miers
Editor: Isabel Venero
Production Manager: Maria Pia Gramaglia
Designer: 40 Worth St. / Michael Schmelling

2025 2026 2027 2028 / 10 9 8 7 6 5 4 3 2 1
ISBN: 978-0-8478-4062-5
Library of Congress Control Number on file

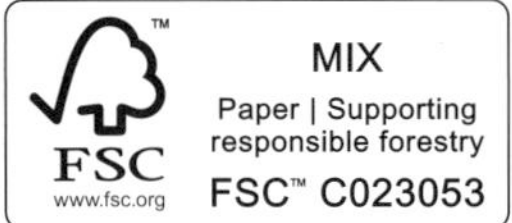

Contributor Biographies

Jarrett Earnest is a writer and curator living in New York City. He is the author of *What it Means to Write About Art: Interviews with Art Critics* (2018) and *Valid Until Sunset* (2023). He edited and wrote the introductions to *Hot, Cold, Heavy, Light: 100 Art Writings 1988–2017* by Peter Schjeldahl (2019); *The Young and Evil: Queer Modernism in New York, 1930–1955* (2020); *Painting is a Supreme Fiction: Writings by Jesse Murry, 1980–1993* (2021); and *Feint of Heart: Art Writings 1982–2002* by Dave Hickey (2024). Earnest hosts Angelic Transmissions, an art talk show on East Village Radio.

Natasha Stagg is the author of *Surveys: A Novel* (2016); *Sleeveless: Fashion, Image, Media, New York 2011–2019* (2019); and *Artless: Stories 2019–2023* (2023), all published by Semiotext(e).

Photo Credits Dan Allegretto: p. 263. Charles Benton: pp. 15, 54–55, 70, 77, 78, 81, 109, 134–35, 137, 138–39, 141, 187, 223. Dan Bradica: pp. 13, 35, 36–37, 49, 57, 66–67, 89, 83, 85, 125, 128, 133, 170–72, 173, 175, 188, 210–11. Dan Bradica Studio: p. 193. Nicolas Brasseur: pp. 18–19. Melissa Castro Duarte: pp. 91, 131, 220–21. Ethan Chang: pp. 88–89. Matthew Grubb: pp. 79, 94, 96, 147, 151. Richard Ivey: pp. 48, 113. Dario Lasagni: pp. 22–23, 26–28, 29, 30–31, 47, 61, 69, 74, 156, 186, 191, 197, 198–99. Joerg Lohse: p. 155. Jeff McLane: pp. 8, 33, 56, 112, 148–49, 150, 202–03. David N. Regen: pp. 102–03, 177. Elon Schoenholz: pp. 10, 45, 106. Christopher Stach: p. 59.

Jacket front: ***Catwoman***, 2016. Oil and acrylic on canvas, 16 x 12 inches (40.6 x 30.5 cm).
Jacket flaps: ***Swan***, 2016. Oil and acrylic on canvas, 72 x 84 inches (182.9 x 213.4 cm); ***Blue Morpho (after Martin Johnson Heade)***, 2015. Oil and acrylic on canvas, 16 x 12 inches (40.6 x 30.5 cm)
Cover: ***Doberman Pinscher***, 2023. Oil on linen, 44 1/4 x 33 1/8 x 1 3/8 inches (112.4 x 84.1 x 3.5 cm).
Courtesy of the artist and David Kordansky Gallery

Jacket back quotation: Richard Maltby, *Hollywood Cinema: An Introduction* (Hoboken: Blackwell Publishers, Inc.), 1995.

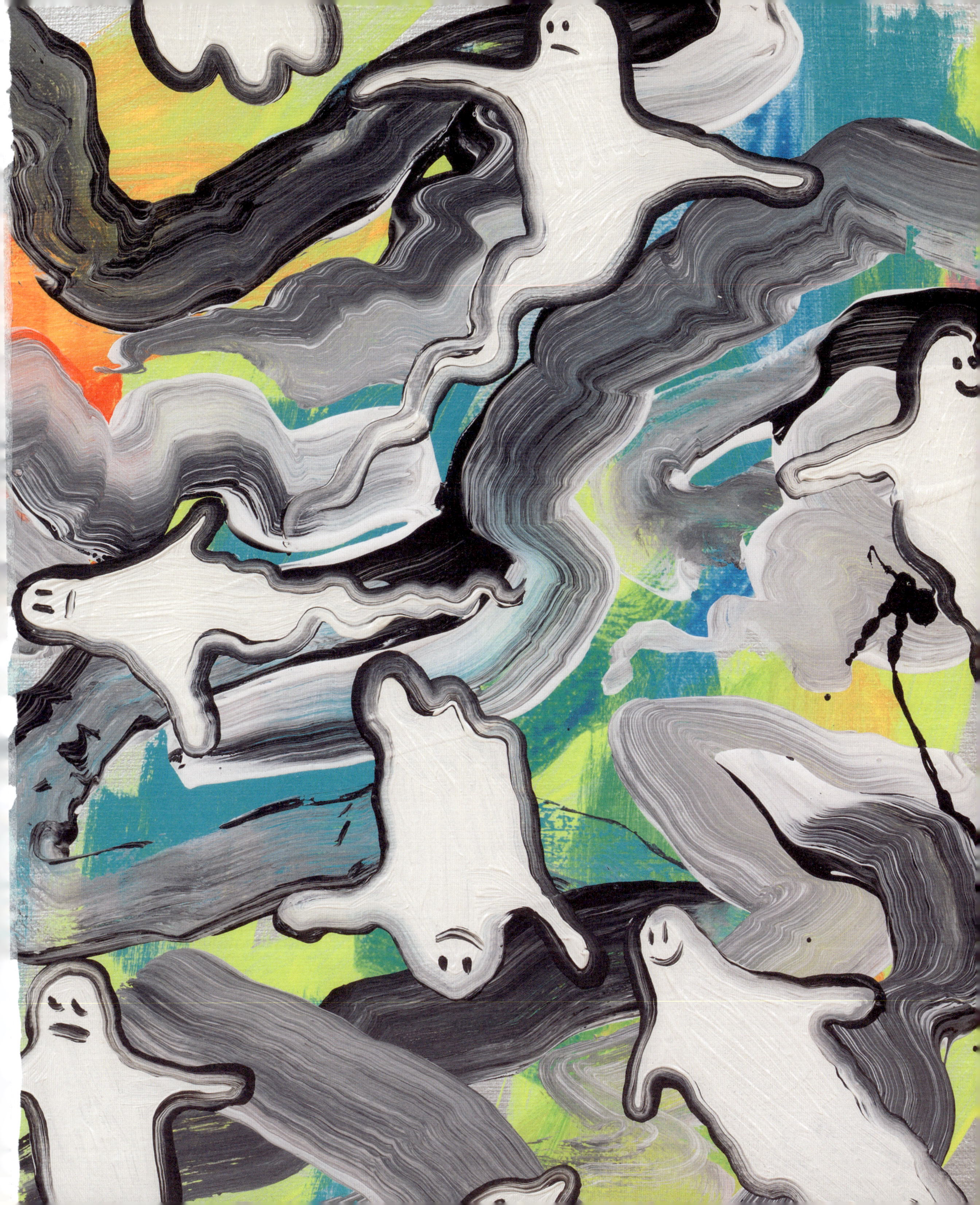

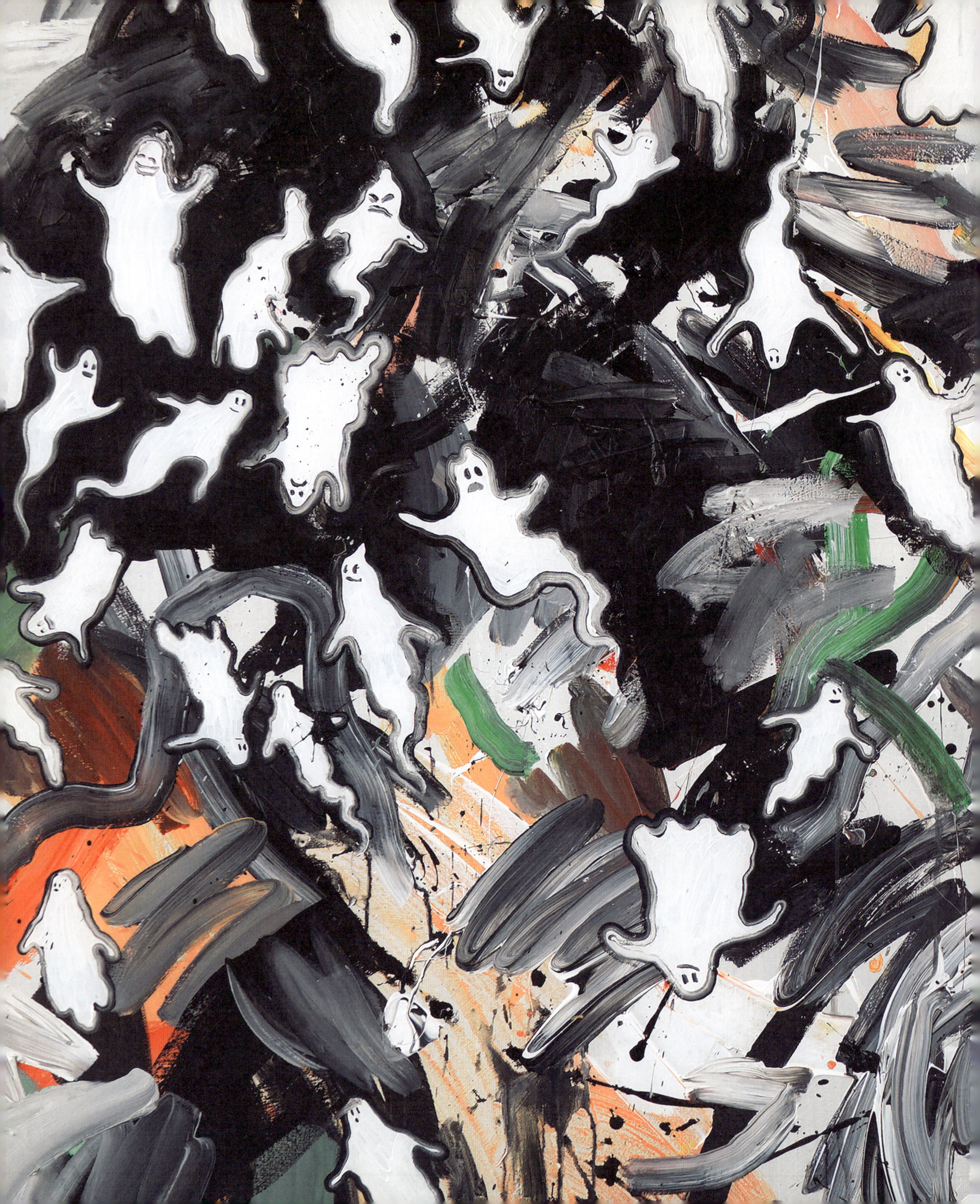